ADVANCE PRAISE FOR *FORCE IN STATECRAFT*

"National security would be more assured when decisions related to the application of force are grounded in mature politico-military understanding and flawlessly executed by a war fighting apparatus rooted in jointness. 'Force in Statecraft', an excellent initiative of the National Defence College, reflects the views of some of India's most accomplished and articulate practitioners in the security management arena. A must-read volume."

– **N.N. Vohra**

Former Governor of J&K, Principal Advisor to the PM, Home Secretary and Defence Secretary.

"The Editors have brought together highly credible names in Indian strategic circles to discuss how the Indian armed forces deal with diverse national security challenges ranging from full-blown wars to bloody insurgencies and the challenge of preparing for an uncertain, technology-heavy future. The book enriches the ongoing debate on India's strategic thought and culture."

– Dr **Arvind Gupta**

Director, Vivekananda International Foundation and the former deputy national security adviser

"Despite having one of the finest militaries in the world, Indian military practitioners have been somewhat reluctant to write rigorously on the role of force as an instrument of statecraft and its implications. This is the first serious attempt to bring together a galaxy of "soldier-scholars" to frame this very important conversation, thereby filling a serious void. As Indian policymakers become more nuanced in their attempts to integrate the use of force into national security policymaking, this collection holds immense scholarly and practical value."

– Dr **Harsh V. Pant**

Professor of International Relations, King's College London &
Director of Research, Observer Research Foundation, New Delhi

This is an outstanding volume with contributions from professionals who have spent much of their careers grappling with the subject that they are writing on: the complexities that states face in using force in a number of different arenas. The distilled wisdom here offer valuable perspectives, even if one does not fully agree with all of it, and a useful balance to those of us who also consider these issues but without the benefit of direct experience.

– Prof **Rajesh Rajagopalan**

Jawaharlal Nehru University, New Delhi

FORCE IN STATECRAFT

FORCE IN STATECRAFT

AN INDIAN PERSPECTIVE

EDITORS

ARJUN SUBRAMANIAM
DIPTENDU CHOUDHURY

KW Publishers Pvt Ltd
New Delhi

in association with

National Defence College
New Delhi

Second Reprint February 2024

ISBN 978-93-91490-92-8 Hardback
ISBN 978-93-91490-93-5 ebook

Published in India by Kalpana Shukla

KW Publishers Pvt Ltd
4676/21, First Floor, Ansari Road
Daryaganj, New Delhi 110002
Phone: +91 11 43528107
Marketing: kw@kwpub.in
Editorial: production@kwpub.in
Website: www.kwpub.in

Printed and Bound in India

CONTENTS

Preface xi

CHAPTER 1

Painting the Landscape 1

Arjun Subramaniam

CHAPTER 2

Limited War 10

Prakash Menon

CHAPTER 3

Evolution of India's Counter-Insurgency Doctrine 30

J.R. Mukherjee

CHAPTER 4

Changing Contours of Conflict in the North East and J&K 48

D.S. Hooda

CHAPTER 5

Left Wing Extremism and Urban Terrorism 64

K.C. Verma

CHAPTER 6

Manoeuvre Warfare: The Past-Present-Future 84

Praveen Bakshi

CHAPTER 7
Pushing the Limits of Endurance:
High Altitude Warfare 104
Rakesh Sharma

CHAPTER 8
Firepower 122
P.R. Shankar

CHAPTER 9
India's Rise: The Imperative of Seapower 141
Anil Chopra

CHAPTER 10
India's Aircraft Carrier Dilemma 157
Arun Prakash

CHAPTER 11
The Future of Undersea Warfare in the 21st Century 175
P. Ashokan

CHAPTER 12
The Enduring Relevance of Offensive Airpower 192
Diptendu Choudhury

CHAPTER 13
Air Transport Operations: Critical Responders
and Vital Enablers 212
Rajeev Sachdeva

CHAPTER 14
The Indian Rotary Wing: Legacy and Prospects 229
Rajesh Isser

CHAPTER 15
Employment of Special Forces in Future Conflict Scenarios 246
Prakash Katoch

CHAPTER 16
Synergy in Higher Defence Organisation 263
Arup Raha

CHAPTER 17
Lessons in Jointness from the Andaman Nicobar Command Experience 282
Sudhir Pillai

CHAPTER 18
India's Nuclear Posture 305
Balraj Singh Nagal

CHAPTER 19
Understanding China for the Strategic Practitioner 325
S.L. Narasimhan

Editors 344

Distinguished Contributors 346

Index 354

PREFACE

In 1962, when Prime Minister Jawaharlal Nehru declared a national emergency in response to the Chinese aggression, Atal Behari Vajpayee, a first-time Member of Parliament, demanded a special session. Nehru agreed, and, on November 8, 1962, Vajpayee famously debated: *"We should not hesitate to accept that by ignoring national security we have committed a big crime against the Nation. By leaving our borders unguarded we have committed a grave sin and we should be prepared to atone for it."* Almost six decades later, in May 2020, the Chinese aggression in Eastern Ladakh has brought India's national security back into the spotlight. Given that India's principal adversaries are two nuclear-armed nations and collusive strategic partners, the long and live unresolved external borders, and the persistent internal security challenges arising out of extremism and external state-sponsored terrorism, India's national security environment is truly unique. The sacred covenant of the military to safeguard state sovereignty and its citizens is no longer limited to its borders and near seas, as threats have multiplied swiftly across all domains.

In a wider perspective, India's economic progress and growth have expanded the contours of its national interest beyond the continental construct. Since future threats and national interests are no longer limited by geography, the security environment can also no longer be limited to the two-dimensional land and sea domains. The air, space and cyber realms provide an all pervasive 'volume of influence' from the third dimension; a dimension which expands the array of military options available to the nation, and must therefore be leveraged more comprehensively. Recent events across the world have forever transformed the traditional approach to national security, and it is no longer the sole preserve of the military. Overwhelming force no longer remains the only option, considering that it's unbridled employment will be economically prohibitive to the nation. Consequently, it will mostly emerge as the last option to tackle security challenges. But a bespoke application of force that is swift, precise, timely and effective, used individually, in part or jointly with other elements of power to achieve desired outcomes, will find greater relevance in the future. While a comprehensive whole-of-government approach is the way ahead, the role of force in statecraft needs to be redefined.

The Armed Forces, which are the principal custodians of force application in India, are at the cusp of a transformational change that would require them to let go of shibboleths of the past and accept newer paradigms. True to human nature, the transformation is running the gauntlet of resistance to change, laying bare institutional limitations, inadequacy of knowledge and legacy mindsets, underpinned by the uncertainty of the future. All elements need to come together, closing the splayed fingers into an iron fist, to ensure security of the nation and the safety of its people and interests. Today, it is also critical to broaden the national security discourse beyond the security establishment to include the legislators, bureaucracy, the strategic community, academia, media, and most importantly the citizen. National security needs to become everyone's concern, which necessitates breaking down silos, flattening hierarchies and changing mindsets. As a more visionary and robust outlook is infused into India's national strategy, a nuanced and sophisticated understanding of what each element of force brings to the table, and what the military means to the nation, is an inescapable imperative. In this context, the role of the National Defence College in developing and nurturing future strategic leadership and policy makers becomes even more critical than what it is today.

The requirement for a more sophisticated and astute understanding of the role of force as an instrument of national security necessitates a close strategy-link between citizens, academia, practitioners of force and policymakers. This thought was dominant when the idea of a book on all the cornerstones of force and their place in India's future security was first discussed with the co-editor. The timing could not have been more fortuitous with the tumultuous changes in the world and the region, and the defining process of change in India's higher security structure which is underway. Time, however, was a singular constraint with the need to publish this volume before events overtook the idea. This endeavour would not have been possible without the support of the Defence Secretary, Dr Ajay Kumar. His intellectual enthusiasm and encouragement have enabled the NDC to push academic boundaries.

Deadlines, challenges and change are no strangers to the NDC and it was heartwarming that each of the writers wholeheartedly supported the project, albeit under the healthy pressure of the deadline! The truly impressive list of contributors, who collectively bring with them almost 800 years of hard earned wisdom in the service of the nation, are thus invaluable partners on this intellectual journey. The College is grateful to them for their thoughts and views, which we hope will help trigger the much-needed strategic debate on the future use of force in India's national security context. All citizens with their rightful stake in national security, need to seek greater knowledge and understanding of force and its keepers. A need that this collection of writings hopes to fulfil.

The book has been a labour of love and the steadfast commitment to see it through. It would have been impossible to realise the dream in less than a year without the herculean efforts of my co-editor, who balanced quality with an impossible deadline, which was met gamely and wholeheartedly by the publishers! They have my sincere appreciation and compliments.

Diptendu Choudhury
Air Marshal
Commandant & Co-Editor
National Defence College

CHAPTER 1

PAINTING THE LANDSCAPE

ARJUN SUBRAMANIAM

A BEGINNING

The National Defence College (NDC), New Delhi has been a repository of rich intellectual debate in the realm of nation-building and national security for over six decades. Its alumni have risen to high positions of power and influence in India and abroad, and the institution is a crucible of strategic learning where strategic opinions and positions are shaped in a collegial environment. The freedom of expression among the members and the speakers is triggered by the umbrella of 'Chatham House Rules,' allowing them to share their wisdom in a refreshingly vibrant intellectual environment. And yet, this collective wisdom has not burst forth into a torrent of writings for posterity. Surprisingly, in comparison to some renowned Think Tanks in India, the institution has not made its mark in the written space apart from the routine journals and seminar proceedings.

This intellectual drought can mainly be attributed to a combination of institutional lethargy and a reluctance to intellectualise military thinking through robust writing by senior military leadership. A colonial mindset has exacerbated the situation by limiting the military mind to operational and tactical musings rather than creating an eco-system that encourages senior military leadership to contribute meaningfully to the development of strategic thought and the continuous regeneration of operational philosophies in a rapidly transforming conflict milieu. The multi-layered vetting and clearance process also inhibits senior leadership from putting pen to paper, thereby limiting the scope of widening the reach of military wisdom and thought. Senior military leadership and security practitioners from other branches of government who display immense intellectual potential at NDC, do not seem to either gather institutional support to build on this competency, or do not see 'career value' in devoting long hours to honing writing and academic skills while still serving, preferring instead to wait until retirement to do so.

THE IDEA

The last few years have seen a significant increase in writing on strategic and military issues in the open domain by accomplished Indian security practitioners after they shed their uniforms, and a trickle from serving ones, albeit within the strict tramlines of institutional propriety and 'company policy.' This is a welcome development and must be encouraged. In the backdrop of this nascent renaissance, the idea for putting together an edited volume emerged as a hybrid concept for proliferating a multiplicity of ideas and thoughts through a collective medium of an anthology of reflections on myriad aspects of force as an instrument of statecraft.

What then was the broad idea behind this collaborative effort? It was to harness the collective wisdom and experience of three generations of military and security practitioners for a growing readership of policy makers, military and security leaders and professionals, young and middle-ranking military officers, academia and the general readers interested in military and security affairs. It was also felt that, as the apex institution of strategic learning in the country, the NDC should claim ownership of such an initiative, reach out to the best practitioner-minds in the country and request them to expound on several operational issues as well as a few strategic and transformative issues. The idea was not to go beyond the areas of expertise of the contributors while still providing guidance in the ongoing process of strategy and doctrine formulation at various levels.

THE PRODUCT

This is a unique product, the likes of which may not have emerged from even the more advanced western war college eco-system for the simple reason that this is a hybrid offering from practitioners that is largely based on historical and experiential learnings, tempered and garnished at places with academic and theoretical support. The volume does not seek to establish academic moorings, nor does it seek to advocate company policy and justify existing Indian military thought. The idea for the book emerged over a cup of coffee during the break period after the 60th NDC course, while reviewing the feedback received from readers of the refurbished NDC Journal, *Kuutneeti*.

As the co-editor of this anthology, I was confident that an outreach to several of these brilliant practitioners would not go in vain, having engaged with hundreds of accomplished veterans over eight years of research that led to the writing of two books on contemporary Indian military history. Thus, began a random outreach to over 20 accomplished practitioner veterans, each with remarkable operational careers and, more importantly, an inclination to put pen to paper and contribute to the development of intellectual capital within security and strategic structures.

The next hurdle to overcome was deciding on the flavour of the book. Should it look at the big picture and dwell on policy, strategy and doctrine, or should it address 'bread and butter' issues of soldiering, operational art and war fighting with a sprinkling of the former? What about technology, space, cyber and the changing character of war, or issues related to the ongoing transformation in military structures and higher defence organisation? The absence of a National Security Strategy and the nascent stage of military transformation meant that we also had a wonderful opportunity of offering differing perspectives on reforms in Higher Defence Organisation and transformation of the Indian military. This is an unfinished agenda that has seen much writing and debate in recent years and could well determine how India makes the transition to 'leading power' status. This was the raison d'être to focus on a hybrid intellectual combination comprising the instrument of force, military core competencies and critical issues of synergy, transformation and China-gazing.

While the initial outreach for potential contributors was mainly to NDC alumni, it was felt that widening the pool would add significant value to the anthology. Consequently, four of the contributors are accomplished non-alumni, including a former Chief of Naval Staff, if in lighter vein, one were to be protective about the NDC brand. The broad themes that make up the anthology are critical and even emotive issues of land, sea and airpower including an examination of joint structures; internal security challenges and inter-agency synergy; and a taste of China. It was also considered important to draw on the experience of three generations of military leaders to offer a holistic package to readers. Consequently, the volume has contributions from soldiers, sailors and airmen who have held important command and field assignments at the highest levels across two decades.

OVERVIEW

Since its independence from colonial rule in 1947, the Indian state has employed the instrument of force with great responsibility and restraint in the best traditions of a maturing democracy. The landscape of external and internal security challenges that India faces has been vast and varied and a subject of much discussion and writing in the recent past, and it was therefore felt that commencing the volume with an examination of the basic nature of limited conflict from an Indian perspective would set the right tone. Orchestration of land power in a full spectrum conflict milieu presents its own set of challenges for the Indian Army as it shifts focus from a predominantly Pakistan-centric and counter-insurgency focus to keeping an assertive and belligerent China at bay along a long and contested frontier that has seen much action over the last decade. In this context, readers will understand why the critical elements of India's counter-insurgency (CI) and some internal security strategies have dominated India's security mindset over the last few decades after looking at them through a chronological and conceptual perspective. As several peripheral hotspots such as Jammu and Kashmir and Nagaland, along with their proxy elements, continue to fester, it is important for policy makers and operational planners to remain in touch with this genre of conflict and ensure that lessons from the past blend with current realities. In the same breath, even though the armed forces have had limited exposure to counter Left Wing Extremism (LWE), or Naxalism as it is popularly known, a detailed chapter on this internal security challenge and the emerging genre of urban terrorism by an accomplished officer from the Indian Police Service was considered important to close the loop on internal security issues.

Among the casualties of a CI-intensive land strategy have been manoeuvre and firepower and revisiting them is essential if the Indian Army is to roll out effective strategies to counter China's People's Liberation Army (PLA), which is strong in firepower and has been inducting light armour onto the Tibetan Plateau to enhance manoeuvre. Concurrently, a Pakistan-light strategy with fewer boots on ground has no option but to rely on offensive airpower to shape the various battlespaces and embrace manoeuvre and airpower and seapower to drive operational effects even as the Indian Army is compelled to beef-up infantry deployment along the Line of Actual Control (LAC). High Altitude Warfare with an emphasis on joint operations merits serious reflection as it will continue to demand much focus as the highest probability of limited conflict with India's principal adversaries exists in that domain.

The seas around India have seen much action over the last decade as the Centre of Gravity of the world's maritime affairs has gradually shifted towards the Indian Ocean Region (IOR) and the Indo-Pacific because of China's rise and its increased propensity to contest these waters. Consequently, the maritime rivalry between the US and China in the Indo-Pacific, the entry of the PLA Navy in strength into the waters of the Indian Ocean and the growing asymmetry between the PLA Navy and the Indian Navy, all focus on how the Indian Navy will respond to these challenges as the primary custodian of India's maritime security. The broad discussion on the relevance of sea power will be accompanied by focussed debates on the need to build a balanced Navy. It is in this context that Indian perspectives on the continued relevance of aircraft carriers from a naval aviator and former naval chief are just as important as an accomplished submariner's clear enunciation of the future of underwater warfare. Both will feature in the section on maritime power.

The Indian Air Force has emerged over the last decade as a critical instrument of statecraft. It has proved to be a decisive element of deterrence and coercion in a 'no war no peace' situation; as a first responder in both offensive and enabling operations; and as a lynchpin of sustaining India's security forces along hostile borders in what can be truly termed as 'Full Spectrum' air operations that stretch across the strategic, operational and tactical domains. As part of an in-depth 'bread and butter' discussion, the continued criticality of offensive air operations, fixed wing transport operations and the growing relevance of rotary wing operations will feature in the airpower section. An IAF focused offering on airpower in no way diminishes the importance of the air arms of the Army and the Navy, which render sterling service in their areas of operation.

India's Special Forces have matured significantly since their baptism by fire as specialised units in the jungles of Sri Lanka as part of the Indian Peacekeeping Force (IPKF) in the late 1980s. Several recent operations conducted by the Indian Army's Special Forces, as well as the active contribution in several areas by the Indian Navy's Marine Commandos (MARCOS) and the Indian Air Force's Garud Force highlight the importance of such forces in future conflicts as they offer high payoffs with calibrated risk mitigation and even deniability.

A case study on the success of the Andaman Nicobar Command could offer instructive lessons as the Indian military grapples with jointness and integration, even as a former air chief offers his views and recommendations for deep and long overdue reforms in Higher Defence Organisation (HDO) without getting distracted by the clutter caused by piece-meal integration.

Military professionals in Indian can never lose sight of the nuclear overhang that exists in South Asia since it will remain a critical component of the escalation ladder in the India-China-Pakistan security relationship. A comprehensive walk-through across the Indian nuclear landscape from a historical, doctrinal and capability perspective is essential to remind policy makers, practitioners and academics of the nuclear overhang in India's neighbourhood. Finally, a detailed examination of China offers instructive guidance for the strategist-practitioner on how to assess India's principal strategic adversary and competitor through a lens that highlights how the former amalgamates enduring historical lessons with ideology and power narratives. This would trigger the right response mechanisms as India's strategic community deals with an ambitious and assertive neighbour that is determined to achieve its strategic objectives vis-à-vis India with focused application of hard power, ambiguous exploitation of the 'grey zone' and the ability to calibrate the escalation ladder.

On a different plane, such a free-flowing intellectual exercise is important for the wider strategic community, policy makers, academia and the wider citizenry that displays an interest in national security affairs. Policy makers in India have a restricted view of military matters because soldiers, bureaucrats, academics and civilians more often than not, 'talk past each other' rather than talk to one another.' This is one of the main reasons for the absence of a robust national discourse on national security and matters military. This initiative may help to contribute in elevating strategic thinking and add to the Indian academic discourse on the instruments of force in statecraft in a modest way.

CHALLENGES

The biggest challenge in putting this volume together was a DNA issue that I have observed and validated during my service and academic career. I have always marvelled at the ability of senior Indian military leadership to articulate verbally, and have been disappointed by their unwillingness to share their experiences in writing for posterity. Brilliant field commanders have seldom left behind a legacy that could be emulated and cast in stone because of a reluctance to buckle down and commit some time and effort to the art and discipline of professional writing. Several questions, such as: Why has the West taken ownership of most Counter-insurgency (CI) and Counter-terrorism (CT) strategies when the Indian Army has been practising it for decades, have remained unaddressed over the years due to a lack of articulation from practitioners? Despite having executed one of the most spectacular vertical envelopment strategies in the post-World War-II era, why have India's armed forces not showcased the Bangladesh Campaign of 1971 as a model for joint operations? Why has the IAF not taken ownership of innovative High Altitude (HA) operations despite extended operations in Siachen and the 'never attempted before' high altitude bombing campaign in Kargil? Or, why has the Indian Navy been reticent about claiming leadership in global anti-piracy operations despite its stellar record? The simple answer I have for this intellectual lethargy over the years has been a general disdain within the entire national security eco-system to institutionalise and intellectualise the business of warfighting.

Much academic writing takes years to break down into the structure of a book or an edited volume because of an obsession with academic pedagogy and structure. While every effort has been made to preserve academic robustness, some contributors have been given sufficient bandwidth to express themselves without insisting on either proving their hypotheses or offering citations by the dozen. In some cases, authors have combined citations and bibliography, while in others they have used styles other than the Chicago style. Their experience and wisdom more than makes up for this departure from typical academic styling.

Edited volumes, such as this one, normally take two to three years from conception to publishing. With a deadline of just about a year, the volume was entirely at the mercy of 19 accomplished and high-profile contributors, all of whom responded to the occasion splendidly, honouring the submission deadlines and responding with speed to editorial suggestions and interventions. Several contributors wrote their pieces in the wake of the pandemic and the resulting family travails. Despite being hit hard by the pandemic, Ms Kalpana Shukla and her team at KW Publishers ensured that the book was published as planned—that by itself is a wonderful achievement. The biggest force multiplier in ensuring that this volume rolled out on schedule was the boundless enthusiasm of Air Marshal Diptendu Choudhury, the Commandant of the National Defence College, who wrote the Preface, contributed a chapter and is my co-editor. He offered valuable advice, inputs and interventions as the project progressed.

Considering that this is NDC's first major publication, there was also a need to be cautious about intellectual and institutional red lines, while also exercising the intellectual autonomy of the institution to provide a level playing field for contrarian and competitive views on issues like the utility of aircraft carriers and submarines, or the importance of fire and manoeuvre irrespective of the genre and nature of conflict. This volume is intended to pave the way for several such broad and focussed deliberations on strategic, national security and military affairs. Finally, it is hoped that this volume is just the start of a steady flow of quality writing from the NDC.

CHAPTER 2

LIMITED WAR

PRAKASH MENON

ABSTRACT

India's concept of Limited War seems to have survived, since its advent into the strategic discourse after the 1998 nuclear tests. Nuclear weapons have changed the nature of military confrontations between India, China and Pakistan and supposedly played a role in most of India's major military confrontations with Pakistan and China. The extent of the role and its impact on the minds of decision makers is difficult to fathom. However, exercise of caution is apparent. Fortunately, none have matched their rhetoric with actual actions. Although force has been exchanged, its escalation has remained tightly controlled by political rationale. Perhaps the political leadership have clarity that force has only restricted utility for solving problems between nuclear-armed powers. But, the probability of deliberate or accidental military situations getting out of political control cannot be ruled out. Therefore, while it is important to understand the mechanics of Limited War, it is better that the concept remains the last resort and best if it is untested.

INTRODUCTION

This chapter will examine the impact of a product of a politico-military imagination on the trajectory of geopolitics in the Indian context. The product is the concept of Limited War, which was born in the Subcontinent from the womb of nuclear weapons when India and Pakistan went nuclear in 1998. Prior to that, though wars were fought in 1947-48, 1962, 1965 and 1971, limits that imposed themselves related to policy that was shaped primarily by the interaction of power, strategy, costs, fear and culture.

With the advent of nuclear weapons in national arsenals, policy on war and its conduct became imprisoned by the fear of escalation to the nuclear level. It was a military problem that was not easily amenable to political control. Force application to achieve political objectives had to contend with the reality that once military forces are unleashed, the military momentum of action and reaction would be difficult to control by the rational hand of policy. The perennial danger in war was that military forces in contact could acquire a logic of their own that gets disconnected from policy objectives. The potential net result could be uncontrolled exchange of nuclear force, posing an existential threat to both. This problem has defied a solution despite the intellectual heft of several generations since Hiroshima and Nagasaki. What happens after the first nuclear weapons have been fired remains an intractable problem. The solution sought must balance two practically irreconcilable paradigms of war between nuclear powers. Yet, simultaneously, both continue to coexist uneasily.

The conventional paradigm of war was on seeking political outcomes through force by imposing one's will on the adversary. The extent of political outcomes achieved was finally decided on the table of political negotiations. A military capitulation by one of the sides would be the ideal way out. In contrast, the nuclear paradigm enunciated by Bernard Brodie, 1946, states: "Thus far, while the chief purpose of the military establishment had been to win wars, after the advent of nuclear weapons, its chief purpose was to avert them."[1] This paradigm turned on its head the notion of victory that was based on the application of conventional force to the extent of imposing one's will on the adversary.

The continued coexistence of the two paradigms and its impact on military preparations for war has been sustained by theories of deterrence and has birthed the Stability-Instability Paradox.[2] There is stability towards the higher level of military force exchange but increased instability at the lower levels. During the Cold War, proxy wars represented the primary form of contestation even when there were continued tensions spawned by the competition in military build-up that was persistent in the name of deterrence. Big wars and direct military confrontations between nuclear powers have been avoided so far, and even if they seemed imminent, political leaders have acted with great caution even as the levels of political rhetoric in a crisis seemed to reflect bravado. But when it came to the crunch, risk avoidance was preferred. But the search for the ceiling that represented nuclear threshold has not been given up though there is broad political acceptance that it is not worth exploring.

Strategists, the world over, are now pursuing a plethora of forms to coerce and achieve political outcomes. The preference is for activities towards the lower end: covert, stealthy and deniable, punches that may not physically hurt as much but are psychologically efficient. The attempt being to create the politico-military conditions for advantage in negotiations. War as previously understood and practised remains a key instrument of statecraft. What has changed are the forms that it is adapting. Some of the forms defy the classical definition of war that stays with the threat or application of violence as the distinguishing line between war and peace.

THE INDIAN CONTEXT

In the Indian context, that distinguishing line has been blurred for long. The Indian Military used to refer to it as No War No Peace (NWNP). Over time, the term has been consumed by other fashionable imported descriptions. NWNP sought to focus on that space, which is now a popular hunting ground of research. The Indians are the most experienced nation in the world with regards to the utility of force under the nuclear shadow. The Pakistanis might also feel entitled to such a claim that could be countered as India has experience with China too. The world can probably take some lessons from the Indian experience.

In the Indian context, Stability-Instability Paradox[3] is clearly evident. The Kargil Conflict was fought a year after both countries carried out nuclear tests and was restricted geographically to an area extending across a linear frontage of over 100 kilometres in the state of Jammu and Kashmir. However, both countries lacked an operational nuclear arsenal worthy of the name. The fact that Pakistan had no operational nuclear weapons in 1999, was admitted by General Musharraf[4] who was the architect for initiating the conflict as its Army Chief.

The role of nuclear weapons in the Kargil conflict is instructive, especially because, despite the deficiency in operational nuclear weapons, the nuclear capability seemed to have played a role. The suspicion of possession was sufficient to induce caution in the political leadership on both sides. Vajpayee's insistence on not crossing the LoC cannot be justified in military terms, and the price of that restriction meant an increased probability of greater loss of Indian lives. But the political value attached to containing and isolating the geographic span of the conflict outweighed the risks to lives. We can only speculate how the conflict would have turned out if the IAF had been allowed to cross the LoC. The military mind would lean towards the notion that the conflict would have ended sooner, saving lives and remaining geographically restricted.

Our focus here is that Vajpayee's decision, whatever it was, reflected caution. Probably, it was to some unknown degree influenced by the destructive power of the nuclear weapons. The nuclear weapon is for certain a politician's nightmare. Even the thought of just one nuclear weapon exploding on any of the nation's cities is unthinkable and the avoidance of that possibility is a major and natural political anxiety. Publicly, the political leadership is to project the will to use nuclear weapons under conditions that are to be clearly communicated to potential adversaries. Such a projection is supposed to strengthen deterrence, prevent wars and keep the nuclear weapons sheathed. But it is also the nub of the politician's dilemma.

INDIA'S CONCEPT OF LIMITED WAR

The concept of Limited War was rolled out at an IDSA Seminar in January 2000, held at the Institute of Defence Studies and Analysis (IDSA). It was there that the Defence Minister George Fernandes and the Army Chief General V.P. Malik expressed the official Indian views on limited war.[5] In his opening address, the Defence Minister explained the rationale of limited war: 'We had understood the dynamics of limited war.... Nuclear weapons did not make war obsolete, they simply imposed another dimension on the way warfare could be conducted.... So, the issue was not that war had been made obsolete by nuclear weapons, and that covert war by proxy was the only option, but that conventional war remained feasible, though with definite limitations, if escalation across the nuclear threshold was to be avoided....'

At the closing address of the seminar, General Malik stated:

'The rationale for limited war is economic considerations, risk of high casualties, international pressure and the nuclear factor.... Limited war is characterised by limitations, which tend to control its conduct and space. It could be limited in time, geographical area, or force level. In the Indian perspective, when we talk of a limited war, it could range from the kind we have been engaged in Siachen since the 1980s, the Kargil War in the recent past, to future wars, which could be fought by us in confined sector(s) along our long frontiers. It is not possible to outline the exact contours of any future war with great deal of certainty.... The whole scope and conduct of limited war would be governed by the end state.'

Jasjit Singh, the Director of the Indian think tank IDSA, in an article 'Dynamics of Limited War', defined limited war as the following:

> 'If nuclear war and total global war are no longer viable propositions as an extension of politics by other means, the only choice available to states to use destructive forces for political purposes is through limited conventional war, sub-conventional war with military-type weapons, and the use of coercive military force without necessarily

> resulting in war. The overall result has been reducing the potential of war down to limited wars…'[6]

Speaking at a seminar in November 2002, General Malik elaborated on the concept of limited war:

> 'The fundamental point for a limited war is that it is a political process conducted for bargaining. The aim is not to win but rather not to lose and fight in such a way that the enemy is forced to settle for peace…. There is a linkage between deterrence and escalation. Capability to wage a successful conventional and nuclear war (if necessary) is an important deterrent. A war may well remain limited because of a credible deterrence…. Continuous control of the escalatory ladder by the political and military leadership is important.'[7]

ESCALATION – THE INTRACTABLE REALITY

Prior to and during the nuclear era, the intractable challenge for politicians and the military has remained the 'control of the escalatory ladder'. This is a problem that has been explained by Clausewitz in his brilliant treatise On War in the early 19th century. The explanatory model called the 'Trinity'[8] portrays three forces at play that could pull escalation

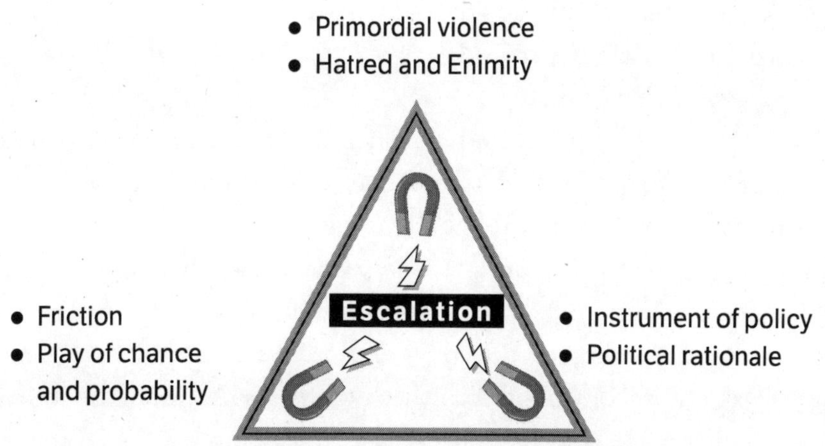

THE CLAUSEWITZIAN TRINITY

in three different directions. Escalation in the model was represented by an imaginary magnet suspended in the middle.

The model represented a nation and the scope for escalation when opposing military forces are engaged. The strength of the forces at play would be determined by the product generated by the clash of similar forces on the opposing side. Thus, the degree of hatred and enmity between the populations or political communities in conflict would ignite the fires of primordial violence that inheres in human nature. From an Indian perspective, for long, at the level of political communities, the degree of Indo-Pak hatred has been progressively growing for various reasons. Recently, in the context of China, especially after Galwan, the memory of 1962 has been revived and has ushered in an intensified sense of antipathy and distrust. However, with trade relations only being slowly impacted, it is incomparable to the popular emotion that Pakistan can trigger in India.

The second source of force has been described by Clausewitz as *Friction*, where the play of *Chance and Probability* is sometimes nearly impossible to control as it is not in human hands and is further complicated by the *Fog of War* resulting from the climate of war that is pervaded by danger, exertion and uncertainty. He compared the difficulty of executing military operations like walking in water and opined that unimaginable things can happen, and worse, many things can go wrong simultaneously. Experienced soldiers will vouch for this. Escalation is an easy victim of this force.

The third force represented human sanity in the form of war being subordinated to political rationale that was encompassed in policy. Self-preservation was the foundational impulse. Everything else was subordinated to it. Of course, self-preservation largely represented the policy making elite. Policy set the objectives of war and was free to moderate it depending on the strength exerted by the other two forces, but it was not in control of the other two forces. Adjusting policy was easier and feasible, and that is how war finally moves to the political table of diplomacy and political agreements.

THE INDIAN EXPERIENCE

In India, the notion of conventional war between nuclear powers is yet to be field tested. Conventional wars between nuclear powers had to be planned and fought under the nuclear shadow. This required policy to embrace doctrines of deterrence to prevent wars that could trigger the use of nuclear weapons intentionally or inadvertently. India's nuclear doctrine of August 1999 and its slightly modified official version of 2003, rejected that Limited Nuclear War can be planned and should be fought. It visualises that the risk can never be justified. Therefore, in both versions, it combined No First Use with retaliation to inflict unacceptable damage. The official 2003 version replaced the earlier 'punitive retaliation' to 'massive retaliation'. The switch of description cemented the disapproval of limited nuclear war. It has also spurned the idea of Tactical Nuclear Weapons as it considers that any use of nuclear weapons of any size will have strategic consequences. However, Conventional Limited war that seeks to change the status quo favourably, remains the focus of military preparations.

India's experience of limited war has been so far confined to brinkmanship accompanied by coercive diplomacy with the pressures built up by the potential military clash being the political weapon in play. The Indo-Pak crisis of 2001-2002 provides some valuable insights when viewed in its context. What was under test was the utility and effectiveness of the Indian concept of Limited War to stop Pakistan from using terrorism as a tool of foreign policy. On 27 May, 2002, the Indian External Affairs Minister responded succinctly to a nuclear threat made by Musharraf during the crisis: "He stated that this was tantamount to nuclearisation of terrorism, adding that 'in this we see an example of how the promotion of terrorism and the threat of nuclear weapons are being held simultaneously. The international community has to take note of the seriousness of these two dangers."[9] The crisis has been the longest military confrontation where both sides were mobilised. Pakistan dealt with the pressure of an Indian attack by political retreats that were tactical, like Musharraf's speech on January 12, 2002.[10] Apparently, succumbing to India's coercive diplomacy and the exertions of the US State Department, President Musharraf spelled out a sweeping domestic reform agenda.

In the early part of the crisis, India relied more on its own threat of Limited War than on international intervention. Simultaneously, for Pakistan, the main political thrust was on highlighting the danger of nuclear war to invite international attention especially intervention by the US to prevent India from launching a war. The US was highly dependent on Pakistan at that time due to the Afghan War, and even had military assets based in Pakistan carrying out operations in support of its operations in Afghanistan.

In the later part of the crisis, in May 2002, as war clouds deepened following a cross border terrorist strike on the Kaluchak military camp in Jammu, India's political thrust shifted its weight to international intervention. Later, the US did indeed play a crucial role in defusing the crisis. The military fallout of the crisis rekindled an old idea that finally became known as the Cold Start Doctrine. The primary land forces objective of capturing large tracts of territory remained. The new doctrine attempted to create capability to launch attacks in the shortest possible timeframe by relocating offensive assets as forward as possible, thus reducing time for mobilisation. Initial thrusts would subsequently be exploited by forces moved forward from depth areas. It is another matter that Pakistan too moved its formations forward and embraced the idea of TNW.

India's central political logic was that capture of territory could act as the bargaining chip for getting Pakistan to stop using terrorism as a tool of foreign policy. The logic had lost all validity even before Indo-Pak nuclearisation. Even if a successful war was fought and territory was captured there was nothing stopping Pakistan from backtracking on terrorism later. Additionally, capture of large tracts of territory may necessitate a counter-insurgency, unless the captured territory was mostly de-populated. Shallow thrusts[11] were advocated by some, but in practice nothing much changed and destruction of Pakistan's military capability continued to be the military aim. Seeking decisive battles remained the military aspiration.

The lessons of the 2001-02 Indo-Pak crisis were internalised by India and Pakistan differently. India's political leadership became sceptical of the utility of war. However, India's military believed that the validity of Limited War was upheld and could be successful, if mobilisation time was reduced and political decision making was done at speed. Pakistan believed that they had successfully used the nuclear factor to prevent India from launching its military. Their belief in the utility of terrorism under the nuclear shadow was strengthened. Later, these opposing beliefs were again put to test when the next big crisis presented itself on November 26, 2008.

THE MUMBAI TERRORIST STRIKE

Politically, with the defusing of the 2001-2002 crisis, the India-Pakistan relationship showed a positive trend. Both countries signed a ceasefire agreement in November 2003 and commenced a Composite Dialogue. This relatively congenial phase endured in fits and starts and it was revealed in February 2007 that India and Pakistan had come close to an agreement based on a non-territorial solution. However, the peace process came under stress with Pakistan-sponsored terrorist attacks beginning in July 2006 with the serial train blasts in Mumbai, followed by the serial blasts in Jaipur in May 2008; a suicide attack on the Indian Embassy in Kabul in July 2008; and several terrorist attacks in Bangalore, Ahmedabad, New Delhi and Guwahati between July and October 2008. India's reactions were limited at the tactical level on the Line of Control (LoC) that included exchange of fire and shallow cross border raids.[12]

On November 26, 2008, Pakistan carried out a major terrorist strike in Mumbai and inflicted substantial causalities, including foreigners. But it did not stir the evocation of Limited War as India chose the diplomatic route for putting pressure on Pakistan to bring the perpetrators to account. The question that begs for an answer is why did India confine itself to political and diplomatic measures despite ample proof of the Mumbai attack being launched from Pakistan? The reaction was in marked contrast to India's reaction in 2001. Several reasons could be construed:

- Though Pakistan initially denied the incident, it condemned the attack and offered to cooperate in the investigation, which was later shot down by its Army. In the weeks following the attack, Pakistan took at least limited action to arrest the perpetrators and raised some hopes in India that the civilian leadership was committed to acting against terrorist groups.
- Military options provided by the Indian military leadership may not have convinced the political leadership that they would resolve the issue of preventing terrorism originating from Pakistan. The military options such as air strikes and ground action could result in a limited war, but how this could facilitate the political objective of getting Pakistan to eschew using terrorism against India as a foreign policy tool was neither clear nor convincing enough. Apart from not achieving the main political objective, considering its focus on economic development, a limited war was not in India's interest.
- Some attribute the military inaction to the personalities involved in the decision-making, especially the Prime Minister, who continued to keep faith in seeking a stable and friendly relationship as part of the nation's grand strategic vision. The fact that the Congress Government was voted back to power in 2009 indicates that India staying with political and diplomatic measures did not have any major impact on its electoral fortunes nor did it find much ballast in the electoral debate.
- Immediately after the Mumbai attack, Pakistan made it clear that if India was to react militarily it would have to shift most of its troops from the western border, thus weakening its effort to counter the US-led Afghan campaign against the Taliban.

> This threat was aimed to get the US to put pressure on India to refrain from retaliating militarily. The US, in fact, did send the Secretary of State Condeleezza Rice, to counsel restraint. India, on the other hand, perceived the possibility that the strategic purpose of the Mumbai attack was a result of a conspiracy between the ISI, LeT, the Taliban and Al-Qaeda to get Pakistan to ease pressure on their bases at the Af-Pak border. An Indian military response could mean playing to the terrorist game plan.

As had happened with the 2001-02 crisis and the Kargil conflict, the Mumbai attack produced divergent internalised narratives on both sides. The divergent narratives provided fertile ground for future misunderstandings and miscalculations. India's views on Pakistan's duplicity were reinforced and the inadequacy of political and diplomatic measures to force Pakistan to give up the terrorist tool as a foreign policy instrument was also internalised. Pakistan concluded that the nuclear factor could be leveraged to seek foreign intervention to restrain India militarily.

LOC FIRING

Since 2007, the LoC has been active and on a slow boil. By August 2014, cross-border firing exchanges increased and had peaked in 2019/20, till a ceasefire was re-established in March 2021. Apart from inflicting casualties and destruction, it also involved displacement of civilian population on both sides. For as long as both sides operate on a free will, LoC firing is a useless exchange of energy. But it can come in handy for domestic politics. Unlike the Congress Governments, the BJP's general inclination has been to be tough towards Pakistan. It is a fundamental ideological disposition. In LoC firing, there was enough scope to show the iron hand to the domestic polity and electoral benefits could accrue with the media whipping up popular passions directed at Pakistan. The Pakistan Army used the LoC firing to boost up the India threat which is the oxygen for the military to remain in power in Pakistan's politics.

Gurdaspur/Pathankot/Uri (2014–2017)

Despite BJP's ideological disposition, the Indian Government had extended an olive branch to Pakistan, which unfortunately had a short shelf life due to the repeated reassertion of a familiar mode of derailment through cross border terrorist attacks. Earlier, the Lahore Bus Yatra by Vajpayee was followed by Kargil in 1999; Manmohan–Musharraf talks were followed by Mumbai serial train bombings and later by the Mumbai strike in 2008. There was a Modi–Sharif meeting at Ufa on July 10, 2015, where they reached an understanding to resume the Composite Dialogue. The Gurdaspur terrorist attack occurred on July 27, 2015. Later, Modi's surprise visit to Lahore on December 25, 2015 for a meeting with Sharif was followed by the attack in Pathankot on January 2, 2016.

Both the Gurdaspur and Pathankot attacks occurred at times when the civilian government on both sides were attempting to restore political relations. In both the cases, it seems, officially, there was no serious thought to any Indian reaction that involved the use of cross border application of force. Pakistan claimed innocence as usual and offered their sympathies. After Pathankot, Pakistan agreed to assist in the investigation and in a surprising move of goodwill their investigating team was given access to the scene of action inside the Pathankot Air Base and areas through which the infiltration took place. After the investigators returned to Pakistan, they went back to the default mode – denial, deceit and obfuscation. A follow up visit to Pakistan by Indian investigators never materialised. These experiences therefore hardened the Indian stand that settled at 'No talks without halting terrorism'. Then followed the Uri attack.

The Uri attack in September 2017 on an Indian Army's administrative location claimed 18 lives and injured several more. The attack was carried out at a time when India-Pakistan relations were at a low ebb due to the Gurdaspur and Pathankot attacks. In addition, Kashmir was witnessing a prolonged phase of violent civil protests that followed in the wake of the killing of a local terrorist leader of South Kashmir, Burhan Wani. On the international arena, the United Nations General Assembly (UNGA) was in session from September 13 to 26.

The culpability of Pakistan was established through electronic tracking, especially the GPS carried by the terrorists. Following a familiar pattern, Pakistan denied culpability, floated conspiracy theories and accused India of trying to distract attention from human rights excesses in Kashmir. Also, another phase of cross-border cease-fire violations commenced with intensive use of mortar and artillery fire. All this was predictable and followed the existing pattern. But what was different this time was the internal political dynamics in India.

The substantial loss of lives coupled with the deterioration in India-Pakistan relations presented a challenge to the Indian Government that was left with no choice but to pick up the gauntlet. The Indian reaction was announced to the world and described as 'Surgical Strikes' on September 29 post the UNGA Session. Indeed, the scope and effect of the surgical strike was a remarkable achievement by India's special forces especially because significant damage was inflicted without suffering any casualties.

The Indian DGMO's statement evoked considerable jubilation amongst the Indian public and the Government projected the 'surgical strike' as a feather in their political cap. In the realm of domestic politics, 'surgical strike' became symbolic of a government that meant business and one that would not hesitate to act in the interest of the nation. The term 'surgical strike' was added to the lexicon of domestic politics and later even used to describe the surprise sprung on the Indian public by a demonetisation exercise aimed against black money. 'Surgical strike' thereafter figured in all the elections held at the state levels and was touted as a major achievement of the Government. To a public that was hungry for action against Pakistan, 'surgical strike' was sweet revenge. The policy of publicising India's military reaction has sustained with the Army now more 'heard' than 'felt.'

From a deterrence perspective, 'surgical strike' had a confused outcome because Pakistan's political and military leadership completely denied India's claims of having carried out military actions across the Line of Control and the Indian Government also decided against providing much proof of the strike. It therefore relieved the Pakistanis from undertaking any retaliatory military action.[13]

India

- Surgical Strikes signalled a switch in Indian attitude regarding use of military power to counter-terrorism.
- It was apparently surmised that Surgical strikes could be an effective military tool to inflict damage on Pakistan to deter it from conducting terror attacks.
- Pakistan's reaction to surgical strikes could be muted or be dealt with and confined to reasonable escalation limits.
- Considerable domestic political benefits could be garnered if the Indian public is exposed to the narrative of India having resorted to use of force and succeeded in causing damage to Pakistan. Action taken must be displayed for public viewing.

Pakistan

- India's response to terror strike is primarily meant for the domestic polity. Nuclear weapons would ensure that no major Indian military action ensues.
- Pakistan can counter any military action taken by India.

BALAKOT

Nearly three years after the surgical strike, the Pulwama terrorist strike took place on February 14, 2019, through a car-borne suicide attack on a Central Reserve Police Force convoy. It resulted in the death of 40 people and scores wounded. A flurry of denials from Pakistan did not impact the popular emotional upsurge in India for revenge. The reaction seemed certain, but when and how? The response was an air strike on a terrorist camp near Balakot in Kyber Pakhtunwa province of Pakistan on February 26, 2017. The speed at which airpower could be applied was leveraged. It was the first such strike against Pakistan since the 1971 war. Pakistan acknowledged the strike but claimed that the weapons had hit uninhabited areas. India claimed that it caused damage and considerable casualties. The next day, Pak Air Force planes attempted a strike in the Jammu area and were intercepted. India lost an aircraft and its pilot was taken prisoner even as the IAF claimed to have downed a PAF F-16. Pakistan claimed to have inflicted damage on Indian military installations and India denied.

The use of airpower deep inside Pakistan was the hallmark of the military action. The psychological messaging to Pakistan was enough that they combined denial of impact with an attempt at reprisal through an air strike. It allowed them to claim success by downing an Indian aircraft and capturing the pilot. Supposedly, the US played a role in the quick return of the pilot.

Following an established pattern, both sides claimed victory that was useful for domestic politics. But the fact that India had used its airpower to strike deep would have set the Pakistanis interrogating their assumptions on the risk-taking ability of India's political leadership. In terms of stability of deterrence under the nuclear shadow, the situation has moved up to a higher level. But both are exploring the ceiling without being able to reach a conclusion. With the August 2019 abrogation of Article 370 and the change in status of the State of J&K, the possibility of Pakistan fishing in troubled waters is a given. While risk taking on both sides is likely to follow patterns that are largely dictated by political rhetoric, it is hoped that strategic caution would be exercised to control the escalation ladder. For what must be accepted is that while nuclear weapons have not kept the peace, they have prevented the 'big fight' that calls into question the utility of force in the context of nuclear powers. That answer will have to await an examination of how the Sino-Indian military confrontation that commenced in the summer of 2020 pans out over the next few years.

LADAKH-2020

Following the visit of Prime Minister Vajpayee to China in 2003, the two sides had decided not to let the border dispute impact bilateral engagements. A slew of agreements signed in 1993, 1996, 2005, 2012 and 2013 maintained the peace. Since both sides had no agreed understanding of the alignment of the Line of Actual Control (LAC), border incidents were not uncommon and were variously described as 'transgressions'. China, despite it being specifically stated in the 1993 agreement, evaded the identification of the alignment. Meanwhile, China began massive infrastructure projects in the early 2000s to improve its connectivity to and in Tibet and Xinjiang with many roads creeping close to the border and improving air connectivity. Three major incidents required diplomatic intervention to resolve them: Depsang in 2013, Chumar in 2014 and Doklam in 2017. All of them were relatively minor compared to China's aggressive moves in Ladakh in 2020.

In March/April 2020, while India's attention was diverted by COVID-19, China, which was carrying out its annual military exercises in Eastern Ladakh, suddenly changed direction and militarily transgressed into disputed areas in Galwan Valley, Gogra-Hot Springs – Kongka La and the North Bank of the Pangong Tso. What was notable was it had as a back-up its reserve infantry and mechanised formations that could easily reinforce the front. Airpower accretions into Tibet also followed. Though the scale of China's operations was not apparent immediately, India mobilised swiftly once it was recognised. The Indian mobilisation though partial also covered other segments of the border.

In June, consequent to an agreement between military commanders, a disengagement was underway in Galwan valley when a clash resulted in 20 Indian soldiers being killed. China acknowledged a couple of casualties much later but some accounts put the figures between 30-40 dead. This incident had a strategic impact and changed the political and strategic texture of the confrontation.

China prevaricated on talks and changed its position consequent to Indian occupation of the Kailash Range in end August 2020, which dominated key areas in the Southern Bank of the Spanggur Tso. After several days partial disengagement took place, and China vacated the North Bank of Pangong Tso and India reciprocated by vacating the Kailash Range. Further disengagement was stalled through the winter with China dragging its feet. Perhaps, this was a result of India overcoming its reluctance about the QUAD, and taking part in a first ever, Heads of States Meeting and coming out with a Joint Statement called the 'Spirit of the QUAD.'[14]

Apart from Galwan, which apparently was more akin to a brawl and reports of some exchange of fire in the Kailash Range, there has been no direct military shoot-out so far. Though both countries partially thinned out during the winter and disengaged from some potential confrontation zones, the summer of 2021 has witnessed significant build-up of combat capability in depth on both sides. Another round of disengagement in August 2021 seems encouraging, but there are still areas like the Depsang Plains that could prove problematic. Notably, in the present military context, both sides have mobilised airpower assets. This raises the possibility of widening the area of conflict even if the ground fighting is restricted in geographic space. Airpower could play a significant role with India having some advantages because it is not handicapped as China is due to having to operate from fewer air bases, nearly all of which are in high altitude. The advent of the potential use of airpower and its escalatory potential is also another reason for political caution in application of force.

China's intentions in Ladakh and its connect with coercing India to prevent a tilt towards the US could provide a plausible explanation. China could believe that threats and occasional tensions on the Northern Border and using it as pressure point may keep India contained in the subcontinent which is a long-term strategy with Pakistan being thus far its main proxy. Additional resources on the Northern Border would also slow down India's ability to strengthen its maritime power. In the present geopolitical context, China might be using the Northern Border in an instrumental role to signal a warning that it can hurt India militarily if it gets closer to the US, which is one of its primary strategic anxieties. With India now diving into the waters of the QUAD, China's strategic objectives have been adversely affected for the time being. But considering the political stakes involved, further Salami Slicings or limited thrusts in places like Depsang, Doklam, Tawang to name a few are not beyond the realm of possibility. Even if these moves succeed, they will simply push India further towards the US, so how China gets out of this self-created trap remains to be seen.

The confrontation is therefore one of brinkmanship aimed for psychological impact on India's political posture in the larger global competition between the US and China. Force is threatened more than applied. Limited War remains untested in practice but the likelihood of short sharp engagements that change the status quo endures. Importantly, the problem of keeping it short refuses to go away. Nuclear weapons were never brought into the equation but its presence in the minds of leaders is definite. Like with Pakistan, utility of force can change the status quo somewhat but cannot resolve the political problems that gave rise to force application. Neither military superiority nor operational virtuosity nor political guile seems to provide any pathway to impose one's will through force. The paradigm that has endured with Pakistan and China is one of Perpetual Confrontation – Crisis – Short and Sharp Force Exchange – Confrontation. In the Indian context, Limited War is not limited in time, it hides perennially in plain sight within the folds of seemingly intractable disputes with neighbours.

SURVIVAL OF LIMITED WAR CONCEPT

India's concept of Limited War survives in theory though its realisation to achieve any germane and substantial political objectives remains on the drawing board. In any case the aim is not to win but create the conditions for peace. Military technology continues to throw up alternative means of force application but that has failed to convince the political imagination that the battlefield can resolve India's political problems with China and Pakistan. With China, it is about acceptance of subordination in the context of its aspiration to become the leading power in the world. With Pakistan, terrorism is used to keep India off balance. Additionally, both countries also pose combined threats. Hard power for deterrence against such threats must be designed even when its utility seems partial. On the basis of that uncomfortable thought, the Limited War as a military concept may endure while constantly unearthing the lower level of the spectrum of force application that can still be psychologically damaging. However, the extent to which it can influence the will of the adversary, especially if its stakes are high, will remain a moot question.

NOTES

1 Bernard Brodie, The Absolute Weapon (New York: Harcourt Brace, Inc., 1946), p. 76.

2 https://theasiadialogue.com/wp-content/uploads/2017/10/stability-instability-paradox-south-asia.pdf

3 https://web.archive.org/web/20170812115507/https://www.stimson.org/sites/default/files/file-attachments/stability-instability-paradox-south-asia.pdf

4 Musharraf Parvez, *In the Line of Fire* (UK: Simon & Schuster, 2006), pp. 97-98

5 Quoted from Prakash Menon, *The Strategy Trap: India & Pakistan Under the Nuclear Shadow* (New Delhi: Wisdom Tree, 2018), pp. 167-68

6 Singh, Jasjit, 'Dynamics of Limited War', *Strategic Analysis*, Vol-24, No.7, October 2000, p. 1205.

7 Malik, VP, 'Limited War' in Singh, Jasjit, ed, *'ir Power and Joint Operations'* (New Delhi: Knowledge World in association with Centre for Air Power Studies, New Delhi, 2003), p. 157.

8 Carl von Clausewitz, *On War*, trans. Michael Howard and Peter Paret (New Jersey, Princeton University Press, 1976), p. 89.

9 Menon, n. 5, p. 120.

10 https://zeenews.india.com/news/south-asia/text-of-musharrafs-speech_31172.html

11 https://www.nonproliferation.org/wp-content/uploads/npr/83ragh.pdf

12 Menon, n. 5, pp. 137-39.

13 Menon, n. 5, p. 147

14 https://www.mea.gov.in/bilateral-documents.htm?dtl/33620/Quad_Leaders_Joint_Statement_The_Spirit_of_the_Quad

CHAPTER 3

EVOLUTION OF INDIA'S COUNTER-INSURGENCY DOCTRINE

J.R. MUKHERJEE

ABSTRACT

This chapter examines the Indian Army's experiences in counter-insurgency operations from Indian Independence till the beginning of the 21st century. The Army's initial handling of such operations, particularly in Nagaland, Mizoram and Manipur, was based on the British Army's pattern of operations in Malaya and was primarily punitive. India's democratic values compelled a progressive change towards greater people friendliness and on the primacy of political aims in such operations. It is in the backdrop of this change that the article also examines the evolution of the Indian Army's counter-insurgency (CI) doctrine during a period of high intensity CI operations against complex proxy threats in the garb of insurgencies.

INTRODUCTION

It has been widely proclaimed that the Indian Army (IA) has emerged today as a responsible and proficient counter-insurgency force. This chapter attempts to analyse the Indian Army's experiences in counter-insurgency (CI) operations and the evolution of its counter-insurgency doctrine from the time of India's Independence in 1947 to the beginning of the 21st century. India faced its highest intensity of counter-insurgency operations during this period, when it was fighting mostly proxy wars styled as insurgencies.[1,2]

While definitions of various terms can be found in the Indian Army Doctrine for Sub Conventional Warfare of 2006,[9] 'Insurgency' in lay terms is, a rebellion by a section of the population against the state, which may include violent acts of terrorism. It is primarily a political struggle which invariably involves the use of force in which the insurgent indulges in acts of militancy. While there is no universally accepted definition of 'terrorist'—'one man's terrorist is another's freedom fighter'—'terrorism in lay terms is use of violence indiscriminately against innocent civilians.'[9] 'Militancy is a condition which experiences the use of violence.' All insurgencies, however, do not include terrorism. All actions by a Government to end an insurgency, including finding political solutions and use of force to end the same, fall in the realm of Counter-insurgency (CI) Operations.

The insurgencies that India has faced over the years have occurred largely in the states of Nagaland, Mizoram, Manipur, Assam, Tripura, Punjab, Sri Lanka and Jammu and Kashmir. India's Police forces have in addition dealt with—the Telangana secessionist, Naxalite, Maoist-Naxalite and the Punjab Movements.[6,9,21,41] This chapter will not discuss the Punjab experience as that will be covered in the chapter on 'Left Wing Extremism and Urban Terrorism' later in the book.

THE BRITISH EXPERIENCE AND INFLUENCE

Prior to independence, the Armed Forces of British India gained extensive experience in dealing with armed rebellion, insurgencies, tribal revolts in India and Burma, the 1857 War of Independence, as well as the Boer Wars in South Africa and the Indian Independence Movement. The British Army also gained vast experience from their operations in Palestine, Malaya, Kenya, Cyprus, Brunei and Borneo, Radfan and Aden, Dhofar (Oman), and Northern Ireland. They learnt from operations by the French in Vietnam and Algeria, the Portuguese in Africa and elsewhere; and the US Army in Vietnam.

Of these, the British operations in Malaya and Kenya were great successes,[8,15,16,20,28,52] as these insurgencies were suppressed by the British with brute punitive force. They used aerial carpet bombing to neutralise insurgents, destroyed forests and crops by aerial spray of herbicides/defoliating agents and used all types of heavy weapons in support of their operations.

British counter-insurgency theory and practice was thus greatly influenced by their campaigns in Cyprus, Malaya and Kenya. The five principles of counter-insurgency that emerged were—a clear political aim; adherence to the rule of law; a co-ordinated plan outlining political, economic, social and military responses; ensuring security of own bases before launching military operations; and lastly, destroying the insurgents' political infrastructure. The key elements of the British strategy were political primacy, isolation of the insurgent, intelligence and suitable military response. This meant close political control over the operations by a civilian vested with political powers. Great emphasis was laid on intelligence by the civil police with a view to take advantage of their local knowledge. This was imperative to isolate the insurgents from the support of the people and by influencing their "hearts and minds". The form of isolation decided on was the resettlement of population away from the insurgents' activity and influence. Elimination of cells of local support by temporary detention and intelligence screening was also considered essential. The Army would then pursue insurgents who had been forced by isolation to retreat into countryside/urban areas. Civilian casualties were to be minimised to avoid alienating the local population. Following that, a sustained military campaign was to be launched. The problem with the above doctrine was that it assumed the enemy to be the colonial rebel native and the concept of counter insurgency was primarily punitive. The British Doctrine also did not cater to dealing with a proxy war and foreign support while evolving border management/counter-infiltration strategies. Consequently, there was an emergent need to exercise due caution before applying the British Strategy to resolve ethnic insurgencies in India.[4,8,15,16,25,28]

THE INDIAN EXPERIENCE

The IA, however, was instructed to execute counter-insurgency operations based on the British model when deployed for the first time in Nagaland, Mizoram and Manipur. The Indian police also simultaneously handled the Naxalite movement in Bengal and the secessionist movement in Telangana using these colonial punitive methods. The Maoist–Naxalite insurgency in Central India was also handled by the police, who initially followed these methods, but subsequently learnt from the IA's evolving methods of handling counter-insurgency.[1,4,22,25] Nagaland and Mizoram initially bore the initial brunt of the above tactics. The IA, however, eventually switched to operating with a counter-insurgency ethos that was sensitive to the fact that the Army was fighting its own fellow citizens, albeit a misguided lot.[1,3,6,20,21,34,37]

Nagaland

The Naga insurgency for independence commenced on a low key from 1947. Government officials and the police were progressively subverted, and the population won over to the rebel cause through propaganda and selective acts of terror—militancy developed into an insurgency by 1956. The Indian Army (IA), which was then deployed to quell the insurgency, found itself at a serious disadvantage as key locations in Nagaland were in the hands of the rebels; the access routes into the Naga Hills District were cut off; and the District administration and police were totally subverted. The IA had to therefore first launch operations to clear the axes and regain control of the important locations in rebel hands. They then progressively launched operations to 'search and hold' on the British model, to gain control over the population centres and attempted to set up posts to dominate the countryside to isolate the insurgents. It is then that the Indian Government agreed to the implementation of the isolation measures adopted in Malaya, i.e. the regrouping of villages and resettlement of almost the entire Naga population along with issue of identity cards for population control. The newly constructed villages were under the direct supervision of Army posts. The old villages were forcibly destroyed. Measures were also adopted to destroy all crops and granaries to deny food to the insurgents. Night curfew became the norm, with strictly controlled exit and entry into these new villages. Interrogation and punitive action became the order of the day. There were regular search and destroy, cordon and search missions and large-scale sweeps, patrols and ambushes to enforce the above and to neutralise the insurgents.

In the words of General Sir Frank Kitson (under whom the author did the Staff College Course in UK), —'get them by the b----- then hearts will follow.'[4,28.] These operations bore fruit with increasing insurgent casualties and the Armed Forces gaining intelligence. Many of the insurgents took sanctuary across the border in Myanmar; it then became essential to earmark border guarding and counter-infiltration forces to stop insurgent move across the border. To release scarce Army resources for mobile operations, more responsibility was handed over to Central Police/Paramilitary Forces and the newly created village guards raised from retired ex- servicemen, for route opening and protection, guarding of the new villages and other tasks. Political action was then initiated to grant statehood to Nagaland in 1963 and elections held, which satisfied the moderates and created a divide amongst the insurgents. Rewards for information and amnesty and a scheme for surrendered insurgents was simultaneously declared, and talks with all Nagas who opted for peace started. Strict orders had by then been issued and enforced for use of only minimum force, to avoid human rights violations and for commencement of civic action schemes to try and win the hearts and minds of the local population. The 1971 war wherein India defeated Pakistan, resulted in a decrease in foreign support to the insurgency and gave impetus to try and reach a political solution. The talks resulted in the Shillong Accord of 1975. A section of the Nagas joined the mainstream, but those against the accord created the National Socialist Council of Nagalim (NSCN), which continued the insurgency with the help of China, Pakistan and Myanmar.[1,3,5,6,11,29,37,48,50]

By 1988 due to a tribal feud the National Socialist Council of Nagalim split in two—the Isaac and Muivah Group (Tankhul heavy) and the Khaplang Group (Northern Nagaland and Myanmar Naga Hills) and a struggle for control of all Nagalim areas ensued. The Naga Insurgency spread to Tirap, Changlang and Lohit Districts of Arunachal, Assam and Manipur, where the Army and Assam Rifles were deployed to control the same. Due to effective counter-insurgency operations, insurgency was partially brought under control.[2,3,6]

The author, then a Division Commander, conducted a major raid on Muivah's Council Headquarters Camp, wherein the Naga insurgents suffered heavy casualties and negotiated for a ceasefire. The talks commenced with the Government, which continue till today. The insurgents consequently were cantoned and not officially permitted to move around with arms in Nagaland. They did, however, surreptitiously do so and continued terrorising the population, collecting taxes, and gaining control of the area from the Khaplang/other factions, while the Armed Forces continued their area domination operations.[2,5,6,47,49]

Mizoram

Insurgency broke out in the Mizo hills in 1966 due to acute dissatisfaction of the Mizo people with the Government of Assam in handling a famine called Mautam. Here, the Central Government lost no time in bringing in the Army and adopting decisive and punitive measures to quell the insurgency. This included the employment of heliborne forces and the limited use of offensive airpower against insurgents of the Mizo National Front (MNF), who had laid siege of a small Assam Rifles garrison in Aizawl in March 1966. Among the fairly harsh measures to control the spread of the insurgency and insulate the population from the insurgents, similar to those taken in Nagaland, were grouping of villages and food control. Most of the insurgents then fled to Arakan in Myanmar. Negotiations then commenced for a political settlement with the Mizo rebels. The positive role played by the Church went a long way in assuaging the hurt of the common citizen and convincing the insurgents of the futility of continuing with the insurgency. Mizoram was declared a Union Territory in 1972 and elections held. The Mizo Accord was signed in 1975 after long-drawn-out negotiations and full statehood was granted in 1987, based on which the Mizos gave up the insurgency.[1,2,14,24,25,37,49,50]

Manipur

Manipur which bordered Nagaland, Mizoram, Assam and Myanmar went up in flames in the late 70s, with Meitei and Naga tribes taking to arms and Kuki/Chin tribes giving sanctuary to Mizo rebels—the IA was again inducted to bring it under control with operations being conducted primarily in urban areas against Meitei rebels. The pattern was like Nagaland and Mizoram, with the exception that grouping of villages had by now come to be considered counterproductive—it was hence done only partially in vulnerable pockets, in areas bordering Nagaland, Mizoram and Myanmar. At that time, almost all border areas of Myanmar were also involved in insurgency against the Myanmar Government as the tribes lived astride the border of both countries and hence gave sanctuary to insurgents in both countries. Hence, counter-infiltration and border management emerged as important operations. Talks were commenced but did not progress due to the multitude of insurgent groups and the Naga problem. Manipur was granted statehood in 1972 and elections were held. Accords/agreements have been ssigned with many of Manipur's insurgent groups, around 35, and surrender and amnesty policies have been partially implemented. The intelligence agencies are active in trying to weaken the main factions through deals/

creation of breakaway factions.[1,2,36,37,39,49,50,52] Due to pressure of the counter-insurgency operations that continues till today, the insurgency is under control but conflict resolution remains elusive as talks continue.

Assam

The insurgency in Assam commenced in 1979 over the issue of demographic change and the Government doing little to control it. Like Nagaland, the Government failed to nip the insurgency in the bud and called in the Army in 1990. By then, grouping of villages, resettlement of population and food controls were taboo. There was also strong public sentiment against human rights violations and regional Governments became sensitive to it. Therefore, when the Assam (United Liberation Front of Assam) insurgency was somewhat brought under control following Operation Bajrang in 1990-91, the Assam Government halted the operations in a few months. In later years, Operation Rhino I and Operation Rhino 2 were launched in late 1991 and then in 2007 after the state government failed to ensure a lasting peace—here again the Army controlled the situation forcing the insurgents to flee to sanctuaries in Myanmar, Bangladesh, Bhutan, Meghalaya and even Nagaland from where they have continued the insurgency, albeit with little impact as Assam is now approaching near-normalcy as a peaceful and functional state.

The Bodo tribal insurgency erupted in parts of Assam in the late 1980s as a reaction to Assamese majoritarian behaviour and illegal migration. This resulted in an expansion of the IA deployment across Assam to cover the tribal belt to include areas inhabited by other tribes such as the Karbis, Dimasas and allied tribes, who had a similar angst. Following the turbulent 1990s and the return of peace to Assam, a major operation was conducted in 2002 in concert with the Government of Bhutan, which launched operations to evict the various Assam and tribal insurgent groups, with troops from the IA's Eastern Command carrying out border sealing/ counter-infiltration operations along the Bhutan border, an operation in which the author was actively involved as the Chief of Staff, Eastern

Army Command. Simultaneous operations were successfully conducted in Meghalaya, Nagaland and Myanmar. Bangladesh was also prevailed upon to evict insurgent groups from their soil. These pressures forced the Assam and Bodo insurgents to the negotiating table.[1,2,6,11,22,39,49,50]

While the IA espoused restraint even while conducting hard kinetic operations in the 1950s, 1960s and 1970s, continued pressures from civil society over Human Rights violations resulted in the formalisation of the IA's Ten Commandments for all troops participating in counter-insurgency operations. First promulgated by General B.C. Joshi, the Chief of Army Staff in 1993, it included, "no rape, no molestation or torture, no meddling in civil administration, respect for human rights, develop interaction with the media, restriction in the use of excessive force, upholding the code of conduct and honoured traditions of the military, avoiding indiscriminate firing or harassment of civilians, impartiality during cordon and search operations, no acceptance of presents or gifts for performance of duty or otherwise, acting within the bounds of the law, avoiding the 'body count' approach in counter insurgency operations and maintaining relentless offensive pressure against terrorists."[1,2,6,11,21,22,23,39,49,50]

Tripura

Tripura experienced tribal insurgency from 1990, again due to demographic disturbances resulting from the large-scale migration of people from neighbouring states. Following a typical trend, the IA and the Assam Rifles moved in to restore normalcy after the State Police and the administration failed to control the insurgency. However, this time around the state administration built on the Army's counter-insurgency and counter-infiltration campaign by instituting robust border management procedures and found a political solution. The operations followed a similar pattern to those in Assam with the exception that a great deal of emphasis was put on border management, counter-infiltration and finding a political solution through development and talks, particularly in the tribal belt and by good administration. The Tripura Government in fact did a splendid job.[1,2,10,11] From an overall state-wise perspective, the scorecard reveals outright successes in Tripura and Mizoram, while the rest of the states have been a mixed bag.

OTHER ISSUES OF IMPORTANCE

Initially, the Army did not even have police powers of search and arrest, as well as protection from prosecution for acts carried out by them during operations. They therefore sought these powers from the Government and were granted the Armed Forces Special Powers Act, which came into play only after an insurgency affected area was declared disturbed under the Disturbed Areas Act. These Acts were accordingly invoked in all insurgency-affected areas. These Acts are strongly agitated against by civil society.[1,2,22,25,37,50]

Overall command of counter-insurgency operations was often critical, with the British favouring a Committee comprising a senior military commander, a police officer and intelligence officers under the chairmanship of the head of the local administration. This was not followed initially as the Indian Army took charge on grounds of the civil administration and police being subverted. In Assam, however, the Committee system of unified command was adopted in the early nineties and others followed suit[1,2,6,21,23,50]

When the Army was initially deployed, it was not adequately trained for counter insurgency. By the 1970s, 80s and 90s, the Army had set up Counter-insurgency and Jungle Warfare Schools and Battle Schools where all troops entering insurgency areas were trained. In addition, training on counter insurgency began to be imparted at the NDA, IMA, Infantry School, College of Combat/Staff College for all officers and at Regimental Centres for other ranks.[1,2,6,21,50]

Tactically, with the grouping of villages having fallen out of favour as a strategy, companies/battalions/brigades deployed in a grid with specified areas of responsibility. In these areas they carried out area domination with a view to isolate the insurgents from the local population. They would carry out patrols, ambushes, raids, cordon and searches and search and destroy operations in these areas. Counter-infiltration and Border Management was an important part of the operations, as was the Winning Hearts and Minds campaign to try and win over the local population and gather intelligence. As the IA became fully embroiled in local conflicts across the north-east, it also became increasingly dependent on the state police forces for various tasks. This was important if the latter were to replace the IA seamlessly when the situation improved and the Army had to return to their primary duties. A great deal of effort was by now devoted to joint patrolling and intelligence gathering in all its facets.[1,2,6,21,37,39,50]

Sri Lanka

It is frequently asked why an Army that had performed admirably in dealing with earlier insurgencies failed during Operation Pawan in Sri Lanka? From an initial strength of an undermanned division in 1987, the Indian Peacekeeping Force (IPKF) in Sri Lanka quickly expanded to about four divisions with its complement of supporting arms and detachments from the Indian Navy, IAF and paramilitary forces. Their deployment was, however, piecemeal and clumsy with a mismatch between the Force's political aims and military objectives. There was little coordination in the plan of action or optimum utilization of available resources. There was no clear-cut command and control of the Force and its senior commanders were at loggerheads with each other. Also, the Force was not psychologically conditioned or trained to combat the 'Liberation Tigers of Tamil Eelam'. The induction of the Indian Peace Keeping Force into Sri Lanka was ill planned and hastily executed with outdated equipment unsuited to the type of operations. Despite the initial welcome, it did not have the support of the Tamils or the Sri Lankans. The IPKF also failed to isolate the insurgents from the local Tamils. Intelligence was totally lacking regarding the terrain and the insurgents—initially even proper maps were not available and the Force failed to initially adapt itself to deal with the situation on the ground or the insurgent tactics in jungle and urban operations. When the Indian Peace Keeping Force finally seized Jaffna, it failed to prevent the escape of Prabhakaran or his cadres and therefore allowed them to fight another day. The Force failed to apply the required force against the insurgents in the dense forests of Sri Lanka. India failed to ensure the support of the Sri Lankan Government and their Armed Forces in the operations. Instead the Indian Peace Keeping Force fought a lone operation in a foreign country without support. Overall the Sri Lanka experience was a bitter pill the Indian Armed Forces were constrained to swallow.[12,33,43,48]

Kashmir

Insurgency in Kashmir can be traced to Pakistan's proxy war against India after its humiliating defeat in 1971. Exploiting the acute dissatisfaction of the Kashmiris with the alleged rigging of state elections by the Central Government and maladministration, Pakistan's Inter-Services Intelligence (ISI) armed and trained Kashmiri and Sikh youth in Pakistan Occupied Kashmir/Punjab for insurgency against India. The Pakistan-sponsored insurgency, commenced from the 80s with typical insurgent tactics of selective assassinations, terrorist killings, abductions, hijacking, ethnic cleansing by pushing the Pundits out of Kashmir and subverting instruments of the Government. The police forces inducted into Kashmir were not trained or equipped to control mass demonstrations or to deal with insurgency. The indiscriminate use of force coupled with widespread arrests and allegations of torture alienated the population further. As the violence escalated, the IA was deployed for both counter-insurgency and counter-infiltration tasks. It then secured the towns, deployed in a grid and systematically cleared the area. By 1993/94, as the indigenous Kashmiri insurgency petered out in the face of resolute IA operations, Pakistan inducted large numbers of battle-hardened foreign terrorists (FTs) to step up operations and expand the same to Jammu. Escalating the conflict, many regular Pakistan Army soldiers operated in conjunction with the FTs. By 1997-98, the insurgency in Jammu and Kashmir had again largely been brought under control, with large number of terrorists killed or captured. The Army had created special counter-insurgency troops—Rashtriya Rifles—and deployed them in a grid; they were extremely effective. Volunteers from the surrendered insurgents were organised into a Special Operations Group called the Ikhwanis and were employed in operations with mixed results.[8,13,18,19,21,26,27,35,37,44,45,50,52]

During the Kargil Conflict of 1999, one of Pakistan's peripheral objectives was to reactivate the insurgency in Jammu and Kashmir by infiltrating as many FTs as possible, while the conflict raged in Kargil. Thus, while the Kargil Conflict raged, Kashmir was on the boil as the insurgency regained momentum with the infiltration of over 3000 terrorists into the Kashmir region at a time when the author was GOC of the Srinagar-based 15 Corps and had to deal with this crisis-like situation.[6,17,18,19,44]

Pakistan' new strategy saw the start of suicide attacks and attacks on Army counter-terrorist operating bases and government installations. Violence in the region reached a peak by early 1999–2000 even as the IA tweaked its counter-infiltration strategy by deploying troops slightly deeper into the forward posts, in two tiers, with reserves to deal with infiltrating terrorists. It was imperative that units involved in counter-infiltration instituted an effective intelligence and surveillance grid that would guide the battalions towards successful operations. Fencing of the border was also approved. This was done by laying extensive linear ambushes covering the gaps between the posts on the Line of Control—the ambushes were extremely successful. It was quite normal for the Army to strike at terrorist launch pads by raids across the Line of Control as well as through heavy artillery fire in retaliation to infiltration bids.[6,18,19,50]

After the redeployment, due to the Kargil crisis, counter-insurgency operations were primarily looked after by the Rashtriya Rifles Battalions. Hotspots, however, were reinforced by normal infantry battalions. A great deal of emphasis was laid on electronic intelligence.

Signal interception and direction-finding equipment was placed at all important areas in the Kashmir Valley so that all terrorist-linked transmissions could be picked up. Intelligence so gained was passed on to all relevant formations. Blocking funding to the terrorists was also quite successfully done. The over-ground insurgent leadership, were closely monitored. Furthermore, by launching people-friendly counter-insurgency operations based on hard intelligence and taking military civic action, troops were largely able to win over the people's hearts and minds. The situation was again brought under control by the end of 2001. This was possible not only because of the actions of the security forces, but also because of the support of the local population. This led to the security forces apprehending the highest number of terrorists from August 1999 to 2002. More than 5000 mainly foreign terrorists had been neutralised and peace was brought back to the Kashmir Valley for a few years—this was unfortunately not exploited by the Government as the Islamist insurgency scenario continued to pose a serious challenge to India.[6,13,21,27,38,39,50] The major lesson from Jammu and Kashmir has been the lack of a rational political aim and a failure to resolve relations with Pakistan without which the problem is unlikely to be resolved.

CONCLUSION

There is little doubt that the Indian Army has emerged today as a responsible and proficient counter-insurgency force. In the early 2000s, the Indian Army Training Command prepared a Doctrine for Sub-Conventional Operations" based on its experiences, which incorporates all the lessons learnt by the Army indicated above and emphasizes that the Army must follow the philosophy of an 'Iron Fist in a Velvet Glove' and conduct counter-insurgency operations with " a humane and people-centric approach, upholding the laws of the land, respecting human rights and use of minimum force to create a secure environment without causing unnecessary collateral damage." The doctrine also advocates the use of overwhelming force against foreign and hard-core terrorists while giving a fair opportunity to others to shun violence, surrender, and join the moderate mainstream of the nation. The importance of military civic action is stressed to assist in gaining popular support. It reiterates that the role of the armed forces is to assist the civil administration to bring down the level of violence, so that the political process can be reinitiated. Isolation of the conflict zone from 'external material assistance' and the interception of external support at the borders are also stressed.[9,19,21,35,45,50]

Notwithstanding the 'Doctrine', it must be emphasized that no counter-insurgency campaign can succeed without a clear and rational political aim; diplomatic efforts must be enhanced to deny foreign support—particularly from China and Pakistan; the radicalised population of the country must be de-radicalised. Without complying with these conditions, it is unlikely that any insurgency with political roots and proxy support can be resolved.

NOTES

1 Author's innumerable interactions with soldiers, ex-soldiers, their families, from the Assam Regiment (all of whom are from the North East – incidentally the author is also married into the North East), local people and his personal experiences while serving in the North East for 26 years in various capacities dealing with counter insurgency and with the Assam Regiment. He has also been in close touch with the North East for the last 57 years including frequent visits and long stays there after retirement.

2. Mukherjee Lt Gen J R, *An Insider's Experience of Insurgency in India's North East*, Ch 2-6, pp. 17-65; Ch. 10-13, pp. 93-129 (London, UK: Anthem Press, Wimbledon Publishing Company, 2005).

3. Author's detailed discussions on the Naga Insurgency with Lt General S K Pillai while serving with the General for many years and his writings see - Lt Gen S K Pillai, Anatomy of Insurgency, Ethnicity and identity in Nagaland, Writings on Conflict and Resolution, Vol 3, Institute of Conflict Management, New Delhi, 1999. Also see for online access at https://www.satp.org/satporgtp/publication/faultlines/volume3/fault3-genpillaif.htm. Accessed on August 12, 2021.

4. Personal hearings of lectures by General Sir Frank Kitson's on the British experiences of counter insurgency while attending the Imperial Defence Services Staff College Course at Camberly, United Kingdom, and interacting with British, United States, French and Commonwealth Army students during the course.

5. Author was personally in touch with both Muivah and Khaplang of the NSCN to try and convince them to come to the negotiating table. In 1977, conducted a major raid on Muivah's Council HQ Camp in the Intaki Reserved Forest, which was very successful and inflicted heavy casualties on them—this resulted in Muivah negotiating for a cease fire and talks for which continue till today.
6. Personal experiences in conduct of counter-insurgency operations in the North East as a Commanding Officer, Brigade Commander, Brigadier General Staff and Division Commander; Punjab, Corps Commander XV Corps commanding operations in Kashmir and subsequently as Chief of Staff of Headquarters Eastern Command in the North East.
7. Author was one of those involved in talks for a ceasefire with the Hizbul Mujahidin in conjunction with the heads of the IB and R&AW. The author had accommodated the Commander (Abdul Majid Dar) and his Division Commanders in great secrecy at his residence in Badamibagh, Srinagar. They had conducted detailed talks with them over a period of two months during which all aspects of the problem and insurgency were discussed. They would all also move out to Downtown Srinagar to hold talks with all other local leaders at night unarmed and in local dress. The talks almost bore fruition—unfortunately they were all assassinated at the behest of the ISI.
8. Alexander Yonah (ed.), *Combatting Terrorism Strategies of Ten Countries* (Michigan: University of Michigan Press, 2002).
9. Army Training Command (ARTRAC). Doctrine for Sub Conventional Operations. Shimla: ARTRAC, 2006, http://ids.nic.in/. Accessed on July 28, 2011. Indian Army Training Command (ARTRAC). Indian Army Doctrine. Shimla: ARTRAC, 2004, http://ids.nic.in/. Army Doctrine can be downloaded at www.indian army.nic.in/indar_doctrine.htm.
10. S R Bhattacharjea, *Tribal Insurgency in Tripura* (Michigan: University of Michigan, 1989) (also Google Books). *Model of Holistic Approach to Counter Insurgency*, Vivekananda International Foundation Delhi, 2016.
11. Subir Bhaumik, *Insurgent Cross Fire, North East India* (New Delhi: Lancer Publishers, 1996) (now also in Google Books) and *Troubled Periphery* (New Delhi: Sage publications India, 2009). *The Agartala Doctrine* (New Delhi: Oxford University Press, 2016), Intro, pp. 1-38.
12. Bhaduri Shankar and Afsar Karim. *The Sri Lankan Crisis* (New Delhi: Lancer,1990).
13. Rahul Bhonsle, "Counter-insurgency and 'Op Sadhbhavana' in Jammu and Kashmir", IDSA Occasional Paper No. 19, 2011, http://www.idsa.in/occasionalpapers/ Counter-insurgency and Op Sadhbhavana in Jammu and Kashmir.
14. Vivek Chadha. "India's Counter-insurgency Campaign in Mizoram," in Sumit Ganguly and David P. Fidler, (eds.), *India and Counter-insurgency: Lessons Learned* (New York: Routledge, 2009), pp. 28-44, at ser 35.
15. Matthew R. Doherty, Small Wars Journal—The Boer War and Malayan Emergency: Examples of British Counter-insurgency pre- and post-"Minimum Force", Dec 2018.
16. James Flint, "Assessing the British Counter-Insurgency Effort in Malaya E International Relations", PCB Library, London, 2015,. Entire Article for analysis of operations at https://www.eir.info/2015/02/11/assessing-the-british-counter-insurgency-effort-in-malaya/JAMESFLINT,FEB11,2015.

17. Government of India, NSC Sect, "From Surprise to Reckoning," The Kargil Review Committee Report (Delhi: Sage Publications, 2000).
18. Sumit Ganguly, *The Crisis in Kashmir: Portents of War, Hopes of Peace* (Cambridge, UK: Cambridge University Press, 1999).
19. Sumit Ganguly and David P. Fidler, (eds.), *India and Counter-insurgency: Lessons Learned* (New York: Routledge, 2009), pp. 189-206.
20. David Galula, *Counter-insurgency Warfare: Theory and Practice* (New York: Praeger, 1964).
21. Namrata Goswami, "Small Wars Journal - Counter Insurgency, Best Practices in India", June 2012; – excellent article on counter insurgency policy and practice in India.
22. Sanjay Hazarika, *Strangers in the Mist* (New Delhi: Penguin India, 2000); *Rites Of Passage* (New Delhi: Penguin, 2000); *Writing On The Wall* (New Delhi: Penguin, 2008); *Strangers No More* (New Delhi: Aleph Book Company, 2018).
23. Wasbir Hussain, "Multi-force operations in counter-terrorism: A view from the Assam theatre," *Faultlines: Writings on Conflict and Resolution*, New Delhi, 2001.
24. V S Jaffa, "Ten o'Clock to Bed – Insouciance in the Face of Terror," *Faultlines: Writings on Conflict and Resolution*, Volume 5, Institute of Conflict Management, New Delhi, 2001.
25. V S Jafa, "Resolution – Counter Insurgency warfare, the Use and Abuse of military Force," *Faultlines: Writings on Conflict and Resolution*, Volume 3, Institute of Conflict Management, New Delhi, 1987.
26. Jagmohan, *My Frozen Turbulence in Kashmir* (New Delhi: Allied Publishers Ltd, 1992).
27. Afsar Karim, Maj Gen (Retd) with the IDR Team, *Kashmir the Troubled Frontiers,* Edited by Capt Bharat Verma (Retd) and Manvendra Singh (New Delhi: Lancer Publishers, 1994).
28. Frank Kitson, *Low Intensity Operations* (Harrisburg, PA: Stackpole Books, 1971).
29. L Kanchan, "Negotiating Insurgencies, the Naga Imbroglio," *Faultlines: Writings on Conflict and Resolution*, Volume 11, Institute of Conflict Management, New Delhi, 2001.
30. Dinesh Kotwal, The Naga Insurgency: The Past and The Future, www.idsa.org (accessed on December 12, 2011).
31. Narender Kumar, "Jammu and Kashmir: The Emerging Contours and the Way Ahead", Manekshaw Paper No. 21, 2010, Centre for Land Warfare Studies, New Delhi.
32. Mathur, Anant. "Secrets of COIN Success: Lessons from the Punjab Campaign", *Faultlines: Writings on Conflict and Resolution*, Volume 20, http://satp.com. Accessed on October 28, 2011.
33. Mehta, Ashok K. *India's Counter-insurgency Campaign in Sri Lanka* (New Delhi: Routledge, 2009).
34. Mahadevan, Prem, "The Gill Doctrine: A Model for 21st Century Counter-terrorism," *Faultlines: Writings on Conflict and Resolution*, Volume 19, Institute of Conflict Management, New Delhi, 2008.
35. Rao, K V Krishna, General, *Prepare or Perish: A Study of National Security* (New Delhi: Lancer Publishers, 1991).
36. Rammohan, E N, "Manipur – a Degenerated Insurgency and Blueprint for Counter Insurgency", *Faultlines: Writings on Conflict and Resolution*, Volumes 11 and 12, Institute of Conflict Management, New Delhi, 2000 and 2001.

37. Rajagopalan, Rajesh, *Fighting the Guerilla like a Guerilla: Indian Army and Counter-insurgency* (UK: Routledge, 2009); Rajgopalan, Rajesh, "Force and Compromise: India's Counter Insurgency Grand Strategy," *Journal of South Asian Studies*, 2007.
38. Rahul, K., "Winning Hearts and Minds: Lessons from Jammu and Kashmir", Manekshaw Paper No. 14, 2009, Centre for Land Warfare Studies, New Delhi.
39. Roy, Shekhar Basu, "Terrorism A Global Menace, New Approach", Volume 17, No 4; Volume 18, No 1, Calcutta, 2009, with articles only on Terrorism and Counter-terrorism by General S Roychoudhury, General V P Malik, General J J Singh (all former Indian Army COAS).
40. Sahni, Ajai, "Responding to Terrorism in Punjab, and Jammu and Kashmir," in S.D. Muni, (ed.), *Responding to Terrorism in South Asia* (New Delhi: Manohar, 2006, p. 69).
41. Sahni, Ajai, "Terror by Another Name," *Faultlines: Writings on Conflict and Resolution*, Institute of Conflict Management, New Delhi, 2004.
42. Shashinungla, "Insurgency and Factional Intransigence – Nagaland the Dynamics of Extortion," *Faultlines: Writings on Conflict and Resolution*, Volume 16, Institute of Conflict Management, New Delhi, 2001.
43. Sardeshpande, S.C., *Analysis of Phase III of IPKF's COIN Campaign Assignment Jaffna* (New Delhi: Lancer, 1992).
44. Sakhlani, D D., Lt Gen (Retd), *Kashmir Saga: A Bundle of Blunders* (New Delhi: Lancer Publishers, 1999).
45. Sinha, Lt Gen S K, *A Governor's Musings, Soldier Statesman Speaks* (New Delhi: Manas Publications, 2006).
46. Singh, Lt General Depinder, *The IPKF in Sri Lanka* (New Delhi: South Asia Books, 1992).
47: Shekatkar, D.B., "India's Counter-insurgency Campaign in Nagaland", in Sumit Ganguly and D P Fidler, (eds.), *India and Counterinsurgency* (New Delhi: Routledge, 2009).
48. Singh, Harkirat, Intervention in Sri Lanka: the I.P.K.F. Experience Retold (New Delhi: Manohar, 2007).
49. Sinha, S.P., *Lost Opportunities: 50 Years of Insurgency in the North-East and India's Response* (New Delhi: Lancer Publishers, 2008).
50. Sahukar, Behram A, "The Indian Approach to Counter-insurgency Operations", 2008, India https://www.scribd.com/document/169818250/.
51. Thompson, Sir Robert, *Countering Communist Insurgency* (London, UK: Chatto and Windus, 1966).

CHAPTER 4

CHANGING CONTOURS OF CONFLICT IN THE NORTH EAST AND J&K

D.S. HOODA

ABSTRACT

The Naga, Manipur and Assam insurgencies (north east region) are the longest-running conflicts in India, while terrorism in Jammu and Kashmir (J&K) is now more than three decades old and one of the major security challenges for India. Resolution of conflicts in these two regions would improve not only internal security but also our external security because there are cross-border linkages that have helped keep militancy alive in these states. Over the years, in the battle between the militants and the state, the nature of the conflict often undergoes a change. Militants change their tactics based on their successes or failures and their armed strength compared to the security forces. Political steps taken by the government contribute to the stabilisation of the situation and the conclusion of ceasefire agreements. Protracted conflicts could lead to a collective sense among some communities of being victimised by the state. This provides popular legitimacy to militant groups, which helps sustain them even when weak. This chapter will trace the changing contours of conflicts in the North East and J&K since the turn of the century. It will also propose some strategies toward resolving these conflicts.

CONFLICT IN THE NORTH EAST

It has been observed that all insurgencies that broke out in North East India are often clubbed under one head for discussions. This obscures the disparate nature of armed movements that have emerged over the region and, in some cases, within a state. In Assam, the demands of the local Assamese, the Bodos, the Dimasas and the Karbis, all of whom formed insurgent groups, are different from each other. In Manipur, a similar situation exists, with the Meitei, Naga, and Kuki armed groups in conflict with each other. If there is one thing that all these cases have in common, it is that ethnic identity plays a crucial role in sustaining armed movements. For decades, the region was economically and socially isolated, and the governance was poor. This permitted insurgent groups to take root with demands ranging from secession to autonomy to a "special federal relationship" within India.[1] Smaller tribal groups view the armed struggle as a means of attracting the government's attention to their demands.

Two distinct features marked the period from 2000 to 2010. The first was a series of ceasefire agreements to bring many groups overground and integrate them with the mainstream. Paradoxically this period also saw heightened violence due to a spate of internecine clashes and targeting of civilians by insurgent groups. In Nagaland, the Government of India signed ceasefire agreements with the two groups of the National Socialist Council of Nagaland (NSCN)—NSCN (IM) in 1997 and NSCN (K) in 2001. Despite this, there was little compliance with the ceasefire ground rules, which stipulate that the militants remain in designated camps, ban movement with arms and prohibit extortion. Both the NSCN factions regularly fought with each other to establish their domination. Most deaths of civilians and insurgents occurred during inter-faction clashes. Fatalities, mainly among the militant ranks resulting from factional clashes, claimed 97 lives in 2004, 99 in 2005, 147 in 2006 and 154 in 2007.[2] There were a total of 201 fatalities in 2008, including 68 civilians, three Security Force (SF) personnel, and 130 insurgents, indicating a dramatic increase in violence.[3]

There was a similar pattern in other states. In Assam, agreements were reached with the Bodo Liberation Tigers Force (BLTF) and the

Dima Halim Daogah (DHD) in 2003 and the National Democratic Front of Bodoland (NDFB) in 2005. Peace talks were on with the United Liberation Front of Assam (ULFA), though they broke down in 2006. This led to a spate of violence in the state. There were a series of attacks and bomb blasts against Hindi-speaking migrant labour, the deadliest of which occurred on October 30, 2008, when the NDFB killed 88 people and injured more than 500.[4] In 2009, inter-ethnic violence in the North Cachar Hills between the Dimasas and Jeme Nagas resulted in 63 deaths and the burning of hundreds of houses.[5] Later that year, the 'Black Widow' militant group, responsible for much of the violence in North Cachar Hills, laid down its arms and surrendered.[6]

In Manipur, the Government of India entered into a Suspension of Operations (SoO) agreement with 25 different Kuki militant groups between 2005 and 2008.[7] Again, there was no immediate impact on levels of violence, which peaked in 2008 at around 500 deaths in militant-related incidents. There were major inter-factional clashes between Kuki groups in 2007 and 2008.[8] There were also accusations that the Indian Army was using the Kuki groups to "drive out the Meitei insurgents from Kuki-Zomi dominant districts like Churachandpur."[9] The ethnic Meitei-Naga-Kuki mix kept Manipur on a tinderbox, and the 2010 and 2011 blockades of highways leading into Manipur by the Nagas sharpened the divide between communities.

Large groups like ULFA (Pro talks) and NDFB (Daimary) entered into SoO arrangements with the government. Jumping on the bandwagon were also tribal groups like the Karbi Longri NC Hills Liberation Front (KLNLF), which surrendered in 2010 with 419 cadres, but less than 50 rifles.[10] In January 2012, a group of 1855 militants belonging to nine groups surrendered before the Union Home Minister P Chidambaram.[11] These were heartening numbers, but it was also evident that militant groups, under pressure from the security forces and seeing the writing on the wall, were exaggerating the numbers of their cadre to take advantage of the incentives being granted by the government for the rehabilitation of militants.

TABLE 1

Total deaths in insurgent-related incidents in the North East between 2008 and the last three years

State	2008	2018	2019	2020
Assam	373	22	3	8
Manipur	496	23	9	7
Nagaland	201	7	4	2
Total	1070	52	16	17

Source: South Asian Terrorism Portal

One viable explanation for the rise in violence in the second half of the 2000-2010 period is that it was the last gasp of steadily weakening movements. It was also an attempt by the insurgents to show that militancy was alive to negotiate better terms for surrender agreements with the government. This view is supported by the fact that the security situation has steadily improved since 2010. The Indian state got the violence under control by combining military force with political persuasion and exploiting differences between various groups. Table 1 compares total deaths in insurgent-related incidents in the north east between 2008 and the last three years.

Although violence has significantly reduced, militant groups are still active. Their focus is on fundraising through extortion, tax collection, forced donations and siphoning off development funds.[12] Even the groups under ceasefire/SoO arrangements openly indulge in extortion and taxation. When the Nagaland Governor, R.N. Ravi, criticised the 'tax' collection by the NSCN (IM), the outfit issued a statement saying, "The Naga nation does not require permission from the Government of India for taxation."[13]

Those groups that are outside the ceasefire agreements (primarily the Meitei groups of Manipur) have their camps in Myanmar. The India-Myanmar border has an arrangement called the Free Movement Regime (FMR) that permits the tribes residing along the border to travel 16-km across the boundary without visa restrictions.[14] This also facilitates the easy movement of militants across the border. While military cooperation with the Tatmadaw (Myanmar military) has been satisfactory, action against insurgent camps has been sporadic. This indirect external support is one of the main reasons for the survival of Manipur and Nagaland-based outfits. Recent reports indicate that the Tatmadaw has incorporated the Meitei insurgent groups into fighting the pro-democracy militia along the border.[15]

Are the conditions in Nagaland, Assam and Manipur conducive to a return to normalcy? It is obvious that the people are tired of the decades of violence and, in some cases, are pushing back against the militant groups.[16] However, some key issues will have to be addressed for a lasting resolution of the ongoing conflicts. As brought out earlier, ethnic identity plays a key role in sustaining the armed movements. Militant groups are seen as protection against the domination of one ethnic group by another. Even within a larger ethnic group, sub-identities differ. For example, the Zeliangrong Naga tribes have their own armed wing that is in opposition to the NSCN(IM).[17]

In finding a solution, New Delhi, in collaboration with the democratically elected state governments in the north east, must consider measures to address the aspirations of different groups through political empowerment, reconciliation and grant of autonomy in certain areas. The model of autonomous councils has worked to control insurgency in some regions. The government and the security forces must also resist the tendency to play off one group against the other for short-term gains. Any sharpening of the divide between ethnicities will only make long-term peaceful resolution difficult.

A resolution of the Naga problem could provide the much-needed impetus to bring normalcy in the region. A Framework Agreement was signed between the government and the NSCN (IM) in 2015, with much fanfare and in the presence of the Prime Minister. However, six years later, it appears that both sides had misread the complexities of the problem as it also affects other states beyond Nagaland, particularly Manipur that also has a sizeable Naga population. The silver lining is that many Naga groups have expressed support for a speedy settlement of the peace process. As a result, the NSCN (IM) could increasingly find itself isolated on its aggressive stance and demand for a separate flag and Constitution.[18] If the Government of India decides to go ahead without the NSCN (IM), it will have to contend with dealing with the armed members of the group who are currently residing in designated camps within Nagaland and Manipur.

Particularly in the light of the current turn of events in Myanmar, there should be a significant improvement in the management of the India-Myanmar border. Seventy-five years after independence, we are still pointing out reasons like terrain and lack of road infrastructure for our inability to manage movement across the border. The Assam Rifles, which is responsible for the India-Myanmar border, operates from bases that are mostly deployed along existing roads. Such a deployment is unsuited for border management. The poor management of the border has led to calls for merging the Assam Rifles with the ITBP, which will then take over the responsibility of the India-Myanmar border.[19] This could only compound problems by having two separate forces (the ITBP and the Army) operating in the border state under two different ministries. The problem is not in the organisation for manning the border, but with the infrastructure that needs to be created to support efficient border management.

While border management needs to improve, the presence of the Army and Assam Rifles in the internal security role could be reviewed. In July 2016, while hearing a case on allegations of fake encounters in Manipur, the Supreme Court had observed that indefinite deployment of the Army under the Armed Forces Special Powers Act (AFSPA) "would be indicative of the failure of the civil administration to take effective aid of the armed forces in restoring normalcy or would be indicative of the failure of the armed forces in effectively aiding the civil administration in restoring normalcy or both."[20] AFSPA is a law that gives India's armed forces "special powers" to "restore the authority of the State" in regions notified as "Disturbed Areas". Areas, or parts of areas, where the "normal" functioning of the state government breaks down, are declared "disturbed". Once invoked, AFSPA protects the armed forces during high-risk operations undertaken to counter "hostile" militancy, insurgency, or proxy wars by neighbouring countries, to "restore normalcy."[21]

AFSPA is an emotive issue in the North East, and with violence levels having come down, the presence of the Army could be reduced. This would have an immediate impact on popular sentiment. However, if political stability is to be achieved, this strategy will have to be backed by a significant improvement in the capability of the police forces in the north eastern states.

Finally, there is a pressing need to speedily complete and streamline the rehabilitation of the surrendered cadre. To encourage armed groups to come overground, the government agreed to very generous terms. Apart from the financial incentive, groups were permitted to stay in separate camps (some with weapons) to facilitate their rehabilitation. Unfortunately, the groups took advantage of this by continuing with fundraising and extortion, often exploiting the common people with greater impunity after their agreement with the government.[22] All camps housing past insurgents should be shut down, and the cadre should return to their homes. The SoO agreement with the Kuki groups was signed in 2008 and has been extended periodically. In 2017, the Manipur Chief Minister N. Biren Singh termed the SoO as a failure due to frequent violations of the agreement.[23] Despite this, the agreement continues to be extended. Of course, the fears of the Kuki community that disbandment of their militant cadre would put them at risk from armed Naga and Meitei groups will have to be addressed.

CONFLICT IN J&K

The turn of the century was the bloodiest period in the history of the proxy war in J&K. A large number of Army troops had been pulled out of the Kashmir region to Ladakh for the 1999 Kargil Conflict. Pakistan took advantage of this to increase the infiltration of terrorists across the Line of Control (LoC). The bloodiest year in J&K was 2001, with more than 4000 deaths in terror-related violence.[24] There was a spate of suicide attacks, the deadliest being the car bomb attack outside the Srinagar Legislative Assembly in October 2001, killing 38 people.[25] Although violence dipped from 2002 onwards, there were a series of high-profile strikes on temples in Jammu and an attack on the families of Army personnel at Kaluchak, resulting in 36 deaths. In the Jammu Region, terrorists targeted the Hindu community and members of the Gujjar and Bakarwal tribes whom they suspected of helping the security forces.

At this point, a series of events and actions came together that helped control the situation in J&K. Pakistan was under tremendous pressure, both from the US following 9/11 and from the one-year-long mobilisation of the Indian Army following the attack on the Indian Parliament in December 2001. This forced Pakistan to scale back some support to terror activities and declare a unilateral ceasefire along the LoC in November 2003, which India then reciprocated.[26] The Indian Army also brought in 27 Mountain Division from Kalimpong for counter-insurgency operations in the Jammu region and raised the Uniform Force (equivalent to a division) of Rashtriya Rifles in 2002. With the ceasefire in place, the Army speedily constructed an effective fence all along the LoC in the Kashmir and Jammu regions, completing it by September 2004.[27] The fence had an immediate impact on infiltration from Pakistan Occupied Kashmir (POK), with infiltration attempts dropping from 2,417 in 2000 to 537 in 2004.[28]

In the Jammu region, the Muslim Gujjar and Bakarwal population turned against the Pakistani terrorists. Fed up with the brutality and sexual exploitation of the local women by Pakistani terrorists, the residents of

Marrah village set up a vigilante organisation, the Pir Panjal Scouts. They provided invaluable help to the Army in one of the biggest operations in 2003—Operation Sarp Vinash in the Hill Kaka area.[29] The locals paid a heavy price for supporting the Army. In June 2004, terrorists sneaked into Teli Katha village in the upper pastures of Hill Kaka and killed twelve Gujjars, including five children.[30] The deaths were tragic, but once the local population had withdrawn their support, it was only a matter of time before the terrorists would be driven out of the area.

The period from 2005 to 2007 was perhaps the best period to arrive at a political resolution of the J&K problem. The 2005 earthquake in the Kashmir region had devastated much of POK, including the terrorist infrastructure. Local Kashmiri youth who had gone across into POK and joined terrorist ranks in the 1990s started appearing at the LoC to surrender to the Indian Army. In 2006, the year following the earthquake, 198 terrorists surrendered, the highest number in the last 21 years.[31] The government took several steps to take the peace process forward. A bus service was started in 2005 between Srinagar and Muzaffarabad to deepen people-to-people links on both sides of the LoC. Additionally, five working groups were set up in 2006 for confidence-building measures in the State; strengthening relations across the LoC; economic development; good governance; and strengthening Centre-State relations.[32] Back-channel talks between India and Pakistan were progressing smoothly. Khurshid Kasur, then Foreign Minister of Pakistan, is reported to have told Steve Coll, an American journalist, that by early 2007, talks on Kashmir had become "so advanced that we'd come to semicolons."[33] Unfortunately, President Musharraf's domestic problems prevented any agreement from being signed, and the chances completely faded after the 2008 Mumbai attack by terrorists from Pakistan.

In 2008, large-scale protests broke out in Jammu and Kashmir over the transfer of forest land to the Shri Amarnathji Shrine Board, exposing the religious fault lines between the two regions. Notwithstanding another round of violent public protests in 2010 following allegations of human rights violations by the security forces, terrorist violence continued to drop, reaching its minimum level in 2012. According to the MHA's Annual Report 2012-13, fatalities in terror-related incidents in 2012 were 102, a little over 2 per cent of the peak figures in 2001. There was a level of disenchantment among the local youth with the idea of militancy, and the number of locals who joined militancy in 2012 and 2013 was 21 and 16, respectively.[34]

From 2014 onwards, there was a shift in the profile of militancy and its exploitation by proxy extremist elements, which triggered an increase in terrorist acts. Greater alienation was visible among the youth in Kashmir, owing in part to their disillusionment with the trajectory of political events that reflected opportunism and was perceived as a betrayal, particularly in South Kashmir, where the People's Democratic Party (PDP) had campaigned vigorously with an agenda of keeping the BJP out of power in the state, but then formed a post-poll alliance with the BJP. This added to the disaffection that already existed in the state over the slow pace of rehabilitation of victims affected by the devastating floods of 2014. Extensive use of social media among the youth assisted in the spread of propaganda and radicalisation. Burhan Wani, a Hizbul Mujahideen terrorist, became a household name after his pictures appeared on Facebook. There was also an ideological shift, with the new breed of local terrorists invoking religion and calling for the establishment of a caliphate in Kashmir.[35] However, it must be emphasised here that extremism and religious polarisation are not the only causes that contribute to radicalisation in Kashmir. A sense of alienation among both the majority Muslim and minority Hindu populations due to several reasons that are beyond the scope of this chapter are also significant drivers of radical thought.

There was a steady rise in the number of local youths joining terrorist ranks from 53 in 2014 to 218 in 2018. Poorly trained and equipped, the local terrorists were no match for the security forces, sometimes being killed within days of picking up the gun. One consequence of this was that whenever an encounter started, the local population would rush to the site and attempt to interfere with the operation to provide an escape route to the terrorist. Stone pelting and clashes between the civilians and security forces became a frequent occurrence, peaking in July 2016 when massive protests broke out after the killing of Burhan Wani by the Army in an encounter. The widespread use of pellet guns by the security forces to quell this round of protests intensified the anger among the people against the state.

Terror-related violence also showed an upward curve with 387 fatalities in 2018, about fourfold the number in 2012. Taking advantage of the unrest in Kashmir, Pakistan increased its efforts to push in terrorists from POK. Estimated infiltration in J&K went up from 33 in 2015 to 143 in 2018.[36] However, it must be noted that violence levels were nowhere close to what prevailed in the early 2000s. The security situation has largely remained under control, although the possibility of isolated high-profile terror attacks remains real.

In August 2019, the Indian Government decided to revoke the special status granted to J&K under Article 370 of the Indian Constitution and broke up the State into two Union Territories. The intention here is not to debate the merits or the demerits of the government's decision but to assess its likely impact on militancy. While the August 2019 decision may have fuelled further alienation and angst in Kashmir while sharpening the divide between Kashmir and Jammu regions, this has not yet manifested in heightened violence and appears to have sucked much oxygen out of the separatist movement and its proxy support from Pakistan. However, should a sense of defeat and frustration emerge among large sections of the population, the situation could boil over and morph into new kinds of protests. It is also a matter of concern that local recruitment in terror ranks is continuing and a sudden increase in infiltration from across the LoC was noticed in the summer of 2021. Of the 203 terrorists killed in J&K in 2020, 166 were locals.[37]

What is the way forward? The situation in J&K is often described as a proxy war unleashed by Pakistan. There is undoubtedly a substantial proxy and state-sponsored element to externally abetted terrorism in J&K, but this part is perhaps easier to handle. The Indian Government has demonstrated a firm resolve to deal with terrorism emanating from Pakistan, and this is showing results. Pakistan will continue to keep the Kashmir pot boiling, but its position has few takers in international circles. Along the LoC, India needs to improve its counter-infiltration posture by modernising the existing border fence. This project has been discussed for many years and now must be expedited. Eliminating infiltration from Pakistan will reduce the likelihood of high-profile terror incidents like the attacks on Pathankot airbase and Uri garrison in 2016, which are taken as morale boosters by the terrorists.

The major challenge from here on will be to address the causes of disaffection among the people, both in Kashmir and Jammu regions. New Delhi needs to be do more in terms of sustained outreach towards the people and providing the necessary healing touch to alleviate the feeling that the people of J&K are treated differently from the rest of the country. John Burton refined the theory of human needs as a basis for understanding social conflict and its resolution. In Burton's view, the needs most salient to an understanding of destructive social conflicts were those for identity, recognition, security and personal development.[38] By examining conflicts in the North East, we find that India has generally followed the human needs approach to resolving ethnic conflicts with significant success. Steps like the grant of statehood and the establishment of autonomous councils were meant to ensure that minorities feel secure about their rights and identities. A similar approach may need to be adopted for J&K, with significant tweaks to the strategies currently on display. The recent outreach by New Delhi is hopefully a recognition that 'healing' is what may be the need of the hour to turn the tide in J&K.

Additionally, tackling radicalisation requires a far more complex approach than has been shown. The focus of our efforts should be on 'disengagement', which is described as a "change in behavior (i.e., refraining from violence and withdrawing from a radical organisation) but not necessarily a change in beliefs."[39] Attempting to alter people's beliefs that have been strengthened over three decades of conflict is a very long-drawn process and unlikely to succeed. Instead, the idea should be to prevent youths from being radicalised and resorting to violence. If the government can genuinely show that it cares for the people through economic and social upliftment, it could stop the flow of recruits into terror ranks. A lasting resolution to the conflict will also need to address the divide between Kashmir and Jammu. The Hindu community has long felt that it has been sidelined in terms of political power and the allocation of resources, and the tragedy of the Kashmiri Pandits and their traumatic dislocation remains a festering sore that needs urgent attention. Unless the grievances of all communities are satisfactorily resolved, solutions will be difficult to find.

CONCLUSION

The internal conflicts in the North East and J&K have plagued India for decades. While the causes of the conflict have their roots in the desire to protect ethnic identity, the nature of the conflict has evolved over time. This is the result of the interplay between the state and the militant groups, both in quelling armed movements with force and through engagement to bring about political reconciliation. In the recent past, India has followed different approaches to deal with the conflicts in the North East and in J&K. There has been active engagement with militant groups in the North East and promise of political empowerment within the Constitution of India. The Prime Minister stated in his speech following the signing of the 2015 Framework Agreement with the NSCN(IM), "Today's agreement is a shining example of what we can achieve when we deal with each other in a spirit of equality and respect, trust and confidence; when we seek to understand concerns and try to address aspirations; when we leave the path of dispute and take the high road of dialogue."[40] In J&K, the approach has been more security-focused, and a people-centric political outreach has taken a backseat there. In fact, a sense of political disempowerment exists after the state was split into two union territories. The government's recent decision to restore statehood could be a breakthrough, but it will have to be accompanied by steps to address the genuine grievances of the people.

Editor's Note: Senior leadership from the Indian Army has consistently offered a roadmap and strategies for resolution of the J&K and North East imbroglios. This assumes great significance in the light of the ongoing rebalancing of forces to address the heightening security threat posed by India's primary military adversary, China. Freeing-up formations engaged in CI/CT operations and reassigning them along the LAC seems to be an unavoidable consequence of this reality.

NOTES

1 Bhaumik, Subir. "Insurgencies in India's North East: Conflict, Co-Option & Change," East-West Center | www.eastwestcenter.org, April 8, 2011, https://www.eastwestcenter.org/publications/insurgencies-india%E2%80%99s-north east-conflict-co-option-change.

2 Routray, Bibhu Prasad. "Beginnings Of An End?" *Outlook*, https://www.outlookindia.com/website/story/beginnings-of-an-end/237654. Accessed on June 20, 2021.

3 "Terrorism Assessment, Nagaland," https://www.satp.org/terrorism-assessment/india-insurgencynortheast-nagaland-2009. Accessed on June 20, 2021.

4 "Bodo Terror Outfit Chief, 14 Others Convicted in 2008 Assam Blasts," *India Today*, https://www.indiatoday.in/india/story/bodo-terror-outfit-chief-14-others-convicted-in-2008-assam-blasts-1440928-2019-01-28. Accessed on July 9, 2021.

5 Goswami, Namrata. "Blood-Stained Hills Of Assam," *Outlook*, https://www.outlookindia.com/website/story/blood-stained-hills-of-assam/261350. Accessed on July 9, 2021.

6 "340 DHD (J) Militants Surrender," Guwahati News - *Times of India*, https://timesofindia.indiatimes.com/city/guwahati/340-dhd-j-militants-surrender/articleshow/5081532.cms. Accessed on July 9, 2021.

7 Chakravarty, Ipsita. "Will Manipur Change Tack in Its Approach to Militancies That Have Riven the State for Decades?" Scroll.in, https://scroll.in/article/838401/will-manipur-change-tack-in-its-approach-to-militancies-that-have-riven-the-state-for-decades. Accessed on July 9, 2021.

8 Dash, Sandipani. "Another False Peace." *Outlook*, https://www.outlookindia.com/website/story/another-false-peace/265744. Accessed on July 9, 2021.

9 Bhaumik, n. 1.

10 *Tribune, The Assam.* "419 KLNLF Ultras Lay down Arms," September 15, 2010, https://assamtribune.com/419-klnlf-ultras-lay-down-arms. Accessed on July 10, 2021.

11 "Largest Surrender By Militants In North East To Chidamabaram," India News, https://www.indiatvnews.com/news/india/largest-surrender-by-militants-in-north-east-to-chidamabaram-13823.html. Accessed on July 9, 2021.

12 Bhattacharya, Rakhee. "Thriving Underground Economy," *The Statesman*, July 5, 2021, https://www.thestatesman.com/supplements/north/thriving-underground-economy-1502978830.html. Accessed July 20, 2021.

13 "Nagaland Governor R.N. Ravi Criticizes NSCN-IM over 'tax Collection'," Sentinel Assam, June 25, 2021, https://www.sentinelassam.com/topheadlines/nagaland-governor-rn-ravi-criticizes-nscn-im-over-tax-collection-544149. Accessed on July 20, 2021.

14 Das, Pushpita. "India-Myanmar Border Problems: Fencing Not the Only Solution," Manohar Parrikar Institute for Defence Studies and Analyses, https://www.idsa.in/idsacomments/IndiaMyanmarBorderProblems_pdas_151113. Accessed on July 10, 2021.

15 Karmakar, Rahul. "Manipur Extremists Caught in Myanmar Conflict," *The Hindu*. May 27, 2021, sec. Other States, https://www.thehindu.com/news/national/other-states/manipur-extremists-caught-in-myanmar-conflict/article34655352.ece. Accessed on July 20, 2021.

16 "Voices against NSCN 'Taxes' Grow Stronger." *The Hindu*. July 2, 2021, https://www.thehindu.com/news/national/other-states/voices-against-nscn-taxes-grow-stronger/article35097896.ece. Accessed on July 11, 2021.

17 "ZUF on Offensive against NSCN (IM) : 07th Sep18 ~ E-Pao! Headlines," http://e-pao.net/GP.asp?src=24..070918.sep18. Accessed on July 11, 2021.

18 Anand, Manoj. "Naga Accord 'draft' Finalised, Demand for Separate Flag Rejected," *Deccan Chronicle*, October 7, 2020, https://www.deccanchronicle.com/nation/politics/071020/naga-accord-draft-finalised-demand-for-separate-flag-rejected.html. Accessed on July 15, 2021.

19 *Hindustan Times*. "Defence, Home Ministries Continue to Fight on Ways to Guard India-Myanmar Border," October 3, 2019, https://www.hindustantimes.com/world-news/defence-home-ministries-continue-to-fight-on-ways-to-guard-india-myanmar-border/story-gsbZpfJcOsa0x7QcRJwLvK.html.

20 NewsClick. "Seventy One Years of AFSPA: Failed State Machinery," January 26, 2020, https://www.newsclick.in/seventy-one-years-AFSPA-failed-sate-machinery.

21 Ibid.

22 Unnithan, Sandeep and Deka, Kaushik. "North-East Rebel Groups Freely Brandish Arms, Extort Protection Money from Locals and Run Parallel Governments," *India Today*, https://www.indiatoday.in/magazine/special-report/story/20121015-north-east-rebel-groups-freely-brandish-arms-extort-protection-money-from-locals-760072-1999-11-30. Accessed on July 11, 2021.

23 *The Indian Express*. "Suspension of Operation with Militants a Failure: Manipur CM," May 20, 2017, https://indianexpress.com/article/india/suspension-of-operation-with-militants-a-failure-manipur-cm-4665661/

23 "Datasheet-Terrorist-Attack-Fatalities," https://www.satp.org/datasheet-terrorist-attack/fatalities/india-jammukashmir. Accessed on July 12, 2021.

24 "Jammu and Kashmir Bomb Blast: Chronology of Major Terror Attacks on Security Forces in Jammu and Kashmir since 1999," India News - *Times of India*, https://timesofindia.indiatimes.com/india/chronology-of-major-terror-attacks-on-security-forces-in-jammu-and-kashmir-since-1999/articleshow/67996629.cms. Accessed on July 12, 2021.

25 Kumar, Hari. "Indian and Pakistani Forces Agree to Cease-Fire in Kashmir," *The New York Times*, November 26, 2003, sec. World, https://www.nytimes.com/2003/11/26/world/indian-and-pakistani-forces-agree-to-cease-fire-in-kashmir.html.

26 "LoC Fencing Completed: Mukherjee," *Times of India*, October 22, 2012, https://web.archive.org/web/20121022112105/http://articles.timesofindia.indiatimes.com/2004-12-16/india/27151889_1_loc-fencing-infiltration-barak.

27 "Datasheet-Terrorist-Attack-Reference-Data," https://www.satp.org/datasheet-terrorist-attack/india-jammukashmir/India-JK-Infiltration-2001-2019. Accessed on July 13, 2021.

28 Swami, Praveen. "Liberated Marrah," *Frontline*, https://frontline.thehindu.com/the-nation/article30220425.ece. Accessed on July 13, 2021.

29 Swami, Praveen. "Resistance and Reprisal," *Frontline*, https://frontline.thehindu.com/the-nation/article30223495.ece. Accessed on July 13, 2021.

30 "Datasheet-Terrorist-Attack-Surrender," https://www.satp.org/datasheet-terrorist-attack/surrender/india-jammukashmir. Accessed on July 14, 2021.

31 Ministry of Home Affairs Annual Report 2006-07, https://www.mha.gov.in/sites/default/files/AnnualReport_06_07.pdf

32 Coll, Steve. "The Back Channel," *The New Yorker*, February 22, 2009, https://www.newyorker.com/magazine/2009/03/02/the-back-channel.

33 Shah, Khalid. "Ideological Shift, Public Support and Social Media: The 'New' in Kashmir's 'New Militancy,'" ORF, https://www.orfonline.org/research/ideological-shift-public-support-and-social-media-the-new-in-kashmirs-new-militancy-60117/. Accessed on July 15, 2021.

34 Service, Tribune News. "Kashmir Militant Releases Video, Vows to Establish Caliphate," *Tribune India News Service*, https://www.tribuneindia.com/news/archive/features/kashmir-militant-releases-video-vows-to-establish-caliphate-124897. Accessed on July 15, 2021.

35 Ministry of Home Affairs Annual Report 2018-19, https://www.mha.gov.in/sites/default/files/AnnualReport_18_19.pdf

36 *The Times of India*. "166 Locals among 203 Terrorists Killed in 2020," India News - *Times of India*, https://timesofindia.indiatimes.com/india/166-locals-among-203-terrorists-killed-in-2020/articleshow/80012563.cms. Accessed on July 15, 2021.

37 Rubenstein, Richard E. "Basic Human Needs: The Next Steps in Theory Development," https://www.gmu.edu/programs/icar/ijps/vol6_1/Rubenstein.htm.

38 Rabasa, Angel, (ed.), *Deradicalizing Islamist Extremists*, (Santa Monica, CA: RAND, 2010).

39 News18. "Full Text: PM Modi's Speech on Historic Deal between Centre, NSCN-IM," August 3, 2015. https://www.news18.com/news/politics/full-text-pm-modis-speech-on-historic-deal-between-centre-nscn-im-1029728.html.

CHAPTER 5

LEFT WING EXTREMISM AND URBAN TERRORISM

K.C. VERMA

ABSTRACT

India faces external threats as a price that it must pay for having a 'tough neighbourhood.' India also faces internal threats due to regional, ethnic and linguistic diversities, as well as fault lines within society created by economic disparities, caste conflicts and religious and ideological differences. Compulsions of an inchoate democracy and demographic pressures further threaten the progress of the nation. Besides serious challenges from its neighbours, India has had to contend with a multitude of internal issues ranging from insurgencies in some parts of the North East to militant movements, first in Punjab and then in Jammu & Kashmir, both of which were aided and abetted by Pakistan. A persisting Left Wing Extremist movement in the hinterland and the threat of terrorist strikes arising from religious extremism are the internal wars that have impeded India's growth and development.

LEFT WING EXTREMISM (LWE)

In 1967, peasant unrest in northern West Bengal and the issue of implementation of land reforms caused a schism in the Communist Party of India (Marxist), with the hardliners breaking away from the party. Charu Majumdar and Kanu Sanyal, the two pro-Chinese leaders in the breakaway faction, spearheaded agitations that encouraged looting of crops and incitement of peasants against the landlords. The lynching of a police officer in Naxalbari area of Darjeeling district, and subsequent police firing in May 1967 that killed ten civilians, triggered widespread violence. Leaders of the Naxalbari uprising formally announced the formation of the Communist Party of India-Marxist/Leninist (CPI/ML) in 1969 at the May Day rally in Calcutta.

The new Left Extremist party, loosely termed as Naxals after Naxalbari, was inspired by the teachings of Mao and it declared landlords, police and revisionists as 'class enemies'. The path of annihilation and violence was advocated for the establishment of a New Democratic State. The CPI (ML) sought to capture state power "through the barrel of the gun" and by taking the revolutionary struggle to the rural areas.

STAGES OF THE MOVEMENT

Since its inception in 1967, the Left Wing Extremist movement has passed through many phases, with little left of the original organisations, leadership or even ideology. The revolutionary movement has suffered numerous splits and equally often coalesced again under different banners. Over the years, ideology has played a role in the dissensions within the party and splinter groups, but the movement has consistently included lumpen elements.

Following its formation, the CPI (ML) steadily increased its influence and activities, with violence peaking in 1970-71, mainly in West Bengal. During these early years, the Naxals relied almost wholly on conventional weapons, like choppers, spears, pipe-guns and sickles. Violence was confined to annihilation of class enemies, including landlords, rich peasants, money lenders and police informers. The early years were also characterised by strong personalities and serious ideological differences, which resulted in leadership splits and expulsions.[1] After the arrest and death of Charu Majumdar in July 1972 and strong action against the party in West Bengal, the movement all but withered away during the Emergency. Different Naxal groups, however, again became active after the Emergency, spreading their influence through their front organisations and alliances with civil liberties and human rights groups.

Between 1980 and the turn of the century, the Maoist groups spread in several states, with different groups holding sway in different areas. The main theatres of violence shifted from West Bengal to Bihar and Andhra Pradesh, even as other states like Kerala, Punjab, Uttar Pradesh, and Tamil Nadu were affected. The People's War Group (PWG) in Andhra Pradesh, the Bihar-based Maoist Communist Centre (MCC) and two factions of the CPI (ML)—Vinod Mishra group and CPML-Party Unity, were the most active. These groups indulged in selected 'annihilations of class enemies', killing of 'police informers', large-scale destruction of government property, attacks on security forces and random violence to disrupt elections. In Bihar, there were frequent clashes between the Naxal groups and 'senas' (private 'armies') of landlords, as also internecine clashes among extremist groups. In this period, the different groups substantially upgraded their weaponry and conventional firearms came to be more widely utilised. The response of the state remained incoherent, with less than effective police action being the only counter.

From the late 1990s to 2004, the Naxal groups spread their activities to several hitherto unaffected states and consolidated their position in their strongholds. An important feature of their activities was the collection of funds through extortions from contractors and corporate bodies. There was steady militarisation as evidenced by the increasing attacks on police and use of more sophisticated weaponry like grenade firing rifles and even country-made rockets. The PWG enlarged its armed units to form a People's Guerrilla Army and established a so-called Central Military Commission to coordinate and supervise military actions. Successes during this period emboldened the Naxal groups to run parallel government structures, hold 'Jan Adalats' and aspire to form a Compact Revolutionary Zone across central India that extended to Nepal.

FACTORS CONTRIBUTING TO THE PERSISTENCE OF LEFT WING EXTREMISM

Left Wing Extremism has persisted for over five decades as a result of a complex mix of ideological, economic, social, geographical, administrative and political factors. Even without the feeble appeal of Maoist ideology, the movement would derive sustenance from the economic realities and lack of development, which represents a huge failure of administration and governance. The worst-affected areas have for long lacked proper healthcare, education, roads, means of communication, electricity, water and maintenance of land records. The problem has been compounded by poor law enforcement and a near non-existent judicial system. Naxals have used this vacuum of governance to expand their influence and recruit cadres by exploiting grievances related to poverty, unemployment, lack of development and a perception among indigenous peoples that they have been denied their traditional rights over 'Jal, Jangal and Jameen' (water, forest, forest produce and land). The sense of deprivation and distrust has also been used to oppose development and construction of roads, as well as to prevent extraction of mineral and forest wealth from these areas. The topography of the forested and hilly tracts of Central India is convenient for sanctuary, while making movement of law enforcement agencies difficult.

The State's strategy for containing Left Wing Extremism has remained security oriented over the years. In counter-extremist operations, the state police forces and Central Armed Police Forces have suffered casualties with disturbing regularity, sometimes in large numbers. The largest numbers of casualties have been caused by explosions of IEDs planted on roads. Historically, the police have remained under resourced to meet the challenge for numerous reasons that range from systemic inadequacies and budgetary constraints to political diktats. In absolute numbers, the police to population ratios are very low. Even against the suboptimal sanctioned strengths, state police forces carry crippling vacancies, which are as high as 50 per cent in some cutting-edge ranks.[2] On the ground, police presence is heavily tilted towards urban areas, leaving a vacuum in the countryside. Generation of intelligence remains a major challenge and working within the silos of state jurisdictions prevents coordinated actions. This state of affairs has been changing, albeit at a slow pace. In recent years, resource allocation in affected areas has improved and matters related to jurisdiction have been overcome to some extent through the creation of Joint Task Forces comprising personnel of two or more states. In the past, inconsistent approaches of state governments and political parties have sometimes complicated matters. On occasion, state governments have initiated 'peace talks' because of electoral compulsions or wishful thinking and unrealistic expectations. The Naxals took advantage of such phases of respite to recover lost ground, enhance operational capabilities and consolidate and expand their influence.

In 1982, N. T. Rama Rao, the then-leader of the Telugu Desam Party, described the Maoists as 'patriots' and 'elder brothers' to secure their support in the elections to unseat the incumbent Congress government.[3] In 1989, it was the turn of the Congress party to secure Maoist support. The experiment lasted two years in which the Naxals went on a rampage and extorted crores of rupees.[4] The PWG was banned in 1992, but the ban was lifted by Rama Rao soon after he became the chief minister. A ban was again imposed in 1996 by his successor Chandrababu Naidu, who lifted it once more to find a 'political solution' in January 2002.[5] The talks, however, failed within months. A similar ceasefire against the Naxals was ordered by the Y S Rajasekhara Reddy Government in mid-2004, with the blessings of the newly elected UPA Government at the Centre.[6] The 'ceasefire' proved infructuous, and the PWG was once again banned in August 2005. The peace talks gave breathing space to the PWG, which was under severe police pressure. It also paved the way for the formation of the CPI (Maoist) with the merging of the two most powerful groups, the PWG and MCC, and several minor outfits. The CPI (Maoist), with the avowed objective of armed overthrow of the Indian state through people's war, escalated violence and spread Naxal activities to many parts of the country, prompting Dr. Manmohan Singh, then Prime Minister, to observe more than once that Left Wing Extremism was the greatest internal threat.

While ideology played a major role during the initial years of the Left Wing Extremist movement's rise, its relevance diminished over the years. The siren song of Marxist–Leninist dialectics, coupled with genuine empathy for the deprived has, however, always found adherents among the urban elite, intellectuals and human rights groups. This has earned them the sobriquet of 'Urban Naxals'. Such activists and supporters give a veneer of respectability to violence and, wittingly or unwittingly, help the Naxals in propaganda, recruitment and to raise funds. Organisations such as the Progressive Writers' Association, People's Union for Civil Liberties, Coordination of Democratic Rights Organisation and others have come to be perceived as virtually front organisations of Maoist groups.

The Left Extremist movement has found some ideological resonance in organisations outside the country too. While the movement initially received support from the Communist Party of China, it was claimed that fraternal links were also established with like-minded revolutionary groups elsewhere. Later, the expansion of Maoist influence was attributable to the perceived success of Maoism in Nepal. Different Naxal groups claimed association with international organisations like the Coordination Committee of Maoist Parties and Organisations of South Asia, the Revolutionary Internationalist Movement, the World People's Resistance Movement, South Asia, the Krantikari Jansangarsh Ekjutta Samiti and outfits involved in the Mumbai Resistance 2004.[7] According to an internal document of the CPI (Maoist) the party had linkages with 21 fraternal groups abroad, including in Peru, US, Italy, Germany, Colombia and the Philippines.[8] The international links, real and claimed, have been more aspirational in nature than for any substantial assistance. Similarly, efforts of Naxal groups in the past to establish links with the LTTE and militant groups in the North-East were largely for propaganda purposes. According to the government, the Maoists lacked "backing from any foreign agency or country."[9]

LEFT EXTREMIST VIOLENCE AND EFFORTS TO CONTROL IT

Naxal groups seek to spread into new areas in a phased manner; first by surveying an area, then advocating and encouraging economic struggles, followed by the stage of resistance. Throughout these three stages, the stealthily increasing influence of Naxals goes unnoticed and state authorities either remain ignorant or in denial. It is in the next two stages, guerrilla warfare and establishment of liberated areas, that the spread of Left Extremism leads to violence. As a result, the number of incidents of violence is not the best measure of the spread of Naxalism. Numbers, however, serve the useful purpose of quantifying the problem.

With the lifting of the ban on the PWG in 2002 and the formation of the CPI (Maoist) in 2004, extremist activities and violence increased steadily. Maoists increased from 55 districts distributed across nine states in November 2003 to 156 districts spread across 13 states by September 2004.[10] Jharkhand, Bihar, Andhra Pradesh and Chhattisgarh remained the worst-affected states, and LWE groups made fresh inroads into Odisha, West Bengal, Uttar Pradesh, Maharashtra, Madhya Pradesh, Uttarakhand, Tamil Nadu, Karnataka and Kerala. From about 1,200 incidents in 2001, Naxal violence in the country peaked in the years 2009 and 2010, which witnessed more than 2,000 incidents. The number of persons killed doubled from about 500 to 1,000. (Appendix A includes a table of incidents of violence, the number of deaths and the statistics for the worst-affected states.)[11]

Furthermore, this period witnessed many bold ambushes of security forces and daring raids to acquire weaponry. Significant features of these attacks were use of sophisticated weapons, extensive use of IEDs to ambush police parties and the involvement of even several hundreds of cadres and supporters in some attacks. (Some major incidents that illustrate the audacious nature of the attacks are listed in Appendix B.)[12]

THE TIDE TURNS

From 2011, Naxal violence began to decline, and by 2019 the number of incidents had fallen to less than 700, from a high of 2,258 in 2009. The number of deaths (202) also decreased to about one-fifth of the 2010 figure (1,005). The gradual improvement has been the result of a combination of many approaches and initiatives by the state and union governments.

In the federal polity envisioned by the Indian Constitution, 'Public Order' and 'Police' are items in the State List. The crucial responsibility of containing Naxalism remains that of the state governments. The Union Government supplements the efforts of the states, coordinates interstate activities and provides intelligence and additional resources when needed and available. The Ministry of Home Affairs (MHA) created the Left Wing Extremism Division in 2006, which has been pursuing a holistic approach.[13] It formulated a 'National Policy and Action Plan' in 2015, adopting a four-pronged strategy encompassing security, development, ensuring rights and entitlements of local communities and managing public perception.

The MHA ensures better coordination and assists the states in modernisation of police forces, deploys Central Armed Police Forces, bears part of the security-related expenditure and for civic action plans and allocates funds for infrastructure schemes in Naxal-affected areas. The Union Government has also made helicopter support available for casualty evacuation. The Prime Minister and the Union Home Minister periodically review the security as well as development activities with Chief Ministers of the affected states. Different state governments have been attempting to upgrade their security responses; strengthen their intelligence capabilities; adopt focussed measures to make essential services such as drinking water, electricity, health and education available to the people; close gaps in essential infrastructure and create mechanisms for public grievance redressal, mass contact and public awareness.

Among the states, undivided Andhra Pradesh was the worst affected and also the first to steadily achieve the upper hand over the Naxals.[14] This was mainly because a specialised police force, the Greyhounds, was formed in 1989 for counter-Naxal operations. While parts of Telengana remain affected by Naxal activities, the overall decline in Left Extremist violence in the state has been remarkable. In Chhattisgarh, the forested tracts have been a stronghold of the Maoists for many years. Bijapur, Sukma, Bastar, Narayanpur, Kanker and Dantewada are the districts hardest hit. The construction of roads in recent years has, however, contributed to reducing the depredations of Naxals and establishing a police presence in remote areas.[15]

In Jharkhand, the capacity of the police remains inadequate. The formation of a special force termed as 'Jaguars', on the lines of the Greyhounds of Andhra Pradesh has, however, showed good results. Successive governments offered incentives for surrender that, even though random in nature, had a positive impact. In Odisha, the early part of the first decade saw increase in extremist activities, which the state government ignored merely because there was no violence. However, in recent years, a combination of police action and a policy of encouraging surrenders has given good results. The state police have been able to assert themselves, especially in the sensitive Kandhamal-Kalahandi border area. In Maharashtra, Gadchiroli district is no longer afflicted as in the past, but the trijunction of Maharashtra, Madhya Pradesh and Chhattisgarh remains a vulnerable zone. The situation has improved in Bihar too, following some development and governance measures, as well as coordinated police action.

THE WAY AHEAD

Over the past decade, Naxal violence has steadily declined, as have the ideological and political understanding of CPI (Maoist) cadres. The movement itself has been finding less traction and levels of recruitment have declined because of sustained pressure by the police. Overall, the area dominated by the Maoists has shrunk across all the affected states. In recent years, many leaders have either been neutralised or have become inactive. Other favourable factors include the impact of construction of roads, communication facilities and a gradual assertion of the administration in the affected areas.

Regardless of the declining influence of Left Wing Extremism, it would be naïve to conclude that Maoists no longer pose any threat to the country. This is underlined by incidents like the one on April 3, 2021, in which a contingent of the CRPF and Chhattisgarh Police was ambushed in Sukma-Bijapur area, resulting in the death of twenty-two security personnel.

Such random incidents can be expected to continue till the movement is completely defeated, militarily and ideologically. Security forces cannot afford to let their guard down even as governance mechanisms continue sustained efforts in all dimensions of development, empowerment of local communities and security.

THE THREAT OF TERRORISM

India is no stranger to terrorism, having witnessed a hijacking as early as in January 1971 when an Indian aircraft on a flight between Srinagar and Jammu was hijacked by two Kashmiri separatists belonging to the National Liberation Front. The militant groups of different long persisting insurgencies in the North East have also sporadically adopted terrorist tactics while attacking security forces or specific targets. It was, however, not till the rise of Sikh militancy and the movement for Khalistan that India saw the systematic and sustained use of terrorism as a strategy.

Sikh militants indulged in acts of terror from the mid-1980s till the mid-1990s in Punjab and other parts of India, and even in some places abroad. The various Sikh terrorist groups, among which prominent ones were the Khalistan Liberation Force, Babbar Khalsa International (BKI), Khalistan Zindabad Force (KZF), International Sikh Youth Federation (ISYF), Dal Khalsa and the Bhindranwale Tiger Force of Khalistan, indulged in frequent shootings, bomb blasts, attacks on security personnel and assassinations. At the peak of militancy, the targeted killings of non-Sikh passengers in buses and trains were common occurrences. Each year, hundreds of people and security personnel were killed. The most prominent act was the assassination of then Prime Minister, Indira Gandhi, on October 31, 1984. In May 1985 more than thirty bombs placed in buses, trains and public places exploded in New Delhi and nearby places, killing 85 and injuring hundreds. The Babbar Khalsa was responsible for the bombing of Air India Boeing, 'Kanishka', off the coast of Ireland on 23 June 1985 in which 351 passengers and crew lost their lives. The former Chief of Army Staff, General A. S. Vaidya, was killed on August 10, 1986. Beant Singh, Chief Minister of Punjab, and 17 others were killed in a suicide bomb attack on August 31, 1995.

Besides the violence that India witnessed during the Sikh militancy, India has also suffered acts of terrorism arising from the growth of Islamic fundamentalism and extremism in Jammu and Kashmir and in the hinterland. Pakistan has found it convenient to weave both into its relentless proxy war against India and employ terrorism as a strategic tool against India.

THE PAKISTAN FACTOR

Pakistan has always been a difficult neighbour, with differences dating all the way back to its creation in 1947. It has foisted many skirmishes on India and two wars, one of which led to its dismemberment. The formation of Bangladesh and the continuing coexistence of Muslims with Hindus in India is a negation of the two-nation theory, the very raison d'être for the demand and creation of Pakistan. Even though Pakistan remains antagonistic to India, it is alive to the fact that an open-ended conflict between two nuclear-armed countries is highly improbable in today's strategic milieu. Caught in this predicament, Pakistan has chosen to adopt the proxy-war route, variously touted as 'bleeding India through a thousand cuts' or 'Operation Tupac'.[16]

When Sikh militancy started, Pakistan established training camps in Karachi and Lahore and channelled weapons, ammunition and explosives to Sikh terrorists. The Inter-Services Intelligence (ISI), Pakistan's main externally focussed intelligence agency, followed a three-stage plan of (i) alienating the Sikh population from mainstream India, (ii) subverting Punjab's administrative machinery and mobilising mass agitations against the government and (iii) launching a reign of terror in Punjab in which the population became victims of violence by the militants and counter-violence by the state.[17] The ISI regards protagonists of Khalistan like Lakhbir Singh, Head of ISYF; Wadhawa Singh, Chief of BKI and Ranjeet Singh 'Neeta', Chief of KZF, as strategic assets and continues to harbour them. It also shelters Hafiz Saeed, Chief of Jamaat-ud-Dawah (JuD) and founder of Lashkar-e-Taiba (LeT) and Masood Azhar, Chief of Jaish-e-Mohammed (JeM), besides providing sanctuary to underworld don Dawood Ibrahim.

Pakistan has also used terrorism to further its national interests. It had no compunctions about supping with the Al Qaeda and playing host to Osama bin Laden, while simultaneously professing to be an indispensable partner of the US in its global war against terror. The ISI has long had a cosy relationship with the Haqqani Network and allowed Pakistani territory to be used by the Taliban for sanctuary and training. Pakistan has also long claimed to be a victim of terrorism, because of the activities of terrorist groups that it has itself created or nurtured.

ISLAMIC EXTREMISM IN INDIA

The Muslim population of India, arguably the second largest in the world, is composed of almost all streams of Islam, and some of the holiest of shrines of Islam are in India. India has a sizeable Shia population and the two main Sunni movements, the Barelvis and Deobandis, also started in India. The worldwide Islamic revivalism of the 1970s did not immediately impact India, but the Muslim community was influenced by other factors, not all of which were related. In the years following Independence, the old guard of the educated Muslim elite lost its traditional influence on the Muslim community and religious establishments. Following the oil boom in the 1970s, a large number of Muslims, especially from Kerala, migrated to the Middle East for employment. From the Middle East, they brought back not only money but also new ideas related to Islamic extremism. Aggressive postures of Right Wing Hindu revivalists, such as the Ram Janmabhoomi movement, had a significant impact on community feeling.

Within the Muslim population, the Jamaat-e-Islami Hind (JIH) and the JI (J&K) have remained the proponents of Islamic orthodoxy. They have been the prime movers of Islamic revivalism, spreading influence through institutions such as madarsas, colleges, study circles, libraries and newspapers. The JIH was instrumental in establishing both—the Students Islamic Movement of India (April 25, 1977) and later the Students Islamic Organisation (October 19, 1982). The insidious influence of education in madarsas by Jamaat-trained teachers in J&K was responsible for converting the tolerant Sufi Kashmiris into a fundamentalist society. The Jammu Kashmir Liberation Front (JKLF) and Hizbul Mujahideen (HuM) used public outrage over the allegedly rigged elections in 1987 to spread terror in the Kashmir Valley. The leadership of the insurgency was soon taken over by Pakistan and POK—based groups like the Harkat-ul-Ansar, the LeT and the JeM. Fortuitously for Pakistan, the withdrawal of the Soviets from Afghanistan freed many ISI operatives, foreign 'freedom' fighters and huge quantities of arms and ammunition for redeployment in Kashmir. Pakistan's efforts to instigate Muslim youth outside Jammu and Kashmir to adopt the jihadi route, however, remained largely unsuccessful till the demolition of the Babri Masjid.

DEMOLITION OF THE BABRI MASJID AND JIHADI TERRORISM

The Muslim community's outrage over the December 1992 demolition of the Babri Masjid and subsequent communal riots helped Pakistan extend its proxy war beyond Jammu and Kashmir and the Punjab. Feeding on religious fervour in the wake of the demolition of the Masjid, several terror modules were established in different parts of India that were directly or indirectly linked to the ISI. These modules engineered bomb explosions in public places, sabotaged rail bridges and tracks and attacked vital installations.

The deadliest attacks took place on March 12, 1993, in Mumbai (then called Bombay). Thirteen explosions ripped through the financial capital of India, killing 257 persons and injuring more than 1,400. The blasts were engineered by the underworld don, Dawood Ibrahim, then Dubai-based, and the Memon family of Mumbai, aided and abetted by the ISI. The perpetrators were selected by Tiger Memon and sent via Dubai to Pakistan for training. Arms and explosives from Pakistan were smuggled into India through the coast of Gujarat and Maharashtra. Besides the serial blasts in 1993, Mumbai suffered other terrorist strikes, the more deadly of which took place on March 13, 2003 (10 dead), August 25, 2003 (52 dead), July 11, 2006 (209 dead, 714 injured), and July 13, 2011 (26 killed, 130 injured). The most spectacular was the attack on the Taj Hotel and other places on November 26, 2008, which left 166 dead and more than 300 injured.

Terrorist attacks have also occurred in the national capital. These include an attack on the Parliament building (December 13, 2001, 9 killed), attack on the Red Fort (December 22, 2000, 3 dead) as well as bomb blasts in public places that took a heavy toll of innocent lives. Other cities such as Jaipur, Ahmedabad, Pune, Ayodhya and Varanasi have also suffered terrorist attacks. Indian Airlines flight IC 814 from Kathmandu to Delhi was hijacked on December 24, 1999, and taken to Taliban-controlled Kandahar. In exchange for the hostages, India had to release three prominent terrorists—Masood Azhar, Ahmed Omar Saeed Sheikh and Mushtak Ahmed Zargar.

Terrorist groups headquartered in Pakistan have carried out the majority of significant assaults in India, but some indigenous groups have also carried out copycat attacks. Terrorist groups in India have also drawn inspiration from or declared allegiance to organisations like the Al-Qaeda and the Islamic State in Iraq and Syria (ISIS) or its so-called Khorasan unit.

STEPS TO COUNTER TERROR

India has adopted a multi-pronged strategy to meet the challenge of terrorism. The Ministry of Home Affairs coordinates counter-terrorism efforts, assisting the States of the Union in capacity building and disseminating intelligence through the Multi-Agency Centres. The ambitious National Intelligence Grid (NATGRID) project for sharing and analysing data for counter-terrorism purposes has been making slow progress. Meanwhile, the

National Investigation Agency, established in 2009, as a specialised agency for investigation of cases of terrorism has matured into an effective counter-terrorist task force. Measures have been initiated to secure the coastline against infiltration and hostile landings. The Union government and some state governments have launched efforts to reach out to the Muslim community and youth to prevent radicalisation. Families of radicalised youth have been supportive of police efforts to wean their family members away from terrorist groups. Traditional Muslim organisations have also played a positive role and supported these efforts. Several Muslim clerics have openly spoken out and issued 'fatwas' against terrorism.[18]

India is a partner in international efforts to counter terror through several Joint Working Groups, as also the Financial Action Task Force (FATF). India supports counter terror efforts of the United Nations, as well as those of regional and multilateral platforms like the Bay of Bengal Initiative for Multi-Sectoral Technical and Economic Cooperation (BIMSTEC) and the Shanghai Cooperation Organisation. Not surprisingly, the SAARC Terrorist Offences Monitoring Desk (STOMD) has remained an ineffective body. Appropriate diplomatic steps are taken to seek cooperation of our neighbours against hostile initiatives from foreign soil. Securing the support of Bangladesh, Nepal and Bhutan to prevent infiltration and sanctuaries has been critical in the overall management of terrorism, as well as in checking the activities of some insurgent groups of the North East.

It is difficult to overemphasise the importance of good governance, an effective criminal justice system, economic well-being and a just and equitable social order in combating so-called root causes. Prevention of disaffection among the minorities and marginalised sections requires adherence to the letter and spirit of our Constitution. On the ground, the states must have an effective apparatus in place to prevent and respond to terrorist acts, in the form of anti-terrorist squads, quick response teams, snipers, bomb detection and disposal units and speedy support from the National Security Guard (NSG) when needed. An efficient intelligence apparatus is essential to prevent attacks and supplement investigations into incidents. The response from the political establishment, the media and people at large requires consensus and maturity, which has sometimes been lacking.

TRENDS AND PORTENTS

In recent years, Pakistan- based Khalistan leaders have not been finding much traction among Indian Sikhs. They, together with prominent activists among the Sikh diaspora particularly in Canada and Germany, have been constantly trying to create pro-Khalistan sentiment, largely through cyber means. The 'Sikhs for Justice', led by US-based Gurpatwant Singh Pannun has been campaigning for secession of Punjab from India. It called for 'Referendum 2020' and exploited the issue of farm laws. Pannun and eight other Khalistan protagonists were designated as terrorists under the enlarged provisions of the UAPA in January 2021 by the Government of India.[19] Efforts of Pakistan-inspired elements to keep Punjab in turmoil continue as witnessed in the targeted killing of Hindu leaders in recent years.[20] Pakistan has added a new dimension to cross-border terrorism by using drones[21] to deliver narcotics and arms to Punjab and Kashmir.[22]

Considering the size of the Muslim population of India, the number of radicalised youth is negligible. Even then, a recent worrisome trend is the indoctrination of educated and affluent Muslim youth, especially through social media and leveraging of issues such as the Citizenship Amendment Act to polarise society.

It is in India's interests to have a friendly and stable neighbourhood, which would have to include a consistent and continuous diplomatic engagement with Pakistan. A meaningful dialogue is, however, possible only in a conducive environment. Equally important are the developments in Afghanistan, which shall bear close watching for safeguarding India's geopolitical interests. The withdrawal of the US and return of the Taliban will encourage radical groups in Afghanistan and Pakistan and this would, in turn, have consequences for India.

APPENDIX A

Left Wing Extremist Violence in India

Year	Incidents	Deaths	AP$ + Telengana	Chhattisgrah	Jharkhand	Bihar	Odisha	Maharshtra
2001	1208	564	461/180	105/37	355/200	169/111	30/11	34/7
2002	1465	482	346/96	304/55	353/157	239/117	68/11	83/29
2003	1597	515	577/140	256/74	342/117	250/128	49/15	75/31
2004	1533	566	310/74	352/83	379/169	323/171	35/8	84/15
2005	1608	677	535/208	385/168	312/119	186/96	42/14	94/53
2006	1509	678	183/47	715/388	310/124	107/45	44/9	98/42
2007	1565	696	138/45	582/369	482/157	135/67	67/17	94/25
2008	1591	721	92/46	620/242	484/207	164/73	103/101	68/22
2009	2258	908	66/18	529/290	742/208	232/72	266/67	154/93
2010	2213	1005	100/24	625/343	501/157	307/97	218/79	94/45
2011	1760	611	54/9	465/204	517/182	316/63	192/53	109/54
2012	1415	415	67/13	370/109	480/163	166/44	171/45	134/41
2013	1136	397	36/11	355/111	387/152	177/69	101/35	71/19
2014	1091	310	22/9	328/112	384/103	162/32	103/26	70/28
2015	1088	230	46/10	466/97	310/56	109/17	92/28	55/18
2016	1048	278	24/0	395/107	323/85	129/28	86/27	73/23
2017	908	263	31/9	373/130	251/56	99/22	81/29	69/16
2018	833	240	23/55	392/153	205/43	59/15	75/12	75/12
2019	670	202	26/7	263/77	200/54	62/17	45/11	66/34
2020	665	183	27/6	315/111	199/39	26/8	50/9	30/8

- ➢ All statistics obtained from the websites/Annual Reports of the Ministry of Home Affairs, Government of India.
- ➢ The columns list the number of incidents/number of persons killed.

$ These figures are for undivided Andhra Pradesh and for Andhra Pradesh and Telengana together after bifurcation in 2014

APPENDIX B

List of Some Major Incidents of Naxal Violence after 2004

1. On February 6, 2004, People's War cadres raided Koraput town in Odisha and in an orgy of violence and looting lasting six hours, took away 505 firearms and 30,000 rounds from the district police armoury, police stations and the district jail.
2. On July 7, 2006, CPI (Maoist) cadres raided a village in Dantewada district, killed 30 unarmed villagers and abducted 45 others.
3. On March 15, 2007, more than 300 cadres of the CPI (Maoist) attacked a police camp in Dantewada district in Chhattisgarh and killed 54 persons, including 15 policemen.
4. On February 15, 2008, in their largest ever loot; four CPI (Maoist) groups raided the Police Training School and the district armoury in Nayagarh in Odisha. In an operation lasting several hours, they killed 15 policeman and one civilian and looted about 1100 weapons, and 2,00,000 rounds of ammunition.
5. On June 29, 2008, CPI (Maoist) cadres attacked a boat in the Balimela reservoir in Odisha, killing 38 police personnel.
6. On July 16, 2008, 21 police personnel were killed in Malkangiri district, Odisha, when the vehicle in which they were travelling hit an IED.
7. On February 15, 2010, CPI (Maoist) attacked a police camp in West Midnapur district, West Bengal, and killed 25 police personnel. They took away about 50 weapons and substantial quantities of ammunition.
8. On April 6, 2010, seventy-six CRPF men were killed in an ambush by Naxals in Dantewada district, Chhattisgarh. The Naxals took away 77 weapons, including 42 INSAS rifles, 6 LMGs, and 2 mortars and many wireless sets.
9. On May 17, 2010, thirty-one police personnel were killed and more than 20 injured when a bus in which they were travelling hit a landmine in Dantewada district, Chhattisgarh.
10. On June 29, 2010, twenty-seven CRPF personnel were killed in an ambush by CPI (Maoist) in Narayanpur district, Chhattisgarh. The extremists looted about 30 rifles, mortar shells, hand-grenades and ammunition.
11. On May 25, 2013, about 250 cadres of CPI (Maoist) attacked a convoy of state Congress leaders in Sukma district, Chhattisgarh, killing 28 persons. Twelve Congress leaders, including founder of the Salwa Judum, Mahendra Karma, were killed and veteran leader Vidya Charan Shukla was fatally injured.
12. On March 11, 2014, sixteen police personnel were killed in Sukma district, Chhattisgarh in an ambush. About 20 weapons were looted.
13. On April 24, 2017, Naxals killed 25 CRPF personnel and injured 7 others in Sukma district, Chhattisgarh. They took away 22 weapons.
14. On July 13, 2018, twenty-four CRPF personnel were killed in the same Sukma area in an ambush.
15. On May 1, 2019, sixteen police personnel were killed in a landmine blast in Gadchiroli district, Maharashtra.

16. On March 21, 2020, about 300-350 Naxal cadres ambushed a police party in Sukma district. In the exchange of fire, 17 security personnel were killed and 15 others were injured.
17. On April 3, 2021 about 300 cadres of the banned CPI (Maoist) ambushed a force of CRPF personnel and state police in the Sukma-Bijapur area of Chhattisgarh and killed twenty-two police personnel and injured more than thirty. A number of Naxalites were also killed.

NOTES

1 Rajat Kujur *"Naxal Movement in India: A Profile,"* at http://www.ipcs.org/issue_briefs/issue_brief_pdf/848082154RP15-Kujur-Naxal.pdf

2 Information related to police strengths, vacancies, etc., has been gleaned from statistics published on the websites of the Bureau of Police Research and Development.

3 Saji Cherian "The States Of Denial by Saji Cherian," *Outlook*, August 23, 2005, https://www.outlookindia.com/website/story/the-states-of-denial/228369

4 Ajai Sahni "'Naxalism' The Retreat of Civil Governance," https://satp.org/satporgtp/publication/faultlines/volume5/Fault5-7asahni.htm

5 *Times of India* "Govt to Hold Fire Against PW," January 29, 2002, https://timesofindia.indiatimes.com/city/hyderabad/Govt-to-hold-fire-against-PW/articleshow/10359096.cms

6 Nihar Nayak, "Unprincipled Peace," July 23, 2004, https://www.outlookindia.com/website/story/unprincipled-peace/224580

7 P V Ramana, "Internal and International Linkages of Naxalites," Dialogue, April-June 2005, Volume 6, No. 4.

8 P V Ramana "The Maoist Global Web," IDSA Comment, April 2016, https://idsa.in/idsacomments/the-maoist-global-web_pvramana_290416

9 Minister of State for Home Affairs, replying to Question No. 248 in the Lok Sabha on April 26, 2016.

10 Sanjay K Jha "Left-Wing Extremism in 2004: An Assessment," February 3, 2005, https://idsa.in/idsastrategiccomments/LeftWingExtremismin2004_SKJha_030205

11 All statistics have been taken from reports of the Ministry of Home Affairs. The states in respect of which figures are mentioned were the worst affected. Figures for Andhra Pradesh and Telengana have been shown together, even after their bifurcation.

12 The listed incidents are by no means comprehensive. They have been gleaned from reports available on the internet. The incidents selected are those in which 15 or more persons were killed, the number 15 having been selected quite arbitrarily.

13 MHA Annual Report 2008, https://www.mha.gov.in/sites/default/files/AR%28E%290809.pdf

14 Niranjan Sahoo "From Bihar to Andhra, How India Fought, and Won, its 50-Yr War with Left-Wing Extremism," https://theprint.in/opinion/from-bihar-to-andhra-how-india-fought-and-won-its-50-yr-war-with-left-wing-extremism/254462/

15 Ashutosh Bhardwaj, "Chhattisgarh Maoists suffering from betrayal, fewer leaders and weapons, and too many roads," The Print, February 10, 2021, https://theprint.in/opinion/chhattisgarh-maoists-suffering-from-betrayal-fewer-leaders-and-weapons-and-too-many-roads/602231/

16 George Perkovich and Toby Dalton, *Not War, Not Peace?* (New Delhi: Oxford University Press, 2016), pp. 141-3. The authors analyse Indo-Pak relations and float the thesis that Pakistan will continue to wage a proxy/hybrid war against India, a major component of which shall remain terrorism.

17 Hein Kiessling *Faith, Unity, Discipline: The Inter-Service-Intelligence (ISI) of Pakistan* (New Delhi: Oxford University Press) (Google Books) Chapter 13, "Insurgency in Punjab".

18 Kabir Taneja, "Deradicalisation as Counterterrorism Strategy: The Experience of Indian States," https://www.orfonline.org/research/deradicalisation-as-counterterrorism-strategy-the-experience-of-indian-states/

19 "Babbar Khalsa International chief Wadhawa Singh Babbar, eight others declared as designated terrorists," https://www.indianarrative.com/india-news/babbar-khalsa-international-chief-wadhawa-singh-babbar-eight-others-declared-as-designated-terrorists-4287.html

20 Pakistan's Khalistan agenda behind killing of 6 Hindu leaders in Punjab, says NIA, https://www.indiatoday.in/india/story/nia-claims-scientific-proof-to-establish-pak-behind-killing-of-six-hindu-leaders-killing-in-punjab-with-aim-to-revive-khalistani-militancy-114489-1-2018-01-15

21 Pakistan dropped weapons via drones in Punjab: Intelligence Agencies, https://www.indiatoday.in/india/story/pak-state-actors-behind-drone-weapon-dropping-incidents-in-punjab-intelligence-agencies-1608026-2019-10-10

22 11 grenades dropped by Pak drone recovered from near border in Punjab, https://indianexpress.com/article/india/punjab-police-bsf-shoot-at-incoming-pak-drone-near-gurdaspur-border-7113601/

CHAPTER 6

MANOEUVRE WARFARE: THE PAST-PRESENT-FUTURE

PRAVEEN BAKSHI

ABSTRACT

Manoeuvre is synonymous with the evolution of mankind and was recorded by Sun Tzu (505-496 BC). Tenets of manoeuvre remained largely untapped in India till the "Lightning Campaign" in East Pakistan in December 1971. General Sundarji, as Army Chief, sparked the renaissance of manoeuvre with his focused modernisation and mechanisation of the Indian Army, giving wings to his successors to test new strategies and doctrines predicated on manoeuvre. The altered character of warfare has given a whole new meaning to the relevance of manoeuvre in future conflicts. India's time has come to transcend from a kinetic, contact-oriented manoeuvre doctrine to the unlimited possibilities offered for practicing manoeuvre in the Grey Zone conflicts of the future, which will be dominated by the domains of cyber, space and information domination. This calls for a fundamental shift from a military-dominated conflict management to a whole-of-government approach that comprehends the nature of manoeuvring.

CONTEXTUAL & HISTORICAL REFLECTION

Manoeuvre evolved and has been practised by animals and humans since the Stone Ages; it only became popular as a concept among strategists much later. The art of manoeuvre becomes more fascinating when multiple hunters and preys are involved simultaneously. Outcomes become more intriguing when a strong adversary is confronted from multiple directions by weaker adversaries, or when few attack a quantitatively larger adversary combining manoeuvre with deception, feint and illusion. The final blow is executed by a concentrated attack from unexpected direction(s).

Manoeuvre as a military thought dates back to Sun Tzu (505-496 BC). He devoted book 7 of his 13-volume masterpiece, *Art of War*, to manoeuvring. Sun Tzu infers, "Rapidity is the essence of war; take advantage of the enemy's unpreparedness, make your way by unexpected routes and attack unguarded spots." Hannibal, the Carthaginian General, is acknowledged to be among the early disciples of manoeuvre warfare during his campaigns against the Romans in 216 BC. Khalid ibn-al-Walid, an Arab Muslim commander, also finds his place of honour amongst successful manoeuvre warfare legends for his success against the Persian Empire at the Battle of Walaja in 633 AD. Napoleon employed pre-emptive moves of cavalry and fast infantry to allow his forces to attack where and when he wanted, enabling force concentration in combination with advantages of terrain. Genghis Khan[1] (1162-1227) is regarded as a legend in manoeuvre theory for charging across Eurasia with his limited force, conquering more land and people in his 25 years than the Roman Empire did in 400 years.

The Marathas derived their power mainly from their masterly use of mobility, particularly in hilly terrain, and yet the two leading generals of the Marathas, Shivaji and Bajirao, have not received their due recognition in modern times, even in the Army of independent India.[2] It is time that we study the generalship of several Indian warrior-rulers such as Rana Pratap and Lachit Barphukan, the latter of whom defeated the Moghuls on the Brahmaputra. Maharaja Ranjit Singh and Hari Singh Nalwa represent the Sikh legacy of manoeuvre, while Rajaraja Chola, many centuries earlier, adopted maritime manoeuvre as a means of expanding his empire into present-day Southeast Asia. India's medieval and pre-colonial generals were as accomplished as their western and eastern counterparts.

Some other notable examples of manoeuvre from history are the Blitzkrieg practiced by the Germans during World War II; the spectacular combined arms manoeuvre by India's armed forces in 1971 led by Leiutenant General Sagat Singh, which resulted in the capitulation of Dacca; and Major General Ariel Sharon's dash to capture the Suez Canal during the Yom Kippur war of 1973. Today's professional officer who understands the integrated battlefield might wonder at the relevance of tactics of the days of yore, but look more closely and lessons reappear. Mobility, shock action and rapid movement continue to disturb the enemy's equilibrium till today.

The cardinal point to absorb is that to restrict manoeuvre to terrain (mountains, plains, deserts) or mechanised operations, limits its value and import. Its execution demands no boundaries or tramlines. Lieutenant General S.S. Mehta,[3] former Western Army Commander and one of the Indian Army's (IA) most ardent proponents of manoeuvre, argues that manoeuvre offers several choices that transcend terrain provided the executor has the verve, exercises command over technology, organisation and training and nurtures the leadership to absorb the risk contingent with it. Manoeuvre embraces speed, shock and economy of effort to generate a fear of the unknown in an adversary, which by itself has exponential value in driving tactical, operational and strategic outcomes. Simply put, it is a strategy which targets an adversary's decision making cycle and tempo with speed, shock and disruption. Lieutenant General A.K. Singh,[4] a former Southern Army Commander and a strategist in his own right, argues that the essence of manoeuvre warfare lies in defeating the adversary's will to fight rather than his ability to fight.

Neither manoeuvre nor attrition can exist without the other; they are two sides of the same coin.[5] The scaffolding is based on which of the two has primacy in strategic formulation. Do you attrite to manoeuvre, or do you manoeuvre to attrite? Manoeuvre warfare looks at styles of warfare as a spectrum, with attrition and manoeuvre at opposite ends. It postulates strategic movement to defeat an adversary more efficiently by targeting key elements of the opposing force, by isolating and destroying them piecemeal and seeking overall capitulation with minimum casualties. Since tempo and initiative are so critical to the success of manoeuvre, command structures are decentralised with more tactical freedom given to the subordinate commanders; this is also known as the directive style of command for manoeuvre warfare.

Lieutenant General V.K. Kapoor, an Armoured Corps officer from the IA, a prolific writer and highly respected strategic analyst, has highlighted the development of the Soviet deep operations theory between 1920-1930 in his thought-provoking article "Fundamentals of Operational Art".[6] General Mikhail Tukhachevsky, the great Soviet scholar warrior, insisted that annihilation/destruction was not the aim of battle and a more scientific approach to operational theory designed on systems logic was essential. With the advent of the Deep Operations theory by late 1937, Soviet Operational Art reached a high state of development and became a principal platform upon which military science developed. General Kapoor argues that the subsequent US "Air-Land Battle Concept" draws much inspiration from this Soviet theory in terms of what constitutes the true centre of gravity of an adversary and where it lies in practice.

INHERITANCE, EVOLUTION & RENAISSANCE

The British rejection of the manoeuvre experience during World War I led to the adoption of the Doctrine of Perpetual Defence, also called the Doctrine of Defence in Depth. By a tragic paradox, this loss of aggressive spirit coincided with the restoration of mobility on the battlefield with rapid advances in the development of mechanised weapon platforms such as tanks, towed artillery and armoured troop carriers. Adding heft to manoeuvre were rapid advances in airpower that facilitated the expansion of the battlefield and offered options to cause combat attrition in an adversary's depth areas. During World War II, it was the Germans, Americans and Russians who embraced manoeuvre warfare, while the British remained glued to the principles of defensive warfare steeped in attrition. This, to some extent, had an adverse impact on the Indian officers within the Indian Army of pre-independence vintage, who saw little of the practitioners of manoeuvre warfare such as Guderian, Rommel, Patton or Tukhachevsky.

Writing in *India Review,* Christopher Clary defines four periods in the evolution of the Indian Army's doctrine.[7] These are: Period of defensive defence from 1947-60s; drift towards manoeuvre following the success in 1971 in Bangladesh; acceleration of mechanisation in the 1980s (Sunderji era); and an emphasis on rapid, limited offensive strikes 2002 onwards (Proactive/Cold Start Strategy). Major General G.D. Bakshi highlights that unlike the Continental Armies of Europe (in specific, the German and Russian Armies), the British Army (till recently) did not recognise the level of Operational Art as a distinct gradation in the functional hierarchy of combat that lay between strategy and tactics.[8] Consequently, the entire post-independence generation of Indian military officers, barring a few like General Thimayya, exhibited outstanding tactical prowess, but failed to grasp the finer nuances of operational art and strategy. It was in these circumstances that the Indian Army was pitchforked into the defence of Kashmir.

The decade from 1962 to 1972 was the most challenging in the post-independence Indian Army's history. Three wars in quick succession with varying outcomes led to the rise of professionalism. The defeat at the hands of the Chinese in 1962 propelled the first round of military transformation in India, while lost opportunities in 1965 revealed an absence of operational design to achieve pre-planned objectives. General A.K. Singh posits that India's armed forces lacked the tools, ethos and training to pursue operational art and manoeuvre warfare, baulking at the employment of the much superior Indian Navy and sub-optimally employing the IAF in reactive operations. The 'Lightning Campaign' in

East Pakistan that resulted in the creation of Bangladesh in December 1971 marked a renaissance in operational art within India's armed forces in more ways than one.[9] It was a brilliant strategic and operational level victory, wherein airborne and heliborne operations, amphibious crossings, naval blockades and air strikes against enemy leadership and centres of gravity were used to speed up the tempo of operations and caused a psychological collapse of the enemy.

During the Lightning Campaign, corps and divisional commanders demonstrated unprecedented initiative and risk-taking skills. Leading the charge into Dacca by employing an expanding torrent concept of attack and bypassing or isolating enemy centres of resistance through vertical envelopment were commanders like Lieutenant General Sagat Singh, the corps commander of IV Corps. Supporting him wholeheartedly were subordinate commanders like Group Captain Chandan Singh (later Air Vice Marshal), who orchestrated the heliborne crossings across the River Meghna, Lieutenant Colonel Himmeth Singh, 4 Guards, Lt Col A.B. Harolikar MVC, 4/5 GR, and Major Shammi Mehta commanding the amphibious Independent tank squadron of 63 Cav, all of whom executed Sagat's daring plan. Contemporary Indian operational art had finally come of age!

General Krishnaswamy Sundarji, India's Army Chief from 1986 to 1988, may well have sparked the renaissance of manoeuvre in the Indian Army after a period of post-1971 slumber. Among the first infantry officers from the post-independence era to have commanded an armoured division, he initiated radical transformation in the organisation, equipment and employment of mechanised forces in the Indian Army. He orchestrated one of the largest manoeuvres by India's mechanised formations in Exercise Digvijay while commanding the Western Army Command, where the freshly minted Russian tanks T-72 were fielded. General Shammi Mehta, who was Sunderji's Military Attaché, recalls a host of doctrinal and organisational changes that were initiated by Sundarji with an eye on emerging conflict scenarios in South

Asia. Mehta recollects that on the day Sundarji assumed his appointment as the Army Chief, he handed over the IA's Perspective Plan 2000 over a 15-year horizon at his very first meeting with Mr Arun Singh, the Minister of State for Defence. Though he didn't have much combat experience, he made up for it with his varied operational assignments and powerful intellect. With his ideas about manoeuvre warfare and nuclear warfighting, Sunderji felt he was well prepared to spearhead the transition of the Indian Army into a potent fighting force.[10]

Sundarji conceptualised and embarked on a series of exercises and operational deployments across all adversarial terrain profiles (plains, desert and mountains), to provide momentum to several ideas for strengthening deterrence in the subcontinent,. Among the several military exercises he conducted, Exercise Brasstacks and Exercise Chequerboard were joint ones with the participation of the national political leadership. They helped provide the impetus for acceptable and doable doctrinal changes that followed. The concept of reorganised infantry divisions for the plains called Reorganised Army Plains Infantry Division (RAPID) took root during these exercises as India's armed forces looked to evolve a combined arms approach to war fighting. General A.K. Singh argues that another battle-hardened armoured corps officer from the 1971 war, Lieutenant General Hanut Singh, complemented General Sunderji and contributed more than his fair share to the art of manoeuvre warfare in the Indian Army. His approach, however, was steady and cautious compared to General Sunderji's flamboyance; a mix of both is required for institutional absorption, according to General Singh.

The IPKF debacle forced the Indian Army to consider whether manoeuvre as a strategic concept was compromised. Did India fall victim to the illusion of strength even as both the LTTE and the Sri Lankan government manoeuvred themselves into positions of strategic advantage? General Shammi feels in hindsight that institutional hubris prevented India from anticipating that manoeuvre would transcend traditional battlefields. He sums up the Sundarji era as one with many firsts: mechanised warfare (as distinct from manoeuvre warfare), the nuclear dimension, doctrine and organisational changes, perspective planning and altering an attrition-oriented mindset. However, it fell short of appreciating the higher call of manoeuvre as a strategic concept. When weighed against Manekshaw seeking time to get ready before intervening in East Pakistan in 1971, the IPKF experience and the readiness to intervene without reasonably clear conflict termination objectives stand out in stark contrast in the realm of strategic foresight and thought leadership while addressing complex security challenges.

TOUGH DECADES: 1990–2020

As the 1990s unfolded, India remained preoccupied with its western adversary, Pakistan, as the latter resorted to a different kind of manoeuvre to shrink the growing conventional asymmetry that was emerging between the two South Asian rivals. This it achieved by leveraging terrorism and proxy strategies as its preferred choice to keep Kashmir on the boil and keep the Indian Army preoccupied with counter-insurgency, counter-infiltration and counter-terrorism operations. Making matters more difficult for India was the overt nuclear weaponisation of South Asia following the acquisition of nuclear weapons capability by both India and Pakistan in 1998. The Pakistan-sponsored insurgency morphed into a vicious proxy war by the late 1990s, emboldened by a declared First Use Nuclear strategy and radicalised non-state actors who emerged as effective proxies.

Convinced that the conventional window was closing, the IA continued to hone its counter-insurgency (CI) capability, without any clarity defining what actions would alter the dynamic. It is in this backdrop that Pakistan planned the Kargil attack, to outmanoeuvre India and seize a sizeable chunk of J&K. Several analysts have suggested that though the operation was tactically brilliant, it was operationally unviable and doomed to strategic failure. India's response was initially hesitant and relied on frontal assaults with heavy attrition—airpower was employed with restrictions that hampered its effectiveness initially. Gradually, a combined arms approach evolved that finally overwhelmed an exhausted adversary. However, the bottom line remained that manoeuvre was largely absent in India's response. It is still debatable whether India's policy of self-restraint limiting its air and ground options within the LoC had any real benefit. This happens when the preoccupation and occupation is restricted to the contact battle. Micromanagement leaves little time for strategic manoeuvres.

The attack on India's Parliament in December 2001 by Pakistan-sponsored and controlled terrorists resulted in widespread mobilisation, resulting in Operation Parakram, a year-long face-off between India and Pakistan. An emerging power like India had every reason to strike back and should have done so in early January, but speculations of why it baulked remain unanswered. This hesitancy sparked a debate within the Indian Army on how to compress operational cycles through a process called provocatively in the West as the Cold Start or Proactive Strategy. The strategy essentially was an attempt to cut down on the time taken to mobilise offensive formations so that the Indian Army could leverage its conventional superiority to realise favourable operational outcomes in the compressed timeframe of the emerging paradigm of 'Limited Conflicts.' Though the strategy was never formally promulgated, it was widely put to practice in wargames and exercises. This heralded a mild though discernible shift in the Indian Army's approach to warfighting on the western front, as a predominantly reactive and defensive mind set was replaced with an offensive orientation premised on manoeuvre. It may be of some interest that Western Command, under Lieutenant General Shammi Mehta, issued a written directive in June 2002 on strategic concepts, replacing several defensive terminologies and practices with the new offensive credo; for example, PIVOT now stood for Pre-emptive Initiation of Violence in the Opponents Territory.[11] The Indian Army's Proactive Strategy can be linked to this understanding of The Pivot.

The last decade has seen the operational focus shift to the Line of Actual Control, with Chumar, Demchok, Depsang, Doklam and Eastern Ladakh occupying centre-stage. On the western front, notwithstanding the surgical strikes and the Balakot air-strike, the LoC has remained live and so has the insurgency in J&K. Following the Eastern Ladakh crisis, a limited two-front war remains a distinct possibility and calls for new joint strategies and complementing doctrines and concepts with manoeuvre as the only driving force that can combat a collusive superiority driven by the might of the PLA. Generals Shammi Mehta and A.K. Singh concur that India's armed forces have developed expertise in set piece battles, but their DNA has not imbibed or embraced the true philosophy of manoeuvre warfare, directive style of command and operational art. There have been a few exceptions, but too few and mainly personality driven to leave a lasting impact.

MANOEUVRE IN FUTURE CONFLICTS: A PERISCOPIC VIEW

The altered character of warfare in the Indian context seems to be biased towards limited or sectoral wars in multiple spatially distanced sectors on two fronts, posing a bigger challenge to the military leadership than the diminishing prospect of all-out war on a single front. Kinetics have yielded space to non-kinetic means of warfare with the focus shifting from contact to non-contact warfare. With the space and cyber domains acquiring a dominant force-multiplier status in all kinds of conflicts, the emergence of ambiguity in what is termed as 'grey zone conflicts' necessitates increasingly complex response capabilities as part of a whole of government approach. With the escalatory matrix in contemporary conflict steepening, the need for a National Security Strategy (NSS) has never been more acutely felt. A clearly articulated NSS would offer focused policy and strategic guidance in the formulation of strategies, doctrines and concepts that ensure the centrality of manoeuvre as an asymmetric element of India's overall game plan to tackle a two-front collusive threat beyond the conventional spectrum. Without well-considered political goals, which can be translated into viable military missions, India's armed forces will have little choice but to plan for reactive and enemy-centric attrition-based campaigns.[12] The time has come for India to transcend from kinetic-oriented manoeuvre warfare to the unlimited possibilities offered for manoeuvre in future conflict circumstances driven by the cyber, space, informational and Artificial Intelligence (AI).

CONVENTIONAL SPECTRUM

In the conventional domain, a rebalancing of forces is underway as India's armed forces seek to jettison their Pak-centric approach and focus on strengthening combat capabilities on its northern frontiers. Several infantry formations, with a sprinkling of mechanised troops are likely to be reassigned from our western borders to the Line of Actual Control. This shift would result in a higher residual ratio of mechanised troops vs infantry on the western border. Thus, the need to imbibe manoeuvre as the predominant strategy by mechanised forces on the western front becomes an even more compelling operational necessity. With the IBG (Integrated Battle Group) concept likely to crystallise into a formal organisation, its continued refinement with the integration of airpower would signal a clear shift towards a manoeuvre-oriented strategy in varied terrain.

Basil Liddel Hart's indirect approach to warfighting that seeks to physically and, more importantly, psychologically dislocate the enemy until it feels compelled to capitulate can be used in conventional wars, when it relies on manoeuvre, as well as in unconventional conflicts or operations other than war, to coerce the enemy without engaging in open battle. In a recent piece, Arzan Tarapore argues that an 'indirect approach' offers several options against a wider array of threats, but has generally been missing from India's strategic repertoire.[13] Tarapore suggests that despite having particular pieces of equipment or nominal mission sets, there are at least four reasons why India has failed to develop workable options using the indirect approach: India's power relative to its adversaries; civil-military relations;[14] organisational culture; and a lack of strategic planning. According to him, India's solution to its military problems has been mass and firepower rather than manoeuvre.[15]

In a recent presentation, Lieutenant General A.B. Shivane,[16] a former Strike Corps Commander and Director General of the IA's Mechanised Forces, forcefully argued that to win future wars quickly, decisively and with minimal casualties, India's armed forces would need to fuse adaptive precision fires with decisive manoeuvre. He rightly stated that technology empowers manoeuvre to dominate time, space, force and information. The Nagorno-Karabakh[17] skirmishes do not provide conclusive evidence of the death of armour. The overinflated claims of both sides have precipitated a rash of new claims of the tank's demise. All it showed was two incompetently trained and equipped military forces that left themselves vulnerable to the power of quickly produced videos making extravagant claims about the potency of drones. Drones will be an increasing threat—but cheap drones are cheap to shoot down as well. Competent modern combined arms combat forces, even without air dominance, can sweep that threat from the sky. As Franz-Stefan Gady and Alexander Stronwell[18] have stated, in the long run, all advanced militaries will have to make the transition from a platform-centric to a more integrated network-centric force structure. In the coming decades, the military that best understands how to combine the two into a hybrid force structure that integrates legacy systems with emerging technologies will have the advantage in high-intensity manoeuvre-oriented combat.

The IA has restructured to have two dedicated Strike Corps for the northern borders, as part of its strategy of deterrence by denial and by punishment. This was a calling late in coming, with half-hearted attempts made earlier in raising of the first Mountain Strike Corps and tasking it for both the North-East and Ladakh. Surprisingly, the IA raised one on the lines of a normal Corps employed in the plains, in place of a Strike Corps suited for the mountains. Instead of a plug-and-play model for a light agile Mountain Strike Corps, it was encumbered with heavy logistic support units modelled on the structure for operating on India's western borders. Thankfully, this extra flab has been shed and another dedicated Corps has been reassigned for Ladakh after due rebalancing of forces. The concept of manoeuvre will truly apply to the employment of both these Corps, to deliver operational effects within a time-sensitive conflict situation that may oscillate between a grey zone to limited/sectoral conflict.

The annexation of Crimea by Russia in 2014, the alleged Russian manipulation of the US elections, or the multiple transgressions in recent times by China at Doklam and Eastern Ladakh, are all evidence of established powers seeking to drive low-cost asymmetric outcomes of grey zone conflict that have the potential of creating disproportionate strategic effects. However, the deterrence value of hard power is in no way undermined by the existence of the grey zone, as witnessed in the recent conflict situation in Eastern Ladakh. Importantly, operational and tactical concepts on employment of mechanised forces in the plains cannot be replicated in the mountains. There are no deep battles to be executed, nor is there space available for concentrated application of mechanised forces in depth. Despite these limitations, mechanised forces have found increasing acceptance as offering significant coercive potential in the mountainous terrain in Sikkim and Ladakh. However, manoeuvre plays out with greater subtlety in barren high altitude terrain when it is employed imaginatively as a networked and integrated force with adequate protection from aerial attack.

The importance of airpower in adding strength to the overall manoeuvre cannot be overstated. Both fixed wing and rotary wing airpower contribute significantly, in all their dimensions, to the overall manoeuvre and need to be better integrated to achieve the desired effects. Given our recent acquisition of impressive strategic lift capability, flexibility in reinforcing mechanised troops for decisive manoeuvre from the western to the northern front and vice versa, has become a distinct possibility, with the concept of Light Tanks and family of similar platforms taking shape. The IA needs to re-strategise to achieve operational effects in the mountains by employing integrated mechanised groups capable of delivering surprise, shock and decisive results, just like the employment of tanks did at Zoji La in 1948. Outdated shibboleths of the plains professing only armour-led operations should give way to transformational deterrence value of mechanised forces being a force in location, or even reinforcing localities captured/dominated by infantry to give it near invincibility, as seen in the recent operation South of Pangong Tso, Eastern Ladakh. The IA needs to seriously address the requirement of Light Tanks, mechanised infantry, attack helicopters, precision fires, responsive air defence, drones, information domination and airpower to out manoeuvre a powerful adversary such as the PLA. Only manoeuvre can create the desired psychological effects to deter an aggressive adversary, both in contact and non-contact conflict, and achieve the desired end state with minimal casualties.

India needs to refocus military modernisation to emphasize certain capabilities over others, and design missions with specific operational effects. Capabilities such as C6ISR, Command, Control, Computers, Communications, Cyber defence, Combat systems (C6), intelligence, surveillance, and reconnaissance (ISR), AI driven operations and cyber warfare have been neglected in favour of combat hardware. India needs to ramp up its defensive and offensive cyber capabilities; integrate technology and synthesise AI with its existing weapon platforms; seek domination of Information operations; develop more robust special operations capabilities, clandestine intelligence operations and partnerships with irregular forces to disrupt militant networks; and engage in more aggressive peacetime military diplomacy to leverage third-party support. Each one of these would directly and indirectly contribute to manoeuvre in the cognitive and unconventional domain.

MANOEUVRE IN GREY ZONE CONFLICTS

In recent years, the genre of asymmetric conflict has gradually morphed in to a reconfigured form of warfare that stays below the conventional spectrum. It largely avoids kinetic contact, offers deniability, targets the social space away from the frontline rather than military objectives in contact, comprises a series of seemingly unconnected campaigns which transform and refine over a period of time to ultimately achieve the political objective. Heather Bothwell defines Grey zone conflicts as security challenges initiated through purposeful aggression that exceeds the bounds of normal competition while remaining below the threshold of conventional warfare. Grey zone conflicts result from adversarial attempts to change the status quo for benefit through gradual belligerence that might be difficult to publicly attribute to the aggressor. Adversaries who initiate grey zone conflicts avoid the costs associated with conventional warfare while miring their opponents in questions involving international law, policy and trade, thereby effectively preventing decisive responses.

The seven hypotheses of future gray zone conflicts espoused by Dr Micheal J. Mazzar[20] are particularly instructive. He claims, among other things, that grey zone conflicts are likely to constitute the default mode of conflict in the coming decades, necessitating new strategies to deal with them. Interestingly, he avers that grey zone campaigns undermine deterrence, which is premised on kinetic tools of war. Of greater value is the strategy he outlines to deal with such campaigns. Some key takeaways for proponents of manoeuvre warfare are: there is infinite manoeuvre space in the grey zone with complete deniability; security measures against such manoeuvre must include both people-centric and military-centric strategies; cyber-attacks will affect people distant from the battlefield, thus offering potential for outmanoeuvring the adversary psychologically. To cope with the grey zone, India's armed forces would need to build redundancies in networks, decentralise decision making, integrate more with not within the Services, but also with other instruments of national power and pick up best practices of other like-minded democracies.

According to Lieutenant General Ton van Loon[21] and Susan Verstegen, in order to manoeuvre in the future environment, a fundamental change in thinking from one focused on military options to one that incorporates the whole context must take place. Next to ground manoeuvre and air manoeuvre, there is a third element that must be taken into account: information manoeuvre. Robbin Laird[22] states that how we shape information dominance is a key part of the evolving approach to manoeuvre warfare. Accelerated warfare means owning the speed of initiative to outpace, out-manoeuvre and out-think conventional and unconventional threats. Defining fifth generation manoeuvre, he states it is the ability of our forces to dynamically adapt and respond in a contested environment to achieve the desired effect through multiple redundant paths.

Grey Zone conflicts are characterised by domination of the cyber and information arena. Countering cyberattacks necessitates not only defensive tools, but also offensive tools that allow for a proportional response in this domain. These tools employed by specially created organisations, are needed to manoeuvre in the cyber and information domains. The German Cyber and Information Domain Command and the UK 77 Brigade[23] are two examples of capability development in this area, but notably the two initiatives differ substantially. The German initiative unites the various units and agencies working in the cyber domain under one roof, thus placing the cyber domain next to the land, air and maritime domains. The British approach is more effect-centric, as it aims to bring together influencing capabilities. The creation of a Strategic Support Force, PLASSF by China in December 2015 was aimed at providing the PLA with the similar capacities and is rated by some analysts as the most potent reform undertaken by China in its transformational theaterisation of the PLA.

For an effective military contribution to a comprehensive approach, close cooperation with the civilian and private sectors is indispensable. In the famous words of former US Secretary of Defence, General James Mattis:[24] 'If you cannot create harmony across service lines, across coalition and national lines, and across civilian-military lines … your leadership in today's age is obsolete'. Militaries should therefore aim at being an effective partner in cross-national and cross-domain cooperation, as well as identify the value of manoeuvre applicable therein. In this role, the military can act as enabler for other indispensable actors and emphatically, should not be in the lead. This ability to synchronise combat effects with other actions aimed at outmanoeuvring the adversary should be the military's pivotal contribution to the comprehensive approach.

Franz Stefan Gady examines Artificial Intelligence (AI) in relation to manoeuvre warfare and posits that it is essentially a computer-based capability to execute human mental processes at superhuman speed.[25] AI-enabled technologies based on machine learning algorithms that accelerate the so-called 'kill chain' by linking sensors and shooters in an internet of things or system of systems architecture could have a profound effect on conventional offensive military operations. Grady reflects that a 2019 US Army wargame concluded that an infantry platoon, reinforced by AI-enabled capabilities, can increase its offensive combat power by a factor of ten, thus significantly tipping the defensive-offensive balance in the attacker's favour. Essentially, AI-enabled capabilities could be used to execute a 21st-century variant of manoeuvre warfare that will depend on making faster and better decisions than an adversary, which in turn will depend on information superiority and dominance in cyberspace. An analyst aptly put it that there is currently no master mechanism to integrate the scores of AI-powered systems operating on multiple platforms, resulting in the 'fog of war' being replaced by a 'fog of systems'. Without strong cyber defences intrinsic to any AI-enabled capability, manoeuvre warfare will most likely not achieve the intended success in the battlespace.

Colonel William J Harkin[26] states that the continued relevance of manoeuvre warfare in current and future conflicts is indisputable; however, in order to successfully confront the exigencies of modern warfare militaries must clearly and unambiguously define the type of conflict they are involved in and apply manoeuvre warfare doctrine with an emphasis on the ability to rapidly adapt to a given situation while simultaneously having the foresight to control the tempo of operations. As the challenges of the 21st century emerge, develop and mature, so must solutions; for just as the nature of warfare is immutable, so is the conduct of warfare constantly changing.

TO CONCLUDE

The Indian Armed Forces have come of age as regards the potential of manoeuvre warfare for future conflicts in varied terrains. The armed forces need to sensitise policy makers on the urgent need to leverage the exponential power of manoeuvre, not only for conventional warfare, but especially in the cyber and information domains, to optimise India's capabilities to tackle the emerging multi-domain, hybrid and grey zone challenges of the 21st century. General Shammi Mehta accurately underlines that manoeuvre has now acquired an urgency as never before; competitive deterrence demands an indigenous contribution of the tenets of manoeuvre in the grey zone—all elements of National power will need to sing the same tune in harmony. To counter these new threats India needs to build nimble pre-war capabilities, which are immune to the compartmentalisation of war, No War No Peace and peace time categorisations. In conformity with the need to create organisational and doctrinal tools to compete in the grey zone, Manoj Joshi highlights that technological innovation and innovative approaches in defence policy are the route towards creating a war-winning military.[27] The art of manoeuvre, as existing in the Army, Navy and Air Force, needs to be synthesised to arrive at a common doctrine to be followed by India's yet-to-be raised Theatres, which could emerge as a powerful strategic tool for executing manoeuvres and providing a range of options in the multi-dimensional kinetic and non-kinetic domains. Only by addressing these issues will the true potential of manoeuvre in future conflicts be fully realised by India.

NOTES

1 Lt Gen VK Ahluwalia, Artillery, Retired Central Army Commander, "Manoeuvre Warfare in the Information Age," CLAWS Issue Brief No. 231, June 2020.

2 Col RR Palsokar, *Bajirao I-An Outstanding Cavalry General* (New Delhi: Reliance Publishing House, Third Edition, 2016)

3 Lt Gen S.S.Mehta, Armoured Corps, Retired Western Army Commander, in conversation with the author.

4 Lt Gen AK Singh, Armoured Corps, Retired Southern Army Commander, in conversation with the author.

5 Lt Gen Mehta conversation.

6 Lt Gen VK Kapoor, Armoured Corps, "Fundamentals of Operational Art: A Contextual Review," *Combat Journal*, March 2002.

7 Christopher Clary, "Personalities, Organisations and Doctrine in the Indian Military," *India Review*, Vol 17, No. 1, pp. 100-21, 2018.

8 Maj Gen GD Bakshi, "Operational Art in Indian Context: An Open Source Analysis", *Strategic Analysis*, Vol XXV No. 6, September 2001.

9 Ibid.

10 Arjun Subramaniam, *Full Spectrum: India's Wars 1972-2020* (New Delhi: HarperCollins, 2020).

11 Lt Gen Shammi Mehta as Western Army Commander; Operational Directive on Strategic Concepts; June 2002.

12 Arzan Tarapore, "India's Use of Force: The Missing Indirect Approach," ORF Issue Brief #106, September 2015.

13 Ibid.

14 For a detailed account refer to Anit Mukerjee, *The Absent Dialogue* (New Delhi: Oxford University Press, 2020).

15 Tarapore, n. 12.

16 Lt Gen AB Shivane, "Armoured Corps; Presentation on Technology Empowered Manoeuvre: Future Prospects," CLAWS Seminar, April 2019.

17 Robert Bateman, "No, Drones Haven't made Tanks Obselete," *Foreign Policy*, October 15, 2020.

18 Franz-Stefan Gady, Alexander Stronell, "What The Nagorno Karabakh Conflict Revealed about Future Warfighting," *World Politics Review*, November 2020.

19 Capt Heather M Bothwell, "USN, Gray is the New Black: A Framework to Counter Gray Zone Conflicts," Joint Force Quarterly 101, National Defence University Press, March 31, 2021.

20 Michael J Mazzar "Mastering the Gray Zone: Understanding a Changing Era of Conflict," US Army War College Press, 2016.

21 Lt Gen Tom van Loon, Susan Verstegen, "Manoeuvring in the Hybrid Environment," *Military Spectator*, Netherland, September 2019.

22 Robbin Laird, "The Manoeuvrist Approach: Past , Present and Future," Second Line of Defence, March 2019.

23 Ibid.

24 Ibid.

25 Franz Stefan Gady, "What Does AI Mean for the Future of Manoeuvre Warfare; Analysis," May 2020.
26 Col William J Harkin, "Manoeuvre Warfare in the 21st Century," Marine Corps Association, August 2019.
27 Manoj Joshi, Pushan Das, "The Future of War in South Asia: Innovation, Technology and Organisation," GP-ORF Series, Observer Research Foundation, March 2021.

FURTHER READINGS

1 Capt Heather M Bothwell, USN; "Gray is the New Black: Framework to counter Gray Zone Conflicts," *Joint Force Quarterly*, National Defense University Press, March 31, 2021.
2 Arzan Tarapore, "Defence Without Deterrence: India's Strategy in the 1962 war," *Journal of Strategic Studies*, 2019.
3 Lt Gen HS Panag, "Indian Army's Dash to Dhaka in 1971 was Operational Brilliance, It Holds Lessons for Ladakh," The Print, December 17, 2020.
4 CLAWS Seminar Report, "Manoeuvre Warfare & Firepower: Application in Future," February 3, 2018.
5. Masood Ur-Rehman, "Evolution of New Indian Military Strategy: Implicationsfor Pakistan," International Islamic University, Islamabad, June 2018.
6 Ayaz Khokhar, "Shift in India's Security Policy Towards Pakistan: From Sunderji to Cold Start Doctrine," Strafasia, November 2019.
7 Ali Ahmed, "India's Limited War Doctrine: The Structural Factor," IDSA Monograph Series No 10, December 2010.
8 Lt Gen Ghanshyam Katoch, "Military Change: Summary of the Most Adaptable," Journal of Defence Studies, Vol 11, No 2, April-June 2017.
9 John Hawkes, Sam Cranny-Evans and Mark Cazalet, "The tank is Dead, Long Live the Tank," Wavell Room; October 2020.

CHAPTER 7

PUSHING THE LIMITS OF ENDURANCE: HIGH-ALTITUDE WARFARE

RAKESH SHARMA

ABSTRACT

Historically, wars conducted at high altitude have favoured the defender and implied engagement between opposing armed forces using kinetic force. In India, the imperatives of high-altitude and mountain warfare are most pronounced, as borders wholly with China and partially with Pakistan are across the Himalayan Range, in the high-altitude realm. Considering that the PLA's victory in modern warfare recognises system destruction warfare by disrupting, paralysing or destroying an adversary's operational systems' capabilities, wars in the Himalayas—whenever they are fought—will be in multiple domains. While these wars may, or may not be driven by historically bound territorial disputes, and could well be related to geo-political rivalries, there is no avoiding the need to create new 'sunrise' capabilities for future high-altitude warfare.

BACKGROUNDER

Warfare has always evolved throughout history and will remain a political act that takes place within and between societies.[1] Its specific character is and will be shaped by politics and societies—by what Clausewitz called the spirit of the age. Winning wars, in the spirit of present and future ages, implies the ability to wage war comprehensively in all domains and then achieve its political aims. In the 21st century, defining victory will be a big challenge facing military strategists, particularly in wars in high altitude (HA) areas. In this context, is HA warfare exclusive, or is it merely one of the several genres of warfare against adversaries where land borders exist in difficult terrain and climatic conditions? Has HA had such over-riding effects that warfare stands frozen in time, when warfare itself is facing immense changes forced by technology? Historically, wars conducted at HA have favoured the defender and implied engagement between opposing armed forces using kinetic force, where victory and defeat was largely equated to territorial gains/losses.

In India, the imperatives of HA and mountain warfare are most pronounced across the entire stretch of the Line of Actual Control (LAC) with China, which stretches from Eastern Ladakh in the west to the eastern extremities of Arunachal Pradesh. The HA border with Pakistan comprises the Line of Control (LoC) in Kashmir, Western Ladakh, the Poonch area of Jammu and the Actual Ground Position Line (AGPL) in the Siachen Glacier Region. In the past, of HA warfare it was stated, "... yet certain regions of the world remain largely unaffected by the full reach of advances in military technology. Thin air, cold weather, and mountainous terrain combine to create a uniquely inhospitable battlefield at HA. The elements of military victory at HA have not dramatically changed. Overwhelming fire, in concert with bold manoeuvre, continues to determine victory on the high-altitude battlefield. The emergence of precision warfare has yet to dominate combat in the timeless environs of the world's highest mountains."[2] It is opined that this quote is relevant in all the conflicts that the Indian Army has fought in such terrain since independence, including contestation on peaks, ridge lines, passes, valleys and plateaus above 5,000 metres.

This chapter examines the scope of HA warfare in the Indian context with modern warfare as the foundation, appreciating the distinct dissimilarities of border lines that India shares with Pakistan and China along the way. In many ways, warfare in icy and frigid HA terrain has remained as if in a time warp. Nonetheless, twenty years after the Kargil War, warfare has moved on, and it is imperative to contemplate on its future scale, scope and typology, even in HA terrain. Along the way, this chapter will also dwell on some of the strategic imperatives and suggest the creation of niche capabilities for India.

HA– STRATEGIC GEOGRAPHY AND STRATEGIC HISTORY

The Strategic Geography of HA Mountains

The Himalayas are a great mountain system that forms a barrier between the HA Plateau of Tibet and Xinjiang, even as its offshoot ranges descend to the alluvial plains of India. The Himalayan Range includes the highest mountains in the world, with more than 110 peaks rising to elevations of 24,000 feet or more above sea level. The soaring heights of the Himalayan mountain range comprise steep-sided jagged peaks, HA deserts like Eastern Ladakh, deep valleys and river gorges like those along the River Brahmaputra and Teesta, lakes like Pangong Tso and Changu, and alpine glaciers such as the Siachen. The Himalayan Mountain Range appears as a gigantic crescent with a continuous snow line that constitutes the sources of most Himalayan rivers. Prominent among these are the Indus, Sutlej, Ganges, Yamuna and Yarlung Tsangpo (Brahamputra in India) rivers. A large part of the Himalayas on the Indian side lie below the snow line, with offshoots of lower mountain ranges experiencing varying degrees of precipitation and typology of forest cover.

In the Indian context, HA and mountains tend to exemplify an incorrect vision of a monolithic, generic mountain range. This basic thought needs to be dispelled at the outset, as it affects strategy and tactics, both of which differ dramatically from sector to sector and ridge to ridge. As a result, while developing strategy and operational/tactical plans, generically templating HA areas is fraught with immense pitfalls.

The mountains exact an immense physical and psychological toll on both local inhabitants and deployed troops. The rarity of the atmosphere (paucity of oxygen) is a major cause of many a serious ailments like acute mountain sickness, high-altitude cerebral oedema and high-altitude pulmonary oedema, all of which mandate well-planned acclimatisation plans for troops. The snow and climatic conditions cause related sicknesses such as shortness of breath, dizziness, loss of appetite, nausea, insomnia, weakness and lethargy and flu-like symptoms, as also frost bite, trench foot, chill blains and heat stroke due to ultraviolet radiation. There is also the likelihood of adverse effects on cognitive abilities, such as memory loss.

HA areas also present extended challenges in the management and sustenance of logistic and supply chains, largely due to paucities in infrastructure, climatic conditions and the vagaries of various operational scenarios. This necessitates stocking and dumping to accommodate extended periods of deployment at posts, which severely restricts the force that can be managed, tasked or retained in such areas. Despite these severe restrictions, the Indian Army and the Indian Air Force have risen to the challenges of high-altitude deployments and live operations with alacrity following the 1962 war with China.

Strategic History of Battles in HA Regions of Himalayas

The Himalayas have been witnessing invasions ranging from Alexander the Great in 326 BC to seven Muslim incursions from Central Asia that resulted in fierce battles. From the Indian military legacy, Zorawar Singh (1786-1841), a Dogra general of the Sikh Empire, stamped his legacy on Himalayan conquests in Ladakh, Tibet and Baltistan. Post-Independence, the Himalayas have witnessed significant warfare, commencing with the 1947–48 conflict between India and Pakistan in Jammu and Kashmir. The tribal invasion, which was actively supported by the Pakistani Army, was pushed back substantially due to resolute offensives, and included the capture of several lofty heights in the Uri area across the Pir Panjal Range. The Indian Army's 7 Cavalry accomplished the unthinkable, by deploying Stuart Tanks at 11,553 feet in Zojila that connected Kashmir with Ladakh. This took the Pakistan military by surprise and stopped their offensive designs into Ladakh. The fledgling IAF too pitched in by carrying out carrying out airlifts into Srinagar, Leh and Poonch, as well as never-before-attempted close air support and interdiction missions at Skardu, Zojila and several enemy positions on the Pir Panjal Range.[3]

The 1962 reversal at the hands of China offered India crucial experiential lessons that left indelible memories. Despite the reversals of the 1962 War, there are sagas of immense valour, raw courage and sacrifice in the battles of Rezangla and Gurung Hill in Eastern Ladakh. During the 1965 and 1971 Wars, the Army captured several heights including the towering Point 13620 astride the Shingo River in the Kargil Sector of Western Ladakh. The capture of Haji Pir Pass and the massif of Bedori in 1965, demonstrated the Indian Army's growing prowess in HA warfare. The Indian Army commands the highest battleground in the world, along the dizzy heights of Siachen Glacier and the Saltoro Range, after it pre-emptively occupied several strategic heights like Bilafond La and Sia La in April 1984. The Indian Army and Indian Air Force have learned much in terms of developing joint capabilities in high and super HA terrain, while still controlling the region in a conflict that has lasted nearly four decades. The Kargil War of 1999, in which Pakistan had stealthily occupied heights in the Drass, Kargil and Batalik sectors above 5,000 metres, was an epitome of courage and resilience of the Indian Army units and the campaign-winning impact of directed and concentrated firepower. It also forced India to evolve an effective joint high-altitude campaign that envisage rapid induction of troops with their associated logistics build-up, and effective application of airpower. During Operation Parakram in 2002, Mirage-2000s of the Indian Air Force were used to evict Pakistani invaders in the area of Kel in Kupwara Sector using a combination of laser guided and conventional bombs. The operation demonstrated a growing synergy between the IA and IAF in HA operations.[4]

It is imperative to mention the recent transgressions, aggression and expansionism by the Peoples Liberation Army (PLA) of China in 2020.

The foundation of the management of the LAC in Eastern Ladakh is based on Protocols and Confidence Building Measures that were a result of four formal agreements of 1993, 1996, 2005 and 2013. The PLA demonstrated deliberate, well-planned and premeditated belligerence by bringing in two mechanised and motorised divisions opposite Eastern Ladakh, before engaging in multiple transgressions. The resolute action at Galwan Valley on June 15, 2020, as well as an exhibition of combined effort of Indian Air Force and Army to mobilise and create the logistical strength to sustain operations over the winter of 2020/2021, appear to have disrupted the PLA's future plans. The game-changer was the riposte by Indian Army units on the night of August 29/30 on the South Bank of Pangang Tso across the Kailash Range in the Chushul Sector at heights of above 5,500 metres astride the Spanggur Gap. Indian troops also occupied critical heights on the North Bank of Pangong Tso, demonstrating that India would respond with force at a time and point of its choice.

India's territorial disputes with China and Pakistan, largely in HA areas, are seriously impacted by the physical and physiological conditions in these areas that predicate a certainty that both the aggressor and defender will suffer significant casualties, distastefully referred to as 'body bags'. When it comes to psychological resilience in the face of casualties, India has historically enjoyed an advantage over both its adversaries during multiple conflicts and skirmishes. This was reflected in the aftermath of both the 1962 war with China and the Kargil Conflict. While the PLA grossly underreported its casualties during the 1962 conflict, numbering 722 soldiers killed and 1697 wounded, only in 1994, the Pakistan Army rarely accepts its military casualties caused by shelling or firing on LoC and has yet to reveal the total casualties suffered during the Kargil Conflict.

Traditionally, it is also accepted across militaries that well-planned defensive deployments and strategies hold an edge at HA, even against resolute offensives with very large force asymmetries of up to 1:12. Dislodging defenders demands extraordinary courage and fighting ability on the part of the infantry and special forces, and has generally been backed by overwhelming firepower, causing a psychological weakening of the adversary's resolve, as was clearly seen during the Kargil war. India's armed forces have few competitors on the global stage, when it comes to the ability to concentrate firepower and exhibit extraordinary resilience at HA.

INDIA'S CONTESTED BORDERS – LOC AND LAC

The LoC: In a Time Warp?

There are significant differences between the disputed HA borders that India has with Pakistan and China. The LoC between Indian and Pakistan does not constitute a legally recognised international boundary in J&K and Western Ladakh, but serves as the de facto border. India constructed a 550-km long fence-barrier called the Anti-Infiltration Obstacle System along the LoC.[5] The LoC is among the most heavily fortified multi-tiered defensive systems in the world today, with forces on both sides deployed in eyeball-to-eyeball contact at several places. The Shimla Agreement prohibits the two sides from altering the Lines by force, but the concept of 'holders-keepers' is still valid there, as Lt Gen Vinod Bhatia explains: 'what you have, you keep; what you hold you keep and what you occupy also you keep.' Lt Gen Syed Ata Hasnain calls it 'grabbers-keepers' concept and defines it as: 'Ány side grabbing a piece of ground for a tactical advantage gets to keep it unless forcibly evicted.'[6] The contention of 'holders-keepers' was demolished in 1999, when Pakistan stealthily 'grabbed' large tracts in Kargil Sector, a move that India countered by launching a full-fledged and never-before-attempted offensive to evict the Pakistani forces, without violating the LoC. The LoC has regularly witnessed sparring with small arms and artillery, interspersed with periodic cross-border raids on border posts by both sides. In February 2021, the ceasefire of 2003 was reiterated by both countries as part of the ongoing attempts to calibrate conflict along the LoC. The emotive and identity driven nature of J&K for Pakistan has resulted in the use of HA areas such as the Kishtwar and Pir Panjal Ranges as conduits for prosecuting infiltration and terrorism in J&K from the late 1980s to reap gains in the sub-conventional domain, that are normally associated with victory in war."[7]

The continuation of LoC in Ladakh is the Actual Ground Position Line (AGPL) that divides current positions of Indian and Pakistani troops in the Siachen Glacier region, with Indian Army holding heights on the Saltoro Ridge. The line extends from northernmost point of LoC at NJ 9842 to Indira Col. The defences are occupied by both sides to over 21,000 feet, restricting warfare, the capture of posts or the use of firepower.

The LAC: Unfrozen in 2020

The LAC is the largely effective and mutually agreed line of the disputed border between India and China. China occupies Aksai Chin in Ladakh Union Territory, and has claimed territories at the eastern end of the Himalayas in Arunachal Pradesh. China also has several other territorial claims on Ladakh and along the Uttarakhand-Tibet LAC. The Indian Army has prepared defences along the LAC that are not physically occupied, although Army units in the area are prepared to occupy them at short notice. Prior to 1993, the LAC witnessed transgressions by the PLA in several HA areas claimed by China, resulting in occasional skirmishes and stand-offs. The major incidents were at Nathu La-and Cho La (Sikkim) in 1967,[8] and Sumdorong Chu (Arunachal Pradesh) in 1986-87,[9] both of which were robustly and successfully countered by India. The PLA does not have widespread prepared defences along the LAC, though there are border outposts, camps and garrisons in proximity. Instead, it leverages its superior infrastructure, network of roads and ISR capability to respond to any perceived Indian threat. The PLA also conducts annual offensive exercises on the Tibetan plateau, as was evident in mobilisation of two armoured/motorised divisions to Eastern Ladakh in 2020, while on exercise in Tibet.

As referred to earlier, various Protocols and Confidence Building Measures based on the four formal agreements of 1993, 1996, 2005 and 2013 have been crucial in maintaining peace and tranquillity along the LAC since 1993. The 1993 Agreement on Maintaining Peace and Stability predetermined that no force or threat of force would be used. The 1996 Agreement laid down CBMs and was like a no-war pact dictating the non-use of military capability against the other side, especially within 2 kilometres of the LAC. The 2005 Protocol included methods to deal with face-to-face situations that may arise as a result of different perceptions on the alignment of the LAC. These included the exercise of self-restraint, no use of force or the threat of the use of force, and a peaceful disengagement and a simultaneous return to their bases. The India-China Border Agreement of 2013 emphasised that neither side would use military capability against the other, and that their respective military strengths would not be used to threaten or attack the other. With the experience of face-offs over the years, a caveat was added that the two sides would not follow or tail patrols of the other side where there is no understanding of the LAC. Though the LAC was not an active border, an underlying contestation of a disputed border existed. Of relevance is that all these protocols and CBMs were put into practice in HA areas that added to the difficulties of monitoring and patrolling along the LAC.

CONTEXTUALISING MODERN WAR-FIGHTING AND HA WARFARE

This section aims to contextualise the broader contours of modern conflict and examine them against the imperatives and limitations imposed by HA terrain. Sun Tzu prophesised that *'all warfare is based upon deception'* and China has consistently demonstrated preference for ambiguity, risk manipulation and controlling the narrative to win without fighting.[10] Henry Kissinger opined that *"... whereas Western tradition preferred the decisive clash of force, emphasizing feats of heroism, the Chinese ideal stressed subtlety, indirection and patient accumulation of relative advantage."*[11] Over the last three decades, several strategies of warfare have emerged from China. 'Unrestricted Warfare'[12] did not restrict itself to terrain such as mountains; rather it nullified the boundary between battlespaces and non-battlespaces, with non-military methods. The Chinese 'three-warfare strategy'[13] is a form of statecraft that encompasses non-kinetic means to achieve political ends. The strategy argues that '*... if the object of war is to acquire resources, influence and territory, and to project national will ...China's Three Warfare Strategy is war by other means.*'[14]

Victory in modern warfare, according to the PLA, recognises system destruction warfare as a most effective and modern way of war fighting.[15] It characterises and understands modern warfare as a confrontation between opposing operational systems rather than merely opposing armies. Despite the vagaries of HA terrain and the differentiation in warfighting, China will attempt future wars by disrupting, paralysing or destroying the operational capability of an adversary's operational systems through either kinetic or non-kinetic attacks:

- PLA will call for strikes that degrade or disrupt the flow of information within the adversary's operational system, even in the HA areas, by targeting key data links and vital information network sites and rendering areas "information isolated."
- Degradation or disruption of these operational systems would include an adversary's command and control (C2), reconnaissance intelligence, firepower capabilities and support systems.
- Striking such operational architecture through kinetic and non-kinetic means is a target-heavy approach, which will require numerous successfully executed precision strikes against various components arrayed around an extended battlefield.
- The principal objective of such strikes would be the disruption of the time sequence and/or tempo of the enemy's operational architecture.[16]

Changing Contours of HA Warfare

Do India's military plans give the correct prescription for the conduct of HA warfare in light of the imperatives of contemporary warfare, both from a western and Chinese perspective? In a report on the competition between India and China, Robert D. Kaplan stated of the *"flattening Himalayas"*, the *"defeat of distance"* and that *"the high wall of the Himalayas no longer separates these two great civilizations."*[17] By several yardsticks, India has been slow to keep pace with China in the realm of doctrinal, strategic and technological transformation. Therefore, conventional Indian concepts of war in HA may be insufficient to cope with the realities of multi-domain warfare of the 21st century. It must, hence, be a priority area for military planners and strategists to surmount the systemic, intellectual and technological challenges of envisioning the contours of a future conflict along the Himalayas, particularly with China.

It will become exceedingly difficult to extract strategic gains from tactical or operational successes following HA engagements, for war will no longer be only a contest of annihilation between opposing military forces across the HA mountains. Victory or defeat in the next war therefore cannot be based on objective criteria like respective casualties, territory occupied or lost, war-fighting capability and infrastructure destroyed of the adversary or vice versa, or prisoners captured by either side. Such warfare may attempt to avoid defensive strength and the offensive-defence doctrine of the Indian Army, to avoid a slogging match and face large casualties. Territorial aggression in mountains/HA could be a subsidiary objective, after significant damage has been wrought by system destruction. Though the PLA may attempt to soften the strong defensive lines across the LAC, the efficacy of such operations is untested and gives a certain amount of breathing space for a suitable counter to an initial assault. The impact of airpower, which will be an important factor in seizing relative advantage through the destruction of combat potential, will be discussed subsequently. However, the altitude, the weather and the machine capability may again hamper the adequacy of manoeuvre and lift. Overall, decisive wars in HA terrain will be as improbable as they will be elsewhere, and war fighters will have to get used to modified concepts of looking at outcomes rather than defeat or victory.

STRATEGISING FOR INDIA—BUILDING CAPABILITIES

India must prepare for tomorrow's war in the Himalayas. As previously said, future wars in the Himalayas will be conducted in multiple domains, some evident now and several that are on the horizon. It is important to strategise for disaggregated or synergised warfare in HA terrain by breaking it down cogently for operational practitioners to train and prosecute it effectively. The following broad parameters of strategising for HA areas are imperative:

Because of topographical friction, the possibility of conventional force-on-force kinetic conflict will remain high, necessitating synergistic and coordinated preparation. Forces could be sustained by a few uninterrupted mountainous axes, aircraft drop zones, or makeshift landing fields.

- Contested and unsettled borders and frontiers will remain important triggers in future wars through the prosecution of limited but high-intensity conflict, even if the larger frame may be related to geo-political rivalries. The likelihood of conventional force-on-force kinetic warfare will remain high, necessitating synergistic and integrated planning as there will be severe restrictions caused by terrain friction. Forces could be sustained by a few un-interdicted mountainous axes, aerial drop areas or make-shift landing grounds.
- Creeping transgressions and stealthy encroachment have been the standard modus operandi adopted by India's adversaries to change the status quo along the LoC and LAC. These have invariably been fiercely contested by the Indian Army, and it would be foolish to anticipate widespread and overt offensive operations at HA against battle-hardened and experienced Indian troops occupying well-constructed linear defences. To ensure that adversaries do not get to capture and control dominating heights even temporarily, there is an emerging need to create and maintain a persistent ISR capability that facilitates adequate warning, preventive and even preemptive capability.

- Operational commanders would need to pay greater attention to the design of battle and the conduct of campaigns to obtain a strategic advantage over the adversary. General H.R. McMaster, a former US National Security Advisor, in the Trump administration argues, *"There are two ways to fight ... asymmetrically, or stupid."*[18] In a future limited conflict that will be fought asymmetrically, the design of battle at HA would have to utilise linear defences as pivots and employing composite Task Forces (TFs) or Integrated Battle Groups (IBGs), sized and composed exclusively for HA.
- Hence, the broad campaign plan must offset and defeat any force asymmetry in the adversary's favour by degrading through a multi-tiered combination of asymmetric warfare, kinetic strike and defensive layout. Asymmetric warfare contextually should encompass using linear defended lines only as trip wires, and saturating the battle space with strong deniability through focused and imaginative use of fire and manoeuvre. The ability to expand the battle space and target logistical sustenance lines, forward lines of ingress and choke points will hold the key to territorial warfare in HA terrain. Imaginative strategies of asymmetric warfare across the battle space to deny the adversary any technological advantage across the HA regions will be critical to blunting any military aggression.
- Recent experiences dictate that capability development in preparation for conventional kinetic operations at HA cannot be put on the back-burner. Substantive offensive capabilities and duly acclimatised, trained and kitted troops and airmen must be available for achieving 'across the hump' success and consolidation. Significant enhancement to third dimension capabilities will provide the requisite deterrence while reducing the salience of massed combat power.
- Timely and target-oriented Intelligence, Surveillance and Reconnaissance (ISR) is critical for the effective and timely

execution of operational plans. For example, in environments such as Xinjiang, Tibet and the Gilgit-Baltistan region, timely correlation of the location and movement of the combined arms formations of the PLA and the Pakistan Army, both in peacetime and delicate less-than-war situations is critical to understanding the level of collusivity in any impending conflict scenario.

- Kinetic and non-kinetic warfare at HA will go well beyond force-on-force engagement. The use of long-range precision guided munitions, hypersonic weaponry, drone swarms, autonomous systems and stealthy operational capabilities must be expected, and plans for survivability and redundancy must be factored-in by hardening our systems against premature destruction.
- To withstand an initial onslaught based on Information and Cyber Warfare (IW) and Beyond Visual Range (BVR) capability, and offer a quid pro quo response, India's armed forces will need to better embrace combinations of technology. Improved processing power, connectivity, machine learning, artificial intelligence, automation, autonomy and quantum computing that will achieve disruptive effects will no longer be the stuff of science fiction. Hence, a joint multi-domain specialisation would indicate the right preparation for future warfare at HA.
- The need of the hour is to create integrated multi-domain task forces that amalgamate sunrise technologies and capabilities within a futuristic joint/integrated fighting formation that can be created without unnecessary accretions and with adequate redundancies. Since logistics is a particularly problematic in HA areas, infrastructural resilience with a modern supply chain system is an imperative, as are delivery means that incorporate multiple aerial modes ranging from fixed and rotary wing platforms, as well as drones, to offer both flexibility and redundancy.

Though a one-size-fits-all strategy will not work against all adversaries, a concerted capability development approach focused on the stronger adversary will offer solutions across the spectrum of adversaries.

SYNERGISTIC EFFECT OF AIRPOWER AT HA

Indian Airpower has some advantages while operating in the existing HA environment of the Himalayas, owing to the location of air bases and the proficiency of its aircrew in HA operations. This advantage, however, is fast eroding by the leapfrogging capabilities being acquired by the PLAAF in countervailing domains such as cyber, electronic warfare, air defence capabilities. Airpower, in synergistic application with cyberspace and electromagnetic domains, space, precision strike vectors and ground forces, can have devastating physical and psychological effects on the adversary. Since both India's adversaries have their forces and reserves garrisoned at some distance from the LAC/LoC, their movement is arduous and time consuming through a select few axials/laterals, despite the infrastructure and air lift availability. With the right planning, emphasis on time criticality, kinetic weaponry and air strikes against critical elements of the adversary's combat power and axes of movement can have cascading effects on warfare in HA. Airpower, in its multiple avatars, will be the first responder, to effectively shape the battlefield. This necessitates a fundamental shift in attitude, given that in every previous HA battlefield engagement, airpower was either not deployed or made a delayed appearance. The existing IAF doctrine and the capability offered, the assessment of success is based on 'effects,' which translates into the untapped potential of targets per sortie rather than sorties per target.

Contemporary airpower, like other domains, also relies substantially on good intelligence, as has been argued that *"airpower is targeting; targeting is intelligence…."*[19] In the collection, collation, fusion and interpretation of intelligence, surveillance and reconnaissance (ISR), geospatial intelligence (GEOINT), signals intelligence (SIGINT), open source intelligence (OSINT), human intelligence (HUMINT), and tactical sensors, it is the speed with which such information can be converted into targeting solutions that holds the key to a first-mover advantage. With precise intelligence, it is not even necessary to use precision-guided munitions all the time, as modern aircraft can deliver unguided ordnance with the same precision.

Apart from the prosecution of an offensive air campaign, the importance of rapid mobility and combat logistical support as a game changer at HA was effectively demonstrated by the Indian Air Force (IAF) during the Eastern Ladakh Crisis in 2020. When combined with the increasing proficiency of the IAF in missions such as air landing and air drops by fixed and rotary wing platforms; insertion and extraction of Special Forces; Combat Search and Rescue (CSAR) and aero-medical evacuation that takes into consideration the importance of the 'golden hour' in survival, Indian airpower is well-poised to play a critical role during any type of HA conflict in the decades ahead. The key to unlocking the campaign-winning potential of airpower is to neutralise sophisticated and state-of-the-art enemy air defences, cyber, space and electronic warfare capabilities.

CONCLUSION

Regardless of the vagaries of HA terrain and the peculiarities it imposes on warfighting, future wars will see the disruption, paralysis or destruction of the operational capability of adversarial operational systems through either kinetic or non-kinetic attacks. Decisive operational outcomes in HA terrain will be harder to achieve as compared to what could be expected in more benign terrain such as the plains. Consequently, war fighters will have to get used to modified concepts of looking at a combination of timing and outcomes as a possible driver of conflict termination. Despite this, contested and unsettled borders and frontiers in HA terrain will remain important triggers in future wars for India through the prosecution of limited but high-intensity conflict. The likelihood of conventional force-on-force kinetic warfare will remain high, necessitating synergistic and integrated planning. The use of long-range precision-guided munitions, hypersonic weaponry, drone swarms, autonomous systems and stealthy operational capabilities must be expected, and plans for survivability and redundancy must be considered by hardening combat systems against premature destruction. Indian Airpower has some advantages while operating in the existing HA environment of the Himalayas owing to the location of air bases and the proficiency of its aircrew in HA operations. One of the key tenets of the IAF Doctrine looks at the quantification of success through the lens of Effects Based Operations (EBO) which simply implies 'targets per sortie rather than sorties per target.' The need of the hour is to create integrated multi-domain task forces that amalgamate sunrise technologies and capabilities within a futuristic joint/integrated fighting formation that can be created without unnecessary accretions and with adequate redundancies. The Erwin Rommel statement, "I would rather be the hammer than the anvil," is apt when it comes to waging war in the HA. This hammer must have multiple domains!

NOTES

1 High altitude warfare in India is an extension of mountain Warfare; hence parts of this chapter are drawn from the author's previous publication. Refer, Rakesh Sharma, "Reimaging Mountain Warfare in the 21st Century,"in A.K. Singh and Narender Kumar, (eds.), *Battle Ready for the 21st Century* (New Delhi: Pentagon Press Ltd, 2021), pp. 106-22.

2 Marcus P Acosta, "High Altitude Warfare: The Kargil Conflict and the Future," Naval Postgraduate School, Monterey, California, June 2003, https://calhoun.nps.edu/bitstream/handle/10945/ 1043/03Jun_Acosta.pdf?sequence=1&isAllowed=y

3 Arjun Subramaniam, *India's Wars* (New Delhi: HarperCollins, 2016), pp. 134-51.

4 Mayank Singh, "IAF acknowledges Bombing Pakistani intruders in Kupwara intruders in Kupwara during 2002 raids," *The New Indian Express*, June 25, 2019, https://www.newindianexpress.com/nation/2019/jun/25/iaf-acknowledges-of-bombing-pakistani-intruders-in-kupwara-during-2002-raids--1994914.html.

5 "LoC fencing completed: Mukherjee," *The Times of India,* December 16, 2004, https://timesofindia.indiatimes.com//india/LoC-fencing-completed-Mukherjee/articleshow/960859.cms.

6 Happymon Jacob, *Line on Fire, Ceasefire Violations and India-Pakistan escalation dynamics* (New Delhi: Oxford University Press, 2019).

7 Hal Brands, "Paradoxes of the Grey Zone," Foreign Policy Research Institute, February 5, 2016, https://www.fpri.org/article/2016/02/paradoxes-grey-zone/. Accessed on December 29, 2019.

8 Probal Das Gupta, *Watershed 1967: India's forgotten victory over China* (New Delhi: Juggernaut Books, 2020).

9 Mandip Singh Lessons from Somdurong Chu Incident, IDSA New Delhi, April 26, 2013, https://idsa.in/idsacomments/CurrentChineseincursionLessonsfromSomdurongChu Incident_msingh_260413.

10 Oriana Skylar Mastro and Arzan Tarapore, 'Countering Chinese Coercion the Case of Doklam', *War on the Rocks*, August 29, 2017, https://warontherocks.com/2017/08/countering-chinese-coercion-the-case-of-doklam/.

11 Henry Kissinger, *On China,* (London: Penguin Books Ltd., 2012), p. 47.

12 Qiao Liang and Wang Xiangsui, "Unrestricted warfare", Beijing, 1999, at https://www.cryptome.org/ cuw.htm.

13 Stephan Halper (ed.), *China: The Three Warfare* (Washington, DC, Office of Net Assessment, Office of the Secretary of Defense, 2013).

14 Ibid.

15 Jeffrey Engstrom, "System Confrontation and System Destruction Warfare, How the Chinese People's Liberation Army seeks to wage modern warfare", Rand Corporation, Santa Monica, California, USA, 2018.

16 Ibid.

17 Robert D Kaplan, *The Revenge of Geography: What the Map Tells Us About Coming Conflicts and the Battle against Fate* (New York: Random House, 2012).

18 Allison Schrager, "The four fallacies of warfare, according to Donald Trump's new national security advisor", Quartz, February 22, 2017, https://qz.com/915438/the-four-fallacies-of-warfare-according-to-national-security-advisor-hr-mcmaster/

19 Phillip S Meilinger, "Ten Propositions," *Airpower Journal*, Spring 1996, p. 2.

CHAPTER 8

FIREPOWER

P.R. SHANKAR

ABSTRACT

Contemporary warfare is largely based on the concept of 'Fire and move'. In the Sino-Indian-Pak adversarial triangle, the space for move is restricted by terrain, whereas firepower may be used freely. The balance between 'fire and move' is shifting towards long-range attritional firepower. It enables engagement from standoff distances and penetrates Anti Access and Area Denial (A2AD) systems. The Long-Range Precision Fires Program of the US Army and the Chinese missile arsenal indicates this shift. Indian artillery, with its rich operational experience, will have to modernise, realign itself and adapt quickly to the evolving battlefield. In the future, artillery will have to simultaneously fight the deep battle with the Indian Air Force and the close battle with the Infantry and Mechanised Forces to deter/ward-off adversaries. This chapter examines the evolution of firepower, its key tenets, methods to enhance it and its emerging roles in the Indian context.

FIRE AND MOVE IN BALANCE

'Fire and move' is the basis of all warfare. Both are indispensable and complementary to one another. They must be in harmony and balance on the battlefield. In the Sino-Indian-Pak nuclear charged adversarial triangle, the space for move is restricted and largely takes place when active hostilities are imminent. On the other hand, firepower is an implied force during peace and an applied force in war. Its longer ranges, lethality and effect can be implied *ab initio* from within friendly territory. It can also enhance and mask manoeuvre if used imaginatively. The effects of firepower are enabled by rapid advances in technologies which extend its reach, precision, lethality and networking. An important shift is taking place in this 'fire and move' balance as the increasing ranges and lethality of firepower today forces an adversary to disperse in depth, thereby restricting his ability to manoeuvre for effect.

LIKELY ENGAGEMENT RANGES

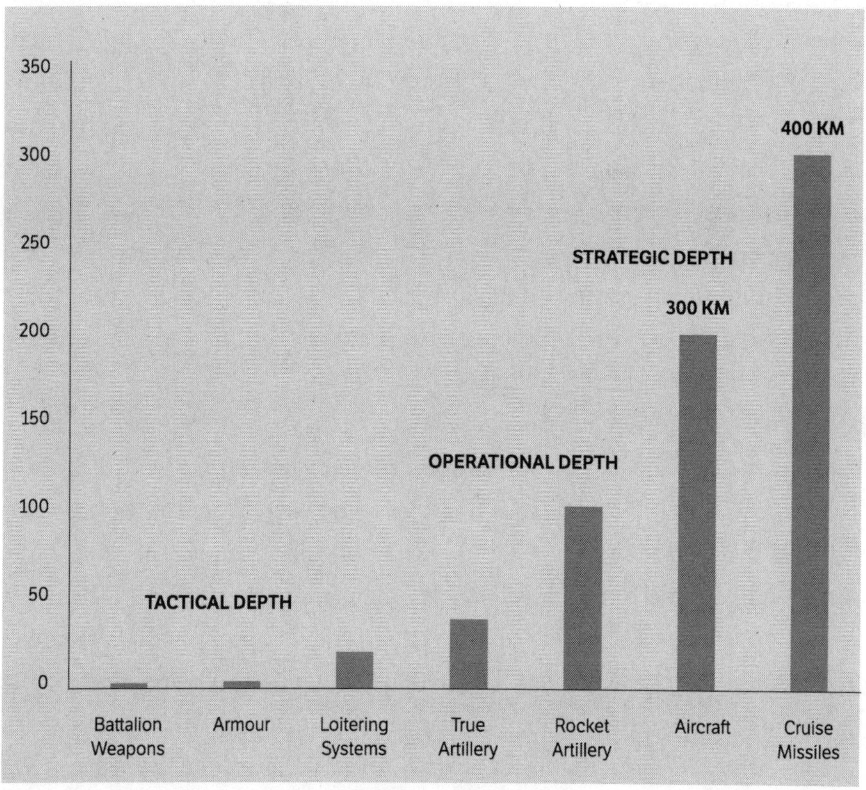

Figure 1: Representative Ranges of Modern Firepower

In the Indian context comprising multi-domain engagement zones, future conflicts are most likely to be fought in the high and medium altitude environs of the Himalayan terrain. Within this template, a conventional war between nuclear-armed countries is becoming increasingly unlikely. Instead, the greater probability is one of extensive military posturing with limited military conflict occurring within acceptable thresholds of violence. According to empirical models from recent times, the potential conflict spectrum includes situations such as the Kargil conflict with Pakistan at one end, and the Sino-Indian clashes in Eastern Ladakh on the other. Escalation control beyond this acceptable threshold is risky and dangerous and it is unlikely that this spectrum will be breached. In most eventualities, firepower will constantly be used for posturing and muscle flexing in tactical and operational depth. The likely engagement ranges (in kilometres) of various firepower systems are shown in Figure 1. These are not the maximum range capabilities of weapon systems, but rather the maximum ranges at which engagements are most likely to take place. Keeping in mind current trends in escalation dynamics as considered by India's strategic establishment, the probability of using ground-based firepower during skirmishes and encounters is greater than using aerial firepower. In a maritime scenario, surface and subsurface firepower will also come into play.

However, once widespread fighting breaks out, firepower is more likely to be applied at the tactical and operational depths with airpower joining the fray for effect. It is unlikely to be applied at strategic depths though the connotation of 'strategic' is rapidly changing as it is quite likely that a small tactical action can have a disproportionate strategic effect. In all cases, it is the author's considered opinion that firepower represented by the Regiment of Artillery is likely to dominate the near battlefield in peace and war. In this context, it is noteworthy that long-range tube and rocket artillery spans the entire battlefield spectrum. It will be complementary to airpower at one end and be directly involved in the contact battle on the other. At this juncture, long-range artillery is a suitable complement for airpower to compensate for the resource crunch faced by the Indian Air Force (IAF) for the foreseeable future. It frees up much of the available airpower for air superiority and deep interdiction tasks. With this as a backdrop, this chapter examines various facets of long-range firepower of the Regiment of Artillery.

EVOLUTION AND DEVELOPMENT OF INDIAN FIREPOWER

In the Indian context, the use of artillery in battle can be traced back to the Mughal period (15th century onwards). Indian Artillery as it exists today is a direct derivative of the Royal Indian Artillery. The derivatives are very clear in terms of organisation, equipment, practices, customs, traditions and institutions. Independent India started distancing itself from the British school of thought as it evolved and grew. Also, as India aligned itself geopolitically with the erstwhile USSR, the Russian influence became more discernible. The shift occurred mostly as a result of the induction of Russian equipment and practices. Technological progress enabled India to design, develop and produce its own firepower. Successful employment of artillery in battles fought by India also enabled the development of concepts and processes best suited to the Indian context. To that extent, Indian Artillery is among the most indigenised arms of the Indian Army and, along with the Indian Navy, the most indigenised element of the Indian Armed Forces.

Until the 1962 Sino-Indian war, Indian artillery consisted primarily of British equipment from the Second World War. The post war expansion started a process of change, when the Soviet 130 mm M46 gun with a range of 27 km was introduced into service. Simultaneously, the 75/24 mm Pack Howitzer, a mountain gun, was introduced into service. Significantly, this was the first gun designed entirely by Indians. By design, it was a complicated, but novel and versatile gun. It could be towed, packed on mules, airlifted and underslung, in a helicopter. Yet it was simple to use and robust in action. The author has a soft spot for this gun since he commanded a 75/24 battery in high altitude terrain several times during his service career. It could be taken almost anywhere in the battlefield and brought into action in minutes.

Until 1971, the Indian Artillery was a 'tube artillery' force. The first shift happened with the induction of the 122 mm Grad BM 21 Multiple Launch Rocket System (MLRS), also referred to as the 'AK 47' of rocket artillery, at the end of the 1971 Indo-Pak War. It is now being used extensively by state and non-state forces universally. The GRAD BM 21 marked the beginning of expansion of Indian Artillery into a rocket and missile force. The second shift happened with the induction of the 105 mm Indian Field Gun and the 105 mm Light Field Gun in the early 80s. Both these guns were manufactured indigenously, and contributed much to gun development as India went on to establish the Field Gun Factory in Kanpur, solely for producing 105 mm guns. In the mid-1980s, the Indian Artillery's third shift saw the introduction of the highly automated 155 mm Bofors. The Grad BM 21 and Bofors changed the way the Indian Army thought about and used firepower. Terms like 'Massed Fire' 'First Salvo Effectiveness', 'Simultaneity', 'Non Linearity', 'Shoot and Scoot', 'Burst Fire Capability' and 'Destruction' entered the lexicon of operational employment and application of firepower. These concepts were successfully implemented during the Kargil War. The 155 mm Bofors was to be inducted into service along with technology transfer and indigenous production and promised a new era in firepower. However, that did not happen due to the now infamous 'Bofors Scandal' that scuttled any possibility for 'transfer of technology' and its subsequent operationalisation. Consequently, after inducting the latest gun technology in the mid-1980s, Indian artillery regressed and stalled. There was a break in indigenous design capability which was revived only three decades later after a concerted effort.

The mid-1980s also saw the commencement of the 'Integrated Guided Missile Development Program', ushering in an age of indigenous design and development of long-range rocket and missile systems.

India achieved its maiden success in the late 1980s, when the 'Prithvi' and 'Agni' missiles were test fired and later integrated into the nation's strategic forces. Along with them, development of an unguided rocket system was undertaken. It has now morphed into the formidable Pinaka MLRS. This century has seen two further developments that have helped to extend and enhance India's firepower. The 'Smerch' rocket system was inducted into service (ex-import from Russia). Along with this, the supersonic 'Brahmos' cruise missile entered service. Both of them have given a new flavour to the firepower capability of the Indian Armed Forces. The 'Brahmos,' with its land, air and sea launched versions, has significantly enhanced the reach of India's strategic firepower. Surveillance and Target Acquisition have kept pace with the evolution of firepower with the induction of Weapon Locating Radars-ANTPQ 37 (ex-USA) and Swati (indigenous) and Unmanned Aerial Vehicles (UAVs) into service.

Until recently, capability development of indigenous medium-range firepower floundered. With the induction of the 155 mm M777 Ultra-Light Howitzer (ULH) and K9 Vajra (Self-Propelled) guns that hoodoo has been broken. The impending induction of the long-range guided Pinaka MLRS will give an edge to Indian firepower on any future battlefield. The future looks promising with more indigenous firepower waiting to be inducted. Along with the evolution of firepower hardware, net centricity of firepower was introduced through the Artillery Combat Command and Control System (ACCCS) and Battlefield Surveillance System (BSS). Additionally, the integrative power of firepower found expression through the Artillery Divisions. The first Artillery Division was raised in 1997[1] and was followed by two more. The sum total is that India has tremendous firepower capability, which is often forgotten and underplayed. Hence a look at the operational evolution of firepower is mandatory.

Operationally, firepower was traditionally used to neutralise an enemy or limit his firepower. It was largely a supportive role to Infantry and

Armour. As a result, artillery was classified as a 'Combat Support Arm,' a proposition that merits a revisit. In the absence of the devastating effects of firepower in peacetime training, infantry and armour-centric manoeuvre warfare occupied pole position during sand model discussions and wargames. Firepower was relegated to the side-lines or taken for granted. Such thinking has stunted the growth of firepower in its entirety in the Indian context. This has been compounded by the Indian Army's extended and widespread commitment to CI operations and small-scale operations. Two instances, however, stand out that have kept firepower relevant and have constantly reminded the military leadership that 'firepower' matters. The first instance being the Nathu La-Cho La incidents of 1967, when heavy fire assaults were carried out on Chinese positions in retaliation to unprovoked firing and heavy causalities to own troops. The Nathu La incident, which went virtually unnoticed until recently, was the first time that India used massed firepower—direct and indirect, to pummel Chinese defences, inflicting thrice the casualties and destroying bunkers in a telling manner.[2] Artillery played a huge role in that short but sharp operation. The lessons of that successful and surgical display of 'firepower' were never developed into operational theory or doctrine. The second instance where 'firepower' proved to be a battle winning factor was during 'Op Vijay' in Kargil. Much has been written about the role of artillery and firepower in the operation. However, India Today's description of the role of artillery in 'Op Vijay', sixteen years later is most instructive:

> *The Kargil conflict once again established beyond doubt that artillery firepower plays a major part in achieving victory on the modern battlefield. Accurate artillery fire reduces the enemy's defences to rubble. Sustained artillery fire gradually wears the enemy's resistance and ultimately breaks their will to fight. By systematically degrading the enemy's fighting potential before a physical assault is launched, the artillery helped to reduce the casualties suffered by assaulting infantrymen. Throughout the offensive phase of Kargil conflict, artillery was called upon to respond to emerging situations and it did so with alacrity*

and telling lethality. The infantry battalions involved in the fighting were the first to acknowledge the immense debt of gratitude that they owe to their artillery comrades.[3]

As range and lethality have exponentially increased, artillery firepower has progressed from a 'neutralisation and suppression' outlook to 'destruction and degradation' practices. Further, the role of own firepower in supressing enemy firepower and interdicting the battlefield has increased with time. In a multi-domain scenario of short and sharp contestations as against prolonged wars, the shock and awe that modern artillery firepower generates in an adversary assumes relevance and adds on to the deterrence value that artillery brings into the contemporary conflict milieu.

KEY TENETS OF EFFECTIVE FIREPOWER

Battlefield domination by firepower will be guided by the time-tested principles of war—selection and maintenance of aim, cooperation, concentration, flexibility, economy of effort, surprise and so on. There are a few prerequisites that will determine the capability of firepower, which will have to be put in place for realistic effect. These prerequisites are reach, effectiveness, protection, speed and simplicity.

The quest to reach out further is primal to any requirement of firepower. The idea has always been to strike the enemy before he can strike us. The neo-modern term for this situation is 'standoff'. The commander can think deeper and wider through 'stand-off'. Extending the range of artillery guns and missile systems, particularly in an airpower light battlefield environment, enhances a commander's ability to shape and drive battlefields in depth. Increasing 'standoff' through long-range precision firepower is a leading trend universally and it is with good reason that one of the top modernisation priorities of the US Army is its Long-Range Precision Fires Program. It provides them with long-range and deep-strike capability, considered to be critical to winning in a fight against peer adversaries like China and Russia.[4] According to a

Royal United Services Institute report, engagement levels are expected to increase by 50 per cent to 100 per cent across most platforms by 2040.[5] China lays strong emphasis on long range engagement with missiles—both in the land and maritime environments. Today, 'standoff' and 'non-contact' are key tenets in multi domain operations. Longer range increases the depth of engagement, expands the area of influence, and improves mutual support. Consequently, it also decreases the number of delivery platforms and reduces logistics. However, there are many caveats attached to increasing reach. The increasing range of tube artillery through the 'gun propulsion' route is reaching its limits. The scope to increase range of guns remains only in ramjet technology. This is a difficult technology to harness in high-spinning gun projectiles. When that is done, there will be a revolution in firepower application. The side that is successful in this field will dominate the battlefield. The other option is to increase the ranges of engagement with rockets and missiles. In all cases, increasing ranges of engagement has certain implications. As ranges increase, accuracy and consistency decrease, to impose penalties on the effectiveness of firepower. As ranges increase, weapon systems become more complicated and heavy. Hence, issues related to cost, deployability and survivability will emerge.

For firepower to be effective in battle, several variables must be addressed, the first of which is 'lethality' of the warhead. The warhead is the true weapon of the gunner, and it must be lethal enough to create the desired effect for the envisaged task. As a result, any ammunition system with a plethora of warheads will dominate. While, warhead technologies are evolving to achieve specified effects, the search to maximise the effect/area with minimum effort is an ongoing quest. Next, to be effective, firepower must be 'accurate and consistent'. The combination of lethality and accuracy will determine the kill probability. It needs to be understood here that firepower must be both dumb and smart. Dumb firepower has a long shelf life, is cheap, reliable and can be sprayed to achieve a widespread effect against area targets. On the other hand, precision firepower is needed to destroy pinpoint/high value targets especially when collateral damage is unacceptable. The trend is to incorporate active seeker munitions to autonomously course correct and zero on to the targets. Precision is a high-tech area that will remain an expensive proposition. The costs get compounded by shorter shelf lives, reduced efficacy due to ageing and unreliability of 'precision' technologies in the battlefield. The cost ratio between dumb and smart ammunition is likely be in the region of 1: 10/20. Overall, the debate is not about whether dumb or precision is better, rather it is about what to use and when, as both are needed in an appropriate mix. A corollary to this is that 'gunner wisdom' tells us that greater damage is caused when more number of small shells are fired as against lesser number of big shells. The devastating lethality of showering an area with submunitions from a carrier shell outweighs the effect of the entire shell. The 'big bang' theory rarely works on the battle field. However, it is not as if the big bang is not necessary. When hardened defences are to be broken, it is only the big bang that will work. This was proved conclusively in Kargil, where the Bofors gun performed this task. Getting the appropriate blend of firepower for the desired effect is the acme of good gunnery!

An important aspect of the effectiveness of fire is placing the 'right amount of firepower at the right place in the right quantum for a desired effect'. This involves surveillance through battle field transparency, target acquisition, precise targeting, communication, observation and task execution. This is a complex process that can be achieved by the use of force multipliers and battlefield enhancers, which enable forces to control and interdict the depth battlefield with a good combination of long range and effective firepower. When combined with airpower, the effect is devastating on an unsuspecting enemy. These 'out of area' unseen effects either prevent the near battle or give an out of proportion advantage to own forces during contact battles, or will promote manoeuvre. The out of area unseen effect is very important in 'conventional deterrence', which is the name of the future game evolving in the Indian operational and strategic contexts. This is an area that merits greater reflection in the Indian Army.

'Mobility' enables concentrating firepower at the right time and place in the right quantum. The old dictum that 'guns must never be kept silent' should never be forgotten. Hence, firepower must be mobile. Mobility of firepower is achieved at tactical levels by 'shoot and scoot', at operational levels by sidestepping and reinforcement, and at strategic levels by airlifting, either as underslung or on board loads in heavy lift helicopters or heavy transport aircraft. While the gun or the rocket system may be transported with relative ease, it is the mobility of ammunition that is the killer and the bigger challenge. Resultantly, there is a need to pre-plan and pre-place ammunition in appreciated quantities so that it is constantly available. That leads us to the fact that having infrastructure to store ammunition at relatively forward locations with good land communication arteries is the key to getting firepower to 'be on time'. In the case of rocket artillery, adequate arrangements must be made for their hides, preparation areas, launch sites and getaway positions.

Firepower is a scarce resource and since the sound of one's own guns booming is morale boosting, friendly firepower must be protected from counter-bombardment, which is a key mission to silence enemy guns. 'Firepower protection' can be achieved by dispersion, intelligent use of terrain and strong local defence. That is basic to any gunner. However, in this manned/unmanned era, the possibility of a third dimension aerial threat should not be overlooked. Further, net centricity implies that adequate protection from cyber attacks must be ensured. The use of decoys is an unexplored option in the Indian context that must be explored in expanded conflict zones.

Firepower is most effective when it is 'simple' to handle and easy to deliver, an aspect that is often lost sight of. Technology further complicates issues as the best technology is that which works in battle, and not necessarily the latest or the most sophisticated one. In the Indian context, firepower systems must work in the given terrain conditions. Complicated systems with too many interdependencies often fail. A simple system, with adequate fall back options is the way forward.

FIREPOWER ENHANCEMENT

Firepower is blind without battlefield transparency, and nothing is worse than using the wrong type of firepower at the wrong time and place. It will be even worse if it is placed over one's own troops. Hence battlefield transparency and situational awareness are fundamental to the effectiveness of firepower. Battlefield transparency is a dynamic multimode iterative process that results from the intermeshing of many issues to enhance the effect of firepower. A good 'information backbone and data fusion' enhances firepower. Artillery Intelligence includes the need to build up an information dataset about terrain, enemy habits, deployment sites and patterns, assets, soft points, capabilities and vulnerabilities. This important ingredient of firepower enhancement and management has been neglected in recent times and must be reinvigorated. With firepower regaining centre stage and technology dominance on the cards, this craft needs reinvention in a new avatar. It also involves preparation and maintenance of target folders with the other services. When this data backbone is fused with surveillance data using AI and networking, firepower becomes predictive in nature.

In the Sino-Indian context, India will be short of firepower in numbers. In such a situation, application of firepower must be technology driven and scientific. The answer lies in 'predictive firepower'. Predictive firepower revolves around sound terrain and target analysis, establishing enemy patterns, responsive logistics, surveillance and networking. It ensures that appropriate firepower is predictively delivered or is ready for delivery across the depth of the battlefield simultaneously, with a fair degree of first salvo effectiveness. Predictive firepower creates surprise and catches the enemy off guard. Every round must be made to count. Precision is an important subset of this capability. In the case of dumb ammunition, availability of continuous and accurate meteorological data is a prime requirement for prediction of the old kind. Predictive firepower creates local overmatch through flexible standoff.

'Surveillance' enhances firepower like nothing else. Surveillance must be three-dimensional, and available 24 hours a day, seven days a week. 'Persistent Stare' is as essential for land based precision fires as it is for complex aerial targeting. Observation Post (OP) officers were the mainstay of surveillance in earlier times. With increase in ranges and extended battle fields, the OP officer grid is reinforced electronically with Thermal Imaging and Observation Equipment, Battle Field Surveillance Radars and Long Range Observation System. Extension into depth comes about with networked manned/unmanned aerial platforms, weapon locating systems and space-based surveillance systems. Networked surveillance enhances battlefield transparency, allowing for more accurate firepower massing, and must be integrated with the fire control grid.

Map 'grids and georeferencing' are required to work seamlessly across platforms, services, and deep into the enemy territory. In simple words, the coordinates and data of a target on ground must be the same irrespective of the source(s) of acquisition of the target or its user(s). China has recently extended its grid into India. That should set alarm bells ringing. India's Armed Forces have a lot of ground to cover in this regard with the need to develop synergy not only between services, but also with Department of Space and other intelligence agencies. A common map grid that is well georeferenced for height is a mandatory requirement for delivery of accurate predictive firepower.

'Netcentric operations' are the way forward. Artillery is the first truly netcentric arm of the Indian Army with the ACCCS and BSS contributing to the complete networking of operational firepower and surveillance. However, new rocket and gun systems need to be incorporated and both systems need to be upgraded with latest hardware. When that is done, efficacy of firepower will multiply manifold. The issue of its cyber security must be addressed by fail-safe communications.

Firepower places huge demands on 'logistics', in peace and war. Firepower will fail to deliver during war/operations, unless a sound logistics infrastructure and procedures are built up during peacetime. Rockets and missiles need special storage conditions, constant maintenance and repair and periodic testing. Further, they are all heavy articles that require preparation and special handling during operations. Ammunition degrades with time and needs to be kept dry and protected, particularly in terrain conditions where space is a premium and moisture content is high.

To be effective, fire must be predicted and guided by observation on the target. For this to happen, 'Sensors need to be integrated with the shooters' and knitted tightly through gridded communications with backups and relays, detailed procedures and rules of engagement with well-defined protocols. These sensors can be UAVs, space-based assets, Special Forces operating in depth or commando OPs. In maritime operations, achieving sensor-shooter integration is even more important since the underwater element also comes into play. The potential of unmanned systems is immense with integration of sensors and weapons on the same platform. These could be either armed UAVs or loitering systems in a single or swarmed mode. Sensor-to-shooter integration is a work in progress in the Indian Armed Forces as more conceptual work needs to be devoted to the depth battle, which is fundamental in this paradigm.

Integration also encompasses 'air space management'. Increased fighter traffic, ground based firepower, air defence assets, and air transported operations complicate and crowd the airspace. As the volume of firepower and delivery platforms go up, so does the demand for better airspace management. Effective engagement will depend on the ability to engage targets seamlessly. This will depend on how best the airspace can be prioritised and managed to enable the right user to use it at the right time as per a time plan. The requirement of airspace management is getting to be more complex by the day, and will need greater coordination and networking in future. Strong sensor to shooter integration and effective airspace management enables a force plus force synergy in the battlefield. Such integration goes beyond conventional thinking on jointness, and it is high time for the Indian Armed Forces to begin thinking on these lines.

ROLE OF FIREPOWER

According to a recent and well researched paper on the 'Future of Fires,' the four main roles of artillery in the modern-day battle field are suppression of enemy fires, striking high-value targets, breaking up enemy force concentrations and providing fire support to enable manoeuvre.[6] These traditional roles of Artillery providing firepower in conventional battlefields will need a major relook in the Indian context. The days of merely supplying firepower in support of infantry and mechanised forces are long gone. The Kargil Conflict demonstrated to everyone the value of destruction and interdiction by artillery; the value addition of well-directed fire will only increase as pressures on commanders will increase to deliver operational outcomes in compressed time-frames. New-look Indian artillery is likely to dominate battlefields in varied terrains, be it against Pakistan or China either as an overwhelming and punishing force, or as a deterrent and coercive a force. In the mountains, the main 'Combat Arms' will be Infantry and Artillery. Also, the main source of firepower in mountains is Artillery since airpower might not be as effective due to the vagaries of weather and terrain conditions.

The neo modern role of firepower is thus intensely strategic in nature. Artillery is now an instrument of 'conventional deterrence'. This component is overlooked in tactically oriented discussions and war games. From a macro perspective, the deterrent role of artillery firepower is becoming increasingly important. This subtle shift needs to be understood better.[7] Nuclear and conventional deterrence theories, scripted largely in the West, will not work in the Sino-Indian or Indo-Pak eyeball-to-eyeball context. On the other hand, suitably tailored conventional deterrence based on different modes of firepower is likely to work.

Modern firepower is discriminatory, can be calibrated and the resulting damage is politically more acceptable than a nuclear holocaust. General deterrence can be triggered, before a crisis occurs through long range vectors, over the long term. When a crisis is imminent or occurs, firepower is a potent tool for immediate deterrence, as well as limited and localised punishment. Hence, conventional deterrence needs to be placed through a credible and transparent system to convey intent. This is now possible due to increased ranges, warhead lethality and precision of conventional firepower. Additionally, conventional deterrence can be focused on counterforce targets with minimal counter value effect. Most importantly it can be delivered at a standoff range through multiple modes. Therefore, conventional deterrence is far more flexible in application than nuclear deterrence. Long Range Precision Fires is the priority program of the US Army's Futures Command for this reason. There are essentially are two modes of conventional deterrence. "Deterrence by Punishment" is the threat to impose unacceptable costs, such as the destruction of an adversary's strategic and high-value targets, in response to unwanted actions. It is offensive by nature. The second mode is "Deterrence by Denial," which is the threat to deny an adversary the ability to achieve its military and political objectives through aggression. The concept is defensive in nature. Firepower is critical in both cases.

Pakistan employs the stability-instability paradox of nuclear deterrence to aggressively pursue a low-cost high-value proxy war strategy. Cross LoC ground/air surgical strikes have deterred Pakistan to some extent, but not to the extent desired by India's strategic establishment. The conflict dynamics along the LoC give an opportunity for India to put in place a credible 'non-contact conventional deterrence' plan using the very same stability-instability paradox. It hinges around the unfashionable but effective attrition through selective air strikes and repetitive ground-based precision strikes. Pakistan should feel the pain of losing something significant, whenever its proxies increase terror activities or engineer an incident in India. Modern guns like M777 ULH and Dhanush have accurate direct firing and night engagement capabilities up to 5-6 km. The Pinaka has pinpoint capability up to 60-90 km. Brahmos extends the pinpoint reach beyond that. Pakistan will contest the battlespace, and India would consistently need to outscale the effort in time and space to rein in the latter through 'Deterrence by Punishment'.[8]

Limited conflict with China has so far been largely averted due to a stability-stability paradigm between both countries. China is employing multi-domain capabilities in space, cyberspace, info space and electromagnetic spectrum for military purposes extensively. Its aggressive intent is constantly reinforced by influence ops. Post the Eastern Ladakh intrusions, it is common knowledge that China is building up forces rapidly on India's northern borders. It will seek a window of opportunity to impose its will through conventional local military action and 'all measures short of war.' This must be thwarted through a 'Deterrence by Denial' capability. The next Chinese aggression is likely to be premised on a quick local victory that India will be unable to counter in time. India needs to deny the Chinese such quick local victories and convince the latter that it cannot achieve its political objectives speedily and at low cost. Through posturing and concerted capability development that includes the imminent threat of firepower causing significant combat attrition, China must be made to understand that the next confrontation with India would be detrimental to Chinese interests and force it to commit and expend sizeable forces and effort. Puncturing the notion of quick local victories is the most effective deterrent against China in the evolving and deteriorating adversarial profile between the two Asian powers. While it is expected that India's current political dispensation may not baulk at using airpower as a deterrent if escalatory compulsions do kick in, the availability of long-range land-based precision fires offers options to put in place a credible non-contact deterrence by denial capability.

Consider the Indo-Pak and the Sino-Indian fronts. Defences and positions will be hardened by the time conflict occurs. Battles will be largely positional and attritional in nature with limited space available for manoeuvre. In this perspective, two issues need to be understood about manoeuvre warfare. Firstly, manoeuvre is feasible only if a hole is punched through the enemy crust. That punched hole is feasible and presaged only on heavy firepower delivery. Following that, firepower must create or hold flanks for mechanised forces to manoeuvre. Secondly, manoeuvre is limited to the extent that is enabled or allowed by both the reach of firepower and the desired limited strategic outcomes. Manoeuvre without the protective umbrella of firepower—ground and air based—is a chimera. Firepower will be an invaluable and mandatory determinant of manoeuvre.

SUMMARY

As India's Armed Forces approach an era of accelerated integration, the role of the Regiment of Artillery is pivotal. Even as the IAF and Indian Navy deploy long-range firepower to keep adversaries at 'standoff' distances, the infantry and mechanised forces along with tube artillery will have to fight the close battle. Artillery will be the firepower bridge in any operational theatre.[9] In this context, the concept of Artillery being only a 'Combat Support Arm' needs a re-examination. This shift is important if jointness and integration is to succeed in India. Firepower has been a battle winning factor in all wars that India has fought. In an era of limited manoeuvrability, firepower will remain an essential component in deterring adversaries and destroying their combat potential if conflict is unavoidable. Technology has now bestowed artillery with tremendous reach, accuracy and destructive capability. With the Indian

Army's Regiment of Artillery embarking on a comprehensive journey of modernisation, both in capability and thought, it will remain a battle-winning factor well into the foreseeable future.

NOTES

1 Most facts pertaining to the evolution of firepower have been drawn from two official publications of the Regiment of Artillery. The Gunner: The Regiment of Artillery publication of 2008 and School of Artillery, Alma Mater of Gunners, 2019.

2 Shubajit Roy, "18 Modi-Xi Meetings, Several Pacts: Killings Breach Consensus, Dent Diplomacy", *The Indian Express,* June 17, 2020, https://indianexpress.com/article/india/india-china-standoff-diplomacy-lac-incident-mea-6462195/. Accessed on June 30, 2021.

3 Ashraf Wani, "Bofors Power Proved in Kargil War", *India Today,* July 25, 2016, https://www.indiatoday.in/india/story/kargil-winning-the-battle-with-bofors-331307-2016-07-25. Accessed on June 30, 2021.

4 Fires Center of Excellence, "Long Range Precision Fires", January 17, 2018, https://www.army.mil/standto/archive/2018/01/17/. Accessed on June 30, 2021.

5 Dr Jack Watling, "The Future of Fires, Maximizing the UKs Tactical and Operational Firepower", RUSI Occasional Paper, November 27, 2019, https://static.rusi.org/op_201911_future_of_fires_watling_web_0.pdf. Accessed on June 30, 2021.

6 Dr Jack Watling, "The Future of Fires, Maximizing the UKs Tactical and Operational Firepower", RUSI Occasional Paper, November 27, 2019, https://static.rusi.org/op_201911_future_of_fires_watling_web_0.pdf. Accessed on June 30, 2021.

7 Michael J. Mazzar, "Understanding Deterrence", Rand Corporation Perspective Paper, https://www.rand.org/content/dam/rand/pubs/perspectives/PE200/PE295/RAND_PE295.pdf. Accessed on June 30, 2021.

8 Lt Gen P R Shankar (Retired), "Non Contact Conventional Deterrence", December 7, 2019, https://www.gunnersshot.com/2019/12/non-contact-conventional-deterrence-by.html. Accessed on June 30, 2021.

9 Lt Gen P R Shankar (retired), "The Core of Theatrisation", June 27, 2021, https://www.gunnersshot.com/2021/06/the-core-of-theatrisation-by-lt-gen-p-r.html. Accessed on June 30, 2021.

CHAPTER 9

INDIA'S RISE: THE IMPERATIVE OF SEAPOWER

ANIL CHOPRA

ABSTRACT

Seapower, specifically naval power, serves not just as an instrument to deter and address military threats in times of conflict, but also to protect and advance far-flung economic and diplomatic interests in times of peace. Seapower, in fact, is indispensible should India aspire to be a nation of consequence beyond its continental periphery. The lack of a powerful Navy militarily confines a nation to its limited geographical location and renders it unable to pursue its interests or exert influence far beyond its borders, all at a detrimental cost to its economic well-being, more so in the contemporary globalised world. Navies are therefore perfectly suited to the modern international order, in which formally declared wars of the industrial era are being replaced by a conflict-ridden 'hot peace'. It is also imperative for India to continue to possess and enhance robust naval capability for manifold reasons, including the Chinese threat, far-flung interests in the Indo- Pacific, energy and trade security and, not least, the heft, influence and political flexibility that power at sea enables.

INTRODUCTION

If 'rise', in the context of nations, refers to the acquisition of the necessary wherewithal to be able to don the mantle of a regional or global power; to be autonomous in defining and pursuing national interests in an interconnected world; and to achieve lasting prosperity and security; then seapower is indeed an imperative to such a 'rise' on the global stage. The advocacy of seapower as an inescapable asset for India to 'rise' is likely to generate a fair degree of scepticism in the governing elites and strategic community of a people who have been continentally focussed for centuries, and often described as 'sea-blind'. Nevertheless, this chapter will argue that seapower is indeed indispensable should India aspire to be a nation of consequence beyond its continental periphery, as indeed warranted by its size, population, location and potentialities. India has all the qualities necessary to 'rise' to considerable heights, but cannot do so without the realisation that seapower is not just an instrument to deter and address military threats in times of conflict, but also to protect and advance far-flung economic and diplomatic interests in times of peace.

The degree and amount to which nations choose to develop various elements of power is a product, inter-alia, of national culture and value-systems, historical experiences, governance models, strategic realism, education and general awareness in the population, and, not least, ambition in the governing elites. This is particularly true of seapower. It has long been recognised that a society with an aptitude for the sea, as well as a government with an inclination to dominate the sea, are fundamental to imparting the necessary impetus and resolve to begin on an expensive, technologically demanding, long-term enterprise. In the context of this chapter, the term 'seapower' shall refer to military, i.e. naval power, as opposed to 'maritime power', which encompasses the whole gamut of activities and capabilities connected with the sea, including the merchant marine, ports, fisheries, constabularies and so on. Regrettably, the recent and widespread usage of the umbrella term 'maritime', especially as an adjunct to 'security', and the propensity of the academic and even strategic discourse to consider navies as but one component of the larger maritime eco-sphere, detracts from due consideration being given to the imperative and utility of hard power at sea, particularly in the prevailing world order , 'rule of law' notwithstanding.

THE ENDURING RATIONALE AND IMPETUS FOR SEAPOWER

The Global System

The Westphalian system of sovereign nation-states remains essentially anarchic, despite the inter-linkages and inter-dependencies of the modern world. There is no central authority that can enforce international borders, despite the existence of the United Nations Security Council. Unfortunate as it may be, 'might is still right' in the global jungle, as evinced in the China Seas, the Crimea and in Syria in recent years. Thucydides' observation that "the strong do what they can, and the weak suffer what they must" remains relevant today. Force continues to be the final arbiter on the planetary canvas, and is regularly resorted to by nation-states—unilaterally, or multi-laterally through military pacts, alliances and 'coalitions of the willing'—and by a host of non-state actors.

The 'rise' of a nation can be said to occur when there is a significant increase in its Comprehensive National Power in a relatively short period of time, accompanied by a perceptible growth of its influence in the international arena. While economic power is the fountainhead, it is only the development and deployment of military power that lends gravitas to a nation's standing, and its ability to affect the outcomes necessary to protect and further its multifarious interests. The relative lack of heft of Japan and Germany post-WWII demonstrates that economic power alone is insufficient to 'rise' in the concert of nation-states.

As 70 per cent of the planet's surface is covered by the ocean, and freedom of the seas is yet enshrined in international law, with no ownership rights on the high seas, or in the airspace above these vast waters, there is no better way to project military power, and gain visibility globally or regionally, other than sustained naval presence in areas of interest, be it in peace-time, crises or conflicts. In times of peace, naval deployment and presence off foreign shores and in distant seas is perfectly legal in times of peace, can be threatening or benign, can coax or cajole, and can be withdrawn at a moment's notice without the stigma of retreat. It thus follows that capable navies are enormously effective instruments of state, and of graded diplomatic signalling, and ultimately of deterrence, especially in this era of 'hot peace'.

However, navies are expensive and require long-lead times and sustained funding to build and operate, all of which calls for resolute national leadership, and an eschewing of political expediency, and short-term distractions. Only powerful, rich and visionary nations can build strong navies, and strong navies make these nations richer and stronger, and lead to long-lasting prosperity, security and great power status. Apart from the chronicled past, this link between seapower and great power is apparent to the present day, as witnessed over the last century by the examples of the US and the Soviet Navies, in the 20th century and the PLA Navy in the 21st. Moreover, the presence and latent power projected by navies facilitates and nurtures commerce to this very day. Trade follows flag, and flag follows trade, as seen by the year-round deployment of Chinese naval assets in the IOR, in tandem with its BRI thrust.

Military Aspects of the Maritime Dimension

The oceans are a single, uninterrupted, inter-connected continuum, with no borders and no fences. Access to any one part of the ocean allows access to the whole. This is applicable to warships as well as to commercial and recreational vessels. Moreover, the ocean belongs to no one—no state, or company or individual. In effect, all navies have legal access to most of the planetary surface. This freedom of manoeuvre of heavily armed warships over the entire globe lies at the heart of the latent threat posed by potent, self-sufficient naval forces deployed for extended periods in areas of interest. Their readiness, proximity and potential for aggression extract considerable leverage, and greatly impact decisions made on land.

Further, 80 per cent of humanity lives in proximity to the ocean—within 200 kilometres of it. This belt bordering the sea is often referred to as the littoral, and it is not only the most industrialised and developed part of the planet, but it is also the focus of most global conflict. Since the late 20th century, the entire littoral has been targetable 'from the sea'—from 'no-man's land', as it were. Attacking targets far inland using a mix of unmanned aircraft/drones and long- range precision munitions, such as cruise missiles, launched from ships and submarines positioned in the high seas, is a capability currently possessed by even medium naval powers, including our local adversaries. The oceans are critical for trade and transportation in a globalised world, and are vital for geo-economic advantage. These Sea Lanes of Communication (SLOCs), are also energy lifelines for many nations, particularly for India, China and Japan. These sinews of prosperity need military protection, and conversely, can be cut and bled.

The seas also are the source of enormous living and non-living resources, and a major factor for food security, mineral sourcing/mining, and perhaps a panacea for water scarcity. This is unavoidably leading to greater maritime conflict, as seen most visibly in the South China Sea, and in the spate of other maritime boundary claims and disputes, leading to naval capacity-building world-wide. Maritime insecurity is on the rise, and nations are struggling to structure multi-lateral maritime security arrangements to address trade and energy insecurity.

Seapower denotes the capability of a nation to wage war at sea, and achieve naval supremacy and military advantage over rivals, peers, challengers and threats. It also refers to a nation's ability to protect and advance its political, economic, and military interests through maritime control. It is, however, impossible for anyone to be in complete control of all the sea at all times. The ocean is simply too vast and the sea cannot be conquered, occupied or barricaded. It can only be 'used' to further objectives. Any control must be established by naval forces on, above and under the surface of the sea. This is a demanding proposition in terms of both force levels and operational effort, and can only be exercised by large blue-water three-dimensional Navies. Thus, intrinsically, the term 'seapower' cannot be divorced from the military connotation.

Technology has only multiplied the military advantages conferred by seapower. Besides attacking the littoral, navies can strike the deep hinterland from neutral waters, and have developed new means of transporting land-fighting power ashore. Similarly, the vastness and relative opaqueness of the ocean make the stealthy ballistic nuclear submarine the most survivable, potent, and effective component of the strategic nuclear triad.

The lack of a powerful Navy militarily confines a nation to its limited geographical location, unable to further its interests or exert influence far beyond its borders, all at a detrimental cost to its economic well-being, more so in the contemporary high-tech globalised world. Conversely, it is axiomatic that nations who possess seapower can hypothetically exercise it worldwide, in terms of military action, power projection, presence, influence and, not least great prosperity, due to seaborne trade and investment. This is precisely why, beginning in the 15th century, seapower has been such a great determinant in the modern era. The rise of professional navies has been coincident with the concept of sovereign nation states. Great powers have always emerged on the strength of their seapower, as seen by the rise of Spain, and, eventually, the British, whose Royal Navy presided over the British Empire and 'Pax Britannica' for over a hundred years. Britain's decline saw the Americans and then the Soviets become naval super-powers. The fates of powerful nations and their navies are inextricably entwined. The exercise of maritime power has not slowed in the 21st century, since powerful nations continue to maintain large and expensive navies, despite the affairs of mankind being mainly centred and resolved on land. Clearly, the benefits accruing from seapower far outweigh the costs.

India has the potential, the latent wealth and the technological base to acquire influence well beyond its shores, by building a world-class Navy.

This process commenced soon after Independence, and in a relatively short time India has built a sizeable, professionally reputed, three-dimensional, blue-water Navy. The rapid growth of the PLA Navy in recent decades reflects the sustained focus of the Chinese Government on acquiring seapower and great power status. A stronger Chinese Navy in the 21st century, with aircraft carriers and nuclear submarines, is clearly causing unease across the world, particularly in the Indo-Pacific. This feature should mobilise the collective will and ambition of the Indian people to pursue and sustain the growth of Indian seapower through sustained funding outlays, rather than being distracted by emergent and fleeting crises.

Attributes of Seapower

Naval forces, which are continually operating in a virtually borderless international domain, have certain unique attributes derived from the nature of the sea itself, and from the characteristics and nuances of international maritime law and covenants. In peacetime, the term 'gunboat diplomacy', while commonly used to convey the coercive power of naval forces deployed in an area of interest, does not even remotely capture the range of missions to which warships can be employed. In war, navies do not defend coastlines. They are instruments of offensive manoeuvre, foraying deep into the ocean, seeking out the enemy, bringing him to battle and destroying him as far away from their own shores as possible.

Warships have access to the territorial waters of all other nations, or 12 miles from the shore, under international law. Such access allows naval forces to be pre-deployed in areas of interest, either covertly or overtly as circumstances require, and thus maritime forces are often closest to crises as they occur, and are able to respond or intervene quickly. Exploiting the access provided by the sea, warships can move hundreds of miles per day over most of the world's surface, unimpeded by terrain or third-party agreements. This enables Navies to quickly respond from over the horizon, yet they may also be easily withdrawn to a distance. Naval forces have integral logistical wherewithal, such as fuel, provisions, water, ammunition and stores that allow them to operate independently, over long ranges, without external support for protracted periods of time. The time taken for ships to be replenished is also minimal. This permits naval forces to sail at short notice, deploy to the area of interest using access and mobility, and remain on station for months on end. The attributes of access, mobility and sustenance accord naval forces the 'reach' to apply national power at long distances from home and for extended periods of time that would otherwise be beyond the sphere of the nations' influence using other components of national and military power. For example, while aircraft may be able to fly to long distances especially with air to air re-fuelling, they cannot sustain at the point of application of power.

Sealift provided by specially designed naval platforms complements the speed of large modern airlift platforms as the principal means of deploying military, logistical, or humanitarian personnel, equipment and store on a large-scale. Sealift enables land and amphibious forces to transit to theatre, position offshore if required, and then facilitates joint power to be brought to bear ashore, especially if basing and overflight permissions are not forthcoming from other states. Once in the theatre, maritime forces can remain on station for prolonged periods of time and are able to quickly adapt to the tempo of the operation. They can signal political resolve and act as a force for deterrence or coercion. The ability of maritime forces to poise in international waters allows the footprint ashore to be minimised or avoided altogether, and the political complications and military risks of committing forces on land can be minimised to the greatest extent possible. Warships operate forward in high-threat environments, and are designed to withstand significant damage before becoming non-operational. The critics overlook this aspect.

At a strategic level, maritime forces can shape and exploit the battle space, exposing an enemy's flank and rear. At the operational level, these forces can manoeuvre from the sea to attack, distract, disrupt and often envelope much larger forces ashore. To summarise, warships stationed in any area provide any national leadership with an abundance of political and military options at short notice. Navies are therefore perfectly suited to the modern world wherein formally declared wars are being replaced by a conflict-ridden 'long/hot peace', in which big and small powers use their military power more for deterrence and coercion, and to contain outright armed conflict.

THE OUTLOOK FOR INDIAN SEAPOWER

The Global Context

Following the collapse of the Soviet Union, China's explosive entry onto the world stage has brought back the possibility of a return to bipolarity in an unstable world that is dotted with a larger number of small, yet heavily armed nuclear powers. In such a geo-strategic environment, seapower will be vital to maintaining peace, on account of the flexibility it offers during periods of crisis/tension. Consequently, apart from the US and China, a host of medium powers, including Russia, Japan, India, France, the United Kingdom and Australia, have significantly increased their naval capabilities since the turn of the millennium, inducting new aircraft carriers, nuclear submarines and sealift platforms. Almost every coastal state has begun to expand maritime capacity building, and even nations like Bangladesh and Myanmar have acquired submarines.

When viewed through the prism of great power rivalry, the world is witnessing an old-fashioned full-fledged naval armed race, this time between the US and China, uncannily reminiscent of that between Britain and Germany before the First World War, and again between the US and the Soviet Union during the Cold War.

While China has embarked on a warship building programme unprecedented in history, the PLA Navy is still a long way from possessing seapower commensurate with its ambitions. It has not yet achieved the capability to deploy globally for extended periods of time with adequate strength in waters other than those of the Indo-Pacific, in general, and the China Sea.. The author posits that China is a great power in all aspects save its ability to fight and project power across the oceans of the world (The editor argues that Chinese airpower is some distance away from global power projection). Its massive naval building program, and acquisition of new weapon, cyber and space capabilities have allowed it to achieve Anti-Access Area Denial in the Western Pacific (WP), but its ability to undertake combat operations outside of the China Seas is questionable, as it is confronted by resident powers like India in the Indian Ocean, and the blue-water capabilities of the Indian Navy, which is not constrained by geography and extended lines of logistic and combat support. Any further strengthening of China's seapower would undoubtedly have an impact on India's influence and standing in the Indo-Pacific, unless India embarks on its own strategy of building seapower and ensuring that it does not get marginalised by the PLA Navy in contested maritime spaces.

To summarise, the current global strategic scenario clearly demonstrates that seapower remains a significant element in power equations in the Westphalian world, despite some scholarship and analyses arguing that this form of hard power is passé, and no longer relevant in a world dominated by economic coercion, diplomatic finesse, aerospace power, and battle-space transparency. The increasingly contested and vast oceanic spaces are progressively occupying strategic centre-stage in our times, and the 21st century has been aptly described as the 'century of the seas'. As it aspires to rise, India would do well to heed this evidence and not be distracted from embracing seapower, as those who seek to preserve the northern frontiers alive intend.

The Indo-Pacific: Turbulence East and West

The Indo-Pacific (IP) concept, developed in 2007, is now obviously the centre stage on which the new global "great game" is being enacted. It is a combination of geography, strategy, connectivity and battle-space. It is the theatre in which Beijing has chosen to challenge both the US, as well as the Asian status-quo, in its pursuit of the Chinese Dream. However, while China is now dominant in the Pacific part of this construct, it is far from being so in the Indian Ocean Region (IOR). China, and indeed the world, recognises that it cannot be a global power until it is a power in the IOR, and its future plainly depends on its ability to do so. This objective, however, can only be realised if India does not possess the requisite seapower and allows itself to be persuaded again into donning continental blinkers. The IP is also an arena in which India must rise beyond just addressing the China challenge, as it can easily bring seapower to bear both East and West. Despite the fact that they are no longer oblivious to the sea, Indian policymakers are yet to capitalise on seapower and are easily distracted by emergent geopolitical events. There were three main drivers that created the IP concept. First, the realisation that Japan alone could not balance China in Asia, especially since US assets were stretched and shared between West Asia and the West Pacific. A rising India, with its powerful, professional Navy, working with Japan, Australia, and ASEAN, may be able to do so. Second, the striking military vulnerability of China outside the WP, combined with China's significant dependence on the IOR for energy, raw materials and markets, could be leveraged by India in the IOR. Finally, the need to protect ever increasing East-West trade, which runs the gamut of choke points and narrow gulfs from turbulent West Asia to the tinder-box of the South China Sea, necessitated India's provision of SLOC security. The IP construct basically added India to the Asia-Pacific balance of power, since it was vital to regulating Chinese maritime behaviour across the huge swathe of contested maritime spaces that have emerged in the Asia Pacific, Oceania and IOR regions.

This was a great opportunity for New Delhi to assure regional ascendency and boost security and prosperity by being able to 'Look and Act' both East and West simultaneously, owing to the momentum and synergies acquired by maritime cooperation with established powers. However, till very recently, India was slow to grasp the moment, as well as the potentialities inherent by being courted by diverse stakeholders, for reasons that are beyond the purview of this chapter. Given the nature of its noisy argumentative democracy, there too many conflicting voices, with many calling for accommodating Chinese power and many others distrustful of any alignment or loss of autonomy. Consequently, India was hesitant to embrace both the 'free and open IP' (FOIP) advocated by the US and Japan, as also the QUAD, reflected in its reticence to invite the Royal Australian Navy (RAN) into the fold of MALABAR. Fortunately, the combination of an unpredictable US president and the miscalculations of an over-ambitious CCP has given New Delhi another chance to stamp its credentials across the IP by exploiting its seapower.

The IP received a boost and gained widespread usage and considerable traction during the Trump administration, as the US called-out Beijing across the board and denoted it as a 'major adversary' in no uncertain terms.

The QUAD is nowhere near a military alliance, neither will it ever be. Even QUAD 2.0 which emerged in 2017, had a far greater canvas of cooperation than just hard security. The Biden Administration has steered Quad on an even more ambitious path, through the mechanism of two Quad Leader Summits held in quick succession, the first virtually in March this year, and the second in person in Washington DC in September. QUAD 3.0 seems to be fashioned on a much broader definition of security as it now proposes joint action on climate change, supply chains, infrastructure projects and many other initiatives.

However, the inherent strategic signalling emanating from this 'concert of democracies' is powerful, and could possibly deter Beijing from overtly aggressive actions in the IP. Whether formally stated or not, it would be apparent to all astute observers that the significant military forces and capabilities of the QUAD members represent a 'Force-in-Being' to borrow from the 17th century Royal Navy concept of a 'Fleet-in-Being'. The very existence of interoperable and combat-ready forces, even when not forward-deployed in a combined fashion, offers a great deal of hard deterrent value. China's concern regarding QUAD can be seen in its bombastic rhetoric with regards to what it has described as an 'Asian NATO'. Beijing's discomfort will be further exacerbated by the recent announcement of AUKUS, an upfront military alliance between Australia, the UK and the US.

It would be apparent that Indian seapower would be critical for meeting emergent threats and furthering far-flung interests in the IP and IOR, by itself, or in tandem with other forces through initiatives like QUAD and MALABAR.

THE INDIAN NAVY: BOOST OR BLOCKADE?

By any standard, the growth of the Indian Navy (IN) in the fifty years since independence has been remarkable. By the turn of the millennium, the IN emerged a strong balanced three-dimensional blue-water force that had stamped its presence in the Indian Ocean, and whose prowess had been acknowledged globally. It is one of the largest ten navies in the world, operating aircraft carriers, nuclear submarines, and is only the fifth Navy to have strategic nuclear capability, giving India the vital third leg of the strategic triad. However, the growth of the IN has sputtered since the turn of the millennium. Instead of growing in accordance with the design of long-term perspective plans, which were created in detail with proper consideration given to the pattern of previous moderate financial outlays, force-levels have remained static, and are poised to see a downward trend. Important long-lead time projects remain unsanctioned, primarily for lack of funds. This does not bode well for the Navy a decade from now.

The disconnect between India's military spending and its threat evaluation and stated ambitions is growing. This has given short shrift to many naval plans, including the replacement of existing platforms. This impacts not only force-levels and military capability, but also credibility in the region and beyond. Inadequate funding also reflects in maintenance of equipment and infrastructure and reduced operational training and deployment, all of which affect readiness and combat efficiency. Even if short-term measures are resorted to, these would only temporarily shore up the defence budget, and cannot substitute for the political and national resolve to fund the military instrument to the degree required. The absence of assured funding seems to have affected the Navy the most, given the long-lead time required for naval platforms to be constructed and inducted.

With India's armed forces undergoing change in a setting of fledgling joint institutions and inadequate cross-domain expertise, the biggest challenge facing military planners will be in the prioritisation of capabilities, be it service-specific or mutually supporting. Asking the Navy to forego aircraft carriers and induct submarines, is akin to asking the Army to disband the artillery to enable more infantry, or urging the Air Force to forego fighter aircraft to acquire more helicopters. The basic components of a Service fight as a composite whole, and prioritising between them would result in a significant reduction in combat capability and credibility. Minesweepers are as important to a Navy as are nuclear submarines or destroyers.

It should be evident to the discerning observer that China's reluctance to formalise the LAC is not only to salami slice when it can, but divert India's attention and resources away from the ocean. This strategy is a recognition of its own vulnerability, but only if the Indian Navy is strong and combat-ready to exploit that vulnerability. Though many within the Indian security establishment realise this academically, the sheer visibility of land conflict, the need to preserve borders, and the political ramifications of any reverses entice them away from the sea. This is understandable, but the long-term implications, even with regard to China, let alone India's regional aspirations and security, must be kept sight of, at least by the institutional memory of the larger strategic community.

CONCLUSION

Whilst the academic and intellectual discourse debates the utility of supposedly vulnerable seapower in the contemporary multi-domain global battle-space, overlayed as it is with air, space, cyber, and hybrid scenarios, the great and medium powers of the world are significantly enhancing naval capability and force-levels, as revealed by even a cursory glance at the naval projects and warship-building programmes across the world. The AUKUS alliance announced in September 2021 has indeed been fashioned around nuclear-powered attack submarines (SSNs) and the connected infrastructure. As may be inferred from the preceding rationale ,it is imperative for India to continue to possess and enhance robust naval capability for manifold reasons, including the Chinese threat, far-flung interests in the Indo-Pacific, energy and trade security, and not least, the heft, influence and political flexibility that power at sea provides.

It does however appear that events of the recent past have brought India to an inflection point. There is every possibility that India will again retreat from the seas on account of the continental threat on its land frontiers, and the Navy be subject to blockades at every turn. On the other hand, it is also possible that New Delhi will seize the opportunities offered by the geo-strategic and geopolitical scenario unfolding in the IP, boost its credentials in the maritime arena, and take its place as a regional power with the credibility derived from being able to act on its interests and commitments.

The outcome will depend to a large degree on whether India's apex strategic leadership comes to believe that seapower can actually deter and moderate Chinese misadventures and aggressiveness on the land borders, and is not just a cerebral, intellectual supposition and linkage. A deployed fleet tends to keep problems at arm's length.

To conclude , seapower is certainly an imperative if India wishes to rise. However, navies are expensive and out of sight of their countrymen. There are no quick fixes, and certainly no immediate political returns. It would therefore not be far off the mark to say that only ambitious nations with visionary, far-seeing leaders, can create and sustain a strong Navy, which will always remain a prerequisite and the prime instrument for power beyond borders.

Bibliography

1 Admiral James Stavridis, "Seapower".
2. Paul M Kennedy, "The Rise and Fall of British Naval Mastery".
3. KM Pannikar, "India and the Indian Ocean".
4. Paul Kennedy, "The Rise and Fall of Great Powers".
5. Geoffrey Till, "Seapower".
6. IHQ, MOD(Navy), "Indian Maritime Doctrine 2019".
7. "Ensuring Secure Seas-Indian Maritime Security Strategy"
8. UK MOD, "British Naval Doctrine, 2011".
9. " Empire" : Nial Ferguson
10. Tom Miller, "China's Asian Dream".
11. William J Bernstein, "A Splendid Exchange".
12. Morrison, "The Two-Ocean War".
13. Alfred Thayer Mahan, "The Influence of Seapower upon History".
14. Daron Acemoglu and James H Robinson, "Why Nations Fail".
15. Robert D Kaplan, "Monsoon - The Indian Ocean and the Future of American Power".
16. Robert D Kaplan, "The Revenge of Geography".
17. Rory Medcalf, "Indo-Pacific Empire: China, America and the Contest for the World's Pivotal Region".
18. Michael Pearson, "The Indian Ocean".
19. Beatrice Nicolini. "Land and Maritime Empires in the Indian Ocean".
20. Julian Corbett, "Some Principles of Maritime Strategy".
21. CSIS brief, "Defining the Diamond: The Past, Present, and Future of the Quadrilateral Security Dialogue".
22. Laxman Kumar Behera, "India's Defence Economy: Planning, Budgeting, Industry and Procurement".
23. Stephen Wilkinson, "Army and Nation: The Military and Indian Democracy since Independence".

CHAPTER 10

INDIA'S AIRCRAFT CARRIER DILEMMA

ARUN PRAKASH

ABSTRACT

For all its perceived strengths and virtues, the aircraft carrier has always stirred controversy and sparked passions. Just as the loyalists point to the carrier's size, reach, mobility and aerial firepower as its strengths, critics focus on its expensive cost, size and vulnerability to bring it down. Over the years, a furious 'carrier debate' has raged in many countries, encompassing the armed forces, politicians as well as the media and academia. No such informed debate has taken place in India, and decision-makers seem to be searching for an answer in the absence of a national security strategy. Air forces, who believe in the 'indivisibility of airpower', see the carrier as a threat to their 'core competencies.' In this essay, the author seeks to address both sides of the carrier debate, and, in the face of an imminent Chinese advance into the Indian Ocean, makes a case for retaining continued faith in the carrier.

INTRODUCTION

Today there are fewer than two dozen aircraft carriers in the world. The huge costs involved in constructing, operating and maintaining carriers have confined this citadel of seapower to a select club of countries that includes, China, France, India, Italy, Russia, Spain, Thailand, the United Kingdom and the United States. It is significant, however, that the number of carrier operating navies has risen from just four at the end of WWII to nine today. While China has yet to disclose the full contours of its ambitious carrier building programme, Japan, a long-time aspirant, is poised to become the program's tenth member, with Turkey and South Korea waiting in the wings.

Despite its growing numbers, the aircraft carrier continues to evoke strong criticism that it is an expensive anachronism, which offers little advantage over lower-cost alternatives. The ongoing debate remains largely centred on enhanced battle-space transparency and key threats like improved submarine capabilities, better anti-ship missiles and, most importantly, the threat presented by shore-based ballistic-missiles claimed to be 'carrier-killers' by China.

In India, national security issues of this nature rank fourth—after politics, cricket and Bollywood—in terms of the interest that they generate amongst the cognoscenti as well as general public. Given this lack of awareness/comprehension, little informed discussion has taken place in India's Parliament, media or academia, about the merits, necessity and affordability of the aircraft carrier. However, within the armed forces, this topic, with its budgetary and operational implications, remains the subject of a rather nuted debate that has remained inconclusive.

Therefore, it would be appropriate for an institution like the NDC, to generate an enlightened debate that addresses the continuing relevance, roles, missions and viability of aircraft carriers in India's future strategic environment. This chapter will hopefully serve as a catalyst for such a process. Before focusing on carriers, it is necessary to highlight the significance of aviation, per se, in naval operations.

AVIATION IN NAVAL OPERATIONS

It is said that when the US is faced with an international crisis, the first question the President asks the Chairman of the Joint Chiefs of Staff is: "Where are the carriers?" This may be an apocryphal tale, but the fact remains that the Pentagon and the State Department consider aircraft carriers as "four-and-a-half acres of sovereign territory", available, at short notice, for leveraging state policy. It is the same for other nations, which consider carriers as potent mobile bases that can be positioned off any shore, worldwide, in a matter of hours or days, not only to project naval airpower—for deterrence, coercion or compellence—but also for diplomatic-messaging, conveying reassurance to friends or rendering humanitarian assistance.

The single most important factor that distinguishes naval airpower from air forces is the fact that navies consider aircraft as an extension of the fleet's weapons and sensors. Airpower is considered an integral component of the maritime operational matrix, and is expected to be deployable within minutes or hours by the naval command-chain. It cannot be just a transient 'helping hand' that must be requisitioned externally, using complex procedures. The utility of tactical airpower (i.e. integral aircraft and helicopters) to the Fleet is based on three key attributes:

- The ability to respond with minimum delay in any geographic location, on a 24x7 basis.
- The ability to reconnoitre and detect targets much beyond the ship's own sensor range.
- The ability to deliver ordnance while the ship remains outside the enemy's weapon danger zone.

There is no single definition of an aircraft carrier, and versions of this ship can vary from 100,000-tonne American behemoths—which require nuclear propulsion, and carry upward of 80 aircraft and helicopters—to Thailand's 11,000-tonne 'VSTOL-carrier.' Other navies, own mid-size carriers of between 40,000 and 70,000 tonnes, which can be driven by non-nuclear propulsion, and carry a mix of 30-40 strike-fighters and ASW helicopters.

The arrival of the STO/VL or 'B' version of the F-35 fighter, has spawned a new class of 'aviation capable' ships. These are the amphibious assault ships, originally classified as landing platforms dock/helicopter (LPD/LHD in US parlance), now being adapted for operation of fixed-wing jets, with or without a ski-jump.[1]

THE CARRIER CONUNDRUM

The traditional justification for aircraft carriers that they provide tactical airpower, independent of land bases, where and when required by navies, is being increasingly questioned by air forces, especially where the 'budgetary cake' is diminishing in size. The emergence of China's 'anti-access and area-denial' (A2AD) strategy seemed to further bolster the case against carriers, and a debate about the justification for building any more of these leviathans continues in many countries.

The essence of the argument against carriers has traditionally been based on the claim that since land-based air forces can perform all its functions, why expend scarce resources on this platform? However, some recent developments, highlighted below, should cause a re-think amongst those, sceptical about the continuing viability of carriers.

- Latest satellite pictures, which show rapid progress of China's third aircraft-carrier, dubbed Type-003, being built in Shanghai's Jiangnan Shipyard, are interpreted as a clear sign that a new class of PLA Navy carriers is on the way. Equipped with electro-magnetic catapults, J-15/J-31 fighters and the KJ-600 fixed-wing airborne early warning (AEW) aircraft, these ships[2] would provide a significant boost to China's maritime power, with consequences for the Indo-Pacific balance of power.
- Britain's two brand new, 65,000-tonne carriers, built in the teeth of opposition at a cost of US$ 8.5 billion, made their operational debut in June 2021. While one is operating in UK waters, the other is leading a multi-national strike-group on a 7-month deployment, half-way across the world, to the Indo-Pacific. Queried about their role, the Royal Navy's Fleet Commander

declared that the two carriers would undertake missions such as: "strategic messaging, power projection, naval diplomacy and trade promotion." This is in consonance with the ruling party's vision of a 'Global Britain,' that includes a 'military footprint' in the Indo-Pacific.[3]

- The much vaunted A2AD threat from China and Russia has been subjected to a critical re-appraisal by US and NATO analysts. It is now believed that not only has the hazard been exaggerated, but that viable counter-measures have become available to mitigate risks. In fact, use of the term 'A2AD' has been discontinued in US Navy documents and discourse on the grounds that it "cedes too much ground to the adversary without adequate evidence."[4]

THE INDIAN CONTEXT

In India, INS *Vikramaditya*, the country's sole aircraft carrier, is expected to be joined by the indigenously designed and built IAC-1 in 2022/23. According to India's 2015 Maritime Strategy, the Indian Navy (IN), in order to discharge its tasks of sea control/sea denial and power projection, is committed to maintaining "two carrier task forces, each comprising one or more carrier battle groups."[5] To account for maintenance cycles and distant deployments, the necessity to field two carriers implies a force of at least 3 such ships. The IN has long aspired to begin indigenous construction of a newer, improved version of the IAC-1, and naval planners have addressed issues about its design as well as financing distribution. In this context, the Navy's requirement for an additional aircraft-carrier has met with stiff resistance from pockets within India's strategic establishment, with the CDS commenting that "Anything on the surface can be picked up by satellites and knocked off by missiles. I think the Navy needs more submarines than aircraft carriers, which require their own individual armadas for protection."[6] Affluent nations have their own logic for maintaining aircraft carriers in their order of battle, but for a rising power like India struggling to cope with multiple crises, there is a need for reflection on this issue. Decisions regarding such critical matters should normally be guided by a nation's security strategy. However, since India has yet to generate such a document, the Indian Navy's Maritime Strategy will have to be a substitute. In this context, let us look at India's past experience in this arena.

INDIA'S CARRIER EXPERIENCE

The Indian Navy's steadfast adherence to the aircraft carrier as the centrepiece of its doctrine and strategy has paid rich dividends over the past half-century. One striking manifestation of this was the contrast between the manner in which the Indian and PLA Navies, almost simultaneously, inducted new aircraft carriers into their fleets in 2012. Over the next four years, the PLAN cautiously approached operationalizing the *Liaoning* and its complement of J-15 Tiger Shark fighters. According to reports, help was sought from the Brazilian Navy after they lost 3-4 aircraft to accidents.

The IN, on the other hand, given its 50 years of carrier operating experience, commissioned INS *Vikramaditya* in 2012 in Russia, and confidently sailed her 12,000 miles to her new home in Karwar. By 2014, the ship and its squadrons of MiG-29K fighters and Kamov-31 ASW helicopters had been worked-up to fully operational status by day and night.

The IN, rightfully takes pride in the critical role performed by INS *Vikrant*'s squadrons of Sea Hawk fighters and Alize ASW aircraft during the 1971 Bangladesh operations. However, it must be acknowledged that the ship was operating in a relatively benign environment because the opposing Air Force was being kept engaged by the IAF. This brings into question, the logic and operational effectiveness of the IN previously relying on a single, small, aircraft-carrier.

While it has been a Hobson's choice, for the Service, faced with tight budgets and a lack of strategic awareness at the national level, the following limitations have loomed in the background:

- Both INS *Vikrant* and INS *Viraat* were "light fleet carriers', the smallest in the carrier family. They were restricted in the all-up weight and number of aircraft that could be accommodated in the hangars and launched/recovered from their small decks.
- The ski-jump, while a useful innovation that facilitated STO/VL (short take-off, vertical landing) operations from small decks, placed limitations on aircraft payload.
- Due to these limitations, both ships could only carry sub-sonic aircraft of limited range and endurance during their operational lives.
- The possible outcome of a Sea Hawk encounter with an F-86 in the 1970s or a Sea Harrier interception of an F-16 in the 1980s and 1990s remained a source of speculation (and concern) for carrier Captains and Fleet Commanders.

However, with a larger carrier like the *Vikramaditya,* capable of operating state-of-the-art fighters, the Indian Navy's operational options have expanded significantly. Given that tactical air support is available around the clock, our task forces can now undertake missions with confidence in the face of air-opposition.

It must be stated here that the oft-mentioned requirement for a carrier to have an "individual armada for its own protection" is a misconception in most instances. Clearly, a carrier's own air-group of fixed-wing fighters as well as airborne ASW and AEW assets, equips it with adequate capabilities for early detection and neutralisation of threats in all three dimensions. Carrying a notional, sanitised 'protective bubble' of 200-250 nm radius all around it, a carrier, actually provides protection to the force that accompanies it, rather than needing protection from a large number of escorts.

While bigger navies may enjoy the luxury of a full 'carrier battle-group,' IN experience has proven that a carrier capable of 20 knots or more needs only a tanker and an escort of 2-3 destroyers or frigates for itself. For specific operations, the battle-group can be constituted on an 'as required' basis. However, it is best if the safety of the carrier as well as its effective employment—whether for force-projection, sea control, or ASW—remains a decision to be taken at a strategic level, with the best available intelligence inputs, rather than being left to the Task Force Commander's tactical acumen.

Two factors need to be borne in mind here. Firstly, the ski-jump restricts aircraft payload, and should be replaced by a catapult on our future carriers. Second, given the new threats facing aircraft carriers at sea, the IN needs to adopt appropriate counter-measures, both in terms of hardware as well as tactics. Against this backdrop, let us undertake a brief examination of the impact of aircraft carriers on seapower.

CONTRIBUTION OF AIRCRAFT CARRIERS

Carrier-borne airpower was instrumental in shaping the course of WWII in almost all theatres. Their role is too well known to be detailed here, whether it was hunting surface raiders like the *Bismarck*, long-range ASW and convoy escort duty in the Atlantic, power projection ashore in the Mediterranean, or over-the-horizon carrier versus carrier combat in the Pacific. The clamour for air support at sea in WWII, saw even merchant ships being equipped with fighters that could undertake a rocket assisted take-off but then had to ditch in the sea. This proved a useful, if desperate, measure and led to merchant ship hulls being quickly modified with a flight deck to create 'jeep carriers' capable of accommodating 15-20 fighters.

The end of WWII saw the US Navy with a massive fleet of 99 carriers and the Royal Navy with 40 such ships of assorted types. Such inventories, however, were unaffordable and began to rapidly reduce after the Japanese surrender. The newly constituted USAF, which claimed global reach with its strategic bombers, offered an alternative to naval aviation in post-War US. A period of inter-Service tension led to the cancellation of the super-carrier USS *United States* and four sister ships. This was followed by the 'Revolt of the Admirals,' which resulted in the resignation of the US Navy Chief and other Admirals in 1949.[7]

Persistent Cold War tensions made it obvious that neither the value of carriers nor the roles assigned to them would diminish. In the seven decades, since the end of WWII, carriers have continued to play a vital role in projecting airpower to exert a decisive influence on distant conflicts. Among the conflicts in which carriers played a key role were the Korean War, the Suez crisis, the long Vietnam War, the 1971 Indo-Pakistan War and the Falklands Campaign.

More recently, the conflicts in the Balkans, Kuwait, Iraq, Afghanistan, Libya and Syria have consistently shown that the not just the US Navy, but also the British, French, Russians and Italians have deployed aircraft carriers as 'sovereign territory' in the Mediterranean Sea and Indian Ocean to project airpower and influence events far from home. The role played by carrier airpower in latter day conflicts has had an impact on not only Chinese thinking, but has also caused the Japanese to modify their two Izumo class LHAs to operate the F-35B STO/VL fighter,[8] with the Turks, South Koreans and Australians likely to follow.

Since the advent of carrier-based aviation, the US has designed and deployed 12 classes of aircraft carriers, three of which are nuclear-powered, and flown over 200 aircraft types from their decks.[9] In the face of constantly developing threats, the USN has been able to maintain the relevance and unique contributions of carriers to US military power by constantly modifying the mix of aircraft in its air-wings.

INDIA'S EMERGING MARITIME ENVIRONMENT

India's central position in the Indian Ocean Region (IOR), astride major shipping lanes accords it both advantages and responsibilities. Jutting a thousand kilometres into the ocean named after it, the Indian peninsula has over 7,500 km of coastline, 200 major and non-major ports, and an exclusive economic zone of over two million square kilometres, which is rich in food and mineral resources.

Over 120,000 merchantmen pass through the Indian Ocean each year, carrying cargo worth a trillion dollars. Both east and west-bound shipping goes through areas where it may be vulnerable to interdiction or interference by states as well as non-state entities, like pirates and terrorists. Since 95 per cent of India's trade and energy is carried by sea, the safety and security of these sea routes is critical to our national growth and prosperity.

While the strategic importance of the IOR is self-evident, India's rapidly growing interests in the Pacific are lesser known. Almost, 55 per cent of India's trade with the greater Asia-Pacific area transits through the South China Sea, and Indian companies have acquired offshore and onshore hydrocarbon drilling rights in littoral states as well as in the Russian Far East. Any attempt to dominate the waters of the Indian or Pacific Oceans would present a grave threat to India's vital interests.

The assumption by India of the role of 'a net provider of security' in the IOR, seen in conjunction with PM Modi's vision of SAGAR or "Security and Growth for All in the Region," places considerable responsibility on the IN. These endeavours necessitate not only the strengthening of India's offensive/defensive capabilities at sea, but also the strengthening of the Navy's non-military roles, which are classified as Benign, Constabulary and Diplomatic.

CHINA'S SHIFT TO THE SEA

China's heavy dependence on Indian Ocean sea-lanes has led to its deep involvement in this region which is practically on India's doorstep. While the 'string of pearls' strategy was crafted for acquisition of maritime footholds, the 'Belt and Road Initiative' with its 'Maritime Silk-Road' component, pushes a far more ambitious maritime agenda linking China's economic and strategic interests in the Indo-Pacific with Europe and Africa.

Accordingly, China's 2015 Military Strategy signalled a shift in maritime focus from 'offshore' to 'open seas', with the PLA Navy (PLAN) mandated to deploy power-projection and sea-control forces in the in the Indian Ocean region (IOR).[10] Starting with anti-piracy patrols in the Gulf of Aden in 2008, the PLAN has steadily gained experience and confidence in operations distant from home, with a small task force maintained in the IOR continuously since then.

With two aircraft carriers already in service, and a third one on the way, the Chinese are rapidly consolidating not only their shipbuilding skills, but also their expertise in the operation and deployment of these complex weapon platforms. Progressive increase in the size of these ships is a clear indication that the ultimate objective of this serial-production programme is the construction of nuclear-powered carriers, in the coming years.

The PLAN has been specifically mandated to safeguard China's interests, as far as the Maritime Silk Road and its vital IOR sea lanes are concerned, and it has adequate 'blue-water' capable ships for this task. However, if PLAN surface forces have not made a conspicuous appearance in the IOR so far, it is due to their lack of organic air cover and vulnerability to India's naval and shore-based airpower.[11] But there should be no doubt that as soon as the PLAN is able to spare an aircraft carrier, it will seek to create a permanent forward presence in these waters, with a PLAN carrier battle-group leading an 'Indian Ocean Squadron'.

PLAN forces deployed in the IOR would not only pose a formidable threat to India's shipping, its peninsular homeland and island territories, but also to IN task forces deployed in distant waters. Such a threat can only be countered with the benefit of an aircraft carrier's protection.

CARRIER VULNERABILITY

Every new weapon system is inevitably followed by one or more counter-measures, and then by prophesies of its early demise. For nearly a century, the carrier has so far managed to survive and dominate the maritime scene. Satellites and other sophisticated surveillance systems have proliferated, making the maritime battle-space largely transparent, and critics claim that a carrier may now have few places to hide.

China, perceiving a grave threat from US Navy carriers, obviously, went to great lengths to evolve what western analysts termed as the A2AD strategy. Centred on the DF-21D and DF-26 anti-ship ballistic missiles (ASBM), amongst other weapons, A2AD added a new dimension to the carrier vulnerability debate. However, the initial panic having subsided, a view has emerged that A2AD is an over-hyped buzzword leveraged to intimidate potential adversaries before the 'match' even begins.

Organic fire control radars cannot acquire targets at claimed (over the horizon) ranges for ASBMs, and targeting data would have to come via networking, from remote aircraft, drones, satellites, and distant land and sea-based radars. Forming such a 'kill-chain' is technically challenging and is vulnerable to disruption at any point in the chain.[12]

It also appears that a number of counter-measures may be available to degrade or defeat the effectiveness of this concept, which has never been tested against a live, moving target. Its efficacy in combat, therefore, remains a matter of assessment and even speculation, particularly in the more open waters of the Indian Ocean. The options available to a carrier group include the following:[13]

- Degradation/destruction of target data sources.
- Mid-course interception using anti-ballistic missile weapons (including high-energy lasers and micro-waves).
- Use of course/speed alterations and decoys/smoke/camouflage to deceive the missile seeker-head.
- Hard-kill measures to achieve terminal destruction of incoming missile.

A technological innovation which has the potential to radically change the calculus of carrier employment is the unmanned combat aerial vehicle (UCAV). A UCAV has double or triple the range and many times the endurance of a manned aircraft, and this opens the prospect of a carrier remaining well outside the enemy 'threat envelope" and discharging a majority of its roles with relative impunity.[14]

In the context of modern combat, no platform can be considered 'invulnerable,' and naval units will suffer in action at sea, if not deployed with tactical/operational acumen. However, notwithstanding its size, a fast-moving carrier is not easy to locate and identify at sea. Even if found, the carrier's air group and escort is capable of neutralising hostile ships, aircraft and submarines before they become a threat. In the worst case, even if it is struck by a missile, the carrier's odds of surviving major damage are far greater than those of any other type of ship.

INTER-SERVICE DISSONANCE

The 1970s had witnessed an unsavoury wrangle between the IAF and IN, over control of the maritime-reconnaissance (MR) role. In 1976, the government directed that the MR role and assets were to be handed over to the IN. The IAF was, however, permitted to retain its shore-based anti-shipping strike role. Initially performed by a flight of Jaguar fighter-bombers armed with anti-ship missiles (ASM), it is understood that a squadron of Sukhoi-30 MKI multi-role fighters deployed in South India have also been assigned this task.

Following an IAF exercise in 2018, media reports claimed that, with these aircraft, "India can dominate the Indian Ocean Region against any military activity including that of the Chinese."[15] Possibly based on such overstatements, claims have been made that this capability will render aircraft carriers redundant! Whether or not the IAF actually intends to expend resources for exercising 'maritime domination,' such reports have caused unease in naval circles. India's armed forces can ill-afford to sow the seeds of another inter-service confrontation over aircraft carriers in an environment already fraught with tensions over the impending formation of Theatre Commands.. At this juncture, it would be pertinent to briefly discuss the viability of shore-based air support at sea.

SHORE-BASED AIR SUPPORT AT SEA A VIABLE OPTION?

The IN is now well-endowed for strike at sea, thanks to its force of ship-borne MiG-29Ks and shore-based P-8(I) Poseidons, soon to be joined by SH-60 helicopters, all of which are ASM-armed. While the supplementing of this capability by the IAF is to be welcomed, it is necessary to remain firmly in touch with reality for a number of reasons.

Firstly, the process of requisitioning of air-effort from the IAF can be a time-consuming and trying affair in time-critical situations. Secondly, in today's crowded maritime environment, obtaining positive identification of (beyond visual range) targets before ASM release could pose serious difficulties for a shore-based aircraft. Last and most important, despite in-flight refuellers, a shore-based aircraft flying in support of a naval force 500-1,500 miles out at sea has severe limitations in 'loiter-time.'

These difficulties are not insurmountable; however, they require intense Navy-IAF coordination and full tactical interoperability, including networking, which are currently not available. Perhaps, they could be developed in a Theatre Command environment. Apart from the practical and operational factors mentioned, it should be noted that the nature and intensity of future conflicts will demand the commitment of assets by IAF to numerous tasks, which include:[16]

- Nuclear second strike
- Acquiring a favourable air situation
- Counter-air operations
- Interdiction operations
- Providing battlefield air support to the Army
- Air-defence of the homeland

Given these constraints, and going by past precedent, it is considered extremely unlikely that the IAF will be willing or able to exclusively place a reasonably large force of Jaguars/Su-30s at the Navy's disposal for anti-shipping strikes.

CAN AIR POWER BE SHARED?

Air power has, unquestionably, become intrinsic to every form of military operations: on land, at sea or in the air. While 'indivisibility of airpower' may have been a good hypothetical construct in the past, it is no longer tenable today. In the current environment of fiscal stringency, far more pertinent is the question: how should airpower be deployed or shared to fulfill the vital operational needs of the Army, Navy and Air Force? The UK, an extremely cost-conscious country, has some lessons for us.

The utilisation of national air assets in UK have been impacted by the Royal Air Force description of airpower as: "Inherently joint, combined and multinational; drawn from all three Services; concerned with the effective exploitation of all air and space power assets; influenced by, and influences, the land and maritime environments." A direct outcome of this outlook has been the pooling of helicopters of all three services to form the Joint Helicopter Command (JHC). With nearly 300 helicopters flown and maintained by tri-Service crews, the JHC is commanded by two-star officers from the Navy, Army and the Air Force in rotation. It has seen successful operational deployments in Iraq and Afghanistan.

In the context of carriers, of even greater interest is the sterling example of 'jointness' demonstrated by the British services on board HMS *Queen Elizabeth* in 2021. The F-35B fighters embarked on board this ship belong to a Royal Air Force unit, No. 617 Squadron. The squadron is manned by a joint crew (including pilots) of RAF and RN personnel and, uniquely, the Commanding Officer of this RAF squadron is a Royal Navy officer.

Given its growing reach and strategic capabilities, which include long-range strike, aerial-refuelling and AWACS, the IAF has the potential to be a powerful ally with whom the IN must actively seek collaboration. This could be a good time for the two Services to get together and develop an Air-Sea Battle Doctrine that would create an effective airpower synergy between IN aircraft carriers and IAF shore-based units, rather than arguing about the "budgetary cake" and hardware.

CONCLUSION

When discussing aircraft carriers, the focus is mostly on their role in conflicts. However, it must be noted that these ships have an equally significant role to play in peacetime as well. Since peace, fortunately, prevails 99 per cent of the time, it is an indicator that deterrence is working. It is only when deterrence fails that war follows. While the 'survivability' of these ships, in a conflict, can be debated endlessly, it is considered that an attack on an aircraft-carrier would constitute a most serious provocation, and one that would be highly unlikely to be initiated by a belligerent nation, unless a major/global conflict is anticipated.

The value that a carrier brings to situations that require, 'maritime diplomacy,' 'presence,' 'show of force,' or 'humanitarian assistance and disaster relief,' has been mentioned. Countries, which have chosen to undertake large aircraft-carrier building programmes like China, have obviously taken account of the risks, vulnerability and costs of such ships, and concluded that the peacetime benefits outweigh wartime risks.

In the current Indian scenario, apart from the balance of forces on land/air, favouring China, there is also the Beijing-Islamabad Axis that awaits activation. Given the difficult situation confronting India on its northern borders, it is logical for decision-makers to explore possibilities in the maritime domain, where India is favourably placed and options exist, both for power-balancing via partnerships as well as direct action via naval deployments.[17]

Despite political indifference and parsimonious budgets, the IN has emerged as a compact yet professional and competent force. However, given China's maritime ambitions, economic strength and prodigious shipbuilding capacity, India will need to enhance its naval force levels significantly. While an 'arms race' is unthinkable, it is believed critical that one or more additional carriers are planned/budgeted in the near future if India is to compete with China in the maritime sector.

Editors Note: The views of the Indian Air Force on its ability to influence the maritime domain should not be construed as dissonance but as elements of a widespread debate on the role of airpower across the spectrum of conflict. Clearly, the best way forward is an informed debate on India's carrier dilemma which the Admiral has initiated with clarity and conviction.

NOTES

1 Larter, David B. "US Navy upgrades more ships for the F-35 as the future of carriers remains in flux", Defence News, https://www.defensenews.com/naval/2020/06/01/us-navy-upgrades-more-ships-for-the-f-35-as-the-future-of-carriers-remains-in-flux/.

2 Funaiole, Mathew P. "China's Third Aircraft Carrier Takes Shape", Centre for Strategic & International Studies, June 15, 2021, https://www.csis.org/analysis/chinas-third-aircraft-carrier-takes-shape. Accessed on June 24, 2021.

3 Storey, Ian. "Can the UK Achieve its Naval Ambitions in the Indo-Pacific?", *The Diplomat*, November 7, 2020, https://thediplomat.com/2020/11/can-the-uk-achieve-its-naval-ambitions-in-the-indo-pacific/

4 June 1, 2020. Accessed on July 5, 2021.

5 Indian Navy, *Ensuring Secure Seas: Indian Maritime Security Strategy* (New Delhi: IHQ MoD (Navy), 2015), p. 22.

6 *The New Indian Express*, February 17, 2020, https://www.newindianexpress.com/nation/2020/feb/17/approval-for-third-aircraft-carrier-may-not-come-soon-indicates-cds-rawat-2104718.html. Accessed on June 25, 2021.

7 *US Naval Aviation.* Goodspeed, M Hill, Editor. Naval Aviation Museum Foundation. 2001. Pensacola, Florida. p. 39.

8 Chang, Felix K. "Taking Flight: China, Japan & South Korea Get Aircraft Carriers", Foreign Policy Research Institute, January 14, 2021, https://www.fpri.org/article/2021/01/taking-flight-china-japan-and-south-korea-get-aircraft-carriers/. Accessed on June 28, 2021.

9 Goure, Dan. "Why the Age of the Aircraft Carrier Isn't Over Just Yet", Real Clear Defence. February 2021 at Why the Age of the Aircraft Carrier Isn't Over Just Yet, realcleardefense.com. Accessed on July 3, 2021.

10 Full Text: "China's Military Strategy (Xinhua)", May 26, 2015, http://en.people.cn/n/2015/0526/c90785-8897779.html. Accessed on June 28, 2021.

11 McDevitt, Michael, A. *China as a 21st Century Naval Power* (Annapolis: Naval Institute Press, 2020).

12 Robelin, Sebastien. "A2AD: The Phrase that Terrifies the US Military", The National Interest, April 9, 2019. Accessed on June 28, 2021, https://nationalinterest.org/blog/buzz/a2ad-phrase-terrifies-us-military-and-china-and-russia-love-it-51597

13 Naval War College Review, Summer 2014, Vol 67, No.3. Robert C Rubel. *Theory of Air Power*, pp. 64-65

14 X-47UCAS, https://www.northropgrumman.com/what-we-do/air/x-47b-ucas/. Accessed on June 26, 2021.

15 *India Today*, April 23, 2018, https://www.indiatoday.in/mail-today/story/iaf-hits-warships-in-deep-sea-carries-out-attacks-on-targets-1217937-2018-04-23. Accessed on July 5, 2020.

16 Prakash, Arun. "India's Maritime Air Power - Outlook for the 21st Century." *Naval War College Journal* Vol 32.

17 Prakash, Arun. "India must formally revive Quad, Seek its Expansion," *The Indian Express,* July 22, 2020.

CHAPTER 11

THE FUTURE OF UNDERSEA WARFARE IN THE 21ST CENTURY

P. ASHOKAN

ABSTRACT

With the advent of space-based surveillance and the growing maturity of long-range strike weapons such as the ASBM (Anti-Ship Ballistic Missile), the viability of establishing effective sea control when engaged in hostilities against a peer or near peer adversary is being questioned. What one is more likely to witness in the future is a battle focused on a contest for sea denial. Under such circumstances, the salience of submarines is destined to grow and it would be wise for a Navy to augment its undersea warfare capabilities. The Indian Navy has had the benefit of maintaining and operating submarines from three different countries of which two classes were constructed indigenously. However, the time has come to dispense with overseas dependency in most aspects of submarine design and construction. The Project 75 (I) under the Strategic Partnership model will be our last opportunity for transfer of comprehensive know-how and know-why in this vital field. There are several new technologies on the anvil that pertain to batteries, propulsion, communications, weapons and sensors. These are at various stages of development and must be studied and, where necessary, incorporated in our India's future submarine projects.

BACKGROUND

In today's world of extraordinary change, gazing into a crystal ball and attempting to make predictions is a risky enterprise. Nonetheless, it is a necessary exercise in order to be adept at confronting security challenges of the future. This is particularly true in the maritime domain, wherein the complexity of platforms and the gestation period to design and build them is measured in decades. The consequent agility to course-correct for emerging threats is low, not only due to financial and technical challenges, but also due to institutional challenges. Organisations and the people who make them commit considerable resources to bring a programme to fruition. It, therefore, becomes difficult to see this colossal effort come to naught due to emergent technological developments that change the fundamentals of the calculus on which the programme was authorised in the first place. Under such circumstances, the tendency is to defend the programme at all costs, clutching at what may even be disingenuous arguments that would not stand the scrutiny of a dispassionate audit. There are countless examples of this in naval history, the most obvious one being the downfall of the battleship—a class of ship that should have been put to rest possibly decades earlier but continued to find favour till the early years of World War II. It was only after the repeated sinking of these behemoths, which included much-glorified platforms such as the Hood, Prince of Wales, Bismarck and Tirpitz, and when not even a fig-leaf of cover remained to justify the monumental expense required to build, man and maintain such assets, did most navies dispense with them.

The corollary to this argument is that the more complex the procurement process is, the less is the motivation to course correct. Even though the arguments for change are clear, they must be weighed against the time, cost and effort required to abandon a course of action and migrate to another. The debate thus shifts to the acquisition of at least some capability, however circumspect, as against the prospect of having no accretion at all. The aforesaid issues are magnified exponentially in the area of underwater warfare as platforms in this domain are significantly more complicated than their surface counterparts. Given the limitations of internal volume, sensitivity to overall weight and its distribution, as well as design complexity, the margins available for change through their life cycle are small. As a result, it is imperative that considerable thought be given to such programmes at an early stage to ensure that the translation from investment to accomplishing national security goals is maximised. This chapter examines the development of undersea warfare and the submarine arm in the Indian Navy (IN) and ponders over its future.

GROWTH OF THE INDIAN SUBMARINE ARM

After the initial acquisition of the Foxtrot, HDW Type 209 and 877 EKM Kilo classes of conventional submarines, the Cabinet Committee of Security accorded approval-in-principle in 1999 for a 30-year Submarine Building Programme involving the construction of 24 submarines over a period of 30 years. This was to be executed in two phases, the first lasting from 2000 to 2012. During this phase, two production lines, Project 75 and 75(I), were to be set-up, one undertaking the licensed production of a single-hulled submarine design and the other for a double-hulled design. Each design was to produce six submarines. This would be followed by a thorough evaluation process in which the best features of each design were to be identified and adopted in the design of an indigenous submarine, 12 of which were planned to be constructed by 2030 under Phase 2 (Project 76).[1]

The contract for the first six submarines (Project 75) was signed in 2005 as part of this ambitious plan, and INS *Khanderi* was commissioned in 2017, five years later than originally planned. The next two submarines were commissioned in September 19 and March 21. The final instalment of this series is planned to be commissioned by 2025. An Acceptance of Necessity (AoN) was accorded by the MoD for the next line of six submarines under Project 75(I) in August 2010, with deliveries set to begin in 2020. Manohar Parrikar, the Defence Minister in 2014, strongly advocated the 'strategic partnership model' in four areas of military hardware, one of which was construction of submarines. The policy took three years to develop and was finally rolled out in June 2017. After considerable deliberation and consultation with stakeholders, Expressions of Interest (EoI) were issued to Indian Yards (the Strategic Partners (SP)) and the foreign OEMs in June and July 2019, respectively. Following a detailed examination of the bids, the MoD Empowered Committee shortlisted Mazagaon Docks Limited (MDL) and Larsen & Toubro (L&T) as SPs and five OEMs: Rubin Design Bureau (Russia), Thyssenkrupp Marine Systems (TKMS, Germany), Naval Group (France), Navantia (Spain) and Daewoo Shipping and Marine Engineering (DSME, South Korea). The RFP, which was supposed to be issued by end of 2020, was finally issued on July 20, 2021.[2] Because of the complexities involved in forming partnerships and making a combined bid, it is anticipated that the contract is unlikely to be concluded before 2024. Going by the thumb rule of about six years for construction (since the design is mature), the first of the class is likely to be delivered by 2030, and the last by 2040.

In 2018, the IN received two state-of-the-art air transportable Deep Submergence Rescue Vessel (DSRV) systems from Ms James Fisher Defence (JFD), ushering in a new era in Submarine Rescue Capability, not only for India but also for the Indian Ocean Region (IOR). With its induction, the Indian Navy has joined a small club of nations having this unique capability. The IN systems are the first third-generation system manufactured by JFD. The contract has also broken new ground in that it covers 'Life Cycle Maintenance and Support' by the OEM for the first time in the country for a period of 25 years. These systems provide the Indian Navy with a robust tool for extending defence diplomacy in the IOR and beyond; the recent MoU for mutual support in Submarine Rescue with Singapore being a pointer in this direction. It will pave the way for the Indian Navy to become a key member of the global submarine rescue fraternity.

INDIGENISATION

Following the induction of the Foxtrots in the 1960s, dormant plans for developing indigenous capabilities were resurrected. Officers undergoing post-graduate training on naval-architecture in the UK and the USSR were encouraged to take up submarine design projects. Meanwhile, during the INS *Khanderi's* Medium Repairs (MR), an unprecedented scale of Transfer of Technology (ToT) on hull and material issues was carried out.[3] It's also worth noting that IN explored indigenously building small submarines along the lines of the Leander Class frigate programme as early as the early 1960s. Discussions began with the famous German designer Dr Gabler, and inquiries were even made with the Swedes and Soviets. However, these could not be pursued due to a shortage of funds. Finally, in 1975, the Apex Defence Review approved the Navy's proposal for construction of submarines. After evaluating proposals from Germany, France, Sweden and Holland, a contract was signed with HDW in December 1981 for four submarines, two of which were to be built in Germany and two in India under ToT.[4]

THE HDW & SCORPENE EXPERIENCE

The HDW contract included a commitment for ToT on submarine construction and transfer of design 'know how' and 'know why' to the Submarine Design Bureau at NHQ. A multi-disciplinary design team of 25 design specialists received training in Germany and acquired the capability to design a single hull submarine. However, no training was imparted in the field of validation of design and linked hydro-dynamic model testing, both of which are critical to submarine construction. Another shortcoming was the non-availability of basic technical specifications of machinery, equipment and components which are essential for designing the various systems on board. In addition to these deficiencies, the utilisation of knowledge and expertise gained was derailed due to a financial scandal and the construction of the fifth and sixth submarines of the class (follow-ons to the two constructed earlier in MDL) was abandoned. Consequently, the skills acquired by MDL atrophied, and workers migrated in large numbers to other yards, including those in Korea. Fortunately, these events coincided with the emergence of the indigenous Advanced Technology Vessel (ATV) nuclear-powered submarine programme, and some of the expertise of the design team was preserved by deploying them on the ATV Programme. However, considerable reorientation had to be done as the strategic boats were of a double hull design.[5]

While the Scorpene contract between India and France for the design and manufacture of six submarines provided for the transfer of a comprehensive set of design know-how documents, access to the compendium of submarine equipment and component data/specifications was not supplied.[6] Consequently, the utility of the ToT has been somewhat limited. Thus, despite the initial progress made in the field of submarine design, Project 75 (I) will continue to depend on ToT from a foreign source. Considering the experience with the HDW and Scorpene contracts, the ToT for Project 75 (I) must have design collaboration with the parent Design Bureau in all disciplines, including systems design, design validation, hydro-dynamic/acoustic/shock/vibration modelling and complete access to design software transfer. The contract should also include access to the compendium of equipment and its specifications. The ToT gained from the collaboration should be shared with R&D establishments, industry and the academia to create an ecosystem for indigenous submarine construction. Training and excellence centres for submarine design at the platform and equipment level should be created, where stakeholders can be trained to upgrade technology and improve skill sets.

CONTRACTS AND EQUIPMENT

While weak contracts may be responsible for the current predicament, the Submarine Design Bureau also remains understaffed and is limited by HR policies in consolidating the expertise acquired while working on the three diverse designs. According to a RAND Corporation study on 'Sustaining

Design Capabilities for Future Projects', the average number of designers required to design a new submarine over a 15-year period is 800.[7]

The personnel assigned to the IN's Submarine Design Group are a fraction of this requirement. An added factor is the limited longevity of tenure. Officers assigned to a submarine design organisation should ideally have a long and stable tenure to see the design process through to fruition, which should take about eight to ten years. The Royal Navy learnt this the hard way during the *Astute* project, when it reduced the number of Royal Navy constructors in accordance with a policy of 'eyes on, hands off'.[8] This cost it dearly, and the decision was rescinded after the delayed delivery of the first three submarines. Given the scarcity of designers and the fact that long-term tenures will always be a cadre-management challenge, it is recommended that the Submarine Design Group undertake only the 'Concept and Preliminary Design', leaving the 'Detailed and Workshop Design' to the construction yard. Further, if it is challenging to assign many uniformed officers to submarine programmes, it would be worthwhile to revive the civilian cadre in submarine design and construction and gradually augment their numbers to meet today's increased requirements.

While India acquired ToT in submarine design at the platform level, there has been no similar transfer of technology in respect of submarine equipment. The requirements of miniaturisation, shock and vibration requirements, and environment specifications have presented a challenge for Indian industry to design and develop such equipment without assistance from OEMs. In the case of the ATV Programme, the pioneers had the wisdom to create the Defence Machinery Development Establishment (DMDE) in the mid-1980s to address this specific issue. The organisation was created to identify and tap the vendor base within the country to manufacture equipment as per the requirements of the platform designer. In the late 1980s, with work on the ATV programme yet to pick-up, recommendations were made to extend the scope of

DMDE to indigenise equipment and components required for the other submarines in commission at the time, i.e. Foxtrot, Kilo and 209 Classes. On security considerations, however, this was not agreed to. In retrospect, if the DMDE had started a parallel effort to build vendors for the conventional submarine fleet at the time, a flourishing ancillary industry would have been established by now.[9] Even before the establishment of DMDE, tentative steps could have been taken in the early 70s to reverse engineer Foxtrot class equipment. This was not pursued proactively, however, due to several reasons that included access restrictions to industry representatives and apprehensions related to copyright violations.

Notwithstanding the above, there have been some success stories. An early example was the indigenisation of submarine batteries, which replaced Russian batteries that were beset with problems related to excessive hydrogen evolution. Indian batteries built by Standard Batteries Ltd (subsequently acquired by Exide) have even been exported to Algeria and Vietnam. Panchendriya, an indigenous submarine sonar, and its successor Ushus have also performed well. In addition, several auxiliary equipment such as compressors, pumps, air conditioning plants, etc., have been indigenised. However, as several of these were reverse engineered from installed equipment without any design data and knowledge of material composition, it has been challenging for them to meet the performance specifications of the original equipment in terms of Noise Vibration (NV) characteristics, reliability, etc. Also lacking was the concept of systems engineering, in which all the equipment and components (made by different vendors) were seamlessly integrated into the system of which they were part. The level of indigenisation in conventional submarines has not progressed to major equipment such as the Diesel Generator or Main Propulsion Motors. Part of the reason is the procurement procedure, where OEMs are reluctant to invest into research on superior material and design facilities due to the small scale of requirements and lack of commitment for further orders. A beginning has been made in the strategic programme with the scaling up of indigenisation to the level of main propulsion turbine and other major equipment, but these are yet to translate into benefits for the conventional fleet.

FUTURE SUBMARINE TECHNOLOGY

Unmanned Undersea Vessels

The roles of submarines are evolving as a response to the ever-changing nature of maritime warfare, which is driven by the vagaries of geopolitics, economics and, most importantly, technology. While there are many types of unmanned vehicles at sea with different sizes, functions, methodology of launch and control, etc., weaponised submarine launched Unmanned Undersea Vessels (UUV) are best exemplified by the Snakehead which is launched from US Virginia Class SSNs and Ohio Class SSGNs. About 10 m in length and weighing about 2.4 tonnes, once its battery is charged by the mother submarine, it can operate autonomously for long durations. It is equipped with an ISR mast, hull mounted sensors which reportedly includes side scanning sonars, and is armed with torpedoes, missiles and decoys. It can be tasked for ISR, mine laying and clearing, scouting ahead of the submarine, anti-shipping, land attack, etc.[10] In fact, it can execute all the roles that a manned submarine can undertake. Such UUVs augment the capabilities of the mother platform by extending the zone of its influence into those areas where it may be risky for the mother platform to operate in. They also help in the conduct of concurrent operations at widely dispersed locations. Submarines can also carry smaller UUVs that can be launched from torpedo tubes and act as forward deployed off-board sensors that are remotely controlled from the mother submarine in much the same manner as is done for wire guided torpedoes. Future submarines are expected to serve as a host platform for a growing number of UUVs of varying dimensions and missions.

The development of contemporary Extra Large Unmanned Undersea Vessels (XLUUVs) is fast approaching the point where they will be capable of matching the performance of manned submarines and even posing a threat to them. The XLUUV Orca, for which the USN has placed orders in February 2019, is reportedly launched from the shore, can operate autonomously for about six months, has an endurance of 7500 NM and can dive to 300 m. It is stated to be able to traverse about 150-200 NM on batteries at a speed of 3 knots, after which it charges its batteries using its Diesel Generator (DG) and snorkel mast.[11] Its endurance in terms of the total deployment period and indiscretion rate is at par with most conventional submarines, though its payload is much smaller. Several XLUUVs, with payloads customised to meet the demands of the mission, can deliver better results at a lesser cost and with considerably lower risk, as compared to costly manned platforms. It is for this reason that most major navies are actively pursuing XLUUV programmes. During the annual parade held in Beijing on October 1, 2019, the Chinese unveiled the HSU 01 miniature submarine, a submersible measuring about 10 m in length and 2.5 m in diameter with twin propellers and two masts.[12]

The biggest limitation in autonomous UUV operations is the lack of reliable underwater communication at extended ranges, resulting in the absence of a human being in the decision chain. While problems related to collision avoidance can be resolved through the incorporation of robust AI algorithms that synthesise sensor data to effectively control the propulsion and control surfaces of the vessel, ceding control of weapon release is far more complex and is fraught with technical as well as ethical issues.

In April 2016, DRDO/NSTL developed a prototype AUV. In addition, NIOT has deployed a low cost AUV Samudra that undertakes deep-sea exploration based on pre-programmed inputs. Fitted with an on-board image processing unit, it can undertake path detection, obstacle avoidance and target identification while submerged.[13] While designing UUVs with autonomous propulsion and payloads (barring weapon release algorithms) is relatively easy, the most challenging aspect of submarine-launched UUVs is the recovery system. Unless the submarine has something like a large Dry Deck Shelter, launch and recovery would have to be done from either torpedo/missile tubes or tubes specifically designed for this purpose. The miniscule tolerances demand precise control of the UUVs while in the process of docking.

Propulsion

Modern day Air Independent Propulsion (AIP) systems can provide 15 to 20 days of dived endurance at low speeds, but must be replenished ashore after this resource is expended. Lithium Ion Batteries (LIIBs) have no such limitations. In sharp contrast to traditional Lead Acid Batteries, they have a much higher capacity (higher dived endurance), quick charging rate (less time snorkelling), can be discharged deeply without damaging the battery (extend underwater stay if tactical conditions don't permit charging) and a much longer service life. However, there are safety concerns due to the evolution of explosive gases and thermal runaway, which could be disastrous in the closed environs of a submarine.

Therefore, even though LIB technology has been in vogue for over two decades, the adoption for submarine application has been slow, with only the Japanese starting to use them on operational submarines. The Japanese Marine Self Defence Force (JMSDF) has fitted LIB in the 11th and 12th boats of the Soryu Class in March 2020 and March 2021 respectively and has removed the Stirling AIP in favour of an additional LIB bank.[14, 15] South Korea has reportedly started prototype development of a similar battery in September 2020, which will be installed in Batch II of the KSS-III submarine programme.[16]

The traditional propulsion method of a shaft and propeller has practically reached its limit of efficiency and reduction of cavitation noise. In most modern nuclear submarines, this has been replaced by a pump-jet that produces lesser cavitation and is consequentially more silent. The main drawback with the pump-jet is that it tends to be heavy and is therefore not conducive for installation on most conventional submarines. The Chinese claim to have developed a rim-driven propulsor where a shaftless rotor is driven directly by electromagnetic force, thereby dispensing with the shaft and gear box.[17]

With regards to prime-movers, the development of High Temperature Superconductivity Motors (HTSMs), with current carrying capacities of nearly 150 times that of traditional copper cables has enhanced the power to weight ratio of propulsion motor by several times.[18] While the HTSM is still in the research and development stage and many years away from operational exploitation, Permasyn motors, which are compact, silent and maintenance friendly, have made their debut in the Indian Navy in the Scorpene Class (Project 75) and are likely to remain the mainstay of future conventional submarines.

Communications

With the ever-growing need of submarines to be integrated with surface forces, there is a need to reduce latency with respect to communications to the barest minimum. While Very Low Frequency (VLF) and Buoyant Cable Antenna (BCA) antenna provide continuous communication capability at depth, there are operational limitations imposed by any streamed body. With the availability of Satellite Communication, submarines can come to periscope depth and exchange communications in seconds. The use of High Data Rate (HDR) antenna operating in the EHF range and capable of data transfer at the speeds in the order of Gbs/sec have cut short this exposure, even when large volumes of data need to be transmitted. Further, HDR antenna can lock on to a communication satellites and transmit point-to-point pencil beams thereby minimising the probability of interception/ interference.[19] Likewise, high endurance Expendable Communication Buoys with a communication link to the submarine either through optic fibre or acoustic means can enhance the capability of communication at depth.

Sensors

Wake detection systems have been in use in the Soviet Navy since the 1960s, where they were called *Sistema Obnarusheniya Kilvaternovo Sleda* and appear in literature with its Russian acronym (COKC).[20] Little is known regarding the employment of COKC as a sensor, similar to the Blue Green Laser, though the Russians used it successfully for homing torpedoes. While a wake homing torpedo can sense a wake and use it to home on to a ship up to three to four minutes after its transit, COKC can reportedly detect the wake of a ship for periods ranging from 30 minutes to several hours after it has passed through an area. The system is based on multiple technologies, including the differential temperatures caused by the discharge of warm water from the submarine's reactor cooling system or diesel cooling water in the case of conventional submarines. There are also reports that the system can detect radio nuclides left by nuclear submarines. There are reports that the Trafalgar Class SSNs of Royal Navy are also fitted with such systems.[21]

Weapons

The greatest threat to a submarine is from an airborne ASW platform, especially dunking helicopters, because the submarine previously had no self-protection capability against them. A Submarine Launched Anti-Aircraft Missile (SLAAM), similar to the Interactive Defence and Attack System for Submarines (IDAS) fitted on the German 212 class submarines, can launch small projectiles through torpedo tubes (4 per tube).[22] Modern submarine sonars can detect the presence of low-flying ASW aircraft and offer general direction and targeting information. The mere knowledge that such a system can be a deterrent to an airborne ASW platform that has been completely insulated from being targeted by a diving submarine.

CHANGING OPERATIONAL ENVIRONMENT

What are the parameters that should be carefully considered while undertaking an informed discussion on the future of undersea warfare? The underwater domain continues to remain considerably opaque. Apart from acoustics, sensing below the surface continues to remain a challenge. Approaches using novel techniques, such as Blue/Green lasers, have fallen short of expectations. Much newer methods of using quantum clocks to sense time dilations produced by the interaction of a submerged submarine with the earth's gravity field, as well as the use of super sensitive magnetometers based on SQUID (Superconducting Quantum Interference Device) technology, are still in their infancy. What has happened, however, is an explosive proliferation of acoustic sensors in the oceans. While these were initially based on fixed seabed arrays, such as the well-known SOSUS (Sound Surveillance System) installed in the GIUK (Greenland-Iceland-UK) gap, the focus is now shifting to mobile sensors, either using powered submersible ROVs (Remotely Operated Vehicles) or far simpler and inexpensive Sea-gliders that utilise rudimentary buoyancy engines to move from place to place. Data scooped up by their sensors are typically dumped in large processing centres ashore, which use all the tools available at their disposal to generate a comprehensive Underwater Domain Awareness (UDA) picture. However, the limitations of acoustic sensors in terms of range, classification ability, as well as ability to extract relevant data from an increasingly noisy ocean persist. Thus, improvements in ocean transparency are iterative and evolutionary in nature.

Unlike the undersea domain, major changes are currently underway insofar as the surface domain awareness is concerned. Space-based surveillance is expanding at an unprecedented rate, driven by reusability of rockets, miniaturisation and the increasing adoption of commercial technology in the manufacturing of satellites. Several constellations of satellites, have already started to be placed in orbit, albeit for communications and internet services at this juncture. A distributed surveillance architecture based on small satellites will profoundly impact sea-surface domain awareness, making hiding at sea impossible in the near future. Surface warfare will, therefore, shift from being a game of poker to a game of chess with complete positional disclosure of both parties being a planning assumption.

Along with this advancement is the maturation of long-range strike weapons, the most potent of which is the ASBM (Anti-Ship Ballistic

Missile). These have the potential of giving shore-based forces the ability to influence the maritime battle thousands of kilometres away from the coastline. The further development of ship- and air-launched ASBMs extends reach even more. While ship-borne missile defence capabilities may partially address this threat, the dice is loaded against the surface platform due to the finite number of weapons that can be carried, the cost difference between a ballistic warhead launched from a reusable rocket versus an expensive fully expendable BMD missile, and the fact that a ship must preserve its ability to float and move to continue to fight. One could even argue that, given the all-pervasive nature of the ASBM threat in a realm of assured sea surface domain awareness, the era of sea control may come to an end, with competing sea-denial dominating the nature of the battle at sea. As a result, one can anticipate that the importance of submarines as a weapon of war in any nation's military structure is only going to expand. This trend is evident in the growing number of submarine operating nations as well as the increasing submarine fleet strength of established submarine operating navies.

Given a long-range weapon and accurate targeting data, the launching platform does not need to travel vast distances to be effective. The weapon does that for you. This addresses the tyranny of distance that all conventional boats with their battery and speed limitations suffer from. Thus, although comprehensive battlefield transparency frees you of the requirement to operate within the radii of maritime reconnaissance aircraft or at choke points, enhanced weapon range frees you from the necessity to physically move a submarine close to its target to employ it effectively. Under such circumstances, the preferred area of submarine deployment would be mid-sea in deep waters. This has the added advantage of providing much greater sea room for manoeuvring, especially in places where the likelihood of encountering opposing forces is low.. Acting as concealed mobile missile batteries stationed mid-sea, conventional submarines will be able to influence the conduct of warfare at considerable distances from their patrol areas, a capability hitherto well beyond the reach of such platforms. Thus, while nuclear submarines will continue to have the advantage of rapid deployment at extended ranges and a prolonged endurance capability, conventional submarines will effectively complement them by increasing their lethality with long-range weapons that can be cued using space-based sensors.

CONCLUSION

Maritime combat capability changes can be classified as either evolutionary or revolutionary. What we have witnessed over the last few decades has essentially been evolutionary. Capabilities have obviously improved, but these have predominantly been iterative in nature. It is worth noting that, despite the evolutionary process, submarines have been successful in maintaining their salience as highly effective platforms for conducting maritime warfare. In fact, going by their increasing numbers, one could conclude that their relative salience has increased. With the increased vulnerability of surface platforms driven by assured domain awareness, as well as the increasing proliferation of long-range vectors, the advantages enjoyed by submarines are set to increase even more. Nations would be advised to continue investing in maintaining an effective fleet of submarines through timely acquisitions, planned refits, effective training and quality maintenance.

NOTES

1. Singh, Sushant, "Explained: India's submarine story in deep waters, long way to go." *The Indian Express*, November 13, 2015, https://indianexpress.com/article/explained/explained-indias-submarine-story-in-deep-waters-long-way-to-go/.
2. Siddiqui, Huma. "The wait for more submarines gets longer! Project 75 I gets delayed further." *Financial Express*, March 9, 2021, https://www.financialexpress.com/defence/the-wait-for-more-submarines-gets-longer-project-75-i-gets-delayed-further/2209149/
3. RAdm AP Revi, "India's indigenous submarine design dilemma," *Indian Defence Review*, Vol 27.3, Jul-Sep 2012, September 17, 2012, http://www.indiandefencereview.com/news/indias-indigenous-submarine/2/
4. VAdm GM Hiranandani, *Transition to Eminence*, p. 107.
5. Revi, n. 3

6. Ibid.
7. John F Schank, et al., "Sustaining US Nuclear Submarine Design Capabilities", RAND, National Defence Research Institute, p. 52.
8. John F Schank, et al., "Learning from experience, Volume III, Lessons from United Kingdom's Astute Submarine Program", RAND, National Defence Research Institute, p. 40.
9. Revi, n. 3.
10. Joseph Trevithick, "Snakehead will be the largest under water drone that the US nuclear submarines can deploy," *The War Zone*, December 28, 2020, https://www.thedrive.com/the-war-zone
11. https://www.globalsecurity.org/index.html, Orca Extra Large Unmanned Undersea Vehicles (XLUUVs)
12. H I Sutton, "China Navy Reveals New Large Underwater Robot Which Could Be A Game Changer," October 1, 2019, https://www.forbes.com/sites/hisutton/2019/10/01/china-reveals-new-robot-underwater-vehicle-hsu-001/?sh=cd21acd19910,
13. Singh Abhijit, "Future technologies for the Indian Navy," Observer Research Foundation, February 23, 2017, https://www.orfonline.org/expert-speak/future-technologies-for-the-indian-navy/
14. Mike Yeo, "Japan commissions its first submarine running on lithium-ion batteries," Defence News, March 6, 2020, https://www.defensenews.com/global/asia-pacific/2020/03/06/japan-commissions-its-first-submarine-running-on-lithium-ion-batteries/
15. Xavier Vavvaseur, "Japan Commissions Its 2nd Li-Ion Battery Submarine JS Tōryū," Naval News, March 24, 21, https://www.navalnews.com/naval-news/2021/03/japan-commissions-its-2nd-li-ion-battery-submarine-js-toryu「とうりゅう」/
16. Xavier Vavvaseur, "South Korea's DSME Launches 2nd KSS III Submarine For ROK Navy", Naval News, November 10, 2020, https://www.navalnews.com/naval-news/2020/11/south-koreas-dsme-launches-2nd-kss-iii-submarine-for-rok-navy/
17. Globe Composite Blog, "Is China taking the lead in submarine propulsion", https://www.globecomposite.com/blog/china-submarine-propulsion-technology
18. Power Bulletin, "Super conductor motor for Navy passes full power test", https://www.powermag.com/superconductor-motor-for-navy-passes-full-power-test/
19. Jacob Longacre, et al., "Voices From the Deep, The New Age of Submarine Communications" (based on an article by Frank Wolfe in Defense daily of July 21, 1998, https://fas.org/man/dod-101/sys/ship/docs/voices.htm
20. GlobalSecurity.org, "System of Detection of Wake", Sistema Obnarusheniya Kilvaternovo Sleda
21. Joseph Trevithik, "Royal Navy Sub Appears in Gibraltar with a Wake Detection System", *The Warzone*, May 8, 2019, https://www.thedrive.com/the-war-zone/27913/royal-navy-sub-appears-in-gibraltar-equipped-with-a-wake-detection-system
22. Thyssen Krup Marine Systems Brochure, "IDAS - Interactive Defense and Attack System for Submarines", https://www.thyssenkrupp-marinesystems.com/en/products-services/innovations/missile-system-idas

CHAPTER 12

THE ENDURING RELEVANCE OF OFFENSIVE AIRPOWER

DIPTENDU CHOUDHURY

ABSTRACT

Airpower is inherently offensive in nature, therefore, military aviation is largely associated with offensive airpower. Airpower, as the most recent type of military power, has had to work hard to establish its credibility not only as a potent military instrument, but also as a politico-diplomatic one in the larger national interest. Its global exploitation has depended on several variables that have been the subject of much debate. Nonetheless, there is no doubt about its ability to shape and produce military outcomes, at times, independently, or in collaboration with other instruments of force and statecraft. This chapter examines the Indian context, wherein despite a legacy of constrained usage, offensive airpower has always been a significant joint contributor towards a conventional deterrent capability. It has an equally significant role to play in India's future security challenges in the amorphous sub-conventional realm, and a vitally important role to play in India's future security contexts, by continuing to adopt threat-tailored technologies and adapting its application doctrines and strategies.

BACKGROUND

Offensive airpower is over a century old since the first use of aircraft for bombing at Ein Zara during the Italo-Turkish campaign in 1911. The Indian Air Force (IAF) is 89 years old and has eighty-four years of experience in conducting offensive air operations since its inception as an independent Air Force in 1932 as a result of the enactment of Clause 4 of the Annual Army and Air Force Bill, and its first offensive action in Waziristan in 1937.[2] The IAF has been relentless in its offensive commitment since its fledgling years in the North-West Frontier Province (NWFP), through the Burma Campaign and all the post-independence wars it has participated in, with the exception of the defining 1962 war with China. Yet, offensive airpower is not fully understood and is underappreciated even today within India's strategic community. Some responsibility for this lies with early airpower theorists and experts, as they were caught up in the revolutionary 'what it achieved' and 'could do' in the world wars and the subsequent conflicts across the globe, and were thus blind to what it 'could not'. To posit that victory could be achieved exclusively through the third dimension was an overreach, but the lesson that victory could no longer be achieved in the other two dimensions without it, was undeniable.

When Air Commodore Jasjit Singh, the doyen of Indian airpower, wrote, "dynamics of air warfare revolves around its offensive capability,"[3] he was referring to the historically demonstrated role that airpower has played in all significant wars. Though its offensive use was peripheral in WWI, it was not only dominating in WWII, but the outcome of the war, as argued by Air Marshal Tony Mason, may have been different without the Strategic Bombing Offensive.[4] While the targeting of enemy industries, and communications, undoubtedly created strategic effects, the bombardment of cities as a strategy to target enemy 'morale' and create 'terror', set off a firestorm of debates, as 'civilians living in London, Hamburg, Osaka or Chunking—proved to be surprisingly tough animals'.[5] Post WWII, despite the continued bomber dominance of the US Strategic Air Command through the Cold War, strategic bombing proved to be a failure in Vietnam.[6] Airpower's fighter-centric offensive capability in the Gulf War, with more than 116,000 combat sorties, 88,500 tonnes of weapons over six weeks, which reduced the ground offensive to a mere 100 hours,[7] with a loss of 147 personnel,[8] was a new benchmark for offensive airpower. It was a watershed moment for China's leadership to reorganise and modernise the PLA Air Force (PLAAF), based on contemporary Chinese doctrinal precepts and airpower lessons of the Gulf War.[9]

A PAST OF ESCALATORY RESTRAINT

Since WWII, the offensive use of airpower has ranged from significant in Korea and Vietnam, to decisive in the four Arab Israeli Wars between 1967 and 1982, underscoring that 'airpower has not lost its unmatched ability to project national power in short times over long distances'.[10] Contrarily, in the Indian subcontinent the narrative has been significantly different with airpower being inhibited in its employment during all wars except the 1971 India-Pakistan war. The traditional perception of airpower's escalatory nature, in which the IAF involvement implied ratcheting up the scale of conflict in the escalatory ladder, merits closer examination to arrive at a broader understanding of India's experience with the employment of offensive airpower as a potent instrument of war fighting and statecraft.

In the first Indo-Pakistan war of 1947–48, the British Commander in Chief, who was also the defence minister, and the three British Service Chiefs, keen to include both nations into the Commonwealth, were desperate to avoid an escalation into an all-out war.[11] They were successful in inhibiting the role of the IAF and preventing its participation in full strength,[12] despite the conviction and eagerness of the Indian political leadership and senior IAF officers to do so.[13] Similarly, in 1962, the utilisation of offensive airpower was eschewed due to a misplaced apprehension of escalation and retaliatory Chinese bombing of Indian cities.[14] This perception was an outcome of the Intelligence Bureau's inaccurate assessment of PLAAF capabilities,[15] a lack of assertive IAF views on the payoffs of offensive airpower, and efforts by John Kenneth Galbraith, the US ambassador to India, to influence PM Nehru.[16] He wrote in his journal—*'I had stopped the Indians from employing their airpower because it would either have committed us back to their defences or forced us to refuse to do so and that either decision would have been equally unfortunate.'*[17] This concern persisted into 1965, when the IAF was again prevented from conducting offensive operations on the Eastern front in order to prevent an escalation and possible Chinese involvement. The fear regarding bombing of cities was evidently still in the minds of the political leadership, as shared by the PM with the IAF Air Chief when the latter advised the unfettered use of airpower against Pakistan.[18]

India's traditional escalatory concerns over the use of offensive airpower were disproved in the run-up to the1971 war when repeated Pakistani air attacks on units of the Indian Army, which were engaged in preliminary intrusions into East Pakistan, resulted in two PAF Sabres being shot down by IAF Gnats in November over Boyra, well before war was officially declared. Following the aerial confrontation over Boyra, there was no escalation as India still did not commence[19] offensive action. Even the PAF pre-emptive strikes on December 3, 1971, which coincided with the Pakistan's ground offensive, merely triggered the inevitable war and did not escalate it. In a nuclear scenario, Kargil adequately displayed that offensive air action could be used with the escalatory control of not crossing the LoC. Manpreet Sethi avers that the IAF's peace time air strike in 2019 at Balakot, bust the myth of its 'necessarily escalatory nature'.[20]

OFFENSIVE AIR POWER IN THE CONVENTIONAL REALM

A Historical Perspective

The 1965 war marked the first time the IAF was able to leverage its offensive capabilities in operations other than support for ground forces. However, the political concerns of Chinese intervention forced it to keep almost half its assets deployed in the East, and it was also initially constrained from attacking PAF airfields. Despite the harsh lessons of 1962, joint planning was practically non-existent, and the Army-AF mechanism for Close Air Support (CAS) was at best nascent. On September 1, 1965, the Army Chief brought the Air Chief on board for the first time with an urgent request for air support,[21] eleven days after the Defence Secretary had conveyed the Cabinet's approval for all elements of military power to be used on August 20, 1965.[22] The IAF launched its first strike against the enemy thrust within 29 minutes of the Army Chief's request. Out of a total of 3937 sorties flown by the IAF in the 1965 war, approximately 2,500 were offensive missions, of which 1,400 were dedicated to Counter Surface Force Operations (CSFO).[23]

The 1971 war was an excellent example of joint-services cooperation and harmony, with adequate time for planning and preparation, thanks to General Sam Manekshaw's foresight and his camaraderie with his fellow service chiefs. In conventional conflicts, offensive airpower has been able to produce a wide range of targeting effects across the strategic, operational and tactical realms by parallel and simultaneous application. The IAF's offensive strategy in 1971, led by Air Chief Marshal PC Lal, hailed the IAF's coming of age, from strategic targeting that impacted the adversary's key centres of gravity, to engagement with 'target systems' like 'energy systems' or the 'communication and transport network systems'. A majority of air operations were flown towards offensive strikes, interdiction and CSFO, in the direct and indirect support of surface operations.

Of the total 6,604 combat sorties, 61 per cent were offensive missions, while 35 per cent were dedicated to Air Defence (AD). A total of 3120 sorties were allocated to CSFO between the Western and the Eastern theatres. This included air interdiction, the unsung hero of offensive airpower. In the East—"*a little over two-thirds of IAFs air effort was in direct support of the Indian Army in the land battle*",[24] which was able to severely disrupt the road, rail and waterways networks, over and above counterforce targets. In the Western sector, "*Its long-range interdiction cut down Pakistan's ability to reinforce battle areas*"[25] with systematic attacks on road and railway networks, ammunition and fuel dumps and key bridges. Strategic targeting impacted the fuel supplies and power generation capacity—"*its fuel supplies became extremely scarce and fuel had to be imported in tankers by road from Iran.*"[26] While several targeting strategies that were successful in 1971 remain an integral part of the IAF's offensive philosophy, their importance has faded away while planning and discussing joint operations in a contemporary conflict milieu. This was evident almost three decades later in the Kargil War, wherein the IAF was again restricted in its operations, with the strict mandate of not crossing the LoC. This limiting of unfettered offensive airpower narrows or restricts the scope and range of kinetic applications. The fifty-year hiatus since the last full-fledged use of airpower in conflict has also largely been responsible for the diminished awareness of its major offensive capabilities and roles beyond those that fall in the realm of CSFO. Unfortunately, an awareness of the long-term debilitating effects of strategic targeting on an adversary that offensive airpower can achieve, as demonstrated by Lal's target system strategy in 1971, has slipped into distant memory.

Limited Wars – Offensive Concentration

During the Kargil Conflict, the political mandate of not violating the LoC restricted the range of offensive options and tactics. Consider the effects of allowing the IAF to interdict logistic nodes, supply lines and approaches to enemy-held positions along the Kargil heights across the LoC. The IAF swiftly adapted to the limited war template with restrictive offensive options and flew 7,631 sorties[27] in six weeks, in what was the world's first ever use of combat airpower at altitudes above 15,000 feet.[28] However, this should not be used as a benchmark for the future, as an unrestricted offensive employment may have produced better strategic outcomes through greater attrition inflicted on the enemy's local deployments, while also exposing the Pakistan Army's deniability bluff that it was not involved in the occupation of the Kargil heights.

Offensive airpower is at that heart of decisive and outcome-driven options offered by air forces across the world to policy makers. As Phillip Mellinger posits—*"the adage, 'the best defense is a good offense,' is almost always true in air war."*[29] The IAF's warfighting repertoire and concepts of operations have long been focussed and dedicated to joint operations and the achievement of the larger military objectives. While some portion of its offensive targeting includes strategic centres of gravity, much of it is dedicated to hitting target systems that comprise fielded forces in depth, reserves, fuel, ammunition and logistics nodes—these directly and indirectly enable both the Army and the Navy's operations. It should be noted that this extensive offensive targeting by the AF is over and above the dedicated battle field strikes and interdictions that it conducts over the tactical battle areas (TBA) as a part of its counter surface force operations.

Exercise Gaganshakti, conducted by the IAF in 2018, projected its future outlook of short and intense limited wars. Over 5,000 sorties were flown in the first three days and over 11,000 sorties overall (including 9,000 by its fighters) in 13 days.[30] This was followed with Exercise Vayu Shakti in 2019, which exclusively showcased its full-spectrum strike capabilities by day and night. A comparison of this volume of effort with the total sorties flown in the 1971 War and the Kargil Conflict in 1999, showcases a wide range of offensive capabilities, which included the grey zone, combat persistence and high intensity of operations, underscoring the IAF's offensive commitment. What is not commonly known is that in the IAF Doctrine, the chapter on Joint Operations is an entire one with CSFO occupying the largest section in the chapter on Air Campaigns, and combat enabling operations for surface forces having the largest section in the Combat Enabling Campaign chapter.[31] Yet concerns regarding the IAF's commitment to joint warfare persist within the Army and the Navy.

The Inseparable Twins

Perhaps the greatest misperceptions about offensive airpower among many practitioners, policy makers, the strategic community and the media is the role of role of Air Defence (AD), which is viewed from a narrow perspective of defending airspace rather than its much larger intrinsic linkage with offensive operations. Since offensive airpower cannot ensure immunity from enemy air action, it must necessarily be backed up with AD. The inseparable and dominant aspect that AD plays in all offensive airpower roles, particularly against adversaries with strong air forces, merits serious consideration in all employment of the military instrument of power. After the harsh lesson of losing a large number of aircraft to the initial PAF pre-emptive strikes in 1965, AD was vital for IAF bases. To deny enemy air interference against IA's surface operations, significant AD air effort was flown in all wars over the TBAs. Today, under AWACS cover, air superiority fighters armed with active beyond visual range missiles carry out offensive AD missions over the adversary's territory. They are vital for our Offensive/Defensive Counter Air (OCA/DCA) operations, and CSFO missions against the enemy. In addition to the dedicated TBA Combat Air Patrols (CAPs), DCA missions also provide AD of TBAs. Even during the Kargil conflict, since F-16s had been deployed at Skardu airfield, extensive AD cover was provided to the IAF's offensive missions[32] for two reasons: to deny the PAF any opportunity to interfere with the Indian Army's surface operations using stand-off weapons from across the LoC, and to allow the freedom of IAF air operations. From a joint perspective, the absence of enemy air, and the consequent freedom of surface and air operations enabled by AD missions, was an unappreciated lesson. Since both India's adversaries possess strong air forces, AD will remain the inseparable twin for offensive operations.

A Conventional Deterrent

What many will have missed in the recent swift and extensive IAF activation in the Ladakh region is the intent to undertake all operational tasks and provide support to the entire range of military operations anticipated in a possible high altitude conflict with China.[33] Every

AD, offensive air power and combat support lesson from the Kargil Conflict was addressed during this activation and the deployment has been a deterrent display of high-altitude offensive airpower capability, which would not have been possible without the political signalling of a commitment to use it if necessary. It has enabled significant escalation control and imposed strategic restraint on the adversary.

There is no doubt that China will do all it can to develop its airpower capability in the region in the long run. With the PLAAF's present limitations in the Tibet Autonomous Region (TAR) attributable to issues such as altitude of airfields, the IAF could use this to its advantage to achieve air superiority/favourable air situation in a limited battle zone. The IAF's strategic agility, its dynamic concept of operations and tactics, and the vast combat experience gained in high altitudes during Kargil will work in its favour. Given the challenges of the terrain, a conflict in the region will be an air interdiction driven joint counter surface force operation, where offensive airpower will play a critical role.

Offensive air defence and destruction of enemy AD will dynamically create the necessary favourable air situations to enable precision strikes and interdictions in support of the surface battle. The IAF's advantage of low-altitude bases permits the launch of heavily armed strikes, thus enabling greater weight of attack. The number of its bases and aircraft allow greater combat persistence, higher and swifter turnaround options between missions, greater tactical deployment options and most significantly, a 24x7 day-night operational capability. For now, the IAF retains the advantage, as strategic security compulsions of China's Eastern seaboard, combined with the current capacity limitations of the PLAAF, preclude a simultaneous two-front deployment in TAR. The IAF's offensive and AD umbrella in the region provides the deterrent intent to wrest an invaluable asymmetric advantage in synergy with IA's surface operations, which the adversary is acutely aware of and concerned about. However, it is already working to address this strategic shortcoming. The changed dynamics in the region, and

China's consistent non-adherence to normative border management mechanisms, mean that the IA will have its task cut out, as it can no longer continue with its seasonal manning. With deterrence building in the North and the East continuing to be a security priority of the future,[34] it cannot be limited to a continental perspective. With the Indian Navy willing to 'go into harm's way' to protect the nation, as averred by the Naval Chief Admiral Karambir Singh,[35] deterrence must be comprehensive. Credible offensive airpower will become increasingly critical as India seeks to limit the growing multi-domain asymmetry with its northern adversary.

OFFENSIVE AIR POWER IN THE SUB-CONVENTIONAL AND GREY ZONE REALM

Changed Outlook

The IAF crossed a significant Rubicon in the realm of airpower as an instrument of statecraft at 0345 H on the February 26, 2019, when Indian fighters entered Pakistani airspace for the first time since the 1971 conflict to strike a Jaish-e-Mohammad (JeM) training camp.[36] For the first time a border was crossed in peace time to strike a target well inside the sovereign territory of a nuclear armed adversary, not for a military objective but for a political one. The offensive use of airpower in a sub-conventional context sent a coercive political message, implying that any unacceptable act of terror on Indian soil would invite swift and lethal retribution. With this, India joined an exclusive club of very few countries that have utilised offensive airpower as an instrument of coercion in a less-than-war situation, heralding a paradigm shift in India's response strategies to provocation by Pakistan.[37] Though executed for the first time in 2019, similar strikes were considered in 2001 after the Parliament attack, and again in 2008 in the aftermath of the Mumbai attack. Punitive air strikes officially became a part of the lexicon in the IAF's sub-conventional warfare doctrine in 2012, and have offered options for exercising asymmetric conventional deterrence in a no-peace-no-war situation.

The preponderant focus on economic growth and development, as well as globalisation, has diminished the appetite for conventional full-scale wars between nation-states. This has made room for the grey-zone-hybrid-sub-conventional warfare paradigm warfare that is kept below the threshold of escalation to direct military action. Though state behaviour has essentially remained stable, non-state actors are not restricted by normative behaviour and have expanded the range of their capabilities to upset status quo and unsettle the established global order. With adversaries now having entered civilian spaces, the offensive use of airpower must be regarded not just in the conventional context, but a sub-conventional one as well. Military institutions are no longer the fortresses they once were, as they are vulnerable to both kinetic hard-kill threats and soft-kill measures dispensed by adversaries they were not trained to fight. The face of war has truly become indistinct![38] The biggest challenge of grey zone threats is that they tend to blur the military and civilian domains. Therefore, threat response and mitigation no longer remain within the responsibility, domain or even capability of a single service or agency. They demand multi-service/agency approaches with flatter operational chains. Given the increased civilian risk factors, political decision making and clearances remain a challenge. The role of offensive airpower in grey zone warfare in the Indian context will depend much on these future trends and the ability of policy makers to understand airpower better.

Grey-Zone Dynamics

The use of offensive airpower in internal security and Counter-insurgency (CI) operations within the geographical confines of the Indian state has been steadfastly eschewed by the Indian government, since its use in North East Frontier Agency, Nagaland and Mizoram in the 1960s.[39] After a Maoist attack killed 76 CRPF members in 2010, the Government had contemplated use of offensive airpower. Air Chief Marshal P.V. Naik, the IAF chief at the time had stated in an interview that *"the military was trained to inflict maximum lethality"* and *"are not trained for limited lethality,"* and that the IAF would join the operations against the Naxals if a decision was taken.[40] While he drew unfair criticism, the point that the lethality of kinetic airpower limits its utilisation due to the degree of destruction and the possibility of collateral damage to innocent civilians was not lost on the government, which restricted airpower to non-kinetic roles only. There was also the aspect that such employment would be an acknowledgement of the prowess and reach of the Naxalites.

Offensive airpower has been extensively used against Islamist factions, insurgents, rebel groups and terrorist elements in urban and non-urban environments, by the US, Russia, Israel, the Saudi led Arab coalition and Turkey. Air strikes have been increasingly used in conflicts as a convenient kinetic option in support of state and non-state actors, often without committing boots on ground. The regional challenges and high likelihood of continued sub-conventional threats arising from the 'Talibanisation' of Afghanistan, may make use of offensive airpower an unavoidable politico-security necessity in the future. In such a case, some key takeaways from across the world are relevant:

- Fighters remain desirable for use due to their weapon choice, active control, and tactical flexibility. While high speed is a disadvantage for target acquisition, low speeds put aircrew and aircraft at risk as there have been fighter losses to shoulder fired SAMs. Keeping out of the lethal envelopes, however, reduces accuracy and has led to high collateral losses to civilians in limited conflicts like Syria, Yemen.
- Helicopters are slower and provide greater tactical flexibility, particularly in operations in conjunction with Special Forces. Their use in Afghanistan and Iraq highlighted the vulnerability to high calibre machineguns and SAMs, which was compounded by unfavourable terrain like mountains and urban zones, where traditional detection and countermeasures proved ineffective due to low altitudes and dispersion of threats.[41] The Soviets lost 333 helicopters in Afghanistan to anti-aircraft guns and shoulder

fired SAMs,[42] and the more recent losses in Syria underscores their vulnerability. IAF helicopters have been hit on numerous occasions during anti-Naxalite operations, but constrained offensively by strict rules of engagement.

- Intelligence, Surveillance and Reconnaissance (ISR) is a vital aspect of grey zone operations in order to search, find, fix and engage targets. Given the terrain, high mobility of hostiles, dispersed operations and their ability to merge with innocent civilian population, real time ISR is a critical pre-requisite.[43] In urban zones, this becomes critical to prevent civilian collateral/fratricide especially when the hostiles use them as cover or human shields.
- Use of armed Remotely Piloted Aircraft (RPA) are an increasingly popular trend. Today there over 36 countries which have armed drones,[44] 10 are developing them and 12 have carried out drone strikes. There are also 10 non-state actors which have armed drones, including the Hezbollah, ISIL, Boko Haram, Houthi rebels, South American drug cartels, etc. In a recent webinar, Air Chief Marshal RKS Bhadauria discussed how the low cost and easy availability of simple disruptive technologies like drones with small state and non-state actors have made them lethal, agile and capable of disproportionate effects.[45] The use of drones by several terrorist groups and the ISI, for arms trafficking in Punjab and J&K are on the rise with upgraded versions with higher payloads, and can easily be adapted for weapon delivery. Offensive use of swarm drones has already heralded its arrival in targeting Russian bases in Syria and the Aramco oil facilities in Saudi Arabia.
- In grey-zone operations, airpower provides a range of viable options based on the desired end state, degree of lethality, extent of acceptability of collateral damage, and political will. Once these are clear, the extent of multi-agency integration needed, the choice of platform, weapons and tactics to be used to counter the threat scenario, and, most importantly, the real time

ISR requirements, are best left to the practitioners.

THE FUTURE CONTEXT

What are the functions and missions of offensive airpower from an Indian perspective that could impact the course of future conflicts across the spectrum? Five wars, two collusive strategic partners as neighbours, 6,917 km of hostile land borders and an increasingly contested Indian Ocean Region (IOR), ensures that conventional conflict retains its pole position in the panoply of security threats that India is likely to face in the near future. Since future conventional conflicts in India's contested neighbourhood would occur under a nuclear overhang, they are likely to be short, swift and intense. Consequently, their limited outcomes will be dictated by which belligerent is able to drive speedier operational outcomes that could possibly result in advantageous strategic outcomes. Offensive airpower will unarguably emerge as a decisive instrument that could precipitate such outcomes because of its inherent characteristics of speed, reach, flexibility and precision. These could cause serious degradation of an adversary's combat potential and cause disproportionate psychological effects, all of which will impact outcomes. While it may not significantly alter adversary state behaviour, the willingness to use airpower will possibly continue to serve as a restraining factor in state sponsored sub-conventional actions as evidenced by tempo of Pak-sponsored terrorist activity in J&K after the Balakot strikes.

The IAF's offensive capabilities will need to be doctrinally and strategically geared for the two vastly different realms of conflict. The collusive-conventional scenario will need the robust twins-offensive strike capability and offensive AD to produce decisive outcomes. Long-range weapons for stand-off precision targeting, electronic advantage, space and net-centric ISR support and offensive air dominance are mandatory prerequisites. Joint planning and synergised execution will be precursors to execution, while surprise, deception, training and tactics will prevail.

While in the realm of conventional conflict, strategies and tactics of offensive air employment are well established in the IAF, the same cannot be said about doctrinal and operational precepts to counter grey zone threats. In the words of Wylie—*'But planning for certitude is the greatest of all military mistakes, as military history demonstrates all too vividly.'*[46] For the elusive grey zone threats, a wide basket of conventional, sub-conventional and mission support capabilities, whether in service, inter-service or interagency, will need to be exploited asymmetrically with adaptable tactics and agility of response, to produce desired outcomes. Offensive applications will vary, contrary to the convenient 'one size fits all' perception of use of airpower by non-practitioners.

Without delving into the fixed wing versus rotary wing issue, the growing desire of surface forces to deploy helicopters for offensive airpower in conventional combat should be viewed with caution. Helicopters have a very high vulnerability to ground fire and MANPADS in conventional conflicts. The failed US attack helicopter strike in Medina, Iraq in 2003, where one AH-64 Apache, out of 30, was shot down and 29 were heavily damaged, changed the US Army Aviation's employment philosophy, limiting further missions to close support. Such operations were best conducted in close coordination with support systems, intelligence and jamming, and under air dominance conditions,[47] a situation that the IAF may not have luxury of operating within. On the other hand, helicopters provide more tactical options in the sub-conventional operations than fighter aircraft, particularly in benign AD environments. Therefore, both offer offensive utilisation options and must be exploited to their full potential. Armed RPAs, while appealing, are not a replacement for manned platforms, and their applications in a disputed aerial environment are restricted. According to John F. Lehman, *"We do not need large numbers of exquisite platforms, such as the MQ-9 and RQ-4, to deliver the ISR and strike needs of counter-insurgency."* The Pentagon is considering a major reduction of the USAF's RQ-4 Global Hawk fleet due to its vulnerability to SAMs.[48] Cheaper and expendable commercial RPAs tailored for offensive missions provide greater future employability options.

Advanced active and passive sensors, precision guided munitions, multi-spectral designation and targeting pods, offensive and defensive EW capabilities, data-linked networks, and ISR fusion are a standard fit in contemporary offensive air operations. However, these come at prohibitive costs and need to be carefully calibrated in the light of the emergence of advanced disruptive technologies like artificial intelligence, robotics, quantum tech, space and cyber capabilities, nano technology, directed energy weapons, hypersonic weapons and platforms, all of which could have immense scope of applications in offensive airpower. General M.M. Naravne, India's Army Chief recently exhorted the nation's armed forces *"to pay adequate emphasis on the available disruptive technologies that have dual use and are being driven by commercial entities and innovations"* adapted into the Indian context.[49] However, there is a catch. The sheer allure of advanced technologies makes it very easy for the military to get 'swept away' with their future prospects. They are expensive, research intensive, are works in progress, have niche limited applications, and not an end in themselves. Most importantly they have a limited shelf life, till the 'counter' is produced or the 'next one' comes along. The IAF would be wise to recall that, given their costs, they should be cherry picked to suit future roles, applications and strengthen core competencies, amidst competing budgetary demands.

CONCLUDING THOUGHTS

Martin Van Creveld, an airpower sceptic, emphatically declared a decade and half ago that there probably would not be any airpower by 2020, citing the argument that inventories would be reduced due to wear and tear rather than combat.[50] Lawrence Freedman counters Creveld by arguing that *"the real argument to be made is about the declining utility of all types of military power"* and yet *"few commanders would wish to fight their land wars without air superiority."* [51] While the IAF's inventory of offensive assets has hit an all-time low, there is a realisation within India's strategic establishment that this free-fall must be checked. The rapid advancements of the PLAAF recently prompted the USAF Chief of Staff Gen. Mark Welsh to caution the House Appropriations Committee in 2016, that China's aircraft numbers would be as big, if not bigger than, the US by 2030.[52] With the increase in China's military cooperation, the PAF too can be expected to improve and expand its inventory beyond the JF 17 Block III with the J 11B, which is the Chinese version of SU 27, and possibly the export version of the FC 31 stealth fighter. Thus, from a future security perspective, speedy restoration of the IAF's combat bench strength needs no reiteration.

Offensive airpower is thus a future military necessity, whether used collaboratively in the continental or maritime realms, or as an independent hard power instrument in the wider national interest. After shedding the shibboleths of its escalatory nature, a much wider view and assessment of extensive offensive targeting undertaken in the wars of the past needs to be taken from a holistic and strategic military perspective. This will enable a greater understanding of its salience and continued relevance in a conventional security framework. A closer examination and analysis of the IAF's extant offensive targeting philosophy and concept of operations will lead to a greater appreciation of its joint warfighting credentials and commitment. But this is not enough. The IAF has to widen its offensive repertoire to stay ahead of the sub-conventional grey zone challenges and threats. Future amorphous threats will necessitate the leveraging of all options including offensive airpower, collectively or selectively. Use of offensive airpower outside the military domains comes with its red lines and often-narrow exploitation constraints. It needs agile tactics, out-of-the-box approaches and the ability to plug and play with other services, forces and agencies, to produced tailored outcomes. This is an area where not only the IAF, but the entire security system has a lot of work to do. It will need to plan, invest and absorb cutting-edge technologies tailored to suit India's future requirements. Considering that the conventional and expanded hybrid threats are a future reality, IAF's offensive airpower will have to stay ahead of the curve by adapting its doctrines and strategies to safeguard the national goals and security interests.

NOTES

1 http://hansard.millbanksystems.com/commons/1933/apr/03/clause-4-relations-between-royal-air

2 Pushpindar Singh, *Himalayan Eagles Volume I*, The Society for Aerospace Studies, New Delhi, 2007, p. 45.

3 Air Commodore Jasjit Singh, *Air Power in Modern Warfare* (New Delhi: Lancer International,1985), p. 19.

4 Air Vice Marshal Tony Mason, *Air Power: A Centennial Appraisal* (Brassey's (UK) Ltd, 1994), p. 60.

5 Lee Kennet, Ed. R. Cargill Hall, Special Studies, "Air Force History and Museums Program", 1998, p. 629.

6 Mark Clodfelter, *The Limits of Air Power: The American Bombing of North Vietnam* (New York: Free Press, 1989).

7 Eliot A. Cohen, "Gulf Air War Survey," 1993, https://media.defense.gov/2010/Sep/27/2001329802/-1/-1/0/AFD-100927-062.pdf. Accessed on April 2, 2021.

8 https://dcas.dmdc.osd.mil/dcas/pages/report_gulf_storm.xhtml. Accessed on April 2, 2021.

9 Diptendu Choudhury (2020) "Expanding Role of PLAAF in China's National Security Strategy", *Strategic Analysis*, 44:6, 521-41.

10 Shmuel L. Gordon, *Air Superiority in the Arab-Israeli Wars 1967-1982, A History of Air Warfare*, (ed.), John Andreas Olsen (New Delhi: Vij Books), p. 155.

11 Srinath Raghavan, *War and Peace in Modern India* (Ranikhet: Permanent Black, 2010), p. 125.

12 Jasjit Singh, *Defence from the Skies* (New Delhi: KW Publishers, 2013), p. 55.

13 Dr Sudhir S. Bloeria, *The Battles of Zojila, 1948* (New Delhi: Har-Anand Publications Pvt. Ltd., 1997), p. 220.

14 Singh, n. 12, p. 94.

15 B N Mullik, *My Years with Nehru: The Chinese Betrayal* (New Delhi: Allied Publishers Pvt Ltd., 1971), pp. 350-1.

16 JK Galbraith, *Ambassador's Journal, A Personal Account of the Kennedy Years* (Boston: Houghton Mifflin Co. Ltd., 1969), p. 487-509.

17 Ibid. Journal entry dated December 6, 1962.

18 Air Commodore Jasjit Singh, AVSM, VrC VM (Retd), *The Icon, Marshal of the Indian Air Force, An Authorised Biography* (New Delhi: KW Publishers, 2011), pp. 152-4.

19 Lal, Op Cit, pp. 154-5.

20 Manpreet Sethi, Op. Cit., p. 175.

21 RD Pradhan, *1965 War the Untold Story* (New Delhi: Atlantic Publishers, New Delhi, 2007), p. 22.

22 Singh, n. 12, pp. 123-4.

23 The number of sorties has been extrapolated from MOD's Official History of the 1965 War by BC Chakravorty, edited by SN Prasad, 1992; Jasjit Singh's *The Icon* (New Delhi: KW Publishers, 2011), pp. 219-76; Air Vice Marshal AK Tiwary, *Indian Air Force and its Wars* (New Delhi: Lancer), pp. 125-55; PVS Jan Mohan and Samir Chopra, *The Indo Pakistan Air War of 1965* (New Delhi: Manohar Publishers, 2009).

24 SN Prasad, *Official History of the 1971 War*, History Division (New Delhi: MOD, 1992), p. 614.

25 Ibid., p. 450

26 Singh, n. 12, p. 146.

27 Benjamin Lambeth, *Airpower at 18,000': The Indian Air Force in the Kargil War*, https://carnegieendowment.org/2012/09/20/airpower-at-18-000-indian-air-force-in-kargil-war-pub-49421. Accessed on April 22, 2021.

28 Jasjit Singh, *Kargil 1999: The Fourth Round* (New Delhi: KW Publishers, 1999), p. 140.

29 Col Phillip S. Mellinger, "10 Propositions Regarding Air Power, School of Advanced Air Power Studies", Air Force History and Museums Program, 1995, p. 19.

30 https://indianexpress.com/article/opinion/indias-stunning-exercise-gagan-shakti-shows-how-force-can-be-used-without-war-to-deter-adversaries/

31 Op. Cit., Basic Doctrine, pp. 57-74, pp. 75-85, pp. 113-6.

32 Lambeth, n. 27.

33 https://timesofindia.indiatimes.com/india/indian-air-force-geared-up-for-combat-role-in-china-border-area/articleshow/76788189.cms. Accessed on April 10, 2021.

34 Shivshankar Menon, *Times of India*, New Delhi, April 25, 2021, p. 13.

35 https://www.republicworld.com/india-news/general-news/navy-day-2020-navy-chief-says-indian-navy-is-combat-ready-for-any-challenges-from-china.html

36 https://www.indiatoday.in/india/story/indian-government-s-full-statement-on-surgical-airstrike-in-pakistan-1465217-2019-02-26. Accessed on April 25, 2021.

37 Manpreet Sethi, *Airpower at Balakot, Strategic Advantage of Airpower* (New Delhi: KW Publishers, 2019), pp. 171-177.

38 Qiao Liang and Wang Xiangsui, *Unrestricted Warfare: China's Master Plan to Destroy America* (Panama: Pan American Publishing Co., 2002), p. 25.

39 http://www.indiandefencereview.com/news/air-power-against-the-maoists/2/

40 https://timesofindia.indiatimes.com/india/iaf-chief-not-in-favour-of-use-of-air-power-against-naxals/articleshow/5770051.cms

41 "Between 2001 and 2004, US Army lost 44 helicopters to enemy fire and accidents. Christian FM." Liles and Christopher Bolkcom, "CRS Report for Congress, Military Helicopter Modernisation: Background and Issues for Congress", The Library of Congress, June 24, 2004.

42 Mohammed Yahya Nawroz and Lester W. Grau, "The Soviet War in Afghanistan: History and Harbinger of Future War", Fort Leavenworth, KS: Foreign Military Studies Office, 1994, p. 7-11.

43 Op Cit, Basic Doctrine, pp. 57-74, pp. 108-12.

44 Peter Bergen, Melissa Salyk-Virk, David Sterman, "World of Drones, International

Security", last updated July 30, 2020, https://www.newamerica.org/international-security/reports/world-drones/

45 https://timesofindia.indiatimes.com/videos/news/drones-in-the-hands-of-non-state-actors-make-them-more-lethal-iaf-chief/videoshow/80014701.cms

46 J.C. Wylie, *Military Strategy: A General Theory of Power Control* (1967; Annapolis, MD: Naval Institute Press, 1989), p. 72.

47 Anthony H. Cordesman, "The Strength and Weaknesses of the AH 64 and other Attack Helicopters", The Iraq War: Strategy, Tactics and Military Lessons, CSIS, Washington, 2003, pp. 317-32.

48 https://www.airforcemag.com/article/the-future-of-coin/. Accessed on April 26, 2021.

49 https://www.business-standard.com/article/current-affairs/need-to-identify-dual-use-techs-that-can-be-used-for-military-army-chief-120082501797_1.html. Accessed on April 26, 2021.

50 Martin Van Creveld, *The Rise and Fall of Air Power*, (ed.), John Andreas Olsen, Op Cit, p. 369.

51 https://www.foreignaffairs.com/reviews/capsule-review/2011-05-01/age-airpower, accessed on April 27, 2021.

52 https://www.wearethemighty.com/mighty-trending/chinas-airpower-may-overtake-the-us-air-force-by-2030/. Accessed on April 27, 2021.

CHAPTER 13

AIR TRANSPORT OPERATIONS: CRITICAL RESPONDERS AND VITAL ENABLERS

RAJEEV SACHDEVA

ABSTRACT

The ability to rapidly position and sustain forces at a place and time of one's own choosing is a fundamental component of combat power. The Indian Air Force's (IAF) Air Transport Fleet has proved its ability to transport military equipment and forces between theatres for routine and special deployments. It has executed humanitarian assistance missions across the world, and evacuated thousands of stranded diaspora from distant conflict zones. The IAF's track record of deploying air transport platforms across the spectrum of conflict and in diverse trouble spots has allowed it to emerge as a powerful instrument of diplomacy and statecraft that furthers state policy and facilitates power projection as India progresses to becoming a leading power in the coming decades.

INTRODUCTION

Demonstrating attributes of speed, reach, flexibility, versatility, concentration of force and responsiveness, the IAF's Air Transport Fleet has emerged as a credible element of Indian airpower with its diverse mix of multi-role platforms that switch easily between several missions that straddle the entire spectrum of conflict. Over the years and with the gradual accretion of platforms and capabilities, the IAF has developed world-class expertise in diverse force multiplier roles. Among these are Special Operations, Air-to-Air Refuelling (AAR), Airborne Warning and Control Systems (AWACS), Intelligence, Surveillance and Recce (ISR), Casualty Evacuation (CASEVAC), Search, Rescue, Mercy Missions and airborne command platforms for National Leadership.

The Indian Air Force provides unique war fighting capabilities that are essential to both service specific and joint operations. Within the basket of both offensive and enabling airpower capabilities, the ability to rapidly focus combat power and resources where required offers any nation a first-mover advantage. Airpower is frequently, and notably in the opening stages of a conflict, the primary manifestation of combat power used against an adversary. One of the critical components of this capability is the ability to rapidly position and sustain forces at a place and time of one's own choosing. This pivotal capability is an essential ingredient of modern operations and supports the desired effects to deter, dissuade or inflict combat attrition on an adversary. While other forms of military power have some degree of inherent mobility, the scale of flexibility and responsiveness that the IAF's air transport and helicopter fleets provide is essential for driving the desired outcomes in war, less-than-war situations and routine military deployments and sustenance in diverse and hostile terrain such as the ones in which the Indian Army is deployed.

INDIAN LANDSCAPE AND THE CHALLENGES

Terrain

India has one of the most diverse landscapes and climatic variations spread across its geographical expanse, all of which complicate the conduct of operations across the spectrum of conflict. To the south, it has vast coastal regions along with island territories. To the west, it has deserts, salt pans and marshy lands. The north east has thick and inhospitable forests and hilly terrain rising to heights of between 5,000 and 15,000 feet. To the north, it has the mighty Himalayas, mountains that range in height from 15,000 to 25,000 feet. Within this widely disparate terrain lie contested borders that must be defended without any respite by the Indian Army and a sprinkling of border protection forces.

The Responsibility

Among the principal doctrinal aims of the IAF's Air Transport Fleet is to sustain these widely dispersed forces by providing mobility and logistics support between and within theatres of operation during peacetime, less-than-war-situations and during conflict. Air mobility has always been a key enabler in all major conflicts across the spectrum of conflict that India has experienced since independence. Surface forces and offensive air forces cannot deploy quickly or maintain themselves in combat without the logistical and air mobility support supplied by the IAF's transport fleet.

High altitude terrain of various hues presents the most significant operational challenge to the IAF's air transport fleet. Dropping zone operations have to be executed flawlessly with little margin for error. Routes and terminal dropping areas are extremely dangerous at several places due to limited manoeuvring space in narrow valleys that are flanked by towering peaks. Strong winds and mountain waves add to the degree of difficulty for pilots, and even an accurately dropped load can drift off track. Missing targets often results in the load being irretrievable due to difficult ground terrain, necessitating another mission to make the load reach its designated user. The entire Siachen glacier,[1] and most posts along the LAC, are air maintained by aerial delivery and airlanded operations at forward airfields and Advanced Landing Grounds[2]—the ALGs. These operations are well-complemented by the IAF's large and expanding helicopter fleet that provides the last-mile connectivity.

Island territories and archipelagos present their own set of challenges for Air Transport operations. Until recently, constraints of permitted aircraft performance, limited endurance, lack of GPS devices, unreliable and readily available meteorological reports and poor long range radio telephony hampered overseas operations. However, with the fleet and satellite upgradations, the operational capabilities of the fleet to connect the Islands with the mainland has improved manifold. As India builds joint capabilities on its island territories to counter the growing presence of China in the region, the dependence on timely and sustained air transport operations has increased significantly.

The volume of peacetime loads that are air-dropped or air-landed by the IAF annually is well over 30,000 tonnes, a huge tonnage by any measure. In the early 1990s, the tonnage projected by the Army and the civil administration and transported by the IAF's Transport fleet was approximately 7,500 tonnes in the J&K Sector and another 7,500 in the North East. With the construction of strategic roads in the north eastern border areas by the Border Roads Organisation (BRO), the sustenance requirement along the north eastern borders has reduced to a mere 1,000 tonnes (a reduction by 87 per cent), whereas the requirement in the J&K and Ladakh Sector has gone up by over 300 per cent, due to the collusive threat emanating from China and Pakistan.

MILITARY AIR TRANSPORT OPERATIONS

Fixed Wing Transport operations provide all the classic airpower attributes of speed, reach, flexibility, versatility and concentration of force. Consequently, they have come to play a key role in the projection of military power. It is, therefore, essential to understand the principles and the conduct of air transport operations. For ease of understanding, air transport capability of modern air forces, such as the IAF, can broadly be divided into three categories: mobility and sustenance, special missions and force multipliers.

Mobility and Sustenance

At the strategic level, also termed as strategic airlift operations, these involve the transportation of passengers or military equipment between theatres for routine deployments, reinforcement, projection of influence and capability, and even the evacuation of stranded citizens/military personnel from troubled spots around the globe. Operational and tactical airlift, or theatre airlift, is used for rapid and responsive movement within an area of operations to meet specific operational and tactical objectives. It primarily consists of the carriage of passengers and cargo within a theatre (Intra-theatre). Typical missions flown in direct support of surface forces include air landed missions into prepared or semi-prepared airfields also called Advance landing Grounds (ALG) in the Indian context. They also include air dropped missions that involve a paradrop of troops or the airdrop of tactical mission payloads into the battlefield if no suitable airfield for air landed missions is available.

Special Missions

As the capability of air transport forces across the world improved significantly in terms of stealth, reach and precision, so did their usage in the genre of military operations termed as Special Operations.[3] These include multiple missions like airborne assault and the insertion and extraction of Special Forces, both of which could use the air landed or air dropped option.

Force Multipliers

The increasing versatility of the military transport aircraft has led to a realisation that they can be employed in much more than just traditional roles of mobility. The number of roles and missions that have evolved over the last four decades is testimony to the increasing flexibility of airpower and its all-pervasive impact, not only in the military domain but also in the realm of statecraft. While this section will merely touch upon the diverse force multiplier roles that have been assigned worldwide, the IAF-specific section will delve into how the IAF has leveraged this capability effectively. Air-to-Air Refuelling operations (AAR),[4] Airborne Warning and Control Systems (AWACS),[5] Intelligence, Surveillance and Recce (ISR),[6] Casualty Evacuation (CASEVAC), Combat Search and

Rescue (CSAR) and Missions of Mercy are among the widely embraced force multiplier missions.

HISTORICAL VIGNETTES

The First India-Pakistan Conflict

The early years of the IAF's transport fleet saw it playing an impactful role during the first India-Pakistan conflict of 1947-48 with its modest fleet of Dakota aircraft from 12 Sqn.[7] This oldest transport squadron of the IAF was tasked with carrying out independent India's first ever air landed operation in a battle zone; it was an operation that saved Srinagar and laid the framework for how the state of Jammu and Kashmir looks like today. On October 27, 1947, three Dakotas carrying troops from the First Battalion of the Sikh Regiment (1 SIKH) touched down in Srinagar in the nick of time to save the airfield from imminent capture by advancing lashkars (tribal armies) embedded with regulars from the Pakistan Army. The Daks, as they were affectionately called, flew incessantly for the next three weeks without oxygen and de-icing equipment, both considered an absolute necessity for operations at high altitudes and cold weather, as they inducted 161 Brigade into the Kashmir Valley. In 1947-48, a crisis was developing at Poonch, which was literally under siege as Lashkars and the Pakistan Army shelled the town incessantly with their howitzers. Poonch would have fallen by early 1948 had it not been for three timely actions. The first was to divert elements of 161 Brigade to relieve Poonch. The second was the hasty construction of a kuccha airstrip to support a risky but possible landing by Dakotas to sustain the besieged town through air landed and air dropped operations. The third was the air landed induction of light artillery into Poonch, which would allow the garrison to offer a befitting response to the enemy fire, an operation that was executed by day and night in extremely hazardous operational conditions. The relief and sustenance of Poonch for almost a year compares favourably with the Berlin Airlift that took place soon after the siege at Poonch was lifted. In early 1948, Pakistan launched Op Sledge to seize the areas of Skardu, Kargil and Zojila, and ultimately wrest control of the Leh valley. Even as a column of Indian troops attempted to breach the Zojila pass and open the second land route from Manali, Air Commodore Mehar Singh led the first airlanded task force into Leh, as Dakotas from 12 Squadron opened an airbridge to Leh by ferrying in 250 soldiers of Second Battalion of Fourth Gorkha Rifles. It was an operation that saved Leh.

Airborne Assault to capture the Poongli Bridge

One of the key catalysts of the collapse of the Dacca garrison in December 1971 was the psychological impact of the Tangail airdrop. As the Indian Army's 95 Brigade was advancing on Dacca from the north, it was assessed that a foothold in Tangail would greatly assist the operation. Accordingly, 2 PARA was tasked to launch an Airborne Assault to capture the Poongli Bridge on the river Jamuna. The air assets used by the IAF were large by any standards, consisting of six AN-12, two Caribous, 20 C-119 Packets and 22 Dakotas. On December 11, 1971, two Caribous were used to drop 60 hessian cloth dummies as a feint at P minus 20 min on a separate DZ. The dummies were fitted with pyrotechnics to simulate small arms fire. At the same time, the Pathfinders landed on the main DZ. The main assault troops, who embarked from three airfields, Dum Dum, Kalaikunda and Guwahati, were dropped in the landing zone at 1630 h and captured the bridge by 1900 h. The capture of the Poongli bridge allowed the advancing Indian Army, to avoid the heavily fortified main road to Dacca and push all the way up to Mirpur Bridge at the gates of Dacca. With other Indian forces converging onto Dacca from multiple directions, this was the straw that broke the camel's back and forced the unconditional surrender of 93,000 troops at Dacca on December 16, 1971.[8]

Innovative use of Transport Fleet for Bombing

The IAF worked for years to improve its bombing capability, and thus employed An-12 transport aircraft for bombing during 1971 conflict to disrupt Pakistani formations attempting to cut-off Kashmir from the rest of India. These missions inflicted heavy casualties Pakistani infantry and armoured formations. After the IAF achieved air superiority in the western sector (and air supremacy in the eastern sector) during the Bangladesh Liberation War, the bombings were done at night.[9]

The concept to deploy An-12s for bombing was first mooted in 1967 and this innovative idea was encouraged by the Chief of the Air Staff, Air Chief Marshal Arjan Singh and sustained by his successor, Air Chief Marshal P.C. Lal. The aircraft's rear 35 mm turret gun was activated and a rear radar was installed even as it was configured to carry 28 to 36—500 pound bombs for carpet bombing. On December 3, 1971, the day the war began with Pakistani pre-emptive airstirkes against several IAF bases in the western sector, six aircraft of the 44 Squadron, led by the CO himself, bombed Pakistan Army's Changa Manga ammunition depot in the forests for two days. In the next round, a Pakistani artillery concentration around the Haji Pir pass was attacked and a Pakistani artillery brigade was seriously degraded. The aircraft, which were based in Bareilly, were then tasked with attacking Pakistan Army's 18 Division at Fort Abbas, the water works at Suleimanke and military installations around Bahawalpur. In the absence of sophisticated navigational aids, all target acquisition by night was done by astral means or on 'mental' DR (Dead Reckoning), resulting in highly effective and accurate bombing that surprised the Pakistanis.

Out of Area Contingencies

The coup d'état attempt in 1988 that threatened to overthrow the government of President Gayoom in the island republic of Maldives, presented the IAF's transport fleet with an opportunity to showcase its capabilities in the first joint Out-of-area-contingency operation that was launched by India in response to an SOS from a friendly neighbour.[10]

The airlanded assault on Hulule airfield in the Maldives, code named OP CACTUS, was launched by the Indian Air Force and Indian Army on November 3, 1988, to foil the coup and rescue the President of Maldives. The operation, which commenced on the evening of November 3, 1988, and was spearheaded by Ilyushin Il-76 aircraft of the Indian Air Force, airlifted elements of the 6th Battalion of the Parachute Regiment (6 PARA), a company from 3 PARA and the 17th Parachute Field Regiment from Agra Air Force Station and flew them non-stop over 2,000 km to land at the Malé International Airport on Hulhule Island within nine hours of the appeal from President Gayoom. The paratroopers restored control of the capital to President Gayoom's government within hours, and as some of the mercenaries fled toward Sri Lanka in a hijacked freighter, they were intercepted on the high seas by two frigates of the Indian Navy and handed over to the Maldives government.

Strategic Airlift

The successful evacuation of 111,711 Indian citizens from Iraq, Kuwait and Jordan in 1990 by Air india and the IAF, which operated 488 refugee flights over a 59-day period set a world record. Similar missions were carried out from Lebanon in 2006 (Operation Sukoon), Libya in 2011 and Yemen (Operation Rahat) in April 2015. Operation Rahat, involved the deployment of C-17 aircraft of the IAF and Air India's aircraft to airlift thousands of people in distress.[11] The recent evacuation of India's diplomatic mission, Indian citizens stranded in Afghanistan, Afghans of Indian origin, and even several distressed Afghan citizens from Kabul was led by IAF C-17s which flew several missions over almost two weeks.

Humanitarian Assistance and Disaster Relief (HADR)

Also, termed as mercy missions by aircrew across the world, the IAF's transport fleet has always been an early responder during disaster relief operations at home and overseas. The Tsunami that hit the Andaman and

Nicobar Islands and all the nearby island-states around India, including Sri Lanka and Indonesia, at around 0645 on December 26, 2004, served as a test bed for the transport fleet. Not only did the IAF render speedy relief to India's own island territories that were devastated, it also swung into action with spare capability to join rescue efforts in Sri Lanka and Indonesia. Exemplifying this spirit was a lone Dornier at Carnicobar Airfield whose crew started the aircraft and taxied it to the highest point on the runway. In the absence of any other communication, they connected with Chennai and appraised them about the situation at Carnic. The crew flew three shuttles between Carnicobar and Port Blair from the damaged runway, with no navigation aids or Air Traffic Control, to evacuate individuals in critical need of medical assistance.

Whether it is the repeated and effective responses to earthquakes, floods and forest fires, or the more specific responses to the Bhuj earthquake,[12] Kashmir or Nepal earthquakes,[13] or the execution of 'mercy missions' from areas of influence and interest, the increasing sophistication of airlift platforms such as the C-130 and C-17, has helped the IAF's transport fleet contribute significantly to the IAF's doctrinal articulation as an instrument of diplomacy and statecraft.

Assistance during Pandemic[14]

On February 27, 2020, 76 Indians and 36 foreign nationals from Bangladesh, China, Madagascar, Maldives, Myanmar, South Africa and the US were evacuated from Wuhan (China). As a gesture of goodwill to China, the aircraft also carried medical supplies as a symbol of goodwill. "The IAF aircraft has landed. Mission completed. On to the next," was tweeted by the External Affairs Minister S. Jaishankar, after an IAF's C-17 brought back 58 Covid stranded Indians from Iran on March 10, 2020. This was the second such evacuation by the Air Force.

Bolstering India's fight against a devastating second wave of infections, IAF's transport fleet flew sorties round the clock, bringing in critical aid from abroad and distributing life-saving medical equipment and oxygen cylinders, across the country. The IAF is conducting continuous relief measures as part of the defence services support to civil authorities. 'Operation Sanjeevani'[15] is already in full swing with deployment of a large number of wide-bodied aircraft and helicopters all across the country to shift medical supplies and associated equipment. Under this operation, the IAF has already sent aircraft with medical aid including vaccines to almost 70 countries including all the regional neighbours. Since March 25, 2020, the IAF has flown hundreds of sorties ferrying over 336 tonnes of medicines, ration and other essential supplies to various parts of the country.

Special Operations and Force Multipliers

Of all the contemporary air transport capabilities that any leading power must possess, the realm of Special Operations has witnessed substantial capability accretion in the IAF. The IAF regularly trains with the India Army's parachute brigade and Special Forces units from all the three services in near realistic conditions and has the capability to execute a swift brigade-sized airborne assault in large formations of over 40 aircraft with a mix of all types, the An-32, IL-76, C-17 and C-130 bunched together. A great deal of coordination and precision is displayed to synchronise the force with its equipment, integral firepower and mechanical transports at a single location in the shortest possible time frame from multiple directions and all this in the cover of darkness. The window for such dominance in time and space is dependent on several factors and is sometimes called dynamic air dominance. The induction of the C-130J has added teeth to this mission and enabled effective small-team insertion of specialised forces along with their combat equipment into combat zones in varied terrain.[16]

IAF force multipliers based on air transport platforms such as Air-Air-Refuelling (AAR), Airborne Warning and Control Systems (AWACS), Airborne Early Warning (AEW), Communication Intelligence

(COMINT) and Electronic Intelligence (ELINT) act as tri-service enablers that allow operators to plan and execute missions that were hitherto considered complex and complicated to execute. They have literally changed the way full spectrum operations are planned and conducted. With the induction of airborne tankers in the IAF based on the IL-76 platform (IL-78), combat ranges of IAF and Indian Naval fighter aircraft have expanded to cover India's articulated area of influence from the Malacca Straits to the Gulf of Aden while operating from the mainland with full load.

The IAF's 'Eyes in the Sky' or AWACS is again a unique aircraft that combines a Russian aircraft (IL-76) with an Israeli system based on the Phalcon radar that offers significant value to both offensive and air defence operations. By plugging-in easily to the IAF's Integrated Air Command and Control System (IACCS),[17] it offers operators and commanders excellent situational awareness and decision-making tools for the effective conduct of the entire range of offensive and enabling air operations.

Like several modern air forces, IAF aircraft and aircrew constitute an important element of the country's airborne intelligence apparatus comprising COMINT and ELINT platforms with various payloads in the form of cameras and sensors that help map and create adversaries' electronic mosaic or orbat.

Casualty evacuation is a crucial task in contemporary wars and conflict as the 'golden hour' can be the difference between life and death. This particularly holds good in potential conflict zones in hostile terrain that stretches across thousands of kilometres along the LoC and LAC. This mission, which is most effective when performed in concert with the IAF and Indian Army helicopter fleets, entails the availability and positioning of aircraft with specialised medical facilities at forward airfields to create a 'medical bridge.' While most transport aircraft of the IAF can be modified for this role, it is the C-17 in its MEDEVAC and ambulance configuration that can be a game-changer in both conflict and natural disaster scenarios.

THE FUTURE

SAGAR—A Vision for Mutual Growth

The economies of many of the littoral countries depend heavily on commercial ports, the shipping industry and most importantly, the enormous natural resources that enrich these waters with a profusion of marine life. For India, of course, the Indian Ocean is of vital importance with an extensive coastline of around 7,500 km, including 36 islands of Lakshadweep and 572 islands of the Andaman and Nicobar. India's EEZ is 2.4 million square kilometres in size, and the sea accounts for 90 per cent of its commerce volume and nearly all of its oil imports.

In his very first year as Prime Minister, Mr Narendra Modi stressed on an integrated approach towards the Indian Ocean Region and named it SAGAR[18] (Security And Growth for All in the Region). This vision for the region is to safeguard its organic unity while advancing cooperation. To fulfil the vision, a capability is required which can link up all the Nation States in the region. The contribution of the Indian Air Force's transport fleet in realising this objective has been unique, and it has proved its efficiency in responding speedily to several contingencies in the IOR using its HADR and Non-Combat Evacuation (NCE) mission capabilities.

In 1988, Operation Cactus (Maldives) demonstrated that the strategic airlift capability of the IAF was central to the swift and efficient response of the Indian Military that rendered the operation brief and bloodless. Relief operations during the Tsunami (2004) and the contribution of the IAF's transport fleet during the conduct of Operation Rainbow and Castor to help Sri Lanka and Maldives search for missing fishermen, are examples of the expanding capabilities of the IAF's non-kinetic capability in joint operations during peacetime, Operation Neer 2014 was conducted to alleviate the water crisis at Male and is among the several examples highlighting the importance of airpower in maritime domain.

Capabilities of IAF in IOR

Maritime air operations received special focus during the IAF's largest-ever air exercise, Gagan Shakti-2018,[19] when special attention was paid to maritime air operations as IAF Su-30 MKI multi-role fighter aircraft and Jaguar maritime strike aircraft flew deep into the Indian Ocean. They practised delivery of long-range weapons such as the cruise missile BrahMos[20] and long-range Harpoon missiles to refine offensive and defensive tactics against maritime targets. An operational range capability was also demonstrated by flying the Su-30 MKI all the way to Malacca Straits, which was only achievable with the employment of force-multipliers and enablers such as the AWACS and Air-to-Air Refuellers (AAR)—the IL-78 FRAs. When one considers the Indian Navy's existing maritime air operations and surveillance capabilities, as well as the IAF's quickly expanding enablers and force multipliers, there is ample reason to be optimistic about projecting power into the IOR and the near realms of the Indo-Pacific. When paired with a permanent base in the Andaman and Nicobar Islands, there is ample evidence to suggest that airpower has an important role to play in accomplishing India's maritime objectives associated with both the economic and security dimensions of the SAGAR initiative.

Platforms & Technology for the Future

Tasking dictates the fleet requirement and is generally a mix of heavy lift with carrying capacity of 20-30 tonnes per aircraft, medium lift with a 10-15 tonnes payload, and for tactical missions, the IAF requires aircraft for an aerial delivery of 4-8 tonnes per mission The IAF has traditionally required a fleet of roughly 50 aircraft for communication duties.

For the first three decades after independence the IAF had a mix of An-12 aircraft (10-15 tonnes), Packet Fairchild (4-6 tonnes), Caribou and Dakota aircraft for the Air Maintenance and Logistics support, whereas Avro with Boeing 737-200 were deployed for Strategic communication duties. The fleet is generally modernised and upgraded due to ageing issues once in 30 years. In the early 1980s, when the entire fleet was in crisis, Avro aircraft were inducted for Air Maintenance and inter-island communications. The fleet was thus modernised with fourteen IL-76 aircraft (40 tonnes) and 124 An-32 aircraft (4-6 tonnes), resulting in the decommissioning of An-12, Caribou, Packet Fairchild and Dakota aircraft.

With the rise in national aspirations and an increase in strategic requirement of India, the Transport Fleet was augmented 30 years after the induction of IL-76 and An-32 fleet with eleven C-17 Globemaster aircraft (with a max varying capacity of 78 tonnes) and twelve C-130J Hercules aircraft (a tactical aircraft with 20 tonnes capacity). The mid-level An-32 and Avro aircraft will soon be replaced with the C-295 (6-9 tonnes capacity), 16 of which will be flown down from Europe with the remaining 40 aircraft being produced by the Tata Group in India. The IAF is also looking to acquire a fleet of over hundred 100 passenger Medium Transport Aircraft (MTA) for which plans have already been initiated.

For the foreseeable future, the IAF's Transport fleet will primarily comprise 11 Strategic lift C-17 aircraft, 10 heavy lift IL-76 aircraft, 12 C-130J for strategic missions, 56 C-295 for and tactical airlift and 100 aircraft for military communications with the finalisation of MTA. IAF has already acquired Boeing 777, Boeing 737-700 and E-135 Embraer aircraft for Strategic Communication duties. As force multipliers, IAF will continue to maintain the FRAs, AWACS and the ELINT aircraft for enhancing its war-fighting capability.

CONCLUSION

The role of the IAF's transport fleet has been unique in statecraft because of its efficiency to respond speedily to contingency situations and its inherent characteristics of range, mobility and flexibility. Other than countless rescue missions within the country, many nations have benefitted from the HADR and Non-Combat Evacuation (NCE) mission capabilities of the IAF's Air Transport Fleet. While the IAF's strategic airlift capability has been repeatedly demonstrated in the IOR region, its other enabling capabilities act as strategic instruments of statecraft. These can be effectively leveraged for the collective well-being of the region, particularly among India's maritime neighbours and island states that are the focus of the SAGAR initiative. Air transport aircraft directly support power projection and expansion of influence. With the advent of more capable and versatile aircraft, air mobility operations, with all its enabling and force multiplier roles, will be intrinsic in developing future concepts of operations.

By all yardsticks, air transport forces will remain an indispensable instrument of national defence policy and power projection in the foreseeable future as India seeks to increase its influence in the region and build adequate state capacity on the path to becoming a leading power in the decades ahead.

NOTES

1 Andrew North, "Siachen dispute: India and Pakistan's glacial fight," bbc.com/news/world-asia-India-26967340, 12 Apr 2014. Accessed on June 26, 2021.

2 Deepshikha Hooda, "IAF to have 7 operational Advanced Landing Grounds in Arunachal Pradesh in a month," July 13, 2018, economicstimes.indiatimes.com/news/defence/IAF. Accessed on June 26, 2021.

3 Major Aryea Gottlieb, "The Role of SOF Across the Range of Military Operations," *Air and Space Power Journal,* June 1, 1987, pp. 1-7.

4 E Tonline, "What is air to air refuelling for aircraft & how it works?" July 30, 2020, economictimes.indiatimes.com/news/defence. Accessed on April 20, 2021.

5 Editors of Encyclopaedia Britanica, "AWACS aircraft and military technology," britanica. com /technology/AWACS.

6 Air Mshl BK Pandey, "AEW&CS - IAF's Eye in the sky," issue 09-2012 DRDO, sps-aviation.com/story/?id=1062t

7 Arjun Subramaniam, *India's Wars – A Military History 1947-71* (Noida: HarperCollins Publishers, 2016), p. 105.

8 Soumyadip Mullick, "1971 war: How Army para—dropped Infantry into East Pak," https://www.thestatesman.com/bengal/1971-war-army-para-dropped-infantry-east-pak-1502940334.html. Accessed on June 26, 2021.

9 Gulshan Luthra, "IAF's Innovative use of Transporters as Heavy Bombers," April 2013, https://www.indiastrategic.in/topstories1980_IAF_use_transporters__bombers.htm. Accessed on March 13, 2021.

10 Gp Capt JV Singh, "Out of Area Contingencies," https://www.geospatialworld.net/article/logistics-extending-the-reach/, January 4, 2014. Accessed on March 23, 2021.

11 Shreya Pareek, "Did you know that the largest Air evacuation in history was done by India?" February 18, 2015, https://www.thebetterindia.com/15179/heres-need-know-largest-air-evacuation-history-india/. Accessed on March 31, 2021.

12 Josy Joseph, "Earthquake hits India," https://www.rediff.com/news/2001/jan/26quak24.htm, January 2021. Accessed on April 7, 2021.

13 All India, Press Trust of India, "Nepal Earthquake: Indian Air Force, Army made 2223 sorties, rescued 11200 People," June 6, 2015, https://www.ndtv.com/india-news/nepal-earthquake-indian-air-force-army- -2223-sorties-rescued-11200-people. Accessed on May 16, 2021.

14 Shreya Dhodiyal, "The Distance IAF Has Covered In Fight Against Covid-19," May 27, 2021, https://www.news18.com/news/india/55-times-around-the-globe-thats-the-distance-iaf-has-covered-in-fight-against-covid-19-3781889.html. Accessed on June 7, 2021.

15 Special Correspondent, "IAF Airlifts 6.2 tonne Essential Drugs to Maldives," April 2, 2020, https://www.thehindu.com/news/national/iaf-airlifts-62-tonne-essential-drugs-to-maldives/article31240436.ece. Accessed on April 2, 2021.

16 Air Marshal Anil Chopra, "Air Elements in Special Ops," June 6, 2020, http://www.indiandefencereview.com/news/air-elements-in-special-ops/. Accessed on May 3, 2021.

17 Indrastra Global Editorial Team, "India's Integrated Air Command & Control System (IACCS): A NCW Milestone," September 28, 2015. '*IACCS*', https://www.indrastra.com/2015/09/ANALYSIS-IACCS-257.html. Accessed on May 27, 2021.

18 MEA Press release, "MISSION SAGAR: A major Milestone in India's Engagement with IOR Countries," July 1, 2020, https://www.mea.gov.in/press-releases.htm?dtl/32803/MISSION+SAGAR+A+major+Milestone+in+Indias+Engagement+with+IOR+Countries. Accessed on May 12, 2021.

19 *Times of India*, "Gagan Shakti 2018: All you want to know about India's biggest military Exercise," April 18, 2018, https://timesofindia.indiatimes.com/india/gagan-shakti-2018-all-you-need-to-know-about-indias-biggest-military-exercise/articleshow/63814321.cms. Accessed on April 4, 2021.

20 Army Technology, "Brahmos Supersonic cruise Missile," https://www.army-technology.com/projects/brahmossupersoniccru/

CHAPTER 14

THE INDIAN ROTARY WING: LEGACY AND PROSPECTS

RAJESH ISSER

ABSTRACT

This chapter traces the history of operations of Indian military helicopters since their inception in 1954. Innovative and can-do approaches of military commanders and aircrew are major highlights that are covered. It is a broad canvas covering conflicts of 1962, 1965, 1971, IPKF Ops in Sri Lanka, the Kargil War, and actions within the country. There is little doubt that helicopters have demonstrated a ubiquitous presence in several crisis situations that India has faced. India's greatest security challenges lie in the Himalayas, and that is where its rotary wing element of force and statecraft will play a decisive role. A concept of operations involving legacy and newer acquisitions is also discussed. A Fourth Industrial Revolution, convergence of fast-evolving technologies, and disruptive strategies and tactics promise a revolution in how conflict scenarios will emerge in the future with a complex mix of manned-unmanned teaming on the battlefield. Some of these issues with an eye on future rotary wing transformation have been explored.

A HISTORICAL PERSPECTIVE

By the early 1950s, the Indian Air Force (IAF) had already embarked on an ambitious expansion and modernisation plan. The Government had given its approval for induction of modern aircraft and equipment. Vampire jet fighters had entered the IAF in early 1948 and moves were afoot to induct the French Ouragon (Toofani) jets and C-118 Packets, a medium capacity tactical transport aircraft. It was around the same time that the versatile and ubiquitous helicopter entered the IAF with the acquisition of a few Sikorsky S-55 and Bell-47 IIIG Helicopters. The first such unit, 104 Helicopter Unit (HU) was formed on March 10, 1954, at Palam, New Delhi.[1]

1962, 1965 and Counter-insurgency

The fleet was still in its infancy when tensions were rising on the border with China in 1961, when the government decided to deploy Army units all along the border to check likely Chinese intrusions as part of the infamous Forward Policy. The entire area was remote and undeveloped, without any surface communications. The task of maintaining the Army was thus naturally given to the IAF. When the fixed wing transport aircraft like the DC-3 Dakota, C-119 Packet and the Russian AN-12 quickly geared up to start air maintenance to forward airfields and Advance Landing Grounds (ALGs) either through para-dropping or air landed operations, the equally important task of liaison, communications and casualty evacuation was the responsibility of the IAF's fledgling helicopter fleet.[2] In July 1962, the Bell 47s of 104 HU were actively involved in casualty evacuation in the Galwan valley of Ladakh. This was the first time that the Bells had operated above 10,000 feet AMSL. Throughout the period of tension and later the actual fighting in 1962, helicopters of the first three units of IAF tirelessly and fearlessly evacuated several casualties, and brought timely succour to the injured by way of urgently needed medical supplies and other essential stores and equipment.

In the East, facing the Chinese were the undermanned and ill-equipped troops of the 4th Infantry Division with 7 Brigade, which was deployed as far forward as the Namka Chu rivulet. Defensive build-up in the area was difficult because of the single, tortuous, road that wound its way across difficult terrain from Tawang to the Namkachu valley. For reconnaissance and liaison flights, some of the Division's Bell 47s from

No. 105 HU flew up and down valleys carrying Corps, Divisional and Brigade commanders.

Two Bell 47s were located at the helipad at Zimithang, and were soon employed to lift casualties from the improvised helipads up at Lumpu and Tsangdhar once the conflict broke out in October 1962. Four Mi-4s were based at Tezpur, the headquarters of 4 Corps in the plains of the Brahmaputra, and these too ran the gauntlet of Chinese ground fire while flying in reinforcements and supplies and evacuating casualties from the advanced landing pads. Several helicopters were shot down in the Tawang and Walong sectors as a result of hostile fire and severe weather circumstances, although this did not deter the Mi-4s and Bell 47s from continuing to operate courageously through the conflict.[3] On one such mission on October 1962, Squadron Leader V.K. Sehgal became the first war casualty from the IAF when his helicopter was fired at by the enemy in the border regions of NEFA. Air Chief Marshal P.C. Lal paid glowing tributes to these gallant pioneers of the helicopter fleet in his book "My Years with the IAF."[4] Another hero of the fleet was Squadron Leader A.S. Williams, the Commanding Office of 107 HU, who was awarded the Vir Chakra for his heroic exploits.

During Operation Gibraltar, the covert operation to seize Jammu and Kashmir (J&K) by Pakistan in August 1965, a helicopter task force was formed to assist the fighting against armed infiltrators or Razakars who had entered Jammu and Kashmir in August 1965. Initially consisting of two squadrons, it was later expanded to three and was instrumental in helping the Indian Army check the influx of Pakistani raiders and infiltrators. The task force was mainly based in Srinagar and carried out 79 offensive sorties against infiltrators from August 20, 1965, to the end of hostilities. These suitably modified IAF helicopters, bombed and strafed positions of infiltrators in many areas around Haji Pir Pass, Tangdhar, Badgam, Mandi, Budil, and the hills around Gurez. This was the first time that these medium-lift utility helicopters were used in the offensive role, and the modifications were done in a matter of days.

While these offensive sorties did inflict some damage on the enemy, more importantly, they certainly exerted a great demoralising effect on Pakistani guerrillas.[5] This invaluable support finds a worthy mention in "War Dispatches", the story of the Indian Army's Western Command written by its commander, Lieutenant General Harbaksh Singh.

The baptism of the IAF helicopter fleet in counter-insurgency operations took place during the early years of the Indian Army's operations against Naga insurgents as detachments from Mi-4 units in the east operated in support. However, the coming of age of the helicopter fleet occurred during the Mizo insurgency from 1966 onwards as several quick reaction operations, including an abortive attempt to raid an MNF camp in East Pakistan near the Mizoram border were flown. It was here that the term Special Heli-Borne Operations (SHBO) entered the lexicon of joint Army-Air Force operations of the Indian Armed Forces during an operation to relieve the siege of Aizawal in early March 1966. 5 Para, one of the first Army battalions to move into the Mizo Hills, was involved in the operation along with Mi-4 helicopters and was subsequently based at Aizawl and employed as a fast reaction unit to intercept MNF cadres on the move.[6] Helicopters offered high mobility to troops, and a tremendous element of surprise. Several such missions were undertaken with 5 Para, 13 Kumaon, 8 Sikh, 18 Punjab, 1& 6 Assam Rifles, 16 Jat, 5 J&K Rifles and other battalions. An enemy that had been sitting unchallenged for days or weeks could suddenly, without warning, find itself under assault from troops brought in by helicopters. Pilots had just read about the exploits of similar air mobility operations then ongoing in Vietnam and were willing to undertake such missions. Major General Sagat Singh, the commander of 101 Communication Zone, which was entrusted with operations in Mizoram, leveraged his experience with 110 HU in Mizoram to plan audacious helilifts during the Bangladesh War in 1971 when he was the General Officer Commanding 4 Corps.

The 1971 India-Pak Conflict and Sri Lanka

While helicopters as war-machines, vital suppliers and gunships were first employed in France's Algerian Campaign in 1950, it was the Vietnam War that thrust them to the forefront as a game-changer in such dirty wars. Helicopter employment was only limited by a commander's creativity and risk-taking limits. The whole world sat up and took notice—and so did a few Indian commanders during the war for liberation of East Pakistan in 1971. The first to do so was Lieutenant General Sagat Singh, the maverick corps commander of IV Corps, one of the formations that was tasked with offensive operations towards Dacca from east. He had seen what the Mi-4s could do in terms of SHBO and vertical envelopment in Mizoram. Supporting him in leveraging the potential of the Mi-4s was one of the IAF's most audacious middle-level commanders, Group Captain Chandan Singh, who Sagat designated as his Air Force task-force commander, an appointment that never really existed at the time. In just one week, they coordinated the most audacious series of operations with just over a squadron worth (11-15) of Mi-4 helicopters from 110 and 105 HU. General Sagat had seen what Mi-4s could do during the 1966 Mizo campaign by Indian joint forces and despite being tasked to carry out a secondary attack into East Pakistan from the east (Tripura), he exploited the potential of 11 Mi-4s of 110 HU in Kumbhigram at his disposal to emerge as the spearhead of the Indian Army's advance on Dacca. With impeccable teamwork Sagat and Chandan Singh a never-attempted-before vertical envelopment operation that outflanked the static Pakistan Army defences and produced spectacular operational outcomes that only the fog of war throws up.

Sagat and Chandan used Mi-4s to launch whole battalions and brigades across innumerable waterways, including the mighty Meghna River and its tributary, the Surma, to first bypass and bottle up the Sylhet Garrison with merely a battalion, and then heli-lifted two brigades to the doorsteps of Dacca. This left Dacca vulnerable and forced its garrison to surrender.[7] Though Sagat was made to wait for other formations to catch up, the series of heliborne operations that he executed were game-changers that accelerated the collapse of the Pakistan Army in East Pakistan and hastened the creation of Bangladesh.

Another major operation that saw extensive employment of IAF helicopters was Operation Pawan, the Indian Peace Keeping Force (IPKF) operations in Sri Lanka from October 1987 to March 1990. While the most important and extensive roles were airlift of supplies, troop lift and reinforcements, helicopters were also used in the offensive role.[8] On October 23, 1987, a detachment of Mi-25 gunships from 125 HU from Pathankot was inducted into Jaffna. Their very first mission was against LTTE concentrations at Jaffna Jetty with front guns and rockets. It was a highly effective and coordinated action that forced the LTTE cadre to stay away from roads and waterways, and restricted their movements to night only. Hundreds of similar actions were done in joint operations over the next three years in roles such as: suppressive fire in general area of the intended landing zones of own tactical helicopters; area bombing/strafing of known jungle hideouts; armed escorts to tactical helicopters engaged in SHBO; and fire support to own troops from 'Op Call' position (on ground at forward helipads).

The IPKF concept of operations was based on operations of a large unit (usually division strength) involving close supervision and direction from higher command. The IPKF's reliance on conventional techniques would ultimately cost it dearly. Except for a few tactical successes and several individual acts of gallantry, IPKF operations did not deliver any meaningful operational or strategic outcomes. The only IPKF forces that managed some success were Para (SF), who used methods that resembled those of the LTTE. The SF realised the importance of intelligence and mobility, especially regarding jungle routes, inhabitants and activities of LTTE. Difficult and time consuming, the intelligence gathering was essential to the success of such operations, as was the coordination with helicopter crews, who responded with courage and professional excellence.

Kargil, UNPKO and Anti-LWE Ops

Helicopters were used extensively during the Kargil conflict—from armed-attack role with rockets and cannons to regular ones at high altitudes such as troop mobility, resupply and casualty evacuation.[9] After one Mi-17 was shot down by a Pakistani Stinger as it did not have a self-protection suite, the armed role for Mi-17s was stopped. But aircrew continued being innovative in conjunction with ground commanders. One such mission in which the author took part involved four disassembled, 105 mm mountain guns to be carried in the Mi-17 cargo compartment to distant high-altitude sites close to the action so that they could be effectively used in the direct firing mode. The need to have dedicated attack helicopters for action in the Himalayas was acutely felt during the Kargil conflict.[10] Capping the effort was sustained casualty evacuation operations by IAF and Indian Army helicopters.

IAF helicopters have played a key role in the success of all Indian Army deployments to UN peacekeeping operations in the Democratic Republic of Congo (DRC), Sierra Leone, Somalia, and Sudan, often in extremely trying and dangerous operational conditions. These have been documented and acknowledged both within the UN and in India as a role-model of jointness in deployment and operations. Two exemplary case studies in the efficacy of helicopter operations in UN missions are DRC and Sierra Leone under UN Chapter VII. Even though all roles in the book were tasked, the forceful peacekeeping in the Congo for almost seven years was conducted with care and calibration with no collateral damage.

As per Government of India (GoI) guidelines, IAF has employed its helicopters in anti-Left Wing Extremism (LWE) operations only in select non-kinetic roles. These include reinforcing troops of the Central Armed Police Forces (CAPF), evacuating casualties and mortal remains, providing air logistics support to those deployed on ground, besides carrying out aerial reconnaissance over hilly and mountainous areas of this region. The operation mainly covers the states of Chhattisgarh,

Bihar, Jharkhand, Maharashtra, Andhra Pradesh and Odisha. Earlier constrained by a series of mine and IED blasts, CAPFs have now been able to increase their footprint over a larger area, as their reliance on roads as the sole means of supplies has gradually reduced. Such operations are now conducted with the knowledge that should any casualties occur, IAF helicopters will be dispatched immediately to evacuate them. This is in keeping with the tenet that a combatant's morale can be lifted by the knowledge that he would be transported to safety should he/she get injured during operations.

Siachen Ongoing

During Operation Meghdoot in 1984, the Indian Army, ably supported by the IAF, seized control of the heights dominating the Siachen Glacier to prevent a similar move by the Pakistan Army. IAF Il-76s, An-12s and An-32s transported stores and troops, and airdropped supplies to high altitude airfields, while Mi-17s, Mi-8s, Chetaks and Cheetahs ferried men and material to dizzy heights, far above the limits set by helicopter manufacturers. In fact, this incredible performance at the extremes of temperature and altitude is a benchmark for high altitude rotary wing operations. The Siachen Glacier lies in one of the most inhospitable regions, and contains some of the highest peaks and most glaciated regions of the world. Prior to the current ceasefire that is holding since 2003, there was a constant threat of enemy shelling and attack by IR guided Man Portable Air Defence Systems (MANPADS). Both sides have lost several helicopters and crew to direct enemy action. Among the several examples of good joint innovative action was when IAF Mi-17s airlifted medium artillery guns in marginal weather conditions and under incessant enemy shelling to posts beyond Bilafond-La (over 17,000 ft high).

CONCEPTS IN ROTARY WING EMPLOYMENT

Persistent conflict and asymmetric approaches by adversaries is a given in the contemporary conflict milieu. Low-intensity and short-duration conflicts in highly confined but fast-paced battle-spaces are more likely to occur than wider conventional wars. Though offensive airpower would play a vital role, boots on the ground and combat support missions of airpower would be critical for the success in such tasks. Airpower in High Altitude (HA) operations will play a pivotal role, especially in providing tactical mobility, logistic support and fire support besides numerous other support roles. Possible scenarios for sub-conventional operations in J&K, parts of the north east and along the borders with Nepal, Bhutan and Myanmar include counter-insurgeny, counter-terrorism, and even localised battles like Kargil. Some of these could be fanned by adversaries and competitors like Pakistan and China. Highly mobile light infantry and Special Forces adequately supported by fixed wing, UAVs and helicopters may help contain them from growing into more serious confrontations. Lessons from recent campaigns clearly suggest the need for a revamp of man, machine, tactics and multi-agency work culture.

Air-Land Ops and the High-Altitude Campaign

Missions like battlefield interdiction, Battlefield Air Strikes (BAS) support, and armed reconnaissance can be carried out by AH units in conventional Air-Land Operations either independently or in cooperation with other elements. As parallel operations emerge as a non-negotiable paradigm of contemporary conflict, AHs with increasing stand-off capability can contribute significantly to the counter-air campaign by suppressing enemy air defence systems that constitute a forward tier of defences. Similarly, they also possess the ability to continue with offensive operations in the Tactical Battle Area (TBA) in a contested aerial environment, albeit with greater risks, should own fixed wing assets find it difficult to engage surface targets. This could prove critical in a limited and high intensity conflict. It's also becoming more popular to equip helicopters with Air-to-Air missiles (AAMs), which offers new possibilities for rotary wing operations over the TBA.

Under normal circumstances, BAS at high altitude are high-risk missions for both high-speed fixed-wing airpower and attack helicopters. While fixed-wing platforms have evolved their own tactics to stay clear of SAM envelopes and deliver precision weapons and even dumb bombs from medium altitude and great distances, they are more suited for interdiction rather than pin-point targeting against concealed and static targets on hilltops. Even though both the Russians and the Americans have suffered significant attrition while employing helicopters of various kinds in Afghanistan, they continue to offer significant value with improved survivability techniques, such as terrain masking techniques and skilful employment of defensive suites and stand-off weapons.

Battles in the mountains will primarily be for holding on to passes, dominating heights and roads, all under multi-tier fire from the enemy. The point here is that terrain will force compartmentalisation of action and, therefore, the necessity of independent sub-unit action, including calling in of firepower (artillery or airpower) at a much lower level than the battle in the plains. It is in such a combat milieu that innovative pairings between Unmanned Aerial Vehicles (UAVs), helicopters of several kinds, Special Forces and Forward Air Controllers can significantly impact the tactical battle in several ways. As a whole chapter is dedicated to firepower, this chapter will only mention that attack and utility helicopters can successfully contribute to the maximisation of firepower for effect in the mountains. Among the key operational requirements of the futuristic Indian Light Combat Helicopter, which has undergone extensive operational trials in Eastern Ladakh in recent months, must be to cater to High Altitude operations with greater survivability, stealthy manoeuvre and precision firepower.

HELICOPTERS IN FUTURE BATTLEFIELDS

Multi-Domain Interoperability

Multi-domain operations stretch across a spectrum of conflict from Hybrid Warfare to low-intensity security situations and require capabilities that are responsive and adaptive. Warfighting in such an environment is about networking in a secure redundant communication environment with other capabilities in every domain. From a practitioner's perspective, the AH-64 Apache, which has recently been inducted into the IAF, is a perfect platform to explore the utility of helicopters in a full-spectrum environment. It incorporates the latest in technology and concepts in warfighting and conflict-management, and its open architecture with modern high-capacity datalinks and network capabilities allows plug-ins that India's armed forces would need to incorporate in the future. In fact, the Israelis have shown that it can be quickly converted from an anti-armour role to targeting terrorist leaders with precision and stealth (night). In 2011, NATO even used it in the littoral domain operating from naval ships.[11] Its array of weaponry and self-protection suites allows it to engage at stand-off ranges in all terrains—deserts, jungles, urban settings, and most importantly, mountains where India's future conflicts would most likely occur. Lessons learnt in employment of Apaches in Afghanistan have allowed modifications in equipment and tactics to be effective at altitudes.

The future holds much promise for the Apache based on several trials being conducted in the US and NATO. Among these are newer predictive maintenance with multiple sensors and avoidance of brownouts through sensors and symbols. Moreover, AH-64 pilots collaborate with unmanned platforms at various levels of control. This will allow better effectiveness in targeting and survivability. The quartet of Apache, Chinook, C-130 J and C-17 offer a capability to deploy Special Forces anywhere overseas where Indian interests are at stake. These are machines that can stretch 'jointness" to 'truly integrated' responses.[12]

Current thoughts on helicopter employment use the term Combat Support (CS) and Combat Service Support (CSS) missions. While the former provides operational support for combat units, the latter is responsible for all logistical functions such as supply, maintenance, transportation, casualty evacuation to the combatants to complete their mission. CS missions include Special Forces action, personnel recovery and quick-reaction capability. The ubiquity of helicopters on the tactical battlefield is their prime capability as indispensable assets.

The visualisation is that from bringing small task forces into battle to providing all kinds of support, such as weaponry and situational awareness, helicopters are expected to play a vital role. A truly integrated battle will mean all roles, especially firepower support, which will have to be coordinated and synergised with fixed-wing unmanned and manned aircraft.[13] Attack helicopters would be among several airborne sensors and shooters of the joint force.

A 2012 Congressional Research Service report classified 31 per cent of US warplanes in service as unmanned. The Israeli Army is clear that swarm operations by unmanned systems executing several battlefield roles would be a core concept in the future.[14] Any involvement of humans would mainly be dictated by high complexity of decision-making along with possible ethical and moral dilemmas.

Even medical and health support has undergone a paradigm shift after the First Gulf War. The concept of forward-basing large surgical units was found unsound in modern-day battles.[15] Moving critical or even stabilised cases within the 'golden-hour' to hospital care in rear areas was found to be more efficient and effective. Larger helicopters with trained personnel and on-board ICU-care are now fulfilling this function. Looking ahead, unmanned helicopters could be employed when the risks are too high for manned helicopters in a combat zone. The recently acquired CH-47 Chinook would fit this role very neatly.

The Urban Challenge

In the Indian conflict milieu, high-intensity operations in dense and chaotic urban settings may not yet be the norm. However, if India's armed forces are headed for greater convergence and interoperability with strategic partners and a continued role in UN Peacekeeping and Peace Enforcement Operations (UNPKO), it must think and train about the urban challenge. COVID-19-like pandemics, climate change and the fight for resources, such as water and food, have the potential to create conflict situations in urban spaces that may warrant the use of force beyond what is employed currently.[16]

Urban warfare is a unique genre of conflict, which offers the defender an advantage of stealth and the ability to surprise while executing ambushes and hit-and-run tactics. It is a fertile ground to exercise anti-access and tactical area denial by the defender. On the other hand, issues such as avoiding collateral damage and civilian casualties will only complicate matters for the attacker (presuming ethical conduct). It is precisely in such contexts that teaming special forces (SF), helicopters, unmanned air and ground vehicles will offer significant advantages like ubiquitous transparency that will allow specific acts of precision attacks on leadership and other lead elements of the enemy. The most obvious advantage is reduced exposure and vulnerability to ground forces, as well as shaping the battlespace for them to dominate the ground and ensure presence, which is vital to force a combat end-state that is linked to conflict termination/resolution.

Enabling Special Forces

In limited wars and less-than-war situations, helicopters and their aircrews would be most needed to help Special Forces (SF).[17] The efficacy of SF is mainly dependent on their ability to surprise and shock with their unconventional and sometimes unpredictable methods and timing. For this aviation support has to be of the best quality in terms of capabilities and adaptability. Additionally, aircrew will be forced to deal with adverse environmental conditions such as weak or no light, low-flying in perilous terrain, and the possibility of browning and whitening out when close to the ground. The skill-levels required are undoubtedly the highest in piloting, indicating the need for care in recruitment and training. Simply put, aviation limits may curtail SF's freedom to operate as flexibly as possible.[18]

Special Forces have a unique and innate adaptive ability, and are employed to respond with agility against unpredictable enemies. They are masters in asymmetric approaches to problem-solving. Achievement of tactical surprise, a key in such campaigns, is enabled by speed, stealth, and agility, along with superior technology. The ability to appear at an unexpected place and time of one's own choosing, with an offensive mindset, enables retaining initiative and surprise. This is an effective asymmetric counter to the advantages of experienced insurgents, i.e. local tacit support, early warning networks and local terrain knowledge. A paradox is that the characteristics that render SF an ideal choice for dispersed and geographically isolated insurgency is largely premised upon mobility, responsiveness, and firepower provided by airpower. In an SF environment of hyper-competence and sense of purpose, operations are characterised by clear mission orders and appropriate technology that allows dispersed command, control, and execution. Employment of airpower must reflect complementary response structures of command and control.

Advances in technology and tactics allow acute target discrimination and weapon effectiveness of air-delivered weapons. Precision weapons can achieve unthinkable accuracy and overwhelming firepower in support of light and agile SF; additionally, they dramatically reduces fratricide and collateral damage. Persistent ISR can provide appropriate flank protection and early warning. Mobility and effective firepower can allow even 'lighter and more lethal' SF. Terrain following radar, varied flight profiles, all-weather abilities, standoff ISR for threat and detection avoidance, and offset landing zones allow stealth in a true sense. This force structure from an Indian perspective requires deeper reflection in terms of acquisition plans, training and interoperability.

Convergence of Technologies

Current rotorcraft developments are aimed at high availability (modularity and low life-cycle costs), increased loads, speeds and manoeuvrability, higher safety standards, and increased survivability among others.[19] When coupled with agile and encrypted communication, robust networks with redundancy and built-in resilience, the potential for leapfrogging capabilities is immense if one adds-on better man-machine teaming within and outside platforms. While rotorcraft are testing speeds of 500 kmph, speed is not everything. Manoeuvrability, survivability and sustainability may have larger bearings in combat. Even reducing the noise levels of an approaching rotary wing may be a game-changing proposition. Survivability will include looking into battle-damage tolerance, advanced metallic and composite usage, crash-impact mitigation mechanics, and better structural design to take impact from ballistics.

Helicopter manufacturers are working feverishly on aspects such as real-time threat data and analysis, distributed aperture systems for spherical protection with manual and auto triggering, kinetic, passive and active sensors, and countering attacks by unmanned aerial systems. In simple words, a fully adaptable, automated and integrated electromagnetic operations self-protection system. Another key concept in avionics is having an open-architecture frame to adopt future developments including some disruptive ones. It must be able to adapt to future advanced avionics, active control systems and tactical data links. For example, developments in active control system are aiming for automated takeoff/landings as well as autopilot control.

We already have prototypes of coaxial rotors along with pusher props, fans or propellers, or advanced tilt-rotors. Experiments to modify rotor blade-shapes in flight to optimise noise reduction or aerodynamic efficiency are at advanced stages.[20] The Defense Advanced Research Project Agency (DARPA) in the US is investigating smart material actuated rotor technology or SMART, which includes piezoelectric material use. It holds promise of not only better efficiencies and longer ranges, but also reduction in human errors, higher maintenance fault tolerance and redundancy, lower weight and higher reliability.

Maintenance concepts will aim for modular replacement rather than rectifications. Along with better monitoring methods and diagnostic tools linked to ground stations, zero maintenance will be the ultimate aim. Pre-emptive maintenance will incorporate means to detect fatigue and damage precursors and real-time analysis. A Health Usage Monitoring Systems (HUMS) is one such networked and integrated mechanism that uses real-time data collection and analysis to drive up operational availability through pre-emptive maintenance and cut down costs. AI-driven diagnostic models can provide advanced anomaly detection and vibration monitoring to improve diagnostic and analysis capability.

CONCLUSION

This chapter has touched the legacy of Indian military helicopters since inception in 1954, and the innovation that defined their employment in war and peace. In fact, rotary-wing aircraft have played a key role in nearly every crisis that India has faced in the last six decades. It has also traced current thoughts on their usage especially in the mountains. India's greatest security challenges lie in the Himalayas, and that is where its rotary wing will play a decisive role. The future is sure to bring a complex mix of manned-unmanned teaming on the battlefield, and some of the issues have been explored here.

Editor's Note

The rotary wing fleets of the Indian Army and Indian Navy have contributed significantly to operations and HADR over the last five decades. They do not find mention in this chapter only because there is insufficient bandwidth to include all stakeholders in military aviation.

NOTES

1 Isser, R. *The Purple Legacy: IAF Helicopters in Service of the Nation* (New Delhi: Pentagon Press 2012).

2 Roychowdhury, Shankar. "China's Air Power: Implications for India." *CLAWS Journal* Summer 2010, www.claws.in. Accessed on September 1, 2019.

3 Isser, R. "Exploring Indian Airpower Doctrine & Debacles in the Himalayas," Vivekananda International Foundation (VIF) Paper, July 2020, pp. 7-8, www.vifindia.org. Accessed on

November 1, 2020.

4 Lal, P.C. *My Years with the IAF* (New Delhi: Lancer Publishers, 1986), pp. 207-16.

5 Isser, R. *Airpower in Irregular & Hybrid Conflicts: The Indian Context* (New Delhi: The Book Line, 2017).

6 Isser, n. 1.

7 Cardozo, I. "The Battle for Sylhet," *Scholar Warrior*, Spring 2020, pp. 98-105.

8 From interviews with Commanding Officer on the respective Helicopter Squadron's War Record Book. This was an effort to collate IAF helicopter fleet's contribution, subsequently published as *The Purple Legacy* (New Delhi: Pentagon Press, 2011).

9 Bedi, Rahul. "Paying to Keep the High Ground", *Jane's Intelligence Review*, Vol. 11 No. 10 (October 1999), pp. 27-31.

10 CLAWS. *20 Years After Kargil Conflict*, Seminar Report, July 2013, pp. 9-14, www.claws.in. Accessed on June 15, 2021.

11 See NATO, ATP-49, 'Use of Helicopters in Land Operations – Doctrine.' NATO Helicopter Inter-Service Working Group. Apr 2012. website of NATO. *NATO Future Helicopter*, https://www.defensenews.com/digital-show-dailies/paris-air-show/2017/06/16/nato-s-future-helicopter-the-alliance-s-strategy-to-modernizing-its-rotorcraft-capability/. Accessed on June 17, 2021.

12 Rajesh Isser. 'Asymmetric Competition Ahead for Indian Air Power,' Manohar Parrikar Institute for Defence Studies and Analyses. *Journal of Defence Studies*, Vol. 15, No. 1, January-March 2021, pp. 1-24.

13 Jon Harper, "The Rise of Skyborg: Air Force Betting on New Robotic Wingman," *National Defense,* September 25, 2020, www.nationaldefensemagazine.org. Accessed on November 10, 2020.

14 Israelis urged to prepare for battlefields dominated by robots, http://www.spacedaily.com/reports/Israelis_urged_to_prepare_for_battlefields_dominated_by_robots_999.html. Accessed on November 10, 2020.

15 Bastian, N., Fulton, L., Mitchell, R., Pollard, W., Wierschem, D., and Wilson, R. "The Future of Vertical Lift: Initial Insights for Aircraft Capability and Medical Planning," *Military Medicine*, Vol. 177 (2012).

16 Ministry of Defence. *Strategic Trends Programme, Global Strategic Trends – Out to 2045*, Fifth Edition (London, UK: Ministry of Defence, 2014).

17 *Afghanistan war: Why helicopters are critical to US and NATO forces*, www.csmonitor.com

18 Miklós Szabó, "The Future NATO Rotorcraft Force—Capability Requirements through 2030 and Beyond", *JAPCC Journal*, Ed. 23 Winter 2016, https://www.japcc.org. Accessed on December 15, 2020.

19 "Vibhram" a novel helicopter design by a team of post graduate students, https://www.iitk.ac.in/aero/design-competition. Accessed on June 12, 2021.

20 Hoffman, F.G. "Will War's Nature Change in the Seventh Military Revolution?", *Parameters* 47(4) Winter 2017-18, pp. 27, https://ssi.armywarcollege.edu/. Accessed on June 10, 2021.

CHAPTER 15

EMPLOYMENT OF SPECIAL FORCES IN FUTURE CONFLICT SCENARIOS

PRAKASH KATOCH

ABSTRACT

Special Forces provide multiple low-cost and high-gain options to governments for achieving military, political, economic and psychological objectives especially in conditions of grey zone and sub-conventional war. Such operations are conducted during peacetime and across the spectrum of conflict—from no war no peace situations, to limited conflicts and war. Their employment at the strategic level on politico-military missions can provide rich dividends in shaping the environment in the nation's favour as an extension of foreign policy. India has considerable Special Forces potential in the backdrop of an adverse strategic disadvantage vis-à-vis China and Pakistan arising out of the prevailing collusive security threat that the latter pose. Building of Special Forces capability with diverse competencies to offset this disadvantage needs to be addressed. There must be a national policy for using Special Forces either separately or in combination with irregular forces and as a nucleus for special operations or continuously running deep coalitions against adversaries.

COMING OF AGE

Special Forces are specially organised, trained and equipped to achieve military, political, economic or psychological objectives by unconventional means in hostile, denied or politically sensitive areas. These operations are conducted during peacetime, no war, no peace, conflicts and war.[1] According to Stephen Cohen, "The task of Special Forces is the proxy application of force at low and precisely calculated levels, the objective being to achieve some political effect, not a battlefield victory." They often operate as small bodies without direct support.

In 1963, the CIA helped India raise the nucleus of the Special Frontier Force (SFF) by recruiting Tibetans in exile. Presently, the SFF also has Special Action Groups (SAGs) that are entirely manned by Army personnel on deputation. SFF units and sub-units have been deployed in operational areas in the past, including during operations for the liberation of Bangladesh and in 2020 in eastern Ladakh to confront the PLA.

The 'Meghdoot Force', raised and utilised as a commando unit behind enemy lines during the 1965 Indo-Pak War, was a forerunner to the Indian Army's Special Forces. With the addition of two such units, all three were deployed under the IPKF in Sri Lanka. These Parachute (Commando) units were later renamed Parachute (Special Forces). The prefix 'Parachute' remains because these units are part of The Parachute Regiment. Since then, the number of these units has expanded and they have been continuously deployed in counter-insurgency (CI) and counter-terrorism (CT) operations, as well as UN missions.

The Marine Commando Force (MARCOS) of the Indian Navy was initially raised in 1987 as the Indian Marine Special Force (IMSF). Deployed under the IPKF in Sri Lanka it undertook multiple successful operations. In 1993, the MARCOS seized a ship in support of the UN that was smuggling arms to Somalia.[2] It has since been used in anti-piracy operations and continues to be deployed for CI-CT operations in J&K and Ladakh.

The Indian Air Group (IAF) developed the 'Garud' commando force in February 2004. Tasks of the Garud include direct action against targets like enemy radars, special reconnaissance, rescuing downed pilots in hostile territory, establishing and providing air-traffic control airbases on foreign soil and base protection of critical IAF assets and installations including airfields. Though not a primary task, the Garuds have also operated alongside the Rashtriya Rifles in CI and CT operations in J&K.[3]

The National Security Guard (NSG) of India was established in 1986. It is a specialist CT force with two components: Special Action Groups (SAGs) manned by Army personnel on deputation and Special Rangers Groups (SRGs) manned by personnel from the Central Armed Police Forces (CAPF). The SAGs are at the forefront of operations, while the SRGs are trained and tasked to provide the outer cordon during complex operations. SAGs are also trained for anti-hijack operations.[4] The NSG has played a pivotal role in internal security, with many successes including Operation 'Black Thunder', 2008 Mumbai terrorist attacks and the elimination of terrorists from Akshardham Temple in Gujarat.

After years of deliberations over raising a Special Operations Joint Command, the Armed Forces Special Operations Division (AFSOD) was established in 2019, bringing together Special Forces personnel from all three branches of the armed forces. However, it remains a work in progress with minimum force levels and without integral support elements.

SPECIAL FORCES AS STRATEGIC INSTRUMENTS OF COERCION

With the use of direct military force becoming riskier for states in terms of escalation, cost and lives, the importance of coercion as a powerful instrument of statecraft is becoming more apparent in contemporary times as states seek to counter adversaries without going to war. Given the limitations of both hard and soft power, there is a continual need to identify non-military or indirect ways to deter, coerce, weaken and even punish an adversary who threatens a state's security and national interests.

It is imperative to identify alternate approaches in the economic, cyber or information domains to secure or re-invent existing structures within the panoply of hard security measures that do not risk uncalibrated escalation, while retaining the effectiveness to influence adversary's behaviour. Special Forces are one such element of the latter.

According to a study conducted in the US, the three most cost-effective instruments of coercion available to the US are: first, financial sanctions to deliver calibrated economic pain with precision, from targeting individuals to hurting targeted sectors for slowing economic activity; second, support pro-democracy opposition by leveraging global information networks, media and NGOs, to undermine a regime that is inimical towards US interests, and; third, offensive operations as high-return and high-risk options. The last option, if skilfully targeted and calibrated to avoid collateral damage, could be very effective. The report, however, conveniently ignores the widespread and successful employment of US Special Forces in tandem with the above options and proxy entities in what is termed Operations Other Than War (OOTW).[5] Surely, the three above options cannot be the only coercive options within the framework of coercive diplomacy, and if they are, how effective will they be in the absence of threats of force and, if necessary, the limited and selective use of force in a discrete and controlled manner?

The Chinese concept of 'Unrestricted Warfare' as outlined by Colonels Qiao Liang and Wang Xiangsui in their widely-acclaimed book, *Unrestricted Warfare: China's Master Plan to Destroy America*, is a more direct and all-encompassing paradigm of coercive choices below the threshold of war. They outline military tools that complement hard power like biochemical, ecological, space, electronic, guerrilla, terrorism; trans-military tools like diplomatic, networks, intelligence, psychological, smuggling, drugs, virtual; and non-military tools like financial, trade, resources, economic aid, regulatory, sanctions, media and ideological. Together with this is China's 'Political' Warfare, psychological operations and 'Legal Warfare' through illegal territorial claims.[6]

How can Special Forces be used as instruments of strategic coercion? This necessitates looking beyond only direct-type of actions. In this context, it would be prudent to examine the Chinese strategy of 'Deep Coalition'. A 'deep coalition' may consist of one or multiple nation-states, civil society organisations, narco-mafias, private corporations with vested interests, individual speculator(s) and other components. Deep Coalition involves players at many levels of the system; it is multi-dimensional with all groups operating concurrently in a continuous flow – multiplying, fusing into others, and so on.[7] With its numerous references to the political role played by non-state players ranging from credit rating agencies to narco-mafias, and its emphasis on the 'civilianization of war' thesis, Unrestricted Warfare as articulated by the Chinese embodies the concept of 'deep coalitions,' in all but name. This mutation is much like the way modern technology is impacting the battlefield and it is also at the same time blurring the concepts of who the participants of war are? It is emerging that non-professional warriors and non-state organisations pose an increasing threat to sovereign nations. Should Special Forces be part of such 'deep coalitions', preferably embedded within the nucleus and armed with new skill sets?

For India, it is also vital to maintain a robust "Out of Area" (OOA) capability. Here too Special Forces have an important role in conducting a vast range of missions. These could vary from being the spearhead element of the Rapid Deployment Force(s) (RDF) or used independently or in conjunction with other elements of National Power. The OOA capability can be used to protect interests, expand influence or assist a foreign government, should there be a need like the situation that emerged in Maldives in 1988 when President Gayoom requested India's immediate assistance to foil a coup.

THE IMPORTANCE OF SPECIAL FORCES IN CONTEMPORARY WARFARE

Sub-conventional conflict, including the use of irregular forces, has become the norm within the larger construct of hybrid warfare that encompasses most forms of contemporary conflict. Use of irregular forces is not a new phenomenon, but has gained prominence, with nations big and small exploiting its potential to the extent that sub-conventional capacity has become the currency of geopolitical power. Most analysts agree that sub-conventional operations will dominate the conflict landscape in the future. Asymmetric and hybrid operations have emerged as tools with greater strategic value than conventional operations, with nuclear weapons offering greater deterrent value.

An important facet of present-day wars and conflicts is that most of these are fought within civilian population centres, blurring the distinction between combatants and civilians. In such scenarios, it is important that collateral damage be kept to the minimum, if not avoided altogether. Furthermore, in the face of warfare in the broad sense that will unfold on a borderless battlefield, it is no longer possible to rely on conventional military forces and weapons alone to achieve national security in the larger strategic sense, nor is it possible to protect these stratified national interests. Warfare is in the process of transcending the domains of soldiers, military unit and military affairs, and is increasingly becoming inclusive for politicians, scientists and even bankers. All this exemplifies the value of 'deep coalitions' discussed above. This type of battlefield milieu requires specific precision actions, for which the Special Forces are best suited, albeit with broader skill sets.

India's security challenges are increasing rapidly. The China-Pakistan anti-India nexus clearly manifested itself through 2020 during the Chinese aggression in Eastern Ladakh and Pakistan's military mobilisation in Gilgit-Baltistan.[8] Chinese Foreign Minister Wang Yi explained in an article titled "An Iron Friendship Firming in a New Era," published in the Pakistani media on March 2, 2021, that no matter how regional and international landscapes may evolve and what challenges and risks may arise, China will continue to work with Pakistan to strengthen their iron friendship. Wang Yi stated that relations between the countries have become a strategic asset that both sides cherish.

The growing nexus between China and Pakistan is a major challenge for India, which must be watched alongside Pakistan's rapidly deteriorating geopolitical situation.[9] Pakistan continues to support multiple radical and terrorist groups to destabilise India, with Turkey planning to send mercenaries to bolster the proxy war in J&K.

China looms large not only over India but the entire Indo-Pacific region with its revisionist and expansionist agenda—both in military and economic terms. It continues to lay claims to large tracts of Indian territory and apparently has no intentions of resolving the border problem with India. Having drawn Nepal into its strategic sphere and building a threatening posture around the Doklam Plateau in Bhutan, China may pose future challenges to India through Nepal and Bhutan. Re-energising of the China-Myanmar Economic Corridor (CMEC) may see PLA presence in that country under pretext of guarding the CMEC and allied projects, like the China-Pakistan Economic Corridor (CPEC). With the potential of increased Chinese presence on India's western flanks resulting from pipelines and infrastructure running through Afghanistan and Iran to the warm waters of the Persian Gulf, India is staring at an 'encirclement strategy' with Chinese marines bound to make their presence felt sooner than later at Iranian ports and Kyaukpyu Port in Myanmar, adding to their presence in Gwadar, Pakistan. While the PLA presence on India's eastern flank needs to be viewed in conjunction with China's illegal claims to large portions of the State of Arunachal Pradesh, its increasing presence on India's western flank must be seen as a strategy to erode India's operational maritime advantage in the Indian Ocean Region (IOR).

Consequently, the inevitability of a growing strategic asymmetry with China in this space is a given. Consequently, the importance of Special Forces operating independently or as force multipliers in conjunction with other forces is essential for responding to a wide spectrum of crises and opening up possibilities of a reduction in asymmetry. Situations precipitated by terrorism, subversion, insurgency and proxy wars by neighbouring countries or by non-state actors operating from their territory will continue to pose major security challenges for India with the possibility of limited conventional conflicts adding to the proliferation of such threats. Ambiguity and a marked divergence from traditional risks characterise security challenges today and it is likely to be so in the future also.

Operations by Special Forces are of two categories: those conducted in support of and in conjunction with individual service actions or joint operations, and those conducted partially or fully independently. The latter, which needs added attention in the prevailing security scenario that India faces, are usually conducted in hostile, denied, or politically sensitive environments to achieve military, diplomatic, informational, and/or economic objectives by employing military capabilities for which there is no broad conventional force requirement. These operations often require covert, clandestine or low-visibility capabilities. The difference between the two is that the latter differ in the degree of physical and political risk, operational techniques, mode of employment, independence from friendly support and dependence on detailed operational intelligence and indigenous assets.

Special Forces provide governments with a variety of low-cost and high-return options like controlling the escalation, overt or covert operations with deniability, reaching the adversary's vulnerable areas and limiting collateral damage while targeting critical strategic points. As a clandestine extension of the country's foreign policy, these actions are typically coordinated with the country's intelligence agencies.[10] According to Lieutenant General A.S. Kalkat, former Overall Force Commander and GOC IPKF, and later Army Commander, Army Training Command, "Special Forces has been an idea whose time had long come, however it is only in the recent past that our military leaders and higher defence authorities have recognised their vast potential. It is not as easy as introducing another weapon in our armoury, it has to be regarded as a Weapon of War."

LESSONS FROM RECENT SPECIAL FORCES EMPLOYMENT

Indian Special Forces are mostly engaged in CI-CT operations particularly in J&K and in the north east. They have contributed immensely in elimination of terrorists in these regions since they spearhead most operations. Three prominent operations conducted by Special Forces in recent years offer significant lessons for future employment.

Operation 'Hot Pursuit'

India's north east is infested with multiple insurgent groups with external linkages. The region is witness to a growing China-Pakistan nexus that seeks to keep these alive. Despite an intelligence sharing protocol with Myanmar, several insurgent camps thrive along the Indo-Myanmar border. On June 4, 2015, an Indian Army convoy was ambushed by insurgents using improvised explosive devices, rockets and automatic fire in Chandel district of Manipur state in the north east, resulting in heavy casualties. Two militant organisations owned responsibility for the attack; National Socialist Council of Nagaland, Khaplang Group-NSCN(K) and Kanglei Yawol Kanna Lup (KYKL). After the ambush, the insurgents crossed the border retreating to their camps inside Myanmar.

For the riposte, the mission allotted to the Special Forces was to hit the insurgent camps of the NSCN(K) and KYKL involved in the June 4 ambush. All intelligence inputs led to pinpointing the locations deep inside Myanmar's forested area through difficult terrain. Two teams were formed for the mission with a combined strength of 70 Special Forces personnel under an overall commander. They were all dressed in the uniform of the infantry battalion stationed in the region. The operation was planned on foot, with helicopters on standby in case of an emergency. Both teams were thoroughly briefed and rehearsals were done.

Reaching the staging areas, the teams were to traverse through forested hilly terrain to reach a hilltop in vicinity of the insurgent camps. With two Burmese-speaking guides from an Indian village, they crossed into Myanmar at first light on June 8. Enroute they encountered five civilian hunters whom they secured and took along, reaching the hilltop at sunset. The attack was to begin before sunrise on June 9. However, speculative firing by the insurgents during the night from the camps below necessitated a modification in the plans. Instead of one, two teams were assigned for direct assault, with a third covering the rear to prevent being encircled and enabling a safe exit.

The raid was meant to capture the insurgents during their morning meal, as their daily routine included two meals a day, at 0500 hours and 1500 hours, for which they collected in the dining area.[11] The raid began at 0400 hours, with RPG rockets taking out the two sentry posts and the six sentries, followed by heavy volume of automatic fire. The assault teams disengaged after causing much damage with automatic weapons, grenades and RPGs during the 45-minute fight that took place in three areas within the camp. The insurgents suffered heavy casualties. One newspaper quoting ground sources, reported 38 insurgents were killed and seven others were wounded. The Special Forces teams suffered no injuries and reached base by noon on June 9.

Among the several lessons it is seen that hard intelligence-driven operations are bound to succeed when accompanied with detailed briefing, rehearsals, surprise and a high degree of mental and physical toughness of the raiding party. A working knowledge of insurgent's language was essential, for which Burmese-speaking guides were hired, and observing the camps from a hilltop through the night was a wise move considering that speculative fire by insurgents would confirm their locations. Overall, one of the raids was a clinical operation and executed with finesse, while the other raid was less successful, reaching a camp which was found empty, possibly as a result of a tip-off about the likely operation.

Cross-Border Raid on Terror Launch Pads—'Surgical Strikes'

In the wee hours of the morning of September 18, 2016, four heavily armed terrorists of Pakistan-supported Jaish-e-Mohammed (JeM) entered the Indian Army post at Uri in J&K using accomplices from the Indian side. They lobbed incendiary grenades and fired automatic weapons; some grenades set the diesel dump afire. Most of the casualties were from burn injuries. All four terrorists were killed. They were carrying items with Pakistani markings, including maps, GPS, explosives, a matrix sheet of codes and notes in Pashto, besides AK-47 rifles and under-barrel grenade launchers. Following this, the Pakistan war machine went on high alert with F-16s flying over Islamabad at night. Pakistan's prime minister, defence and foreign ministers and Army Chief threatened war in case India attempted to attack Pakistan.

A list of 35-40 terrorist training camps in Pakistan occupied Kashmir (POK) with their locations was widely known by several constituencies within India's security establishment and this was regularly updated. Pakistan co-locates most of these camps with regular Army posts, so that an attack on them could be portrayed as an attack on the regular Army. In some cases, the two are merged. Ahead of these terror-training camps are forward launch pads. These are also close to Pakistani posts, but in the gaps on lower ground, along the infiltration routes. Trained terrorists are staged forward to launch pads, awaiting commands to infiltrate, mostly while under cover fire from Pakistani posts.[12]

The Indian Army's Northern Command had for some years tabulated and prioritised the various options for attacking these launch pads, which also included assessed casualties to the attacking parties at each target. From this list, specific targets to be attacked were approved by the government. However, these were not revealed to the raiding Special Forces columns till the last minute. At the political level, Pakistan got no indication that India would respond to the terror attack at Uri by sending in Special Forces. The targets selected were widely dispersed, albeit the two opposite Uri were about half a kilometre apart. The columns selected to raid all targets were from two Special Forces battalions under Northern Command, who over the years had cultivated 'assets' for intelligence gathering.

By midnight on September 20, all the columns had marched forward on foot to their respective stations near close to the LoC in Uri, Poonch and Kupwara. The columns remained doggo in this location, awaiting further orders. By midnight of September 26, orders were received for 'remaining on standby' and columns were given their respective targets. The next few hours involved surveying and monitoring the LoC and the route beyond, briefings, final preparations and checking of weapons.

Shortly before noon on September 27, the green signal arrived for attacking respective terrorist launch pads. Northern Command coordinated the movement of all columns to ensure that the LoC was crossed simultaneously and with due caution to avoid alerting the enemy. It was usual practice for Pakistani posts to undertake speculative firing including illuminating ammunition at night. However, none of the columns were directly engaged, indicating the enemy did not suspect anything. Short of the targets, the Team Leaders took stock to monitor the enemy movement and location of sentries. In some cases, there was speculative fire from the launch pads also. The columns remained under forest cover for few hours looking for the right moment to launch the raids.

The raids began by shooting the sentries dead, followed by firefights that in some cases lasted about an hour. Terrorists attempting to run into the forest were gunned down. The return journey was most difficult as enemy posts now fully alerted and opened up with medium machine guns to rocket-propelled grenades and ammunition of every kind, short of heavy artillery. The columns crossed the LoC before sunrise on September 29 after taking a circuitous route under continuous fire. Terrorists at the launch pads suffered heavy casualties. No casualties were suffered by the Special Forces columns.

Pakistan was deceived into believing that India would not resort to cross-border raids. Human assets and all source intelligence helped streamline attack plans. Maintaining radio silence throughout and attacking columns with last minute targets ensured a high level of secrecy. Precise coordinated movement of all the Special Forces columns and attack in widely dispersed locations paid off in keeping the enemy off guard.

Operation 'Snow Leopard'-2020

As part of the Chinese aggression in Ladakh during 2020, the PLA not only intruded in the areas of Pangong Lake, Galwan, Gogra-Hot Springs and Depsang, but also launched a premeditated attack on Indian troops on June 15 with crude weapons at Galwan without warning, despite having agreed to withdraw. However, China was surprised by the fierce response from Indian troops in Galwan during the night of June 15-16, and suffered around 40 casualties during the skirmish.

Following the skirmish and despite five rounds of military-to-military talks at Corps Commanders level to disengage in eastern Ladakh, China remained obstinate, showing no inclination to move back. In this backdrop, the Indian Army launched Operation 'Snow Leopard' on the South Bank of Pangong Lake on August 29th and 30th to strengthen its presence in the region and operate multiple pressure points for China. Since these heights overlooked PLA positions, including their garrison at Moldo, the Indian Army assessed that they could force the PLA to seriously consider pull-back options as part of a larger de-escalation process.

Preparations for 'Operation Snow Leopard' had begun in early August after a concerted build-up of Indian forces. Among the strategic heights identified for occupation were Black Top, Gurung Hill, Rezang La, Magar Hill, Rechin La, Helmet Top; all heights around Chushul and Kailash Range covering the Spanggur Gap. Accordingly, teams were prepared from the SFF and Army's Special Forces personnel, adding high altitude acclimatised troops from other units with each team tasked to occupy specific heights and secure sustainable supply lines. The Indian Army took control of posts dominating Chinese posts on south and north banks of Pangong Tso. China protested and attempted to launch a counter attack, but baulked as it recognised that it would be futile to attempt to displace Indian forces from positions of overwhelming advantage. Despite Chinese claims that these heights were on Chinese territory, India was clear that the heights were on Indian Territory before the 1962 Sino-Indian War and were never occupied by either side since. It was therefore rightly termed as a preventive operation.

Operation 'Snow Leopard' particularly frustrated the PLA because it had inducted two motorised divisions into Ladakh and there were enough PLA troops to occupy these heights simultaneous to the earlier intrusions in the areas north of Pangong Tso. It was particularly galling to China because the SFF manned by Tibetans, was part of Op 'Snow Leopard'. This operation gave India tremendous strategic advantage, with heights like the Kailash Range providing a launch pad for further operations if China upped the ante.

The infirmities of PLA troops in high-altitude terrain of Ladakh were noticeable. For the premeditated attack at Galwan on June 15, PLA inducted specially trained troops, possibly Chinese Special Forces who did not fare well against Indian troops. The PLA may have used Special Forces to counter Op 'Snow Leopard,' but they were unsuccessful. This shows that the Special Forces concept needs expansion, particularly for quickly occupying heights and passes in high altitude areas along the border with China.

CRYSTAL GAZING

India's emergence as an Asian giant is expected to be hampered by major security difficulties posed by its main adversaries, China and Pakistan. While the former would want to limit India's strategic space and keep it confined to South Asia, the latter is unlikely to shed its perception of India as an existential threat. Consequently, India will continue to face the spectre of simmering insurgencies, proxy wars and terrorism including CBRN terrorism, as well as threats to its land and sea borders. While continuing to prepare for full-spectrum threats, much conflict will remain in the grey and sub-conventional zone. It is amidst such a conflict landscape that building of Special Forces capability with diverse competencies assumes great importance.

India is yet to define its national security policy but it needs to address the adverse strategic disadvantage it faces vis-à-vis China and Pakistan at the sub-conventional level. The Special Forces operations in Myanmar and POK discussed above indicate a reactive philosophy of employment rather than a proactive approach. Lost opportunities in the past have included: not infiltrating the LTTE during Operation Pawan; no effort to target terrorist leaders in Pakistan-POK; no effort to exploit dissent in Gilgit-Baltistan that could have prevented the CPEC from being built— failing to recognise that Special Forces do not create insurgencies, but rather exploit existing dissent; no joint operations with Afghan Special Forces even though Pakistani Army regulars are operating in Afghanistan and no deterrent developed against China's sub-conventional war on India. A proactive approach for employment of Special Forces in recent times could have considered the stealthy occupation of the Karakoram Pass when PLA intruded inside the Depsang Plains.[13] From 1950 to 1972, the CIA launched a thorough covert action campaign in Tibet through India and Nepal in support of Tibetan rebel forces in close collaboration with the US Departments of State and Defense. The CIA ceased these operations in 1972 after US President Richard Nixon decided to embrace China. This is the type of capability India needs against its adversaries/likely adversaries. There are hosts of dissident Uighurs, ETIM, Balochis, Sindhis around the world who are looking to support insurgent movements in China and Pakistan. The Indian Army is reportedly studying Tibetology, but what about Uighurs, Kachins and infiltrating Chinese proxies in Myanmar?

India must define a policy for employment of Special Forces that delineates their pro-active employment at the strategic level. Chinese Special Forces are assessed to be embedded in development projects around the world. India needs to establish multiple deep coalitions against adversaries, in concert with strategic partners where required.[14] Special Forces should be central to any asymmetric response. The key lies in achieving strategic objectives through application of modest resources with the essential psychological element.

This transformation requires skills and competencies that Special Forces should possess in addition to the handling of various types of weapons, communications, explosives, surveillance equipment, transportation, modes of insertion/extraction, camouflage, survival, IT, basic medication and the likes. Knowledge of customs and traditions of the target region and disguise, are essential to merge with the local population and infiltrate terrorist and other organisations. Psychological and cyber operations, civil affairs, handling civilian modes of transport and drones, as well as knowledge of critical points of intended targets and installations would be required.

The notion that Special Forces are meant for only cross-border strikes up to a certain distance and that strategic responsibilities are best left to other specialised government agencies must be reconsidered. India should learn from the CIA acting in synch with Pentagon and USSF, also from Pakistan, which has similar processes in place. The Army, Navy and Air Force have their integral Special Forces while the government has the NSG to deal with situations. There is no reason for the AFSOD not to be employed for strategic tasks in concert with organisations R&AW and NTRO.[15]

According to Lieutenant General Vijay Oberoi, former Vice Chief of Army Staff and Colonel of The Army Special Forces Regiment, "India essentially needs a Special Forces Joint Command (SFJC), but we seem to have settled for a Special Operations Forces Division. In my view, this is a regressive move. The concept of AFSOD really amounts to again frittering away SF resources, or coming back to the old dispensation of set-piece formations, which would be anachronistic on the future battlefield. In my view, a SFJC independent of geographical joint commands as fielded by the US Military is essential." Policy makers need to take this seriously. Special Forces should be central to asymmetric response, including against irregular forces. A physical attack is only the extreme and potentially most dangerous expression of asymmetric warfare. The key lies in achieving strategic objectives through application of modest resources and the essential psychological element.

NOTES

1 Cohen P Stephen, *The Idea of Pakistan*, Brookings Institution Press, Washington DC, 2004.

2 Business Today.in, "Centre deploys MARCOS in eastern Ladakh as part otri-service operation", November 28, 2020, https://www.businesstoday.in/current/economy-ssedpolitics/centre-deploys-marcos-in-eastern-ladakh-as-part-of-tri-service-operation/story/423283.html#:~:text=MARCOS%20have%20been%20deployed%20to,Eastern%20Ladakh%2C%20government%20sources%20said&text=The%20Central%20Government%20has%20deployed,lake%20area%20in%20eastern%20Ladakh.

3 *Hindustan Times*, "Five things to know about IAF's Garud commandos", October 13, 2017, https://www.hindustantimes.com/india-news/five-things-to-know-about-iaf-s-garud-commandos/story-YxOvfnMX3QgGjM32jCBcNP.html

4 Katoch, Prakash and Saikat Datta, *India's Special Forces—History and Future of India Special Forces* (New Delhi: Vij Books India Pvt Limited, 2013).

5 David C. Gompert, Hans Binnendijk, "The Power to Coerce", Rand Corporation, Santa Monica, California, 2016.

6 Blank, Stephen, "The Chinese Concept of 'Unrestricted Warfare': Global Competitors Up The Ante", Second Line of Defense, April 11, 2014, http://www.sldinfo.com/the-chinese-concept-of-unrestricted-warfare-global-competitors-up-the-ante/

7 Ibid.

8 Katoch, Prakash, "The China-Pakistan Threat", *SP's Aviation*, March 8, 2021, http://www.sps-aviation.com/experts-speak/?id=522&h=The-China-Pakistan-Threat

9 *Greek City Times*, "Turkey is preparing Syrian mercenaries to fight in Kashmir: report", December 4, 2020, https://greekcitytimes.com/2020/12/04/turkey-syrian-mercenaries-kashmir/

10 Katoch and Datta, n. 4.

11 Katoch, Prakash, *Special Operations Case Studies—Lessons for India* (New Delhi: Lancer Publications, 2019).

12 Ibid.

13 Katoch and Datta, n. 4.

14 Katoch, Prakash, "Special Forces in India", *Indian Defence Review*, Jan-Mar 2013, http://www.indiandefencereview.com/news/special-forces-in-india/#:~:text=While%20Special%20Forces%20should%20be,dangerous%20expression%20of%20asymmetric%20warfare

15 Katoch, n. 13.

CHAPTER 16

SYNERGY IN HIGHER DEFENCE ORGANISATION

ARUP RAHA

ABSTRACT

Since Independence, all national security challenges to India's sovereignty have highlighted the limitations of the higher defence organisation (HDO). This has caused periodic churn among governments and the strategic establishment, including the military, urging actions to address the shortcomings in the system. Reforms are essential in every organisation and institution to keep up with the changing environment, evolving threats, challenges and opportunities, and this is especially so when clear shortcomings have emerged over the years. The focus on Jointness is very crucial, but it cannot be limited to only the three Services, as it must be seen from a wider perspective to include the entire HDO. The institution of CDS along with DMA is a desirable step forward in bringing about reforms, mainly in the military organisation of HDO and partially in the functioning of the MoD, for greater jointness and efficiency. It is relevant to remember that both hierarchical organisations, and the 'tradition-bound' Indian ethos and culture, do not accept revolutionary changes. Therefore, reforms in the Indian Military systems should be progressive and a step-by-step approach to change is desirable.

INTRODUCTION

Before discussing the need for reforms in HDO, it is important to note that the citizens of India hold India's Armed Forces in high esteem and as the last bastion during times of crisis and distress. They are a symbol of secularism, national integration and have remained apolitical even as they have consistently and dedicatedly contributed to preserving the nation's sovereignty and internal stability. A steadfast allegiance to the Indian Constitution and the People is their signature trademark.

All national security challenges to India's sovereignty since Independence, have brought to the fore the limitations of the higher defence organisation (HDO). This has caused periodic churn within governments and the strategic establishment including the military, urging actions to address the shortcomings in the system. Expert Committees and Group of Ministers (GoM) have occasionally highlighted flaws and recommended corrective measures to the government. Several of these were implemented in a wide range of spheres, which included changes in organisational structure of the Armed Forces and Intelligence Agencies, enhancement of force levels and acquisition of advanced weapon systems and equipment. Recent reforms towards strengthening national security have also focussed on military indigenisation aimed at achieving strategic autonomy, licenced manufacture of state-of-the-art weapon platforms, and upgradation of space capabilities, nuclear weapons and ballistic missile technology.

While the recommendations of the various committees mainly dealt with the reforms in the Armed Forces, HDO and a few other departments, they rarely touched upon areas of political and bureaucratic oversight. Many recommendations were either ignored or implemented half-heartedly, resulting in structural gaps, organisational lacunae and sub-optimal working efficiency.

NEED FOR REFORMS IN HDO

The recent political initiatives, such as the appointment of a Chief of Defence Staff (CDS),[1] and creation of the Department of Military Affairs (DMA)[2] in MoD, are aimed at implementing the long-overdue recommendations of Kargil Review Committee (KRC), Group of

Ministers (GOM) and Naresh Chandra Task Force (NCTF).[3] The mandate by the Government is centred on promoting jointness in procurement, training and staffing for the Services through joint planning and integration of their requirements, and facilitation of restructuring of Military Commands for optimal utilisation of resources by bringing about jointness in operations, including through establishment of joint/ theatre commands.[4]

Reforms are essential in every organisation and institution to keep up with the changing environment, evolving threats, challenges and opportunities, and this is especially so when clear shortcomings have emerged over the years. In retrospect, the way the organisational structures of the Army, Navy and Air Force have evolved, reveals inherent drawbacks. In retrospect, the drawbacks are obvious in the establishment of multiple operational (war-fighting) Commands in the same geographical area. Such an arrangement affects co-ordination, prioritisation in allocation of war-fighting resources, jointness of operational plans, joint training and execution of war-plans. It is well understood that while no organisational structure and arrangement can be predicted with certainty for the future, the methods of yesterday are no longer suitable for tomorrow. Meaningful reforms cannot be postponed any longer.

The focus on Jointness is very crucial, but it cannot be limited to only the three Services; it must be seen from a wider perspective to include the entire HDO. The process of creating Integrated Functional Commands and Theaterisation of the Armed Forces requires an analysis of the roles, responsibilities and the charter of the CDS and the DMA, as well as the functioning of other organs of HDO. Considering the enormity of changes proposed and the desired outcomes of the reorganisation, an accurate perspective on the quantifiable changes, the efficiency models, reduced decision—action cycles, and all previous shortcomings of the system need to be identified and benchmarked. Just reorganising the hierarchy, and the charter without checks, balances and oversight is not enough as proven by the somewhat ad-hoc reorganisation attempts of the past. The prevailing national environment is different from the past as India's citizenry is more concerned and engaged with national security. In view of the wide range of challenges and threats faced by the nation, greater transparency, accountability and responsibility is therefore a given in all matters of security, both on part of the HDO and the Services. Thus, mere creation of posts and organisations is no longer acceptable in the process of the transformation, unless it can produce the desired outcomes.

THE INDIAN CONTEXT

The HDO of powerful nations in the post-World War II era evolved gradually keeping with their national aspirations, national strategies, international security perspectives and the various technological changes. While the type of governance sets the datum, most HDO's include appropriate structures for:

- Political control over the Military.
- Bureaucratic oversight in fiscal matters, acquisition of weapon systems and equipment for capability enhancement, creation of infrastructure, administrative support, and so on.
- Organisational structure of the Army, Navy and Air Force, both individually and combined, to deliver on the military objectives determined by the Nation.
- This is where the Allocation of Business Rules (AoB)[5] and Transaction of Business Rules (ToB)[6] of the GOI come into play for the efficient functioning of the top echelons—Political, Bureaucracy and Military. The security outcomes produced by the military instrument of national power will fall short of national and constitutional expectations unless the three top echelons of HDO function in unison, demonstrate, and ensure integration both in spirit and action.

It is neither possible, nor appropriate, to follow the template of HDO of powerful nations like the US, China or Russia because of several structural aspects. The constitutional framework, economic status, national resources, national aspirations, threat perception and mitigation are among the most important. Next come the evolved priorities, which include international commitments, desired global influence and strategic footprint, aspirations for global leadership roles, interventions and expeditionary actions. For example, the US has global presence, reach, influence and commitments, and hence its HDO structure plays an important role in the US National Security Strategy.[7] The US has immense resources to meet its aspirations and support its global strategic footprint. China is a rising superpower, building up its economic and military capabilities to challenge American hegemony, and is rapidly expanding its strategic footprint to fulfil its own historically driven aspirations. Therefore, the HDOs of these nations have undergone restructuring over the years to meet their global commitments and aspirations. While India has neither territorial ambitions or current expeditionary commitments, the threats it faces are no longer limited to its geographical borders. India must also protect its legitimate strategic interests and territorial integrity against two collusive, nuclear-powers as adversaries. It also lacks the economic heft and resources, except for human capital, to become a global force in the short-term horizon. The Indian HDO, therefore, must be unique, structured and empowered in a way that all the military instruments of power, whether used independently or jointly, may be fully utilised in mitigating India's specific national requirements. Since India's rise towards becoming a 'leading power' is still a work in progress, and is unfolding gradually, it is imperative that its HDO structures be adaptable to these national transformations.

CURRENT CHALLENGES OF THE HDO

India has a robust national security architecture comprising organisations, institutional bodies, policies, directives and mechanisms to achieve national objectives. It has tiered decision-making structures that function with a process-based approach, and has four important constituents: First is the Cabinet Committee on Security (CCS), which is headed by the Prime Minister with several Cabinet Ministers as members, like Raksha Mantri (RM), External Affairs Minister (EAM), Finance Minister and Home Minister.[8] It deliberates and decides on important matters related to India's Security; The next is the Ministry of Defence (MOD) under the political leadership of the RM, along with a team of Secretaries and elements like DRDO, DPSUs, Scientific Advisor, FADS (Financial Advisor), CGDA, etc. It also includes the three Service Headquarters helmed by the COAS, CNS and CAS, and the latest addition to the list being CDS with the DMA. The third is the Defence Planning Committee (DPC) headed by National Security Advisor (NSA) equivalent to a Cabinet ranked Minister, and Defence Acquisition Committee (DAC) chaired by RM. Finally, there are several policies, guidelines and directives for smooth functioning of HDO, like RM's Directive (Mil Strategy), Union War Book, Defence Acquisition Policy (DAP), AOB and TOB rules of GOI, etc.

In terms of its architecture, on the face of it, the Indian HDO is well structured. However, the gap between the mandate and actual functioning of the near-perfect structure, is remarkably wide. There are several aspects of HDO that require urgent remedial actions.

- **National Security Strategy (NSS).** The absence of a well-articulated NSS document is a huge handicap for the political, bureaucratic and military leadership. Many prior judgments demonstrate the inadequacy of knowledge on matters military and national security perspectives on important issues in the security domain. In the absence of an NSS, the HDO has a 'what do we do?' reactive approach to national security rather than a 'this is what we do' pro-active approach. The change towards a proactive outlook will be possible once the contours of the NSS define the strategic aspirations, goals, and benchmarks of India's security interests. The golden rule should be that the decisions are in conformity with the broad guidelines of the NSS.

- **Military Strategy (RM's Directive).** The RM's written directive issued from time to time is considered to be the Military Strategy (MS) for the Nation, MOD and the Armed Forces. Ideally, the MS should be formulated within the contours of the NSS but since this document has not been formalised, the MS has little sanctity in ministries which matter, especially the Finance Ministry, which provides budgetary support. The review of the MS is irregular and is prepared with independent Service-wise inputs merged together to form the directive. In the absence of an integrated approach, the employment of the military instrument gets somewhat detached from comprehensive national power, which impacts planning and jeopardises mitigation of emerging threats. The prioritised Long Term Integrated Perspective Plan (LTIPP) of the Armed Forces is thereafter prepared based on the MS, and it would be ideal if the MS and LTIPP receive CCS approval, thus ensuring their sanctity for structured capability building.[9]
- **Expertise on National Security.** India's founding architects intentionally chose to keep the military isolated from governance structures for reasons that are well-known and beyond the purview of this chapter. It has also been observed that specialisation in national security affairs has been largely absent within political and bureaucratic structures. While learning on the job for a political leader may be acceptable, specialisation in various facets of national security within the bureaucracy is essential. This grooming could involve graded exposure to courses in Defence Services Staff College (DSSC) in Nilgiris, course at College of Defence Management (CDM) Hyderabad or Army/Navy/Air War colleges and finally undergoing the one-year course at National Defence College (NDC) in Delhi. The curriculum at NDC comprehensively deals with all aspects of national security and strategy, to prepare senior Military and Civil Services officers for working cohesively in HDO. Similarly, the Military leaders too need exposure

and knowledge on the overall functioning of the government departments, legal and financial management aspects as a part of their career progression. Consequently, the inclusion of selected middle-ranking and senior military officers in Phases 4 and 5 of the career training of bureaucrats would pave the path for better synergy in the MoD.

- **Overcoming Mistrust.** Even though India's military has remained impeccably apolitical, secular, fought external adversaries over the previous seven decades to protect sovereignty, and has professionally filled fissures and cracks arising from insurgencies and other internal security challenges, there have been times of mistrust between diverse instruments of national security. The Department of Military Affairs (DMA) should be able to overcome this challenge in the overall functioning of HDO.
- **Efficacy of Chairman Chiefs of Staff Committee (COSC).** The jointness amongst the three Services should have improved significantly after the establishment of the post of Chairman COSC and HQ IDS under COSC in October 2001.[10] The flaw was in the ad hoc manner it was constituted, and the dual-hatting of the Chairman instead of a permanent incumbency. Perhaps, the Government, which did not wish to create one more four-star General post of a permanent Chairman COSC or CDS, instead created a titular appointment with little authority and limited consequence. The creation of HQ IDS, on the other hand, did help in laying a strong foundation for jointness amongst the Services, and in providing a launch-pad for an empowered CDS in the of end 2019.[11] Turf battles are common to all militaries, but they are reduced to manageable levels by appointing a CDS in most countries, where he has the decision-making authority and is able to influence the hardliners in each Service who suffer from inflexibility, single-service mind sets and work in narrow operational silos. Needless to add, the CDS must have in-depth

knowledge of the capabilities and option each Service provides, both individually and jointly, be fair in ensuring equality amongst all independent services, ensure that national security remains a combined responsibility of all, as against the present perception of single service dominant approach, and provide the best military option to the nation against future threats and challenges, and finally, be mature in views and articulation.

The bigger problem that confronts India's Armed Forces is the non-availability of the wherewithal to fulfil its mandate, that includes inadequate resources, funds, assets, equipment and weapon systems for capability building to mitigate the wide range of threats. To build a war-fighting capability through the implementation of the LTIPP, there must be an assured and credible defence budget. Unless unforeseen circumstances necessitate a reduction in allocations, the yearly rise in Capital and Revenue heads must be established. Though certain ball-park figures are available towards annual increases in allocations, they are rarely adhered to. The long gestation period, normally exceeds 10 years in acquisition projects, and at times non-release of promised funds jeopardises the execution of LTIPP and operational capabilities, with an accompanying risk of technology becoming dated even before it is inducted into the Services.

The acquisition of major equipment is notoriously 'process-driven' and not 'outcome oriented', with little accountability from the stakeholders. Purchases are fast-tracked in emergency or crisis situations, which does not help in meeting the contingency since major inductions have a considerable lead-time to fructify and operationalise. The authorities responsible for completion of acquisition processes have turned over-cautious, launching themselves on a fault-finding mission rather than working a way out to fructify the project based on operational, diplomatic and strategic needs. It is perhaps a natural response to sustained orchestration by vested political interests against a big-ticket project, since no one wants to be blamed for recommending or approving the purchase when a post-mortem is conducted following a change of government. The opportunistic exploitation by political parties of major acquisitions, has caused immense harm to India's capability building efforts and has impacted the ability of the Armed Forces to deter adversaries effectively.

TASKS CUT OUT FOR CDS AND DMA

The institution of CDS, along with DMA, is a desirable step forward in bringing about reforms, mainly in the military organisation of HDO and, partially, in the functioning of the MoD, for greater jointness and efficiency. It is relevant to remember that both hierarchical organisations, and the 'tradition-bound' Indian ethos and culture, do not accept revolutionary changes. Therefore, reforms in the Indian Military structures should be progressive and a step-by-step approach to change is desirable. A total overhaul of the structure and functioning, based on merely the assumed or perceived success of such reforms in other militaries across the world, and without a detailed knowledge of the problems faced by them, is an immense leap of faith. It will be fraught with many pitfalls and difficulties, especially when the military lacks the 'wherewithal' to support some of the desired changes. The reforms in the military must go hand in hand with reforms in the other elements of HDO to create a strong, credible and dynamic instrument of statecraft. An analysis of the Government directive and its implementation process clearly brings out the tasks that need to be undertaken by the CDS and DMA. Many of these tasks could be executed simultaneously, while a few would take precedence over others, and they are as follows:

- As the integration process advances, the force will be transformed towards a 'lean and mean' force through enhancement of teeth to tail ratio and eliminating duplications and redundancies.
- Implementation of a Tri-Services communication network for Integrated Network Centric Warfare (NCW) capability. A lot of

work must have already been completed in this regard.

- Evolve a contemporary integrated NSS for the RM, covering all military aspects, ranging from individual employment, integrated military applications, and equally importantly, as a part of comprehensive national power to facilitate an 'all of Govt approach'. It must also push for release of this document at the earliest.
- Rework the RM's Directive, Joint Doctrine and the LTIPP based on the military and MoD reforms to achieve the defined national security objectives. Define Jointmanship and set its expectations based on a national outlook. Initiate measures to infuse it into the DNA of each Service, starting by revamping the Professional Military Education (PME) on highest priority. This is important as it will bring about a generational change amongst the future Service officers, but it must be initiated now to have a timely effect.
- Formulate and implement effective tri-Services HR policies towards joint training, career progression and tenanting appointments in joint organisations. There would be a need to fuse and expand parent-Service loyalties towards a larger and integrated military commitment. Each Service will need serious soul-searching amongst its hard-liners who are opposed to Jointmanship in order to understand its importance and find points of convergence.
- Set up Joint Functional Commands like Op Logistics and Training. There are huge challenges in re-structuring the existing network of organisations of each Service to achieve jointness in command and control, supply chain management and training needs. Rather than trying to build from scratch, adapt, modify and restructure only the necessary, with a 'cost to company vs outcome' approach.
- Strategise, plan and develop core competencies for the wide range of future conflict scenarios by leveraging space, cyber,

drone warfare, use of AI, advanced intelligence gathering applications and efficient ISR mechanisms, in all future conduct of integrated military operations and warfare.

- Integration of the operational planning process and the concept of operations for every war-fighting contingency would yield significant benefits. This would mean not a fusion of Service specific plans, but adopting a much-needed 'sitting across the table together' approach to planning by all stakeholders. The CDS and Service Chiefs would be responsible for the integrated plan prepared for all contingencies and activities, whether theatre specific or multi-theatre.

RESTRUCTURING OF COMMANDS

If media reports are to be believed, a lot of progress has been made in providing contours to Air Defence Command, Maritime Command and work is on towards giving shape to Integrated Theatre Commands (ITC) expeditiously, since the appointment of CDS. While the expedience in bringing about changes is understood, the rush to do so was somewhat misplaced.[12] Sensibly, an inclusive and studied approach is learnt to have been adopted by the MoD since. Debates and discussions in the environment indicate the restructured Armed Forces to consist of the following:

- A Unified Air Defence Command defending the entire air frontier of India.
- An expanded single Maritime Command ensuring strategic footprint over the entire Maritime Domain, i.e., Indian Ocean Region (IOR) and parts of the Indo-Pacific.
- Western, Eastern, and Northern Commands are the three 'land-centric' ITCs. The Western ITC would be responsible for countering the Pak-threat, while the Eastern ITC would be China specific. The Northern Command is not planned to be tinkered with presently and remain a primarily Counter-insurgency (CI) and Counterterrorism (CT) focussed structure. While this may be

a fait accompli for a while with the renewed threat of the Taliban's entry into J&K, serious thought over the long term must be given to freeing Indian Army formations engaged in CI/CT for more conventional deployments along the LAC and LoC.

- The allocation of resources to the three ITCs from the three Services would be crucial, especially for the Navy and Air Force, highlighting criticality and conflict of interest in distribution of limited wherewithal amongst Maritime, Air Defence, Strategic Forces Commands and ITCs.
- Clarity would be required in the tasks and responsibilities of Andaman Nicobar Command (ANC), the first Tri-Services operational Command that has set the benchmark for jointness amongst the Services. The role of ANC in the IOR and wider Indo-Pacific region is strategically very crucial in a future conflict or for ensuring a dominating presence in peace time.
- Strategic Forces Command (SFC), a very successful Tri-Services Command, would continue to function as before without any major changes.
- Space, Cyber and Special Ops Divisions would evolve in the future as Tri-Services Commands, under the CDS/COSC.

ASPECTS FOR DELIBERATION

In addition to the threat scenario, the creation of ITCs necessitates deliberations on many factors like area of responsibility, assets and concept of operations. There is an opinion amongst some in the strategic community that India could be considered as a single theatre because of its size and limited war-fighting assets, especially with the Air Force and Navy. India's geographical size is less than the Western Theatre of China with which it shares land borders. The area of responsibility of the Hawaii based US Indo-Pacific Command is many times larger than the maritime domain of India, while its Naval and Air Force assets are much larger than the inventories of the IN and the IAF.[13] The Air

Force will find it difficult to distribute its meagre combat aircraft and force multiplier assets like AWACS, AEW&CS and Air to Air Refuellers towards dedicated doctrinal tasking for land-based maritime operations in anti-shipping role, fighter aircraft to Strategic Forces Command for air vector of nuclear triad, Air Defence Command requirements (in peace and war), the ITCs for Counter Surface Force Operation (CSFO) and Counter Air Operation (CAO) campaigns and IAF's strategic targeting requirements of industry, leadership, fuel and energy, etc.[14, 15]

In terms of operations, the Indian Army believes in having all formations under the firm command and control of the relevant top Commander. This is a very relevant aspect from the point of view of tasking and mobilisation of reserves for an effective operational campaign. However, for the IAF these two aspects are intrinsic in its time tested and operationally proven strategy of centralised planning and decentralised execution. This strategy of airpower employment is common to all Air Forces of the world and is not exclusive to the IAF. Despite the reduced combat aircraft resources, the IAF has successfully exploited its multi-role combat fleets to switch operational roles (CSFO, AD, CAO) and missions (Strike, escort, offensive and defensive combat air patrol, ISR, etc.) seamlessly and between theatres to achieve concentration of force at the most crucial battle. This was amply proven based on the demonstrated performance in Exercise Gaganshakti.[16] Distribution and control of critical air assets, as also management of airspace between offensive and defensive air elements of ITCs and AD Command, would remain a challenge. Even with advances in the quantity of air assets, a lot of brainstorming would be necessary to evolve methodologies to harmonise the concept of air operations. Management of airspace would need much-improved co-ordination amongst operators, robust Standard Operating Procedures (SOPs), command and control protocols, prioritisation of air tasking, etc. Network Centric Warfare capabilities will certainly facilitate efficient airspace management, especially over Tactical Battle Areas (TBA).

RESPONSIBILITIES OF CDS

The CDS as the single point advisor to the Government, currently wears three hats. First, as the functional head of Tri-Services Operational Commands (SFC and ANC), Space, Cyber and Special Operations Divisions—likely to be upgraded to Operational Commands; second, as Chairman of COSC, ably supported by the three Chiefs and CISC, controlling joint training, defence intelligence, communication networks, procurements, budget management, HR issues, International Military Co-Op Exercises (military diplomacy), HADR and aid to civil authorities. Finally, as Secretary DMA, dealing with MoD policies, co-ordination with other Ministries like Railways, Shipping, National Highways, Home Affairs (NSG, para-mil-forces), Civil Aviation, MEA, HRD, Telecommunications, etc.[17]

The situation is perhaps more complicated and tougher than the dual-hatting of the Chairman COSC earlier. The responsibilities of the CDS are likely to increase manifold with the operationalisation of Air Defence Command, Maritime Command, ITCs and other Integrated Functional or Support Commands like Joint Training Command and Operational Logistics Command. Restructuring the Military involves a lot of work, in not only determining the contours and structures of the Commands but also defining the role and responsibilities of CDS, COAS, CNS & CAS, Theatre Commanders and Commanders of Functional and Support Commands. There are many challenges in streamlining the functioning of senior commanders and staff in the process of integration and it may take several years to achieve harmonised functioning. To enhance jointness amongst the Services, the Chairman COSC and the three Service Chiefs would need to sit together on all promotion boards of star ranks, selection of both command and staff appointments in joint organisations like HQ IDS, ANC, SFC, etc. Presidential awards list for distinguished service like PVSM, AVSM, and those for gallantry would have to be determined by the COSC members under the Chairman, for final approval of RM. These steps would ensure that performance in joint organisations would receive due recognition and encourage an integrated military mindset as against single services loyalties. The CDS and Service Chiefs would be required to attend all war-games and major Command/ITC level field exercises to fine-tune the fused joint operational/contingency plans. Attendance at the RM would be desirable for greater sanctity of such plans.

ENHANCING EFFICACY OF HDO

Simple modifications in roles and responsibilities will not make the HDO more effective. It must establish legitimacy and presence for the military instrument of power as a vital element of CNP. It must leverage the requirements of the military in today's world of competing demands, governmental priorities and shrinking budgets. Good teamwork, co-ordination, responsiveness and information flow are the hallmark of an efficient and integrated HDO. This will need to be done in several ways.

The quality of interaction between military leadership and the Prime Minister sets the trend in Civil-Military integration and relationship down the hierarchy. Despite the several burning issues that the PM deals with, regular interaction between the apex military and executive leadership during these transformative times is desirable if meaningful change is to be made in HDO. The ruling regime's perspective on national security issues and events is shaped as much by political considerations as it is by the desire to achieve national security goals.

The Raksha Mantri is the true lynchpin of the HDO, who prepares the canvas for jointness and enhanced Civil-Military relations of the entire organisation. The incumbent's knowledge and experience in governance, and of being a senior heavy weight in the Cabinet used to dealing at the strategic levels, are equally important factors. The RM would have to be a pragmatic leader who would not get bogged down by bureaucratic process and forcefully argue the MoD cases to convince the CCS, based on national interests and strategic necessity, and where necessary, use his discretionary powers for approval. In the acquisition of weapon systems, the emphasis is often on the commercial aspects while downplaying the crucial operational factors with strategic implications, which impact the security needs of the Nation. The RM's success and effectiveness in CCS meetings ignites the MoD with vigour and dynamism. This has a cascading effect in building good relations and Jointmanship between the military and the bureaucracy.

The NSA, currently a Cabinet Minister rank appointment, is the real interface between the military leadership and the PM. A warm and cordial relationship between military leaders and the NSA, with mutual trust as the basis, is essential in shaping and providing an integrated and appropriate military response on matters of national security. Even though the NSA's plate is full of additional responsibilities, there is a need for more regular engagements with military leadership towards employment of the military instrument in the national interest. For example, the NSA's role as the Chairman of Defence Planning Committee has a direct bearing on military capability building effort with strategic implications, necessitating a greater and more regular engagement with the top military leadership.

The Parliamentary Standing Commitee on Defence, comprising Members of Parliament from various political parties, is critical to the HDO in exercising supervision over all MoD activity and India's defence preparedness. Several structured interactions are held between the Committee members, high-ranking MoD officials and the military leadership on pre-determined issues. Some of the members justifiably, raise concerns of their States and political constituencies on recruitment, job opportunities in the military and setting up of military stations in respective States. However, in a fast maturing democracy such as India, the Committee must become a more knowledgeable, empowered, and influential organisation for reviewing defence readiness. Up-to-date knowledge of the current and future capabilities of each service will enable the committee to become an influential stakeholder in the process of helping the military continuously upgrade its capabilities, war-fighting potential and expedite budgetary support for futuristic capability development. It would also enable independent oversight of the entire HDO and its working. If major political parties groomed some of their young leaders on issues of national security and strategy, it would promote an enhanced understanding of national security at the national level and among citizens. Orientation on national security aspects through familiarisation courses at National Defence College in Delhi, would enable them to contribute effectively in the Parliament, as well as in the functioning of the Standing Committee on Defence.

CONCLUSION

Reforms in the operation of all tiers and instruments of the Higher Defence Organisation are required to achieve greater jointness, with the restructuring and integration of the MoD and the Armed Forces being the principal ones. The 'Mantra' for rapid development of India's hard power and deterrence capabilities lies more in the quality of the integration of political, bureaucratic and military structures. For efficiently tenanting appointments in HDO, bureaucrats and politicians should be exposed to and familiar with the complexities of national security and military instruments. Similarly, senior military leadership needs to emerge out of its operational cocoon and quickly assimilate the finer nuances of statecraft. Unless political leadership drives all this from the top, synergy across diverse agencies could be an issue. The challenge of reforming the Armed Forces into Integrated Commands, both functionally and for warfighting, is extremely difficult. Further effort would be required to fine-tune HR management as well as command and control protocols in order to achieve harmonised functioning in the new organisational architecture. However, the proposed jointness would increase efficiency up to a point, beyond which the armed forces' capability would be defined by the induction of appropriate and potential war-fighting capability.

NOTES

1 Cabinet approves creation of CDS, single-point military adviser to govt, *Business Standard*, PTI, New Delhi, December 30, 2019, https://www.business-standard.com/article/pti-stories/cabinet-committee-on-security-approves-creation-of-chief-of-defence-staff-119122400586_1.html. Accessed on June 25, 2021.

2 Ministry of Defence, Creation of New Department of Military Affairs, posted on February 3, 2020, 8:30 PM by PIB Delhi, https://pib.gov.in/PressReleasePage.aspx?PRID=1601813. Accessed on June 25, 2021.

3 "GOM Report on national Security", 2001, https://www.vifindia.org/sites/default/files/GoM%20Report%20on%20National%20Security.pdf. Accessed on June 25, 2021.

4 Ministry of Defence, n. 2.

5 Government of India (Allocation of Business) Rules, 1961, https://www.cabsec.gov.in/writereaddata/allocationbusinessrule/completeaobrules/english/1_Upload_1187.pdf. Accessed on June 26, 2021.

6 "Transaction of Business", Cabinet Secretariat, Government of India, https://cabsec.gov.in/writereaddata/transactionofbusinessrulescomplete/completeaobrules/english/1_Upload_30.pdf. Accessed on June 26, 2021.

7 "National Security Strategy of the United States of America", December 2017, pp. 45-52, https://trumpwhitehouse.archives.gov/wp-content/uploads/2017/12/NSS-Final-12-18-2017-0905.pdf. Accessed on June 26, 20121.

8 https://cabsec.gov.in/writereaddata/cabinetcommittees/english/1_Upload_3031.pdf. Accessed on June 26, 2021.

9 "Defence Acquisition", https://www.ids.nic.in/defence-acquisition.php. Accessed on June 27, 2021.

10 "Headquarters Intergrated Defence Staff celebrates its 20th Raising Day", https://pib.gov.in/Pressreleaseshare.aspx?PRID=1660684. Accessed on June 27, 2021.

11 Shaurya Karambir Gurung, "Army Chief General Bipin Rawat appointed as Chief of Defence Staff", *The Economic Times*, December 31, 2020, https://economictimes.indiatimes.com/news/defence/army-chief-general-bipin-rawat-appointed-as-chief-of-defence-staff/articleshow/73036179.cms?utm_source=contentofinterest&utm_medium=text&utm_campaign=cppst. Accessed on June 27, 2021.

12 Amrita Nayak Datta, "Why setting up integrated theatre commands should not be rushed—former service chiefs explain", The Print, July 17, 2021, https://theprint.in/defence/why-setting-up-integrated-theatre-commands-should-not-be-rushed-former-service-chiefs-explain/697900/

13 https://www.pacom.mil/About-USINDOPACOM/USPACOM-Area-of-Responsibility/. Accessed on June 27, 2021.

14 https://bharatshakti.in/wp-content/uploads/2015/09/Joint_Doctrine_Indian_Armed_Forces.pdf, p. 25. Accessed on June 27, 2021.

15 https://defenceforumindia.com/threads/basic-doctrine-of-the-indian-air-force-2012.42530/. Accessed on June 27, 2021, pp. 39-123.

16 Arvind Gupta, "Significance of Exercise 'Gagan Shakti-2018'", https://www.vifindia.org/article/2018/may/07/significance-of-exercise-gagan-shakti-2018. Accessed on June 27, 2021.

17 https://indianexpress.com/article/explained/explained-what-are-roles-powers-chief-of-defence-staff-6195264/. Accessed on June 27, 2021.

CHAPTER 17

LESSONS IN JOINTNESS FROM THE ANDAMAN NICOBAR COMMAND EXPERIENCE

SUDHIR PILLAI

ABSTRACT

With the appointment of the Chief of Defence Staff and greater political oversight over military transformation, India's armed forces are now compelled to embrace jointness. Building on the experience gained from the establishment of Joint structures in the aftermath of Kargil, such as the Andaman Nicobar Command (ANC) and Headquarters Integrated Defence Staff (IDS), will serve India well. Service parochialism will have to be overcome through joint acculturation of selected military officers. Conventional mindsets, as institutionally ingrained, will need to be changed to keep pace with the changing character of war and conflict and the continued impact of technology on the Revolution in Military Affairs. Jointness is not about sacrificing single-service ways to accommodate the ways and means of other or more dominant services. Rather than waiting for a crisis to force such a change, it is about synergising them together into a meaningful whole through transformative education and training of future commanders and staff officers.

JOINTNESS IN THE AFTERMATH OF KARGIL

Following the Kargil War, a Group of Ministers (GoM) suggested to the Indian government that *'Modern warfare demands a much higher degree of coordination in operations and management by all the three Services, than ever before"*. They were following up on the recommendations of the Kargil Review Committee (the K. Subrahmanyam Committee) and Task Force (of experts) on Management of Defence (headed by Shri Arun Singh).[1] A multi-pronged approached to furthering military jointness was endorsed as a policy imperative.

Among the many steps taken, the Government of India sanctioned the post of Commander-in-Chief Andaman & Nicobar Command (CINCAN). Thus, by September 2001, a '*Unified Combatant Command*'[2] would be created. The CINCAN (from any of the three military services) was assigned authority over a geographic Area of Responsibility (AOR). He was made singularly and entirely responsible for missions within his AOR. This geographic combatant command is the only 'AOR' for an Indian Commander in Chief (CINC) that overcomes the lacunae of overlapping geographical AsOR for other Commanders in Chief of the three military services of India, each breaching that principle of 'Unity of Command'. Thus, the CINCAN uniquely ended up with the three military service components and the Coast Guard Region placed 'under command'.

A case in point is the lack of a unified military command that hampered early response and effective command and control during the Mumbai Terror Attacks of 2008 (26/11). A few critical findings are highlighted as follows:

- Though Marine Commandos from Western Naval Command and a battalion under the Mumbai Sub-Area, with counter-insurgency and counterterrorism training and experience, reached Taj Mahal and the Trident-Oberoi Hotels, the military's first-responders were constrained due to limited and sub-optimal coordination.[3]

- A military system of subsequent handover to the National Security Guard (NSG) (a specialised outfit under the MHA), or the NSG being detached and attached under military authority, are pointers for evolving the doctrinal basis for joint and 'interagency' and command and control mechanisms. Such processes should have been in place rather than waiting for the arrival of the NSG and orders from different ministries, agencies and command headquarters!

As a former Chief of Staff (2012-2014) to three CINCAN (drawn from each of the three Indian military services), the author of this chapter has had a ringside view of the efforts to further collaborative processes at India's only joint command, the Andaman and Nicobar Command. Upon completeing a fixed two-year rotational tenure as CINCAN, Lieutenant General N.C. Marwah was appointed as Chief of Integrated Staff to the Chiefs of Staff Committee (CISC) in November 2012. General Marwah continued to engage with the COSC to take ahead the joint necessities with an advanced understanding of the issues. After a visit by the Indian Defence Minister (RM) to HQ ANC for a first-hand briefing, the RM directed the COSC to visit ANC and take ahead the joint command's imperatives and India's efforts at jointness.

Despite these early transformative attempts at jointness, the Indian military has remained hostage to institutional or organisational parochialism, and continues to offer lukewarm support to jointness, despite some renewed momentum following the creation of the post of CDS. Indians tend to view the word parochialism in a pejorative sense (in negative terms). However, viewing the dissonance through a sociological lens may permit a greater acceptance of cultural traits and the creation of an expansive mindset that is essential for true jointness. This chapter examines how institutional socio-centrism is a millstone around Indian efforts at jointness. The ANC could be that 'crucible of a concept' to take jointness beyond organisational parochialism in the

Indian context, rather than through any big-bang reforms that could face headwinds and internal opposition.

CASE STUDIES IN JOINTNESS

The Indo-Pak Kargil War

The Pakistan Army launched Operation BADR in the winter of 1998-1999, with Northern Light Infantry elements heading an intrusion into the Mushkoh, Dras, Kargil and Batalik sectors of Jammu and Kashmir. This armed intrusion would lead up to the Kargil conflict and Operations Vijay and Safed Sagar. While Operation Vijay was the Indian Army operation to evict the intruders, Safed Sagar would see India unleashing airpower in the J&K region for the first time after 1971. In an article analysing the use of airpower in such situations, AVM Arjun Subramaniam writes, "Had the Indian Army taken the IAF into confidence from day one and developed a joint plan to evict the intruders instead of trying to use it as an afterthought, armed helicopters could have joined the fight after sufficient degradation had been inflicted by fixed wing aircraft and artillery."[4]

His narrative highlights the shortcomings in joint operational planning, a lack of common collaborative mechanisms and the absence of a proper joint doctrine or a unitary command system, which are crucial to resolving functional differences or ambiguities.

Air War for Kosovo

While the intrusion in Kargil was ongoing, airpower was being employed in another conventional solo show of force in Operation Allied Force at about the same time.

A RAND Arroyo Center analysis reveals lessons from the conflict that merit attention:[5]

- Allied Force was not fought classically like a joint (multiservice) and combined (multinational) operation; this is when one looks at it from perspectives such as collaborative planning, operations, integrating air and ground capabilities, etc.

- The absence of joint or combined planning resulted in reduced operational effectiveness, thereby delaying victory.
- This "disjointedness" could have had severe consequences if Milosevic had not capitulated, and offensive ground operations may have been required.
- Given the Serb tactics of dispersion, coupled with concealment and sporadic use of their air defences, NATO's air only strategy ran into serious problems.

NATO's Supreme Allied Commander Europe (SACEUR) and US European Command (USEUCOM) Commander sought direct attacks against ground force targets given their analysis of Yugoslav ground forces as the Centre of Gravity (COG). The Air Component Commander, Commander Allied Air Forces Southern Europe, recognising the difficulty of doing severe damage to ground forces, judged attack of fixed targets as the best way forward.[6] Towards balancing differing philosophies, as in ALLIED FORCE, the military-way is ideally enunciated through a clear joint doctrine with 'Unity of command' as an important group dynamic to enforce tough decisions when faced with differing perspectives.[7]

The 1991 Gulf War

While the Persian Gulf War of 1991, also called Operation Desert Storm, achieved stated strategic objectives, service-based organisational biases influenced strategy and operations, as evident from the following:[8]

- In the days following the Iraqi invasion of Kuwait, the Operations Plan presented by the CINC of the US Central Command (CINCCENT), Gen Schwarzkopf primarily called for using land forces and assigned a minor supporting role to airpower.

- Schwarzkopf appointed, Lt Gen Chuck Horner, a USAF General as Joint Force Air Component Commander (JFACC). The Army, Navy, and Marine Corps viewed the JFACC with scepticism and were prone to throw many a spanner into the works.
- Despite his insistence on preparing the battlefield in front of the Army, Marines, and coalition forces, Schwarzkopf eventually recognised the value of the stand-alone air campaign and allowed it to run for six weeks before initiating ground combat operations.

The ambiguities and differences in planning and operations ran deep, but were resolved through extensive consultative planning processes. This was facilitated by a joint organisational structure that included at the Apex the Joint Chiefs of Staff (with Gen Colin Powell as Chairman). Thus, the final plan went ahead with a prolonged air campaign (OP INSTANT THUNDER) serving as Offensive Campaign Phase 1 of the four stages that was OP DESERT STORM.[9]

Operation Weserübung

History is replete with many examples that highlight military commanders' discretion, and such norms have been evolved and cemented given the changing face of military reform. An outstanding example of joint operations is Operation *Weserübung*, the German invasion of Scandinavia in 1940. The classical joint operation involved significant land, sea and air forces.

- Hitler overcame service parochialism and rivalry among the three military services headquarters by tasking a joint planning staff assembled at the Armed Forces High Command (*Oberkommando der Wehrmacht* or OKW) to prepare detailed plans after preliminary plans emerged from reports submitted by staff officers drawn from each of the services.

- Significantly, the operational staffs of the services were excluded from the planning process. By personally taking leadership of Weserübung, Hitler bypassed the Luftwaffe, which would play a dominant role in the actual operation The Principal planner was Captain Theodor Krancke, Commanding Officer of the cruiser Admiral Scheer, who was assisted by a small group of Army and Air Force officers.[10]

TWO DECADES FOLLOWING KARGIL

A Chinese Prod

The year 2020 saw India having to ward off a significant border standoff with China. The violent escalation, posturing and de-escalation serve as yet another reminder of the severe security challenges that India confronts in the challenges posed by China's military modernisation and increasingly aggressive policies. The Chinese challenge serves as another reminder that India needs to constantly review, update, and replace military strategies, operational concepts, organisational constructs and equipment.

In an occasional paper for the Observer Research Foundation, Manoj Joshi has highlighted the unwavering commitment and leadership of Xi Jinping in the transformation of the People's Liberation Army (PLA) which he unveiled during the Third Plenum in 2013. While a great deal of media attention focuses on the PLA's hardware acquisition, the transformation in PLA command and control, organisation, employment and doctrine demands greater attention of Indian leadership, both in government and in the military.[11] Toshi Yoshihara, a professor at Georgetown University and a visiting lecturer at the India's Naval War College, has pointed to the rise of a 'Military-Intellectual Complex', as against a 'Military-Industrial Complex' that drives PLA military modernisation and transformation.[12]

Implementation Inertia

In India's case, Prime Minister Narendra Modi has thrown down the transformation gauntlet at the Indian military, and the ball is now in the court of the three services. Suppose Mr Modi were to take advice hypothetically from Ben Gurion, Israel's first Prime Minister, he might have received the following famous quote: 'Of all the deficiencies of our military, lack of discipline is the most severe, and above all at the highest levels.[13] Mr Modi could borrow a leaf from Xi Jinping and ensure close monitoring, lest another opportunity for reform is squabbled away at the altar of parochialism.

Chris Dougherty, a Senior Fellow in the Defense Program at the Center for a New American Security, puts it succinctly when he opines: *'Would-be reformers of India's armed forces often seek to surmount these strategic obstacles through one of two approaches: advocating for increased defence budgets 'to raise all boats with the tide', or by recommending a massive reorganisation of the Indian military along the lines of the U.S. Goldwater-Nichols reforms or the restructuring of China's People's Liberation Army (PLA).'*[14] Suggestions like his 'to create more regional and functional joint warfighting commands' is under serious consideration, prodded by PLA moves along the LAC and in the Indian Ocean. Dougherty's other suggestion, 'to increase the day-to-day use of joint task forces', needs India to take a deep dive into tenets of organisational theory and Joint principles, an imperative in reforming and modernising its conventional military capabilities. Regrettably, multi-disciplinary academic studies on such issues are missing in India's strategic discourse and await the creation of a National Defence University!

CDS—India's Goldwater-Nichols Moment?

The Government of India (GoI) recently overcame inertia, compelled by past necessities such as political consensus and even internal dissent from within the services, and appointed General Bipin Rawat as India's first CDS on January 1, 2020. It also created a Department of Military Affairs (DMA) under him, which hived off several functions from the erstwhile

Department of Defence. With this, a significant recommendation emerging from the wide-ranging reviews that took place after the Kargil War was followed up on, albeit after overcoming the inertia of two decades and that of several governments! Having said that, an optimal approach to jointness can be crucial if we are to accomplish the entire effort properly. Much work remains to be done before we can call the CDS' appointment as India's 'Goldwater-Nichols moment'.

DIFFERING PERCEPTIONS

In his book *Joint Operations: A Short Military History*, Roger Beaumont, Professor of History at Texas University and an early chronicler of joint military structures, captures very succinctly the challenges in jointness. He writes, "Like schools of thought in art, the intensity of partisanship on issues of jointness has sometimes approached the level of emotion held toward foes in war, for it touches closely on the critical bonding and cohesion that lie at the heart of military institutions, and their predisposition to see the world in "them-us" terms."[15]

In writing this chapter, about jointness for inter-service and multi-organisational target groups, a need exists to try and fuse different perspectives and attempts to arrive at a multi-domain understanding of 'how and whither jointness'. Views about jointness, as may be put forth by one service, can be anathema to another. Such views have plagued every effort at integration and jointness the world over.

Doctrinal Framework

The synergistic benefits of jointness are generally well understood in a bipartisan manner. However, the moment one seeks a way ahead for the services to formally work together, diverse perspectives emerge from the woodwork.[16] Given this truism, "*Principles of Jointness*" by Captain Robert C. Rubel, a former US Navy fighter pilot, could hopefully serve to enlighten, as against a 'fragmented approach' to Joint principles:[17]

- The '***Principle of Complementarity***' states that merging services into unified organisations (such as joint task forces) can compensate for weaknesses in one Service by leveraging the strengths of others.
- The '***Hierarchy Principle***' advocates that the degree of jointness (or cooperation among the services) is inversely proportionate to the number of command echelons. Flatter organisations are prone to effective internal collaboration.
- The '***Necessity Principle***' states that jointness at the lower echelons of command tends to increase in the face of an enemy. A major lesson of the Pacific War in WWII is that true unity-of-command can be achieved only on the field of battle.[18]
- This principle indicates that lower levels have successfully integrated following another facet of joint dynamics that is '***synchronisation***'. Tactical units tend to self-synchronise with units of other services.
- The '***Cohesion Principle***', which emerges from many war studies, states that joint arrangements that disrupt unit cohesion negate benefits by reducing morale and efficiency. The level at which jointness disrupts cohesion is usually thought to be the upper tactical level (division, battle group, wing, task force).
- '***Integration***' (attaching elements of one Service to another) is fraught with hazards. Logistics can become cumbersome, and formation efficiency can be impaired, despite the additive effects of the attached elements.
- '***Diversity***' helps than impedes. Competition (in both ideas and practice) leads to better outputs in strategy development or even in performance. Strategies are ideally discourse-based and must represent all stakeholders' interests than be an imposition from one person or organisation.
- Rather than waiting until forces are locked in combat, '***proactive jointness***'—the ability to achieve effective cooperation before a

fight would be preferable. Proactive jointness is an inherently top-down policy matter and is thus inhibited by the hierarchy principle.

Military Bureaucracy and Parochialism

Barry Posen, Professor of Political Science at MIT, has focused on bureaucracies and parochialism in examining the military doctrines of France, Britain and Germany. He summarises that military departments and services are naturally parochial, as are all bureaucracies, by outlining the following:[19]

- The national security functions of the modern state are divided among specialists. These specialists, particularly professional soldiers, live their lives and accomplish their tasks in highly structured, complex organisations.
- Towards optimal performance, military organisations train and educate their personnel to conduct business in a specific manner. Those people are socialised, or trained, such that they tend to prepare their subordinates according to the same rules.
- Because the business rules and the organisations that formulate those rules tend to become "institutionalised," organisations responsible for certain functions have parochial ideas on how those tasks should be carried out.

Parochialism, or inter-organisational rivalry, is recognised widely as a phenomenon called socio-centrism. Such rivalry being natural in a bureaucracy, must and can be managed.[20] Compounding matters in an Indian context, parochialism is facilitated by vague or absent guidance— such as the lack of a centrally articulated national or military strategy. Logically, such advice could have helped distinguish priorities among means and ends.

Jointness in the CDS/DMA Era

Organisational theory suggests that the current efforts at military transformation spearheaded by the CDS could derail unless more multi-domain brainstorming is conducted to understand and think through jointness in greater depth and expanse. Organisational theory is very revealing on why integration is not an easy act to follow. While there is a dependence of each Service on the other in various scenarios, each tends to imply that they can get the job done themselves, and their primary theorists will push such a narrative. These are tactical narratives, and operational level perspectives would suggest otherwise. Given such parochial bottlenecks, organisational theory suggests that a better way to integrate diverse functions in an organisation is to organise by mission rather than by function. A functional structure provides clarity, is economical, and facilitates learning one's jobs; however, it focuses on efforts rather than results.[21] The doctrinal underpinnings of the joint task force, which should be the principal method of command and control in 'theatre'—flows from the Principles of Hierarchy because it makes organisations flatter and the Principle of Necessity that flows from the mission imperatives.[22]

JOINT TRAINING, EDUCATION & INTEROPERABILITY

In 1989, US Congressman Ike Skelton had described the process of joint acculturation as: "the mutual understanding and rapport that develop when students from all services study in mixed seminars and share the ideas, values, and traditions of their services, when they solve joint military problems together, and when preconceived notions about the nature of and solution to problems of warfare, learned during service training and education, are challenged daily."[23] India needs its own Skelton panel to review and enforce imperatives in realigning professional military education and training towards jointness.[24]

In addition to officers proficient in their specific service roles, the military needs high-quality officers competent in joint matters to push interoperability in a technology enabled conflict milieu. Structuring a joint education and training syllabi, where cooperative principles and doctrine is ingrained, at least among a selected few, is an essential requirement.

Joint Staff Officer specialisation may see a dilution of single-service parochialism and more significant support for joint principles. Joint doctrines and publications must be carefully drafted and indoctrinated while accommodating or evolving single-service philosophies. The following points may serve to guide:[25]

- In joint organisations, single-service components struggle for independence from legitimate authority, fearful that capricious, uninformed exercise of that authority will upset the delicate balance of internal structure and routine.
- As specialists in their disciplines, single-services and those deputed as component commanders, may feel that they alone are competent to judge on such matters as size, organisation, recruitment, and equipment of the forces.
- Single services fears are worked around in joint organisations through moderating mechanisms as has been in use from ancient Grecian times. The senior military commander, the *Polemarchos*, was replaced by a communal method of Army command and staff, the *Strategoi*. These are systems in vogue even today, as evolved by Prussia in and after the Napoleonic Wars.[26]
- With the Commander and the Chief of Staff from different services (or different countries), a joint (or multinational) moderating role can be evolved from how the Prussian Chiefs of Staff shared with their commanders the responsibility of command. While this may seem like sacrilege to single-service commanders, such moderating mechanisms can help moderate the parochialism of the commander!
- With India finally appointing a CDS, a VCDS (or a Joint Chiefs of Staff) with moderating roles is essential for the necessary checks and balances in India's efforts at jointness.

Geert Hofstede's[28] work on culture can help provide perspectives on such concepts. In a 'large power distance' country like India, one can expect a situation, given very hierarchical organisations, wherein the boss often makes all the decisions, ignoring sound professional counsel. Given the highly-specialised nature of each Service (and even each arm), such approaches can be problematic. If consensus in decision making isn't achievable, are concepts like unitary command and command responsibility & accountability leadership tenets that can break lock-jams?

ANC-DISSECTING THE EXPERIENCE

When the CDS takes the next steps to further jointness or integration of the Indian Armed Forces, there is much that India can learn from the two-decade-long existence of ANC and the functioning of India's lone Joint Command. ANC has seen each service bringing much to the table in terms of ideas and practices, and there is a lot to take away as we seek to engender synergy and joint efficiencies. For this to happen, single-service parochialism must yield to the importance of jointness, as the Joint Commander must be mission-driven and must drive the professional necessities to further jointness wholeheartedly. The CINCAN and joint commanders across echelons, appointed on a rotational or functional basis, often tend to push their single-service concepts that can be anathema to the other services' operational and support logic and the necessities of joint synergy! Modern commanders are critically dependent on their diverse staffs for kinetic, non-kinetic and informational activities of all stakeholders as they pursue mission accomplishment and seek to command and direct. Such understandings led to Prussian concepts like '*the military marriage of the commander and his chief of staff*'.[29] This must emerge as the driving principle in managing diversity.

The Chief of Staff

The COS can be a crucial cog in joint organisations to work modern information-age concepts like Commander's Critical Information Requirements (CCIR),* Knowledge Management, Battle Rhythm, etc.[30] The Chief of Staff is essential to drive such staff systems and discipline the headquarters organisation and processes. The role of the COS needs understanding and evolution to permit the commander the freedom to engage in his command responsibilities.

A Deputy Commander

Modern military organisations additionally cater to a Deputy Commander at each level. A case exists for creating a dedicated post of Deputy CINC, as distinct from the position of Chief of Staff, to ensure more significant support to the commander in his command functions. A Deputy CINC can be a valuable and essential adjunct to the commander's span of control. Currently, the COS is more the de facto than the de jure second-in-command. Lack of a designated second-in-command throws up anomalies, such as when the two-star Commander Coast Guard Region (COMCG), who is sometimes senior to the COS but is not in the command chain, tends to disrupt synergy. Individual Component Commanders, though one-star appointees are also known to question the authority of the COS when single-service aspects come to the fore and when they find support in a CINCAN from their own Service!

Staff Organisation

Modern militaries must contend with an unprecedented ability of diverse forces to transmit, receive, and disrupt data, all while the data grows exponentially in both speed and volume. The sheer volume of information can be detrimental to effective and timely decision making. Such factors "influence HQ organisations and decision support processes as joint commanders seek to apply art and science to understand the situation, frame problems, plan, and execute at the speed of relevance."[31] The organisation of HQ ANC is essentially structured and modelled on the Indian Navy, which in turn has largely evolved out of the Royal Navy. This staff system is organised under three verticals, each of which is overseen by a rotational one-star Chief Staff Officers (CSO) looking after Operations, Personnel & Administration and Technical divisions. In this system, the coordination is done through a bureaucratic machinery overseen by the rotational two-star Chief of Staff (COS).

ANC's experience demonstrates the advantages and disadvantages of attempting to fuse the organisational structures of all the three services. A case now exists to review, reengineer, and realign the organisational structures based on past experience. Such reorganisation could lead to mission-oriented or functional structuring rather than a bureaucratic, hierarchical stove-piped system. Western staff systems have moved away from the Prussian-British 'approach, which divides staffing responsibilities into two or three simple parts' and gives precedence to operational considerations. The French American "bureau" approach, in which the staff is sub-divided into functional directorates, is now widely used.[32] This continental system has almost completely replaced all other approaches amongst Western militaries, including in the UK and erstwhile West Germany. In such approaches, 'intelligence' and 'administration' have co-equal spaces with that of 'operations' than a sub-ordinate status under the domination of the operations officer as was the practice in the German general staffs.[33] In creating efficient organisational designs, management concepts such 'Theory of Span of Control' have been factored in for efficient and time-critical decision making. Such concepts necessitate detailed study and are beyond the scope of this chapter.

Component Commanders

A case for each Component Commander to be upgraded to two-star ranks needs cognisance. The Component Commanders need to focus beyond the limited confines of a 'Tactical Battle Area (TBA)'. Such up-gradation will also permit the assignment of specialist staff to the component headquarters commensurate to the role and responsibilities. Accordingly:

- The Army Component Commander could have under command independent brigade groups for a wholesome embrace of operational level imperatives that span the expanse of the Andaman & Nicobar Island group.

- Under the circumstances envisioned in the Union War Book, the Coast Guard would have been commanded by the Naval Component Commander. Current rank structures prevent such assimilation.
- The Air Component Commander could synergise and ensure unitary command of the air as a doctrinal necessity.

TRI-SERVICE OPERATING AND TRAINING ENVIRONMENT

The littoral environment can be ideal for tri-service employment and coordination because of the complementary capabilities with each dependent on the other. Milan Vego, a respected Professor of Operational Art at the US Naval War College and regular visiting lecturer at the Indian Navy's war college argues, "Perhaps the most important prerequisite of success in littoral warfare is a solid theory developed ahead of time; otherwise, it is not possible to organise and train forces properly. Littoral warfare requires the closest cooperation among the services, or "jointness." It also often requires close cooperation with forces of other nations."[34]

An annual joint exercise in ANC, during its early years, envisaged an airborne operation into an island in the A&N Island group. HQ ANC's joint staff organisation made possible Command and Control of the exercise to be fully taken over by HQ ANC. The complex activity saw the effective use of all components being exercised, including the Coast Guard. As understood, new exercises such as Exercise 'Bull Strike' that was conducted in November 2020 saw innovative and bold new ways of cooperation and collaboration while improving interoperability and synergy.

Such exercises in ANC not only serve as a testbed for defensive operations in the Andaman and Nicobar Islands, but they may also serve as the basis for India deploying Joint Task Forces under a single commander when attempting tri-service operations (unlike structures in OP CACTUS without the necessary unitary command and control integration). From such exercises and operations, joint doctrine and joint publications must emerge and form the basis for ironed-out Command and Control (C2) and support doctrine.

Fusing Diverse Niche Competencies

The Indian military and ANC are a potpourri of experiences and diverse competencies as brought out in the following examples:

- The seamless and speedy turnaround of battalions to and from operational locations in (say) high altitude to the Islands, using Indian Air Force airlift assets, is exemplary.
- At the same time, many large and voluminous loads are shipped in through sealift capabilities as available with the Indian Navy and with ships-taken-up-from-trade.
- Joint Special Forces (SF) camps have seen diverse capabilities in aerial delivery, riverine operations, etc., being fielded by SF from each force, ready for employment in differing environments.
- Maritime search concepts used by the Indian Navy have been integrated into IAF tasking when searching for Malaysian Airlines MH 370.
- Infantry foot patrols in the dense jungles of A&N Islands demonstrate formidable specialist capabilities. An all-service Jaan Pehchan patrol in thick jungles revealed how these are specialised capabilities and infantry competencies.

The list is long, but the niche capabilities of each of our services need collaborative functioning, and effective staff systems under unitary command aid rather than hinder in this regard.

Component Level Continuity and Training

Currently, the Indian military has dedicated certain higher-level tactical formations to joint structures, such as a Mountain Brigade, an Infantry

Brigade and an Infantry Division. The constituent fighting elements of these formations keep cycling out and may never again operate in such specialised environments. Dedicating units and resources for roles in a Joint maritime theatre can help cement lessons and further learning in an enduring and evolutionary manner. Such assignments can go a long way in furthering a specialised joint culture. For example, French Army Regiments, specialised for over two centuries in marinised environments and roles are closely integrated with the French Navy. There are lessons in such practices for each Service!

ANC's experience highlights that each Service is raised, trained, organised and functions to highly specialised ends. The effort should not be to try and amalgamate them into a joint whole. The Army, Navy, Air Force and the Coast Guard's ability to plan and operate in a mutually reinforcing manner is what ANC and jointness must seek to build on. There is virtue in diversity and the competition of ideas and performances. Fusing these into an efficient fighting whole is the challenge that jointness must achieve.

In the last twenty years, the ANC should have helped to 'socialise and train' joint forces by formulating business rules and institutionalising a joint ethic.[35] The ANC provides an excellent opportunity to attune the Indian Armed forces and even the Coast Guard under controlled conditions to experiment and to learn how to further that much-needed ability to work and operate together with jointness as that mantra.

JOINTNESS FOR FUTURE BATTLE SPACES

With severe constraints of resources and a transformational lag, India is attempting to keep pace with China's rapid military modernisation, even as the PLA is preparing to confront adversaries beyond the physical domains of air, land, sea and space. Modern militaries are also expected to demonstrate leadership in abstract fields like cyberspace, electromagnetic and information environments and the cognitive dimensions.

Even in contemporary asymmetric environments, as encountered in counter-insurgency and counterterrorism (CI/CT) operations, the 'other side' has honed fourth-generation warfare skills to negate the effectiveness of modern conventional forces, including airpower. The use of concealment, low-signature infantry/proxy warfare, long-range, affordable rocket fires (as in Lebanon and Yemen) as tactical and strategic tools has led modern militaries to strive for multi-domain tactical operations in which cyber, electronic warfare, air, sensors, information processing, strike, and ground elements are all upfront embedded with tactical forces.[36]

Deployment of technologies like edge-computing (to reduce data-processing bandwidths and OODA-cycle times), artificial intelligence and machine learning look to be the new mantras as conventional forces seek quicker and more precise ability to locate and destroy enemy forces. Security forces need to rapidly detect and destroy stealthy opponents when they momentarily reveal themselves or emit fleeting signatures. *'Locating the enemy and striking him in his prepared hideouts or as he emerges or moves between them will require evolved rapid technical intelligence and not just human intelligence with its time-late limitations"*.[37] Future Cyber Commands and Space Forces must evolve beyond the usual desire for organisations to seek institutional autonomy from the more traditional commands and services, or even parochial debates about who should head such functional Commands. Integration and jointness can be crucial enablers through an evolved command and staff system.

CONCLUSION

The future will require brave new approaches, and no military can assume any superiority as carved in stone. Increased jointness and integration of kinetic and non-kinetic strategies will be essential competencies for tomorrow's battlespaces, as well as in grey zones. Implementing Multi-Domain Operational (MDO) concepts will require increased jointness of the force at the operational (staff) and tactical levels. A 'mission-command' approach to command and control must seek to lower the barriers that impede the achievement of such synergy.

With the appointment of the CDS, the Indian military is being forced to foster jointness rather than allowing the concept to simmer endlessly. Service parochialism will have to be overcome through joint acculturation of selected military officers. Under circumstances that have prevailed in the Indian military thus far, seizing the chances provided by the creation of Joint structures such as the ANC and HQ IDS in the aftermath of Kargil will serve India well. Conventional mindsets, as institutionally ingrained, will need to be challenged as the Revolution in Military Affairs continues to evolve with the rapid march of human progress and technology. Transformation does not imply forsaking one service's ways and means in favour of other services' ways and means. It is about synergising them into a meaningful whole. With the political nod having been given and the institution of CDS a reality, effective implementation and transformation are now the responsibility of military leadership. The political executive will need to ensure that single-service parochialism on this occasion does not side line jointness. Future commanders and staff officers must be educated and trained to realise that jointness at the higher echelons of command and staff cannot wait until faced by an enemy. That may be too late, and would be a betrayal to the lower echelons who are in harm's way.

Notes

1 'Report of the Group of Ministers on National Security,' February 19, 2001 (Government of India, Cabinet Secretariat Notification No.141/2/1/2000-TS, April 17, 2000).

2 Chapter 6 of the US Goldwater-Nichols Department of Defence Reorganization Act of 1986: "A military command with broad, continuing missions and which is composed of forces from two or more military services."

3 Unnithan, Sandeep. *Black Tornado: The Three Sieges of Mumbai 26/11* (HarperCollins, 2014).

4 Subramaniam, Arjun, "Kargil Revisited: Air Operations in a High Altitude Conflict", *CLAWS Journal*, Summer 2008, pp. 187-88.

5 Nardulli, Bruce R., Perry, Walter L., Pirnie Bruce, Gordon IV, John, McGinn, John G., *Disjointed War: Military Operations in Kosovo*, 1999 (Santa Monica, Pittsburgh, Arlington: RAND Arroyo Center, 2002), pp. xiii-xvii.

6 Ibid., xvi.

7 JP 3-0 Joint Operations. Appendix A-2 Chapter 1, Para 2 (f), January 2017. "The US military has codified Unity of Command as one of the twelve principles of joint operations", https://www.jcs.mil/Portals/36/Documents/Doctrine/pubs/jp3_0ch1.pdf

8 Bash, Brooks L., "Leadership and Parochialism: An Enduring Reality," *JFQ,* Summer, 1999, pp. 66-68.

9 Schwarzkopf, Norman and Petre, Peter, *It Doesn't Take a Hero: The Autobiography of General Norman Schwarzkop* (New York: Linda Gray Bantam Books, 1992), p. 318.

10 Hooker Jr, Richard D., and Christopher Coglainese. "Operation Weserubung and the Origins of Joint Warfare" *Joint Forces Quarterly* Summer, 1993, pp. 102-103.

11 Joshi, Manoj, "Xi Jingping and PLA Reform," ORF Occasional Paper # 88, February 2016.

12 Yoshihara, Toshi, "Strategy and Policy Lecture: Rise of Chinese Seapower," US Naval War College, streamed February 7, 2013, YouTube Video, 5:40, https://youtu.be/7P4sOH5JBXE.

13 Cohen, Eliot A. *Supreme Command: Soldiers, Statesmen and Leadership in Wartime* (New York: Simon and Schuster, 2012), p. 164.

14 Dougherty, Chris, "Force Development Options for India by 2030," (Center for a New American Society, 2019), https://www.cnas.org/publications/reports/force-development-options-for-india-by-2030.

15 Beaumont, Roger A, *Joint Military Operations: A Short History* (Westport, Conn: Praeger Publishers Inc, 1993).

16 Patney, Vinod. "Jointness in Armed Forces and Institution of Post of Chief of Defence Staff are Mutually Exclusive," *Journal of Defence Studies* 2, no. 1: 2008; Mukherjee, Anit. "Fighting Separately: Jointness and Civil-Military Relations in India," *Journal of Strategic Studies* 40, no. 1-2: 2017.

17 Rubel, Robert C., "Principles of Jointness," *Joint Forces Quarterly*, Winter, 2000-01, p. 45.

18 Morton, Louis, "Pacific Command: A Study in Interservice Relations," United States Air Force Academy, 1961, https://www.usafa.edu/app/uploads/Harmon03.pdf.

19 Posen, Barry R. *The Sources Of Military Doctrine: France, Britain, and Germany Between the World Wars* (Cornell Studies in Security Affairs, Cornell University Press, 2014), p. 29.

20 Tighe, Dennis W. "Unification of Forces: The Road to Jointness?" Army Command and General Staff College, Fort Leavenworth, KS, School of Advanced Military Studies, 1991, pp. 9-10.

21 "Defence Organisation: The Need for Change. Staff Report to the Committee on Armed Services", US Senate, 18th October 1985 (Washington: US Govt Printing Office, 1985), 614, at https://searchworks.stanford.edu/view/2644288.

22 Rubel, n. 17, p. 46.

23 "Report of the Panel on Military Education of the One-Hundredth Congress of the Committee on Armed Services" (U.S. Congress. House of Representatives 1989), p. 64.

24 Waggener, Anna T. "Joint Professional Military Education", *Joint Force Quarterly* no. 77 2nd Quarter 2015, pp. 55-59.

25 Posen, n. 19, pp. 33-34.

26 Hittle, Brig Gen, James D. *The Military Staff: Its History and Development* (Barakaldo Books, Kindle Edition).

27 White, Charles E., *The Enlightened Soldier: Scharnhorst and the Militarische Gesellschaft in Berlin, 1801-1805* (Kindle Locations 2070-2071). Kindle Edition.

28 Hofsteder, Geert, *Cultures and Organizations, Software of the Mind: Intercultural Cooperation and its Importance for Survival* (London: McGraw-Hill Book Company, 1991), p. 370.

29 White, n. 27.

30 Torruella Jr, Ramberto A. "Managing the Battle Rhythm". Paper presented at the 12th International Command and Control Research and Technology Symposium "Adapting C2 to the 21st Century", June 19-21, 2007, Newport, RI https://apps.dtic.mil/sti/pdfs/ADA481331.pdf

31 US Joint Staff J7, "Third Edition of Joint Headquarters Organization, Staff Integration, and Battle Rhythm: Insights and Best Practices Focus Paper," September 2019. 1, http://www.jcs.mil/Doctrine/focus_papers.aspx.

32 Johnston, Paul, Maj. "Staff Systems and the Canadian Air Force: Part 1 History of the Western Staff System." (Canadian Air Force Journal, Summer 2008), https://bootcampmilitaryfitnessinstitute.com/wp-content/uploads/2015/07/16-staff-systems-the-canadian-air-force-part-1-history-of-the-western-staff-system-johnston-2008.pdf.

33 Hittle, n. 26.

34 Vego, Milan "On Littoral Warfare," *Naval War College Review*, Vol. 68 : No. 2, Article 4, 2015, https://digital-commons.usnwc.edu/cgi/viewcontent.cgi?referer=&httpsredir=1&article=1200&context=nwc-review.

35 Davis, Charles M., "Jointness, Culture, and Inter-Service Prejudice: Assessing the Impact of Resident, Satellite, and Hybrid Joint Professional Military Education II Course Delivery Methods on Military Officer Attitudes" (2017). Doctor of Philosophy (PhD), dissertation, International Studies, Old Dominion University, https://digitalcommons.odu.edu/gpis_etds/16.

36 Ortal, BG Eran, "Going on the Attack: The Theoretical Foundation of the IDF Momentum Plan" (Dado Center for Interdisciplinary Military Studies: 2020), https://www.idf.il/en/minisites/dado-center/vol-28-30-military-superiority-and-the-momentum-multi-year-plan/multi-year-plan-momentum-a-theoretical-framework/

37 Ibid.

CHAPTER 18

INDIA'S NUCLEAR POSTURE

BALRAJ SINGH NAGAL

ABSTRACT

This chapter evaluates India's nuclear posture through several lenses. It first offers a historical perspective and then discusses the political ideas and debates/ discussion on India's quest for a nuclear deterrent. Offering a critique of the initial diffidence in nuclear decision-making and the development of a cogent nuclear policy, the chapter tracks the crystallisation of India's draft and declaratory nuclear doctrine. Assessing the approach of the political leadership and government officials towards the doctrine, the chapter evaluates India' security concerns in the backdrop of its emerging nuclear posture. An overview reveals that India lost valuable time in developing the nuclear deterrent as compared to its adversaries, China and Pakistan, but has emerged as a responsible quasi-nuclear weapons state in the eyes of the rest of the world.

INDIA'S NUCLEAR WEAPONS PROGRAMME: THE INITIAL JOURNEY

The history of nuclear weapons development in India can be traced to Homi Bhabha.[1] After studying overseas, he returned to India and set up the Tata Institute for Fundamental Research (TIFR) in 1945 to promote the study of nuclear physics with grants from the Tata industrial house. Following independence, Bhabha convinced Prime Minister Nehru[2] of the importance of atomic energy research[3] for building an industrial base, poverty alleviation[4] and to extract politico military leverage in the post-World War II era.[5] After the Atomic Energy Commission (AEC) was created in 1948, with Bhabha as its first chairman, the Department of Atomic Energy (DAE) was founded in 1954 under the Prime Minister and the AEC was placed under the DAE, with Mr Bhabha and the PM exercising utmost secrecy over financial and material resources.[6] The Canadian CIRUS (Canada-India-US) reactor was approved by the PM in 1955 by a telegram sent to Mr Bhabha with no other authorisation, leaving the decision to work on nuclear weapons as suggested by Bhabha open-ended.[7] The CIRUS went critical in 1960, and the Trombay plutonium extraction or reprocessing plant was sanctioned in 1958, where the first lot of plutonium oxide and plutonium metal was processed in 1964-65.[8] The CANDU (CIRUS) reactor bought from Canada was modified by Indian scientists to INDU (Indian Deuterium-Uranium reactor), capable of producing plutonium, while the 100 MW reactor Dhruva augmented the plutonium capacity.[9] Indian achieved a semblance of nuclear weapons capability in 1966-67 a few years after China exploded its nuclear weapon in October 1964, however no political directions were given to go ahead with testing. After PM Nehru died in May 1964, his successor, PM Lal Bahadur Shastri was reticent to permit nuclear testing based on India's stand on nuclear disarmament and its poor economic state. Consequently, he only gave the go ahead to authorise studies of underground explosions for peaceful purposes, also called the Subterranean Nuclear Explosion Programme (SNEP).[10, 11]

Following Homi Bhabha's death in a plane crash on January 24, 1966,[12] he was succeeded by Vikram Sarabhai, who had previously worked in the space department. Though Sarabhai was not enthusiastic about nuclear weapons, he did initiate substantial work in the development of nuclear weapons, building the Purnima reactor during his tenure.[13] The Purnima reactors are a series of critical assemblies built to study neutron behaviour in fission and the use of U-233 as a fuel. The Atomic Energy Commission approved the Purnima project in 1969 and Purnima-I went critical on May 18, 1972. As a pulsed fast reactor, Purnima-I operated on much the same principles as a rudimentary fission bomb. This provided scientists at the Bhabha Atomic Research Centre (BARC) with a baseline against which to evaluate the behaviour of a chain-reacting plutonium system and the kinetic response of the system just above criticality.[14]

DEVELOPING A NUCLEAR DETERRENT

During a visit to Bhabha Atomic Research Centre (BARC) in October 1972, Prime Minister Indira Gandhi most likely ordered preparations for nuclear testing.[15, 16] Her decision to test the nuclear device was based on the experience of the 1971 war when the US Task Force 74 with the aircraft carrier USS *Enterprise* sailed into the Bay of Bengal to coerce India. Mrs Gandhi gave the final go ahead to Homi Sethna, who had succeeded Vikram Sarabhai as the Chairman of DAE, to conduct India's first nuclear test at Pokharan in Rajasthan after successfully marginalising the heavyweight opponents of nuclear weapons within her party. India conducted its first underground peaceful nuclear[17] explosion,[18,19] with a yield of 12-15 KT[20] on May 18, 1974. Other than France, most world powers condemned the nuclear test as India had violated the Nuclear Non-Proliferation Treaty (NPT) of 1968/1970. China was critical of the test[21] as it was a nuclear weapon state and was qualified to be a member of the NPT, which came into force in 1970 while US and Canada imposed sanctions.[22] However, Prime Minister Indira Gandhi inexplicably[23] wrote a letter to Prime Minister Bhutto of Pakistan of India's intention not to make nuclear weapons.

The nuclear test of 1974 was not followed up with other tests, presumably due to external pressure, the sanctions imposed and the consequent economic state of India. PM Morarji Desai, who succeeded Indira Gandhi in 1977, was vehemently and staunchly opposed to nuclear weapons on moral grounds and no progress was made during his two-year stint as PM.[24] After returning to power in 1980, it is speculated that PM Gandhi gave the go ahead for preparations for nuclear weapons testing to Dr Raja Ramana, who had by then emerged as the top nuclear scientist in India. It is even believed that Defence Minister Venkatraman went down the shaft that had been prepared for weapons' testing in 1983, however the PM did not execute the test due to US pressure.[25]

Having accumulated stockpiles of 200 kilograms of plutonium,[26] PM Rajiv Gandhi authorised the development of a range of nuclear weapons from 1984 to 1989.[27] However, he did not proceed with testing or an overt programme. From 1991 through 1996, Prime Minister Narasimha Rao followed a similar path, as Indian nuclear scientists developed a wide range of nuclear weapons that were ready for testing by 1995. However, US pressure from the Clinton administration, is believed to have forced the postponement of a test planned for end 1995,[28] even as the Comprehensive Test Ban Treaty (CTBT) was being finalised during this period, which India refused to sign.

The Pokhran II tests were conducted on May 11 and 13, 1998, under the leadership of Prime Minister AB Vajpayee. On 11 May, three tests were conducted: a thermonuclear weapon, a fission weapon and a sub kiloton weapon. On May 13 two sub kiloton weapons were tested.[29] Once again, major powers condemned the test and sanctions were imposed on India. After the Pokhran II test of May 11 and 13, 1998, PM Vajpayee spoke at the Parliament on May 27, 1998,[30] and attributed the tests and the decision to exercise the nuclear weapons option to reasons of national security.

EVOLVING A COHERENT POLICY

Vajpayee underlined the fundamentals of his government's thought on evolving a coherent nuclear policy consequent to demonstrating nuclear weapons' capability by quoting the 1968 resolution of Parliament on the NPT. The key ones are highlighted below:

- India would be guided entirely by considerations of national security, a proposition that manifested itself in the decision not to sign the NPT in 1974 and the Comprehensive Test Ban Treaty (CTBT) in 1996.
- Elaborating his concerns, Vajpayee argued that with the NPT being extended indefinitely and the reluctance of the nuclear weapon states to eschew disarmament, India had little choice considering that its

security environment had deteriorated due to the proliferation of nuclear weapons and missiles in the neighbourhood.

- In an environment of externally aided and abetted terrorism, militancy and clandestine war, Vajpayee reaffirmed that these were weapons of self-defence to ensure that India is not subjected to nuclear threats or coercion.
- Declaring that India's nuclear policy would be marked by restraint and openness, Vajpayee reiterated that his government had already announced that India would observe a voluntary moratorium and refrain from conducting any further underground nuclear test explosions. Vajpayee's statement in Parliament was sober, tempered and calibrated, and based on a conviction of India's security needs. The declaration was accompanied by the presentation of a document to the Parliament of India.[31]

The document presented in the Parliament strengthened the rationale for testing by stating that India believed that it is the sovereign right of every nation to make a judgement regarding its supreme national interests and exercise its sovereign choice. The document went on to argue that India's nuclear policy was marked by restraint and openness. The restraint, which was exercised for 24 years after having demonstrated its capability in 1974, was a unique example of restraint based on strength rather than indecision or doubt.

INDIA'S NUCLEAR DOCTRINAL DEVELOPMENT

India's political and strategic journey to the nuclear tests and subsequent weaponisation was hesitant, intermittent and slow as it took 34 years to become a nuclear weapons state (NWS) after China did so in 1964, and 51 years after it achieved independence. Sceptics, like the author, could argue that national security was sacrificed at the altar of ideology, personal convictions, moralism, idealism and indecision. PM Nehru was focussed on nuclear disarmament, opposed the use of force to settle international problems and carried forward the Gandhian legacy. However, he saw scientific progress as necessary for the development of India and approved the nuclear programme, keeping it shrouded in secrecy and ambiguity. In an environment where non-proliferation and disarmament dominated the international discourse and no nuclear weapon capability in sight on the Indian horizon, there was no substantial discussion in the country on nuclear weapons, nuclear doctrine or policy.

After the nuclear test by China in 1964, there were demands by a few opposition parties including the Jan Sangh Party and some members of the ruling party for a nuclear test by India.[32] The government and the Congress leadership refused to address this demand for a fundamental shift in India's nuclear policy stating that the prohibitive costs of embarking on a nuclear weapons program, India's historic commitment to a nuclear-free world, its belief in Gandhian principles and misgivings about alienating world opinion undermined the case for the acquisition of a nuclear weapons option.[33] After the Chinese tests, Bhabha had articulated the politico-military significance of nuclear weapons by arguing forcefully: "Nuclear weapons coupled with an adequate delivery system can enable a State to destroy totally the cities, industry, and all-important targets in another State. It is then largely irrelevant whether the State so attacked has greater destructive power at its command. With the help of nuclear weapons, therefore, a State can acquire what we may call a position of absolute deterrence even against another having a many times greater destructive power under its control."[34] No heed was paid to Mr Bhabha's views by the political establishment, nor did the military show any interest in creating an environment for debate on the issue.

The nuclear option was kept alive not only by some opposition political parties but also by some Congress MPs, notable among them being Mr Krishan Kant, then a MP and later the Vice President of India, and Mr K.C. Pant, a future Defence Minister. They canvassed for a nuclear deterrent but with a No First Use (NFU) declaration.[35] Among a few senior military officers who spoke or wrote on the nuclear issue, only Maj Gen D.K. Palit, in his book, "War in the Deterrent Age", published in 1966, argued for India to have a nuclear deterrent against China. He contended that a minimum deterrent with survivability and retaliatory capability would be adequate to ensure deterrence.[36] This thought has since remained with the Indian thinkers. A counter view was offered by Major General Som Dutt in an Adelphi Paper published the same year (No 30, London, International Institute for Strategic Studies, 1966, "India and the Bomb"). He made a case that India did not need a nuclear deterrent because China was not a nuclear threat and that a China–India conventional war was not a viable option due to logistics problem for China.

When Mrs Gandhi's took over as prime minister in 1966, the NPT was being actively discussed the world over. When it was finalised at the UN in January 1968, India was not able to push any of the clauses which it sponsored and was outmanoeuvred by the big powers. Three of the great powers—the United States, the United Kingdom, and the Soviet Union-signed the treaty on July 1, 1968, and the NPT came into force on March 5, 1970. Following this, the debate in India shifted to the discriminatory nature of the NPT and Mrs Gandhi got the backing of the Parliament and the cabinet not to sign the NPT and keep India's nuclear options open. By doing so, an Indian leader displayed statecraft and realpolitik on an international issue for the first time since independence. After the nuclear test of 1974, though Pakistan had embarked on its own nuclear weapons programme in 1972, it was only thanks to Mr K. Subrahmanyam, Director of the New Delhi-based Institute for Defence Studies and Analyses (IDSA), that the debate to acquire nuclear weapons was kept alive in India.

In response to the rapid progress in Pakistan's nuclear weapons programme and the production of enriched uranium in sufficient quantities at Kahuta, the first quasi-official statement that India should acquire the nuclear deterrent came from India's Defence Minister, Mr C. Subramaniam in November 1979. Addressing the National

Defence College, he made out a cogent case on why India should go nuclear.[37] After Indira Gandhi stormed back to power in 1980, India restarted its programme for nuclear weapons development in the backdrop of the conflict in Afghanistan that was seeing a covert war being orchestrated by the US and run by Pakistan to ensure the defeat of the Soviets. As a quid pro quo for its support in evicting the Russians, the US clearly turned a blind eye towards Pakistan's nuclear weapons programme. Consequently, India's earlier preoccupation with Chinese nuclear capabilities was redirected towards Pakistan's growing nuclear status. The argument ran along the following lines: The United States, with full knowledge of Pakistan's nuclear ambitions, was nevertheless supplying Pakistan with sophisticated weaponry and potentially nuclear-capable aircraft. Growing evidence of Chinese collusion in the Pakistani nuclear weapons program further fuelled Indian concerns.[38] Apparently, in 1980-81, the Joint Planning Committee comprising the operational directorates of the three services prepared a paper on the induction of nuclear weapons. Though the Chiefs of Staff Committee forwarded it to the Defence Ministry, no action was taken on the report.[39]

As India became aware of the China-Pakistan nuclear weapons collaboration in 1983-84, and reports emerged in the US that China may have tested a Pakistan nuclear device at Lop Nor,[40] Mrs Gandhi approved a missile development programme called the Integrated Guided Missile Development Programme (IGMDP),[41,42] primarily comprising the nuclear-capable Prithvi and Agni missiles. Indira Gandhi's understanding of the need for developing the nuclear triad was also demonstrated by her clearance in 1970 of the Indian Navy's Project 937 for building a nuclear submarine or the Advance Technology Vehicle (ATV).[43] During the mid-to-late 1980s, the nuclear weapons delivery by Jaguar and Mirage-2000 aircraft was examined, with the latter being deemed to be more suited.

THE SUNDARJI-SUBRAHMANYAM THEORETICAL CONSTRUCT

In 1981, Lieutenant General Sundarji, the commandant of the Indian Army's College of Combat Mhow, released two Combat Papers on nuclear strategy titled 'Effects of Nuclear Asymmetry on Conventional Deterrence' (Apr 81) and 'Nuclear Weapons in Third World' (Aug 81), initiating a debate on nuclear weapons in the region. The timing of these papers coincided with Pakistan's clandestine acquisition of nuclear weapons. For the first time, a realist's view of the nature of the Pakistani nuclear threat, Pakistani tolerance limits and a scenario of the likely use of nuclear weapons in the subcontinental context was articulated.[44] Indian thinking on nuclear weapons remained defensive, with retaliatory second-strike options deemed appropriate and engrained in the military.[45] Sundarji initially suggested a limited nuclear arsenal, but over the years changed the requirements to 150 weapons by 1996.[46]

The concept of No First Use (NFU) figured widely in Indian discussions and debates on nuclear weapons, as well as in global and regional diplomatic parleys. This articulation can be attributed to two of the most influential voices in promoting the acquisition of nuclear weapons by India at the time—Sundarji and K. Subrahmanyam, Director of Institute for Defence Studies and Analyses for nearly a decade and a half.[47] Sundarji made the argument that an adversary possessing nuclear capabilities could threaten the concentration of conventional forces on which India's (and Pakistan's) military strategy rested. The countermeasure of dispersing forces with greater reliance on manoeuvrability would require greater resources than India could deploy soon. This implied that India would need nuclear weapons to deter attack on massed armoured forces.[48] This argument "became the core of India's revived rationale for a nuclear weapons programme in the early 1980s".

In one of Sundarji's unpublished papers, "Strategy in the Age of Nuclear Deterrence and Its Application to Developing Countries," which has been described as among his best pieces, the general went through a series of scenarios involving India with or without nuclear weapons and different levels of nuclear build up. He concluded that in all the nuclear-armed scenarios, there would never be a case for the first use of nuclear weapons.[49] Furthermore, Sundarji argued that if India had "a big nuclear edge over Pakistan" then India could diplomatically ensure stability by adopting "a declared policy of non-first use of nuclear weapons, a 'No-war' pact" and a host of other confidence building measures which India can afford to undertake from a position of strength."[50] He saw the NFU as proof of India's responsible status, writing, "For a sober, mature status quo power like India, a unilateral declaration of no first use should be axiomatic."

By the early 1990s, Sundarji was using the NFU to argue that India (and Pakistan) should shift from a position of ambiguity to an overtly nuclear posture because the former would "prevent both from declaring a 'no first use' policy."[51] Shivshankar Menon, an Indian diplomat who served as National Security Adviser to Prime Minister Manmohan Singh, wrote in his book, *Choices: The Making of Indian Foreign Policy*: "A no-first-use policy was not always the natural or easy choice. I remember then Atomic Energy Commission Chairman Raja Ramanna and Chief of Army Staff Krishnaswami Sundarji often talking in the mid-1980s about a future India with nuclear weapons. For Sundarji, the attraction of an Indian atom bomb was its possible military use to neutralise Chinese conventional.

As a physicist, Ramanna was keenly aware of the limitations on the use and of the practical effects of the bomb. He therefore saw it as an enabler and equaliser, not necessarily as a military weapon to be used but as a weapon to enable the achievement of political and military goals. Over time, as India's conventional military position improved, Sundarji's considerations became less compelling. By the late 1990s, it was the advocates of no first use, including defence analyst K. Subrahmanyam, who prevailed. Their views were found politically most acceptable by the political leadership, particularly Prime Minister Atal Bihari Vajpayee, a long-time advocate of nuclear weapons for India with a larger vision of peace on the Indian subcontinent and in the extended neighbourhood."[52]

Another prominent proponent of nuclear weapons for India, and India adopting a NFU posture, was K. Subrahmanyam. Starting in the 1980s, Subrahmanyam repeatedly pressed the importance of India declaring, either in conjunction with Pakistan or unilaterally, that it would not use nuclear weapons first, through his articles in a leading Indian newspaper, *The Times of India*.[53] In 1985, in the context of critiquing a Pakistani proposal for a South Asian nuclear weapon free zone, he highlighted the fact that both China and the Soviet Union had given pledges of no first use and supported related initiatives to suggest that Pakistan and India "negotiate a joint protocol on the model of Geneva protocol of 1925 outlawing the first use of nuclear weapons" and "then invite China and Soviet Union to sign it too." The idea did not find favour with anyone as Pakistan would not acknowledge its nuclear weapons. He went further to speculate that this "could well be the beginning of a global protocol to outlaw the first use of nuclear weapons."[54] A few years later he expanded the scope of the agreement to say that it "must cover the use of radioactive waste as radiological weapons in view of reports that large quantities of highly radioactive wastes have been transferred from certain western countries to others, including Pakistan."[55]

General Sundarji and K. Subrahmanyam were both part of important committees tasked in the 1980s to examine nuclear weapons issues and advise the Prime Minister. The first group followed Prime Minister Rajiv Gandhi's request for an assessment of the "costs of a nuclear deterrent" in 1985. The second was a study group reportedly set up by Prime Minister V.P. Singh in 1990 to "formulate procedures for effective control of the nation's nuclear arsenal and other issues related to nuclearisation"; the group presented its report later to the P.V. Narasimha government. The first committee's report, about which more is known, is believed to have recommended that "India build a minimal deterrent force, guided by a strict doctrine of no-first use and a retaliation against a nuclear attack on India."[56]

The interdisciplinary group set up in 1985 met five times but did not come out with any conclusive recommendations.[57] At the behest of Ramana, in November 1985, a committee was set up by Chairman Chief of Staff Committee under Gen Sundarji; this committee recommended that India should have a nuclear force of 100 nuclear warheads and 100 missiles in 10 years that would cost Rs 7,000 crore.[58] This was followed three years later by the Arun Singh Committee, which examined several command-and-control issues, location and storage of weapons, mating and delivery of the weapon systems among other issues.[59] The chain of command was an important subject for operational use of nuclear weapons, which was examined by the committee.

On January 28, 1987, Indian journalist Kuldip Nayyar interviewed Dr A.Q. Khan, the man who steered Pakistan's uranium enrichment project at Kahuta. During the interview, Dr Khan told Kuldip Nayyar that Pakistan had the bomb, and later denied it. This threat was given in the shadow of a series of Indian military exercises driven by Sundarji called Brasstacks, which Pakistan suspected to be a cover for attacking it. Following this claim by Khan, the IGMP went into overdrive—the Prithvi and Agni missiles were tested in 1988 and 1989, respectively, with the latter being demonstrated for nuclear weapons delivery.[60] Finally, in 1990 the US President refused to certify to Congress that Pakistan had not reached explosive capability, confirming that Pakistan possessed the bomb.[61] In May 1990, as an India-Pakistan crisis unfolded in the shadow of Pakistan's heightened proxy war in the Kashmir Valley, Dr Ramana the Minister of State for Defence said in Parliament "that while India would never use its nuclear capability against any neighbour, if any neighbour were to do so, the country would rise to the occasion."[62] India, by early 1990 had a deterrent, but no doctrine or policy; except for the small group of scientists, most others from the strategic establishment were in the dark.

THE ENEMY AT THE DOORSTEP

As the North Korean M-11 missiles arrived in Pakistan by 1994, the US did not confirm the proliferation and largely turned a blind eye to the evolving China-Pakistan nuclear weapons relationship despite it being in violation of the NPT. It was obvious that the NPT regime in India's neighbourhood had collapsed as China went ahead in assisting Pakistan set up a plutonium production reactor at Khushab.[63] Indian Foreign Secretary, J.N. Dixit, proposed in a non-paper to the Pakistani Foreign Office an agreement on the no first use of nuclear capability. The proposal evoked no response from Pakistan.[64] In 1997, more evidence surfaced on the China-Pakistan proliferation linkage and the US' permissiveness. The fact that the US Administration insisted on a separate agreement with China, on its proliferation to Iran and Pakistan, during President Jiang Zemin's visit to Washington, and that the Chinese signed such an agreement instead of protesting its innocence, proved that Chinese proliferation was a harsh reality affecting India's security.

Pakistan test fired the Ghauri missile on April 6, 1998. The missile, built with either Chinese or North Korean technology, had a range of 1,500 kilometres and could carry a payload of 750 kilograms. Its range would enable Pakistan to target 26 cities in India. This new Pakistani capability reinforced prior perceptions in India about the deterioration of India's immediate security environment.[66] Any remaining qualms about the wisdom of carrying out nuclear tests were set aside in the aftermath of the Ghauri test. Between May 9 and 10, 1998, Prime Minister Atal Behari Vajpayee informed key ministers and the bureaucrats at the highest ranks, as well as the three service chiefs, of his decision to proceed with the nuclear tests.[67] Seven months after the May 11 and 13, 1998, tests, PM Vajpayee announced India's adherence to the No First Use policy in parliament on December 15, 1998.[68] This was a unilateral decision that demonstrated India's restraint and responsible approach towards the use of weapons of mass destruction and to keep nuclear retaliation only as a last resort among various options of deterrence.

The announcement was a stand-alone one as a draft doctrine was still under preparation by the National Security Advisory Board (NSAB), a part of the newly formed National Security Council Secretariat (NSCS).

SIX PILLARS OF INDIA'S NUCLEAR DOCTRINE

On August 17, 1999, the National Security Advisor, Mr Brajesh Mishra, reiterated India's commitment to universal nuclear disarmament when he made public the draft Indian Nuclear Doctrine.[69] The principal reason for the public release of the draft Indian Nuclear Doctrine was to instill greater transparency in decision making and stimulate discussion and debate on critical matters of national security. The draft doctrine laid out six objectives. First, India's strategic interests required effective, credible nuclear deterrence and adequate retaliatory capability should deterrence fail. This was consistent with the UN Charter, which sanctions the right of self-defence. Second, the requirements of deterrence were to be carefully benchmarked while designing the structure of India's nuclear forces to provide for a level of capability consistent with maximum credibility, survivability, effectiveness, safety and security. Third, India would pursue a doctrine of credible minimum nuclear deterrence. The survivability of its weapons was considered vital in this policy of "retaliation only". This was a dynamic concept related to the strategic environment, technological imperatives and the needs of national security. The actual size components, deployment and employment of nuclear forces would be decided in the light of these factors. India's peacetime posture aimed at convincing any potential aggressor that any threat of use of nuclear weapons against India would invoke measures to counter that threat; and any nuclear attack on India and its forces would result in punitive retaliation with nuclear weapons to inflict unacceptable damage to the aggressor. Fourth, the fundamental purpose of Indian nuclear weapons was to deter the use and threat of use of nuclear weapons by any State or entity against India and its forces. The draft doctrine emphasised that India would not be the first to initiate a nuclear strike, but would respond with punitive retaliation should deterrence fail. Fifth, India would not resort to the use or threat of use of nuclear weapons against States that do not possess nuclear weapons, or are not aligned with nuclear weapon powers. Sixth, the imperatives of deterrence would dictate the necessity for India to maintain sufficient, survivable and operationally prepared nuclear forces, a robust command and control system, effective intelligence and early warning capabilities, comprehensive planning and training for operations in line with the strategy and the will to employ nuclear forces and weapons. Highly effective conventional military capabilities would be concurrently maintained to raise the threshold of outbreak both of conventional military conflict as well as that of the threat or use of nuclear weapons.

No preventive, pre-emptive or offensive intent was reflected in the doctrine as India was prepared to absorb a nuclear attack, bear the consequences of destruction and then only retaliate to cause damage to the adversary. The most important aspect of "punitive retaliation only" was a moral high point where NFU also ensured that there was no scope for error or miscalculation in launching nuclear attacks. It also prevented a trigger-happy readiness state, which may have negative consequences for a nation with a very nascent nuclear force, more so in the fog of war.

The formal Indian Nuclear Doctrine[70] was released on January 4, 2003. Its principal tenets were in line with the earlier draft except for two significant changes—substituting "punitive" with "massive" retaliation and including nuclear retaliation against Biological and Chemical attacks against India or Indian Forces anywhere. The term "massive retaliation" did not leave any ambiguity about the quantum of response, hence it was a wise choice to warn adversaries. The two accords prohibit the use of biological and chemical weapons, which have catastrophic implications and can also be supplied by hostile governments to non-state actors or terror organisations. To ensure deterrence against the Biological and Chemical weapons, India rightly declared its policy, putting states on notice which might secretly supply these weapons to the non-state actors or terror organisations.

No state can find fault in either case because both were reactionary responses, placing the onus of responsibility on the initiator for its actions and consequences. An important feature of the doctrine emphasised that nuclear retaliatory attacks would only be authorised by the civilian political leadership through the Nuclear Command Authority. Indicating its renewed commitment to non-proliferation of nuclear weapons, the doctrine highlighted a continuance of strict controls on export of nuclear and missile-related materials and technologies, participation in the Fissile Material Cut Off Treaty negotiations, and continued observance of the moratorium on nuclear tests.

POST DOCTRINAL IDEAS & AMBIGUITIES

There has been no open revision of India's nuclear doctrine since its release. From 2003 to date, official statements attributed to government officials are limited, and none have threatened India's adversaries. There have been, however, a few instances when doubts or questions have been raised on possible changes or reviews that have infused some ambiguity in the process. These have generated some welcome debate, particularly in the realm of NFU. Before the formal release of the doctrine, Prime Minister Vajpayee offered a revealing comment on the NFU in response to threats of a Pakistani nuclear attack in February 2000: "If they think we will wait for them to drop a bomb and face destruction, they are mistaken."[71] In 2010 a quote was attributed to the NSA, Shiv Shankar Menon on NFU, however the official text of the speech at the National Defence College given out by MEA on its website clears the air; it seems to have been misunderstood by some participants.

While the BJP has maintained status quo on India's Nuclear Doctrine since it came to power in 2014 and PM Modi has reaffirmed India's commitment to NFU,[72] at a book launch in 2016, the then Defence Minister, late Mr Manohar Parrikar, stated: "A lot of people say India has a no-first-use nuclear policy, but why should I bind myself? I should say I'm a responsible nuclear power, and I will not use it irresponsibly. A 'written strategy' is a guideline, but the idea of being unpredictable had to be included in any such strategy." Parrikar later stated that this was his individual opinion.[73] In August 2019, Defence Minister Rajnath said, "Pokhran is the area which witnessed Atalji's firm resolve to make India a nuclear power and yet remain firmly committed to the doctrine of 'No First Use'. India has strictly adhered to this doctrine. What happens in future depends on the circumstances."[74] In the backdrop of a deteriorating regional security environment, maintaining such ambiguity while internally debating the issue is important for an emerging power like India as it evaluates and reviews its various security strategies.

SUMMARY

An examination of the development of strategic and nuclear doctrinal thought in India reveals a focus on nuclear non-proliferation and disarmament during the first 17 years after independence, with no major debate or discussion on doctrines or strategies/policies. Mrs Gandhi, however, demonstrated statecraft and a realist approach to India's national security by refusing to join the NPT, facilitating the creation of Bangladesh, approving the 1974 Nuclear test, and laying the foundation for nuclear weapons and considering the nuclear triad. There are no notes or papers available on her thoughts or ideas, but her actions allow us to infer intentions and evaluate the trajectory of the nuclear programme.

After Pakistan achieved clandestine nuclear capability, India continued to be restrained in the development and deployment of nuclear weapons. Doctrinal processes remained restricted to defensive and minimum deterrence and a No First Use (NFU) policy with a hope that Pakistan would accept the policy and join a NFU policy in South Asia. The 1998 nuclear tests brought the genie out of the bottle, despite no triumphalism or braggadocio on the part of India's political and strategic establishment.

The announcement of the NFU in the parliament on December 15, 1998, was an even bigger act of statesmanship by the Indian PM, as he reassured the world and adversaries that the emerging Indian doctrine would be benign, and not offensive or aggressive. Following the introduction of the doctrine, political and military leaders have been very restrained, reserved and dignified, without any threat or bluster as is the wont of Pakistan's political and military leaders. The post-Pokhran II behaviour of India has been restrained and responsible; the open-source data on number of weapons possessed by India clearly shows that India has not accelerated its nuclear weapons programme or precipitated a nuclear arms race in South Asia. No political or military leader has threatened or been aggressive in articulating views on the nuclear doctrine, and the maturity and wisdom shown by the Indian leadership has reinforced India's responsible and restrained approach to nuclear weapons.

NOTES

1 "Sumit Ganguly, "India's Path to Pokharan II: The Prospects and Sources of New Delhi's Nuclear Weapons Programme", *International Security* Vol. 23, No. 4 (Spring, 1999), pp. 148-77, https://www.jstor.org/stable/2539297?read-now=1&refreqid=excelsior%3A75ad611dd77def7b91362377ad779d07&seq=9#page_scan_tab_contents

2 NTI Article on India Nuclear Programme, https://www.nti.org/learn/countries/india/nuclear/

3 Bharat Karnad, *Nuclear Weapons and Indian Security: The Realist Foundations of Strategy* (New Delhi: Macmillan, 2005), pp. 180-85

4 Ganguly, n. 1.

5 Karnad, n. 3, p. 180.

6 Ibid., p. 182.

7 Ibid., pp. 184-185.

8 Ibid., p. 191.

9 Ibid., p. 192.

10 Ibid., p. 235.

11 K Subrahmanyam, "Indian Nuclear Policy-1964-98" (A Personal Recollection), *Strategic Analysis*, 42:3, pp. 293-311.

12 Homi J Bhabha, "Physicist India", https://www.atomicheritage.org/profile/homi-j-bhabha

13 Purnima reactor, https://www.nti.org/learn/facilities/861/

14 Ibid.

15 Karnad, n. 3, p. 297.

16 Subrahmanyam, n. 11.

17 Statement by Minister of External Affairs Mr Swaran Singh on May 21, 1974, https://archive.pib.gov.in/archive/ArchiveSecondPhase/DEFENCE/1974-JAN-JUNE-PRESS%20RELEASE%20JOINT%20COMMUNIQUE%20&AGREEMENT/PDF/DEF-1974-05-21_100.pdf

18 Statement of Ambassador B C Mishra at the Conference of Disarmament Geneva on May 21, 1974, https://archive.pib.gov.in/archive/ArchiveSecondPhase/EXTERNAL%20AFFAIRS/1974-APRIL-JUNE-EXTERANAL-AFFAIRS/PDF/EXT-1974-05-23_113.pdf

19 Statement of Ambassador Jaipal MEA at IAEA Board on June 18, 1974 https://archive.pib.gov.in/archive/ArchiveSecondPhase/EXTERNAL%20AFFAIRS/1974-APRIL-JUNE-EXTERANAL-AFFAIRS/PDF/EXT-1974-06-18_197.pdf

20 Karnad, n. 3, p. 311.

21 Ganguly, n. 1.

22 Ibid.

23 Prime Minister Indira Gandhi letter to Prime Minister Z A Bhutto Pakistan of June 7, 1974, https://archive.pib.gov.in/archive/ArchiveSecondPhase/EXTERNAL%20AFFAIRS/1974-APRIL-JUNE-EXTERANAL-AFFAIRS/PDF/EXT-1974-06-07_154.pdf

24 Ibid.

25 Subrahmanyam, n. 11, p. 300.

26 Ganguly, n. 1, p. 165.

27 Karnad, n. 3, p. 345.

28 Ibid., pp. 345, 367.

29 Karnad, n. 3, pp. 398-402.

30 PM A B Vajpayee Speech at Parliament of India May 27, 1998, https://eparlib.nic.in/bitstream/123456789/756733/1/249.pdf

31 Papers laid at Parliament by PM A B Vajpayee May 27, 1998, https://parliamentofindia.nic.in/ls/lsdeb/ls12/ses2/0527059801.htm

32 Frank E. Couper. "Indian Party Conflict on the Issue of Atomic Weapons," *The Journal of Developing Areas* 3, no. 2 (1969): 191-206, http://www.jstor.org/stable/4189559. Accessed on March 27, 2021.

33 Ganguly, n. 1, p. 154

34 Ibid., p. 152

35 Subrahmanyam, n. 11, p. 294

36 Karnad, n. 3, p. 308

37 Ibid., pp. 308, 331-32

38 Ganguly, n. 1, p. 163

39 Karnad, n. 3, p. 344

40 Subrahmanyam, n. 11, p. 301

41 Ibid., pp. 299, 304, 315, 349

42 Subrahmanyam, n. 11.

43 Karnad, n. 3, p. 298.
44 Subrahmanyam, n. 11, p. 301.
45 Karnad, n. 3, pp. 356-57.
46 Ibid.
47 Kumar Sundaram and M. V. Ramana (2018) "India and the Policy of No First Use of Nuclear Weapons", *Journal for Peace and Nuclear Disarmament*, 1:1, 152-168.
48 Ibid.
49 Ibid.
50 Ibid.
51 Ibid.
52 Ibid.
53 Ibid.
54 Ibid.
55 Ibid.
56 Ibid.
57 Subrahmanyam, n. 11, p. 302.
58 Ibid and Karnad, n. 3, p. 346.
59 Karnad, n. 3, pp. 346-47.
60 Subrahmanyam, n. 11; and Karnad, n. 3, p. 349.
61 Subrahmanyam, n. 11, p. 305.
62 Ibid.
63 Ibid.
64 Ibid.
65 Ibid.
66 Ganguly, n. 1.
67 Ibid.
68 PM Vajpayee Statement in Parliament 15 Dec1998 Debates pp. 318-22, https://www.eparlib.nic.in/bitstream/123456789/759795/1/lsd_12_03_15-12-1998.pdf
69 Draft+Report+of+National+Security+Advisory+Board+on+Indian+Nuclear+Doctrine#:~:text=India%20shall%20pursue%20a%20doctrine%20of%20credible%20minimum%20nuclear%20deterrence.&text=India%20will%20not%20resort%20to,aligned%20with%20nuclear%20weapon%20powers.
70 Indian Nuclear Doctrine Press Release PMO, https://archive.pib.gov.in/archive/releases98/lyr2003/rjan2003/04012003/r040120033.html
71 Sundaram and Ramana, n. 47, p. 160.
72 K Sundaram and M V Ramana p. 159 and "Narendra Modi says committed to 'no first use' of nuclear weapons," at https://www.ndtv.com/elections-news/narendra-modi-says-committed-to-no-first-use-of-nuclear-weapons-557628
73 Sundaram and Ramana, n. 47, p. 159.
74 Rajnath Singh Defence Minister August 16, 2019 Pokhran, at https://pib.gov.in/PressReleseDetailm.aspx?PRID=1582158

CHAPTER 19

UNDERSTANDING CHINA FOR THE STRATEGIC PRACTITIONER

S.L. NARASIMHAN

ABSTRACT

China has grown in strength politically, economically and militarily over the last four decades. It has a festering boundary question with India. This necessitates a thorough understanding of China, particularly by diverse practitioners of statecraft. There are four aspects covered in this chapter. Firstly, China has followed many strategies during her long history, particularly by several successful dynasties. It draws from those strategies to deal with present-day issues. A variety of examples have been provided in this chapter to prove this point. Secondly, there is no doubt that, Xi Jinping has been accumulating power during his tenure as President of China. The implications of this have consequences for India. Thirdly, PLA has been undergoing a major transformation for some time now. India must take note of this and prepare accordingly. Finally, analysts who have been following China have arrived at several findings. These must be put into context and taken into consideration.

INTRODUCTION

Gordon Chang stated in his 2001 book *"The Coming Collapse of China"* that the Communist Party of China is the root cause of many of the People's Republic of China's problems and will be responsible for its collapse in the near future. That prediction has not come true and China has emerged much stronger over the last two decades. As seen by the fact that a large portion of several seminars or discussions is spent on discussing China and its actions, it is evident that the People's Republic of China (PRC) occupies the mind space of all countries, strategists and academics like never before. The PRC's growing military power has become a cause of concern for most countries that have to deal with it. So much so, Graham Allison in his book titled "Destined for war: Can America and China Escape Thucydides Trap?" argues that unless China is willing to scale back its ambitions, or should Washington D.C. accept a subordinate role in the Pacific, a trade conflict, cyberattack, or accident at sea could soon escalate into an all-out war. Such doomsday theories add to the uncertainty of the global international order that is in a state of flux at present. A clear understanding of China is possible with a deep examination of the country through multiple lenses. This chapter offers strategic practitioners a window into how China adapts strategies of the past and deftly contextualises and adapts them to the present. The chapter would also examine Xi Jinping's efforts to consolidate power and its implications on global and regional geopolitics, trends in the modernisation of the People's Liberation Army (PLA) and some practical observations and implications for India's strategists and military commanders.

BLENDING THE PAST WITH THE PRESENT

For anyone who has been observing China over a period of time, it is obvious that China clearly blends its past with the present. Though there was no external threat to China in historic times, the nomads (Xiongnu 匈奴) from the periphery nibbled at the Chiniese territory constantly. Lack of external theats led to a culture of the Chinese emperor, who was considered a descendent from heaven (Tian Xia 天下), making the decisions on all policies. In the modern context, this is supported by the fact that Mao, Deng and Jiang took most decisions by themselves. After a progression towards collective leadership during Hu Jintao's tenure, it seems that the powers are again getting accumulated in Xi Jinping's persona. He has been declared as the core of the party (中国共产党的核心) and commander in chief.

In olden times, the emperor, his family members and senior military officers struggled to gain power. Now, the power struggle occurs between various groups like tuanpai (Communist Youth League 团派) and taizi (princelings 太子). Changes in state policy were influenced by which group had more power, and this is still true today.

China, for millennia, has adopted a written examination based on Confucian Theory to select government officials. These officials shaped China's strategy to a major extent. Even today, China conducts a common entrance exam called "guokao" that attracts more than a million candidates a year (wu, 2019). The recognised standard in governance is a technique known called Song Neo Confucianism, which envisions a hierarchical structure in which everyone understands their position and performs their role according to the existing hierarchy.

Strategic Behaviour of China.

Five core features (Ashley J Tellis M. D., 2000) that have been identified about China's security behaviour from the past are as follows:

- Protect the Chinese heartland through border defence and control.
- Periodic expansion and contraction of periphery and regional boundaries corresponding to the power of the state.
- Frequent use of limited force based on calculations of relative power.
- Self-reliance and non-coercive security strategies to control or appease the periphery when the state is relatively weak.
- Influence of domestic leadership politics shaping the state's behaviour.

There are striking similarities in the strategy followed by China today and the ones outlined above. China is strengthening border defence and control to protect the heartland. Annexation of Tibet, Xinjiang, Inner Mongolia, unification of Hong Kong and Macau all contributed to the expansion of its boundaries. China's use of force against India, Vietnam and in the South China Sea are examples of the use of force against external entities based on pragmatic calculations. At present, China is gaining in strength, therefore non-coercive strategies are not visible. Examples of domestic leadership politics determining strategy are the handling of the 1989 Tian'anmen Square incident and its recent behaviour in Hong Kong.

China's war fighting has always relied primarily on infantry and cavalry. The Mongols and Manchus, with their excellent horsemanship, were very quick in concentrating forces in superior numbers at the decisive location to overcome Chinese defences. This has been the basic idea behind the War Zone Campaign doctrine conceived in the early 1990s by China. Admiral Zheng He's expeditions to South East Asia, South Asia, Persian Gulf and East Africa in the 15th century made a significant contribution to the protection of China's maritime trade routes. The "Malacca Dilemma" (Storey, 2006), which is based on China's concern about Sea Lanes of Communication, will influence China's security strategies and its efforts to increase its influence in the Indian Ocean and West Pacific.

The expansion and contraction of the territory along China's periphery depended upon the strength and stage of the regime (Li, 1996) (Godwin, 1996). As the power of the Han, Tang, Ming and Qing dynasties increased, their propensity for conquest and expansion along the periphery increased correspondingly and vice versa. Presently, China is increasing its influence in the Central Asian Republics, Mongolia, Koreas, South East Asia, South Asia and West Pacific because its comprehensive national power is rising steadily. When the regimes started declining, the Chinese heartland disintegrated into many feudal kingdoms. Examples of such a circumstance are North-South Division (420-598 AD), Five Dynasties and 10 Kingdoms Era (907-960 AD). The current Chinese emphasis on regime security and protection is likely to have evolved from this.

China's strategic behaviour is influenced by Confucius, Mencius and Sun Zi. All three of them advocated contrasting styles with Confucius preferring moral persuasion, Mencius inclined to force application and Sun Zi advocating coercion. Keeping those templates in mind, China is concentrating on building its conventional and asymmetric warfare capability. China will choose offensive force, when it is militarily strong and use of such force results in minimum political and economic penalties (Alistair Ian Johnston, 1998). Consequently, in the existing world order, China's aggression in the East and South China Seas and pushing ahead with the One Belt One Road Initiative is driven by its military and economic strength. Though China has articulated a policy of offensive defence that is based on Confucian theory and is essentially defensive in nature, it frequently justifies any use of force as a principle of active defence (Li, 2006).

Military operations into peripheral areas in the past were followed by establishment of garrisons in those areas. This trend can be seen in reports of new infrastructure build up after the Dolam incident in 2017 and Eastern Ladakh incidents of 2020. Most earlier Chinese regimes were not able to subjugate their opponents because they did not understand the inner strengths of the latter (Hsu, 2000). China's actions in Tibet, Xinjiang and Hong Kong depict such a behaviour. When the Xiongnu from the periphery of China were defeated, they would retreat and return later, but since the Chinese forces had to stay on, they relied on fixed agricultural areas for their support (Barfield, 1989). Mao Zedong's theory of drawing the enemy deep into his own territory has its roots from this.

Non-coercive strategies adopted by China are passive defence, policies of conciliation or joining hands, breaking contact with the outside world, maintaining hierarchical diplomatic relations or the acceptance of more equal interactions (Shepherd, 1993). A combination of all these aspects was used depending on the strength or weakness of the regime, and the peripheral regions were occasionally pitched against one another (Ashley J Tellis M. D., 2000). Supporting Pakistan against the concerns of India is an example of this. Chinese culture, as well as marriages with the adversary's family, were used to secure the alliance of the rulers. This strategy might be compared to the establishment of Confucius centres or China study centres in many countries.

China maintained a cordial relationship with countries by offering trade and cultural incentives (O'Neill, 1987). China has attempted to develop relations with ASEAN and SAARC countries by designating some countries as Least Developed Countries and signing the Regional Comprehensive Economic Partnership. During the Qing dynasty era, China relied on maintaining peace externally, while it grew internally (Yen-p'ing Hao, 1980). A similar policy is the "External Calm and Internal Intensity" that is part of the War Zone Campaign strategy. It means that China projects herself to be a strong nation outwardly while the internal contradictions and its struggle to manage them are not revealed to the outside world.

China has also implemented a policy of ensuring that some states do not maintain relations with countries that oppose it (Hsu, 1960). It is trying hard to wean countries away from maintaining official relations with Taiwan, even offering protection or economic assistance in some instances, and Pakistan-China relations is an example of this.

When the Western countries invaded China in the 19th century, they proved superior to China in several areas of statecraft and imposed a 'century of humiliation' on a proud civilisation. As a result, when the Communists took control of China in 1947, Mao was determined to seize control of Chinese society and expand the Chinese heartland to restore what he saw as a historical equilibrium on the periphery through coercive action. The Century of Humiliation has accentuated the feeling of inadequacy in China's political elite and through them, in the larger societal landscape. Therefore, there is a strong motivation in the Chinese mindspace to undo what it perceives as the wrongs committed on it (O'Neill, 1987). This has formed the basis for the reunification of the motherland to include Hong Kong, Macau, Taiwan and Islands in the East and South China Seas. Moreover, this has made China extremely sensitive to external threats, which may explain its reactions to India-US relations, US-ROK-Japan Exercises and the Quad.

China's current geopolitical strategy combines a capitalist economy within an overarching communist ideological framework. The strategy evolved from a weak-strong state security strategy and encompasses a non-ideological, laissez faire economic growth, maintaining good international relations, playing an increasing role in world affairs and restraint in using force.

Many experts feel that China is adopting the Shi Strategy, which has been followed for centuries by the players of "Go", a game that is in stark contrast to modern day Chess (Lai, 2004). In "Go," the number of pieces on the board increases as the game progresses, in contrast to the game of chess. Physical annihilation of opponent's forces is not the aim of winning in this game (Kissinger, 2011). Relative positioning of own resources to gain maximum influence is the aim. China seems to be following this strategy as seen by its efforts to establish influence in South American countries straddling the Panama Canal, countries that lie astride the Gibraltar Strait, Gulf of Aden, Indian Ocean, Africa and Asia Pacific. As a first, China has established a base for its ships on Anti-Piracy patrolling missions in Djibouti. This could be a precursor to establishing overseas bases by China (Foreign Minister, 2015). Presently China has stakes in 95 ports across the world.

There is a strong relationship between China's historical security tactics and its current security strategies. China will pursue a mix of coercive and non-coercive tactics, with military modernisation allowing the PLA to aid China in implementing coercive methods. China will attempt to adapt parts of the developed Western world's systems, capabilities and structures, as it did in the 19th century. All these are endeavours by China to become a leading player in the comity of nations.

XI JINPING'S EFFORTS TO CONSOLIDATE POWER AND IMPLICATIONS

As soon as Xi Jinping came to power, he lifted the two-term limit for the President and Vice President of China. He also ensured that he was made the core of the Communist Party of China even as he propagated the 'Xi Jinping Thought on Socialism with Chinese Characteristics for a New Era.' This was then enshrined in the Constitution of China, while in harness, which his two predecessors could not do. He declared himself as Commander in Chief of the armed forces and People's Leader, the latter title which was only used by Mao Zedong. He also put forth the China Dream (中国梦), which is to build a moderately prosperous society and realise national rejuvenation of China (中国伟大复兴). In addition to these, four structural events have shaped Xi Jinping's reign. First, he retreated to Maoism as a political philosophy. In November 2014, Xi Jinping as Chairman of the Central Military Commission (CMC) used the occasion of the 85th anniversary of the 1929 Gutian Conference to convene a critical meeting on political work in the People's Liberation Army. Xi addressed the 420 generals and senior military officials present for the two-day meeting, reminding them of Mao's dictum about Party control of the military and connecting the themes to his current anti-corruption campaign (Mulvenon, 2015). Top Chinese leaders were forced to undergo self-criticism sessions, a tool highly favoured by Mao Zedong and taken to extremes during the Cultural Revolution. Under Xi's presidency, self-criticism sessions are becoming more popular (Drillsma, 2018). Such sessions have been held in 2013, 2016 and 2017 prior to the one in 2018.

Second, all companies, both domestic and multinational, are required to have Party committees. During Xi Jinping's tenure there seems to be a push to increase this phenomena. The recent crackdown on technology companies after decades of freedom is testimony to increased political control over corporates. Despite China's authoritarian system, business happens to be a powerful component of China's increasing international standing. Private firms constitute 84.1 per cent of all enterprises, increasing from just 4,43,000 in 1996 to 15.6 million in 2018. This is why Xi Jinping hopes to increase the presence and power of "Party organisations" (dang zuzhi 党组织)—to boost private sector compliance with central priorities (Thomas, 2020), a phenomenon that had tapered off during Hu Jintao's time.

Third, while leaders from Jiang Zemin till Xi Jinping did carry out anti-corruption campaigns, Xi Jinping gave a punitive impetus to the anti-corruption drive. During the period 2012 to 2019, the number of officials subject to investigation increased steadily from 173,000 to 485,000. To date, over 2.9 million officials have been investigated and more than 1.7 million prosecuted (Diallo, 2021). Xi Jinping launched the campaign in 2018 with the slogan "Saohei chu'e,"(扫黑除恶) meaning "sweep away black and eliminate evil". Nearly 40,000 supposed criminal cells and corrupt companies were put out of action, and more than 50,000 Communist Party and government officials were punished for abetting them. The latest campaign has served another function of enabling officials across China to lock away entrepreneurs and other citizens who have gained too much wealth or influence independent of the Party (Feng, 2021). Fourth, beginning on January 1, 2018, Xi Jinping began issuing Training Orders on New Years Eve, mobilising the PLA for exercise. These are clear indications that Xi Jinping is adopting these methods to centralise control.

The consequences of Xi's actions, as stated above, indicate that he is likely to be in power till at least 2027 if not 2032. His stature within China and the communist party seems to be growing and stands only next to that of Mao, albeit with some internal rivalry. Therefore, he is likely to be powerful with minor internal dissensions. Through the anti-corruption campaign, he is likely to have achieved two things: root out corruption to an extent and bring down some political contenders and those making money at the expense of the Communist Party of China. Under Xi, the aggressive behaviour of the PLA is likely to continue as it has in recent times. Therefore, two generations of Indian strategists and military practitioners must be prepared to deal with him being at the helm of affairs in China and closely monitor when hubris emerges in his decision-making ability as was the case with Mao.

PLA TRENDS OVER A TWO-DECADE PERSPECTIVE

The present round of military reforms in the PLA is likely to radically change the way it operates. There are a number of inferences that can be drawn from these reforms. For all these years, the PLA Ground Forces were the most powerful service and dominated the other services in China. Following the reforms, the ground forces are likely to lose their influence considerably. The Chief of General Staff has lost oversight of military training, professional military education, mobilisation, strategic planning, electronic warfare, cyber resources and human resources management. Human resources management has shifted to the Political Works department. With the four general departments being subsumed into the CMC, the latter has got involved in the day-to-day functioning of the armed forces. This may adversely affect the functioning of the armed forces due to excessive political oversight. Prior to the reforms, CMC had a buffer, which allowed it to undertake strategic thinking and planning. Following the reforms, the PLA will concentrate more on combat capability and territorial defence. Separating the resources of General Staff Department to form the PLA SSF will allow all services to make better use of space and information warfare resources. This could enable the PLA to become a force capable of better joint operations.

IMPLICATIONS FOR INDIA'S MILITARY COMMANDERS

India is unlikely to catch up with China in all realms of defence capacity and capability in the near future. Therefore, India needs to make efforts to increase its asymmetric and deterrent capabilities to prevent China from resorting to the frequent use of force to settle disputes or disagreements. The creation of the PLA SSF and increased testing of missiles by the PLA Rocket Force in the recent past will make the PLA capable of launching a long-drawn-out non-contact warfare aimed at reducing the combat potential of the Indian armed forces. Since space and cyber domains do not have territorial limitations and have absolute deniability, actions in them cannot be deemed as acts of war in its true sense.

Since the days of Mao Zedong, China has been following the principle of Active Defence. Active Defence simply means that China can take proactive measures to pre-empt its adversary's attack. PLA SSF will be important to this concept and provide an information canopy to its armed forces. This will reduce the Observe, Orient, Decide and Act (OODA) loop and the time required for PLA to react to any adversary. India needs to prepare itself to face China's active defence operations. To meet that challenge, India's capabilities in space and information warfare need to improve. PLA RF will try to offset the disadvantages that the high altitude terrain in the Tibetan Plateau imposes on the PLA Airforce. Therefore, India should build redundancies in its operational and civil infrastructure and continue to develop an effective defence capability against ballistic missiles.

India must continuously monitor the PLA SSF's space assets and develop systems to protect its own. Since this force possesses most of the space and cyber assets of China, India needs to harden, isolate, and protect critical infrastructure and military networks to defend itself. India should synergise its offensive and defensive cyber capabilities. Currently, there are a number of agencies involved in cyber operations in India. To have a credible offensive and defensive cyber capability, their efforts need to be synergised. According to some accounts, China is developing laser and Directed Energy Weapons (DEW) that might be launched from space by the PLA SSF. To defend against such contingencies, India should protect and harden its networks against such weapons. Rather than engaging in a competitive space race, India needs to concentrate on its niche deterrent and collaborative capabilities in the military domain of space.

The Chinese have always been adept at psychological warfare and the PLA SSF is likely to spearhead that effort. Such efforts are at an extremely nascent stage in India and must be high on the list of capabilities that must be nurtured and developed at a rapid rate for execution both during peace and war. A structure at the national level to prosecute this form of warfare must be created by leveraging the latent expertise that is available in several agencies that currently work in relative isolation.

EXPERIENTIAL OBSERVATIONS

Internal Issues

There is a general belief that the Communist Party of China is a monolith. The truth is, it is not. It has its own share of disagreements and infighting, but it all takes place within the official compound of Zhongnanhai, Beijing's seat of power.. Therefore, it gives a sense that the party is one and unified. As explained earlier, the taizi and tuanpai struggle for power and influence constantly. There are also eight non-communist parties in China that show a face of the country that adheres to principles of democracy. The non-Communist parties of China are neither parties out of office, nor opposition parties, but friendly parties that "coexist over a long period of time, engage in mutual supervision, show utter devotion to each other, and share honor and disgrace, weal and woe" with the CPC. They are parties participating in government and political affairs (Political System and State Structure, n.d.).

Chinese society is more homogeneous than societies from other large nations, India for example. It comprises approximately 91 per cent Hans while the remainder 9 per cent is divided amongst 55 minority communities. Therefore, it is easier to administer and influence for the Chinese government. It also makes it more difficult for outsiders to penetrate the society. Though the Communist Party of China propagates atheism, other religions such as Christianity, Buddhism and Islam can be practised in China at government-approved houses of worship in a controlled way. The priests and religious teachers need to have the approval of authorities. China has reached an agreement with the Vatican about the appointment of bishops for the Churches in China (Mccallister, 2018).

Controlling the Periphery

China has taken great efforts and invested a huge amount to integrate Tibet with the mainland in a several ways. Among these initiatives, some of the most significant have been the improvements in the road, rail and air connectivity to Tibet from the mainland. Another infrastructure-oriented initiative launched by Beijing is the creation of several Xiaokang villages to settle the population in border areas with modern amenities (Arpi, 2020).

Altering the demographic distribution by offering incentives to Han population to start businesses and settle down in Tibet has paid rich dividends. Changes in the school curriculum has been initiated to influence the mind of young Tibetans. Instituting population and resource control measures to ensure that Buddhism is practised as per the prescription of the central government (Cook, 2017) are among the mildly coercive methods adopted to control the local population.

The Uighur problem has been a well-known one. China has recently used a number of segregatory and punitive measures to ensure that the Uighur population remains under control. This has been done by a number of measures, including control of religious practices, "education camps" and movement control measures. Active surveillance measures have also been instituted (Zenz, 2020).

China officially reclaimed its sovereignty over Hong Kong in 1997 and promised to follow the 'One Country Two Systems' model wherein the latter was expected to retain its independence and governance model till 2047. However, soon after, China started taking control of Hong Kong. Since 2019, there has been an increased effort to integrate Hong Kong completely into China. This has been done by enacting the National Security Law and bringing modifications to the election process. Freedom of press has also come under pressure with the owners of Apple Daily being arrested and the Daily itself forced to close down (Enos, 2021).

INTERNATIONAL RELATIONS

The century of humiliation is often quoted as a reason for whipping up nationalism, as well as to explain the aggressive behaviour of China in the South China Sea and elsewhere. China has laid claim to two island chains. It's claim to the first island chain extends roughly across the East and South China Seas. The second chain of islands extends into Western Pacific and passes through Guam. It is quite clear that the Chinese are making all-out efforts to gain maximum influence within the first island chain. They are quite likely to begin spreading their influence towards the second island chain once the areas under the first island chain come under full control of China (Joshua Espena, 2020).

North Korea: The Korean Peninsula is of utmost importance to China. One of the reasons it reacted very aggressively to the deployment of THAAD systems by the US on South Korean soil was to retain influence on the Korean Peninsula. North Korea, the other important country on the Korean Peninsula, has close relations with China. Therefore, China would like to play an active role in all issues related to the Korean Peninsula and North Korea (Rozman, 2021).

China's Influence in UN Organisations: China has worked hard to secure major roles in UN Organisations, particularly those that are essential to it. China has gained influence in WTO, UNHRC, ITU, ICAO, UNIDO, FAO, IMO and similar institutions which matter to it (Kartik Ashta,

2021). Similarly, the Chinese are investing much capital and effort into developing standards that will help Chinese enterprises obtain a competitive advantage in the global market, such as 3 GPP (Berstein, 2018). China is an important contributor to UN's Peace Keeping Operations in addition to keeping a force of approximately 8,000 personnel ready and equipped for deployment. Despite its unwillingness to engage in serious combat in furtherance of peacekeeping or peace enforcement, it currently funds the UN Peace Keeping Operations substantially.

Diplomacy: During the initial stages of the COVID pandemic, China was accused of being the source of the pandemic and still continues to bear the brunt of global suspicion. Several Chinese diplomats posted across the capitals in the world reacted aggressively and critically towards the countries that blamed China. This was also termed as "wolf warrior diplomacy". However, in the recent past, this trend seems to have softened a bit. The softening up may also be a result of Xi Jinping asking his people to make China a lovable country (Steven Lee Myers, 2021) and setting a target of being a world soft power leader by 2035.

Taiwan: In the recent months, there has been growing concern among observers that China may employ non-peaceful measures against Taiwan (Lee Hsi-min, 2021). This fear may not be wrong, as seen from the number of aircraft that have been violating the ADIZ of Taiwan on an almost daily basis. Just prior to the 100th anniversary of the Communist Party of China, a package of 28 aircraft entered the ADIZ of Taiwan. However, the difficulty of carrying out amphibious operations, bringing other parties into the China-Taiwan issue and the capability of the PLA to launch such major amphibious operations may force China to rethink on embarking on any non-peaceful method of reunification of Taiwan.

INDIA-CHINA ISSUES

Boundary Question: The boundary question between India and China has been a thorn in the flesh of bilateral relations between the two Asian giants for over six decades. After being peaceful for almost 45 years, the Line of Actual Control (LAC) in eastern Ladakh saw casualties on both sides after a violent clash in the Galwan valley in June 2020. The LAC is likely to remain under pressure unless there is political momentum to resolve the boundary issue. However, China's actions in 2020 in eastern Ladakh should be seen as a unilateral effort to change the status quo of the LAC and a regressive step in the overall process of normalisation of relations between the two Asian powers. Unless peace and tranquillity is ensured along the LAC, it is unlikely that the bilateral relations will improve in the near future (Narasimhan, 2021).

Economy: There is a misnomer that trade between India and China is to the tune of US$ 85-100 billion and that this is a good way for the two countries to build confidence and mutual trust. However, dis-aggregation of the trade reveals that it is one sided and benefits China in several significant ways. India's trade deficit with China is to the tune of anything between US$ 45 and US$ 55 billion.There are also non-tariff barriers that have been imposed by China over Indian companies, thereby denying their entry into the Chinese market (Das, 2014). Therefore, trade should not be taken as a source that could bring stability in the bilateral relationship.

CHINA'S MILITARY

It is common knowledge that China's defence expenditure has continuously increased and nearly matches that of the US. The modernisation of all forces has been steadily ongoing, and the goals set seem to be on the way to being realised. There is a lot of effort being put into strengthening service jointness and enabling them to be capable of fighting modern wars. An important aspect in the development of capabilities is the civil-military fusion, wherein, the modernisation that has been achieved in the private sector and in the PLA are mutually exchangeable. Towards this, approximately 7,200 patents that were held by the PLA have been opened to the civil sector. Similarly, a number of patents held by the civil sector have been opened up for the usage of the PLA. This effort is likely to improve the modernisation process of the PLA in a faster time frame.

CONCLUSION

From the preceding discussion, it is clearly evident that the China of today follows the successful strategies of the past and adapts them to the modern times. It has been growing rapidly in power and with the adverse security relationship of recent times, this has serious implications for India. India's strategic establishment and its military commanders must take note of and keep close track of PLA modernisation, which is progressing at an accelerated pace in recent years. Finally, interacting with the Chinese raises a lot of practical issues that must be addressed on a long-term basis, even if certain low-hanging fruit seem visible on the near horizon.

NOTE

1 Only about 10 per cent of China's land is suitable for farming. Much of the land lies within the small plain between the Huang He and the Chang Jiang in eastern China. This plain, known as the North China Plain, is China's heartland. Throughout China's long history, its political boundaries have expanded and contracted depending on the strength or weakness of its ruling families. Yet the heartland of China remained the centre of its civilisation.

REFERENCES

Alistair Ian Johnston, "China's Militarised Interstate Dispute Behaviour 1949-92, A First Cut at the Data." *China Quarterly*, 1998, p. 153.

Arpi, C., "China's border villages are a threat to India's defences." *The Daily Guardian*, October 28, 2020, at https://thedailyguardian.com/chinas-border-villages-are-a-threat-to-indias-defences/

Ashley J Tellis, M. D., 2000 *Interpreting China's Grand Strategy* (Washington DC: Rand Corporation, 2000).

Barfield, T. J., *The Perilous Frontier: Nomadic Empire & China* (Cambridge: Blackwell Publishers, 1989).

Berstein, D., "China: We lead 3GPP Wireless Standards." *CircleID*, May 26, 2018, https://www.circleid.com/posts/20180526_china_we_lead_3gpp_wireless_standards/

Cook, S., "Tibetan Buddhism: Religious Freedom in China." *Freedom House*, 2017, https://freedomhouse.org/report/2017/battle-china-spirit-tibetan-buddhism-religious-freedom

Das, D., "Non-tariff barriers, a thorn in India-China business ties." *The Hindu Business Line*, September 21, 2014, https://www.thehindubusinessline.com/news/Non-tariff-barriers-a-thorn-in-India-China-business-ties/article20869784.ece

Diallo, F., "Xi Jinping's Anti-corruption Struggle: Eight Years On". Stockholm: Institute for Security Development and Policy, 2021, https://isdp.eu/content/uploads/2021/04/Xi-Jinpings-Anti-corruption-Struggle-IB-09.04.21.pdf

Drillsma, R., "Xi forces top Chinese officials to conduct self-criticisms." *Taiwan News*, December 28, 2018, https://www.taiwannews.com.tw/en/news/3606243

Enos, O., "The Closure Of Apple Daily: Another Nail In The Coffin For Freedom In Hong Kong." *Forbes,* https://www.forbes.com/sites/oliviaenos/2021/07/01/the-closure-of-apple-daily-another-nail-in-the-coffin-for-freedom-in-hong-kong/?sh=2313cd5b61ba

Fairbank, J. K., *China, A New History* (Cambridge, Massachusetts: Harvard University Press, 1992).

Feng, E., "How China's Massive Corruption Crackdown Snares Entrepreneurs Across The Country." *NPR*, March 4, 2021, https://www.npr.org/2021/03/04/947943087/how-chinas-massive-corruption-crackdown-snares-entrepreneurs-across-the-country

Foreign Minister: "China to Build Navy Base in Djibouti." *Defence News*. France-Presse Agence.

Godwin, P. H., "From Continent to Periphery: PLA doctrine, Strategy and Capabilities Towards 2000." *China Quarterly* (Special Issue 146), pp. 464-487, 1996, http://www.jstor.org/stable/655477

Hsu, I. C., *The Rise of Modern China* (New York: Oxford university Press, 1960).

Joshua Espena, C. B., "The Taiwan Frontier and the Chinese Dominance for the Second Island Chain", *Australian Outlook*, August 13, 2020, https://www.internationalaffairs.org.au/australianoutlook/taiwan-frontier-chinese-dominance-for-second-island-chain/

Kartik Ashta, A. S., *China's Expanding Influence in the UN System* (Mumbai: Gateway House), 2021, https://www.gatewayhouse.in/chinas-expanding-influence-un-system/

Kissinger, H., *On China* (New York: Penguin Books, 2011).

Kondapalli, S., S. L. Narasimhan, "Interviewer", New Delhi, 2014.

Lai, D., *Learning from the Stones: A Go Approah to Mastering China's strategic Concept"Shi'* (Carlisle: Strategic Studies Institute, US Army War College, 2004).

Lee Hsi-min, E. L., "The threat of China invading Taiwan is growing every day. What the U.S. can do to stop it." NBC News, July 9, 2021, https://www.nbcnews.com/think/opinion/threat-china-invading-taiwan-growing-every-day-what-u-s-ncna1273386

Li, N., "The PLA's Evolving War Fighting Doctrine, Strategy and Tactics 1985-95: A Chinese Perspective." *China Quarterly* (Special Issue No 146), 443-463, 1996, http://www.jstor.org/stable/655476

Li, N., "The PLA's Evolving Campaign Doctrine and Strategy." *Rand*, 1-29, 2006.

Mccallister, D., "China And Vatican Sign Agreement On Appointment Of Bishops". *npr*, September 23, 2018, https://www.npr.org/2018/09/23/650853750/china-and-vatican-sign-agreement-on-appointment-of-bishops

Menon, S. S., S. L. Narasimhan, "Interviewer", September 23, 2015.

Mulvenon, J. "China Leadership Monitor, Hoover Institution", 2015, https://www.hoover.org/sites/default/files/research/docs/clm46jm.pdf

Narasimhan, S. L., "Early disengagement & de-escalation along LAC will reduce chances of fresh clashes: Narasimhan." *Economic Times*, June 9, 2021, https://economictimes.indiatimes.com/news/defence/early-disengagement-de-escalation-along-lac-will-reduce-chances-of-fresh-clashes-narasimhan/articleshow/83371456.cms?from=mdr

O'Neill, H. B., *Companion to Chinese History* (New York: Facts on File Publications, 1987).

Political System and State Structure. (n.d.), Minsitry of Foreign affairs of the PRC, https://www.fmprc.gov.cn/mfa_eng/ljzg_665465/zgjk_665467/3579_665483/t17851.shtml

Rozman, G., "China's Role on the Korean Peninsula". *The National Interest*, June 30, 2021, https://nationalinterest.org/blog/korea-watch/chinas-role-korean-peninsula-188904

Shepherd, J. R., *Statecraft and Political Economy on the Taiwan frontier 1600-1800* (California: Stanford University Press, 1993).

Steven Lee Myers, K. B., "China's Leader Wants a 'Lovable' Country. That Doesn't Mean He's Making Nice." *The New York Times*, June 8, 2021, https://www.nytimes.com/2021/06/08/world/asia/china-diplomacy.html

Storey, I., "China's Malacca Dilemma." *China Brief*, 6, 8, 2006.

Thomas, N., "Party Committees in the Private Sector: Rising Presence, Moderate Prevalence", *Macro Polo*, December 16, 2020, https://macropolo.org/party-committees-private-sector-china/?rp=e

Wolters, O., *The Fall of Srivijaya in Malay History* (London: Lund Humphries Publications Ltd., 1970).

wu, W., "China's civil service exam attracts 1.4 million applicants with eyes on the prize of an 'iron rice bowl' job". *South China Morning Post*, November 24, 2019, https://www.scmp.com/economy/china-economy/article/3039116/chinas-civil-service-exam-attracts-14-million-applicants-eyes

www.globalsecurity.org. 12 03, 2015, http://www.globalsecurity.org/military/world/china/24-character.htm

Yen-p'ing Hao, E.-m. W., *Changing Chinese Views of Western Relations 1840-95* (Vol. 11), 1980. (K.-C. L. John K. Fairbank, Ed.) (London: Cambridge University Press).

Zenz, A., "China's Own Documents Show Potentially Genocidal Sterilization Plans in Xinjiang." *Foreign Policy*, July 1, 2020, https://foreignpolicy.com/2020/07/01/china-documents-uighur-genocidal-sterilization-xinjiang/

EDITORS

Air Vice Marshal (Dr) **Arjun Subramaniam** (50th NDC) is the President's Chair of Excellence in National Security Affairs at NDC. He is a retired fighter pilot from the IAF who has commanded a fighter squadron and a flying base in addition to being a doctrinal airpower expert. After his retirement, he has been a Visiting Fellow at The Harvard Asia Center and Oxford Universities, and a Visiting Professor at the Fletcher School of Law and Diplomacy, Ashoka and Jindal Universities. His current areas of focus are international and regional security, contemporary Indian military history, airpower in integrated operations and the India-China security relationship. He is the author of five books, including *India's Wars: A Military History: 1947-1971* and its newly-released sequel in two versions titled *Full Spectrum: India's Wars 1972-2020* and *A Military History of India since 1972: Full Spectrum Operations and the Changing Contours of Modern Conflict*.

Air Marshal **Diptendu Choudhury** is the Commandant of the National Defence College, New Delhi, and an alumnus of the Royal College of Defence Studies, UK. A highly experienced and accomplished fighter pilot, he has over 5,000 hours on frontline combat aircraft. He has commanded a MiG-29 squadron, two frontline fighter bases and has served as the Commandant of the prestigious Tactics and Combat Development Establishment (TACDE). He has held many key staff positions at Air HQs in the areas of Joint Planning, Inspections and Operations. He has commanded the Composite Battle Response and

Analysis Group, two Air Defence Direction Centres and served as the Senior Air Staff Officer (SASO) at Western Air Command, the IAF's largest command. He has planned and conducted several IAF exercises, as well as led three international exercises in the US, France and UAE. He is a prolific writer on airpower strategy and international security having published articles in professional and academic journals.

DISTINGUISHED CONTRIBUTORS

Admiral **Arun Prakash** served as India's 18th Naval Chief and Chairman Chiefs of Staff Committee, retiring in end-2006. A naval-aviator by specialisation, he was awarded the Vir Chakra for gallantry during the 1971 War while flying with an IAF fighter-bomber squadron. Admiral Prakash is a graduate of the IAF Test Pilots School, the Defence Services Staff College and the US Naval War College.

He has commanded a carrier-borne fighter squadron, a naval air-station and four warships, including the aircraft-carrier INS *Viraat*. Later in his career, he commanded the Eastern Fleet, the National Defence Academy and the Western Naval Command. In 2001, he was designated the first C-in-C of the Andaman and Nicobar Joint Command in Port Blair. Many initiatives were launched in the fields of doctrine, strategy, foreign maritime cooperation and indigenisation during his tenure as Chief. Post-retirement, he served two terms as member of the National Security Advisory Board and was Chairman of the National Maritime Foundation. Currently, he occupies a Distinguished Chair in the Naval War College, Goa. He is a much-respected strategic commentator, and writes and speaks on strategic and defence issues. He has published a compendium of his speeches and writings titled: *From the Crow's Nest.*

Air Chief Marshal **Arup Raha** (46th NDC) was the 24th Chief of the Air Staff and served as the Chairman Chiefs of Staff Committee before retiring in December 2016. He is an accomplished fighter pilot with 3,400 hours of flying and has commanded a MiG-29 Squadron and two frontline fighter bases. He is an A2 Qualified Flying Instructor and a Fighter Combat Leader. Air Chief Marshal Arup Raha also served as the Defence Attaché in Ukraine and is an alumnus of the National Defence College. Well versed with joint operations, the air chief served as AOC Advance HQs with two operational Army commands, Western and South Western Commands. He commanded two Operational Air Commands and served as the VCAS before he was appointed as the CAS. His experience as the Chairman COSC for nearly two and a half years interacting with the political leadership, bureaucracy and military leadership of the Army and Navy offered him deep insights into Higher Defence Organisation.

Lieutenant General **J.R. Mukherjee** (34th NDC) was commissioned into the ASSAM Regiment in 1964 and retired from Army service in 2004 as the Chief of Staff, Headquarters Eastern Command. During his service career, he commanded three battalions in the Assam Regt, a mountain brigade, a mountain division, 15 Corps in Kashmir during the latter part of the Kargil Conflict onwards, and served on staff appointments at Army, Command and Corps Headquarters besides having been Head of the Indian Training Team at Botswana Africa. He is an alumnus from the National Defence Academy, Khadakvasla, Staff College Camberley, UK and the National Defence College, New Delhi. He is also well known for his knowledge of India's North East and Kashmir having served in these regions extensively and during more troubled times. He has written several articles for the editorial pages of the *Statesman*, *Telegraph* and the *Ananda Bazar Patrika* newspapers, and three books titled *An Insiders Experience of Insurgency in India's North East*, *History of the ASSAM Regiment* and *A Soldier for Life: My Story*. He is currently the President of the 'Research Centre for Eastern and North Eastern Regional Studies (CENERS-K) Kolkata.

Shri **K.C. Verma** (32nd NDC) joined the Indian Police Service in 1971. Deputed to the Intelligence Bureau in 1976, he dealt with the whole gamut of intelligence and security issues for thirty years, including the North East and Punjab during difficult times. He headed the Narcotics Control Bureau in 2005-2007 and was thereafter Secretary (Security), as also the Internal Security Advisor to the Union Home Minister. He was Chief of India's external intelligence organisation, the Research and Analysis Wing (R&AW), in 2009–10. After superannuation, he served as a member of the Naresh Chandra Task Force on National Security. He is an alumnus of the National Defence College.

Lieutenant General **P.C. Katoch** (40th NDC) is a third-generation Army officer, who superannuated as DG Information Systems in 2009. A Special Forces officer, he commanded a Special Forces battalion under the IPKF in Sri Lanka, a Brigade in Siachen Glacier area, Mountain Division in Ladakh and a Strike Corps in South Western Theatre. He has served as Defence Attaché in Japan with accreditation to Republic of Korea. A graduate of NDC and former Colonel of The Parachute Regiment, he is a prolific writer on international affairs, geopolitics, military, security, technical and topical issues and is a widely-published analyst in India and abroad. He has is the author of three books: *India's Special Forces, Indian Military and Network-Centric Warfare and Special Operations Case Studies.*

Lieutenant General **B.S. Nagal** (41st NDC) is an infantry officer with combat experience from the 1971 war and the Kargil Conflict. He retired in 2010 as Commander-in-Chief of the Strategic Forces Command (SFC) and then served in the Prime Minister's Office as Chief Programme Staff (SPS) till 2012. He has commanded a division and a corps on the Western Front and is an alumnus of the Army Staff College at Camberly (UK), Army War College, Mhow, and National Defence College, New Delhi. He is a former Director of the Centre for Land Warfare Studies and writes extensively on strategic issues.

Lieutenant General (Dr) **Prakash Menon** (44th NDC) is an infantryman with extensive operational experience and has served as a company commander on the Siachen glacier and the Line of Control (LoC) in Kashmir and Kargil. He has commanded a Battalion, Brigade and a Counter Insurgency Force in Central, North and South Kashmir. He was the Commandant of the NDC and Military Adviser and Secretary to Government of India in the National Security Council Secretariat (NSCS). A PhD from the Madras University, he has several published works to his credit and is the author of *The Strategy Trap: India and Pakistan Under the Nuclear Shadow*, and one of the co-authors of *Non Alignment 2.0 and the recently published monograph, India's Path to Power: Strategy in a World Adrift*. He is currently the Director Strategic Studies Programme and Professorial Fellow, Takshashila Institution, Bangalore, Professor Emeritus, Trans Disciplinary University (TDU), Bangalore, and an Adjunct Professor at the National Institute of Advanced Studies (NIAS) Bangalore.

Vice Admiral **Anil Chopra** (44th NDC) holds the distinction of being the Commander-in-Chief of both combatant commands of the Indian Navy, i.e. the Western Naval Command, and the Eastern Naval Command, and the Director General of the Indian Coast Guard. He also commanded the aircraft carrier—INS *Viraat*, the destroyer—INS *Rajput* and the missile corvette—INS *Kuthar*. As Assistant Chief of Naval Staff (Policy and Plans), he was extensively associated with the formulation of the Navy's Force Structure and Financial/Perspective Planning. Admiral Chopra was a Member of the National Security Advisory Board, Government of India, from 2017-19 and a Member of an Expert Committee appointed by the Ministry of Defence to examine measures to enhance the combat capabilities of the Indian Armed Forces. A Distinguished Fellow with a number of think-tanks, Admiral Chopra was stationed overseas for over four years, including as a Senior Fellow at the US Atlantic Council in Washington DC.

Lieutenant General **Praveen Bakshi** (48th NDC) retired from the Indian Army as General Officer Commanding-in-Chief, Eastern Army in July 2017, after 40 years of service, and having orchestrated the military response to the Doklam incident with China on the Sikkim border. An alumnus of National Defence Academy, he was commissioned into Skinner's Horse, which he later commanded. An alumnus of the National Defence College at Delhi, he commanded an Armoured Brigade and a RAPID Division in the desert sector and a Corps in the plains of Punjab and Jammu and Kashmir. The general is currently on the Board of Directors of two Companies, accredited as a Distinguished Fellow with USI, New Delhi, and is a strategic leadership coach and speaker.

Lieutenant General **D.S. Hooda** (48th NDC) was commissioned into the 4th Battalion of the 4th Gorkha Rifles on December 15, 1976. He has commanded an Infantry Brigade in Jammu and Kashmir, a Division in Manipur and the 16 Corps at Jammu. The General took over the command of the Northern Army on June 1, 2014, and retired from there in December 2016. During his tenure, he oversaw the disputed and troubled borders with Pakistan and China, as well as the counter-insurgency operations in J and K. The surgical strikes of September 2016 were launched under his leadership. During his career spanning 40 years, he gained vast experience of counter-insurgency, both in Jammu and Kashmir and the North East. Lt Gen D.S. Hooda is the co-founder of the Council for Strategic and Defence Research, a think tank based at Delhi, and a Senior Fellow at the Delhi Policy Group.

Lieutenant General (Dr) **S.L. Narasimhan** is an Infantry Officer who has commanded a brigade, an infantry division, a corps and retired as the Director General of Military Intelligence. General Narasimhan has been an instructor in the Indian Military Training Team in Bhutan. He has been an avid China watcher for the last 20 years and served as the

Defence Attaché in the Embassy of India in China for three years. He has a PhD in India China Relations, is qualified in the Chinese language and his expertise spans across international relations and internal issues, economy and defence-related subjects of China. The general has written many articles in various journals and magazines. He is presently a Member of the National Security Advisory Board, India, Director General, Centre for Contemporary China Studies and a Distinguished Fellow with Centre for Air Power Studies, India.

Lieutenant General (Dr) **Rakesh Sharma** (52nd NDC) served for 40 years in the Indian Army and has extensive experience in high altitude borders on the LoC and LAC in Harsil (Uttrakhand), North Sikkim, Uri (J&K) and commanded the Fire and Fury Corps in Ladakh responsible for Kargil, Siachen Glacier and Eastern Ladakh—facing both Pakistan and China. He was Research Fellow at Institute for Defence Studies and Analyses and has done PhD in Defence Studies. He was Adjutant General of the Indian Army responsible for the Human Resource Management, and is now a Distinguished Fellow with Centre for Land Warfare Studies (CLAWS) and a member of the Executive Council of the Institute for Defence Studies and Analyses. He is a prolific writer and lectures on geostrategic and military matters.

Lieutenant General **P.R. Shankar** (49th NDC) retired as the Director General of Artillery and is an alumnus of NDA, DSSC, Naval Postgraduate School, Monterrey and NDC, New Delhi. He has held important command, staff and instructional appointments in service. He has vast experience in all kinds of terrain and operational situations which have confronted the Indian Army in the past four decades. He has deep knowledge, understanding and experience in successful defence planning and acquisition. His impetus to the modernisation and indigenisation of Artillery resulted in fructification of major 155 mm Gun, Rocket and Missile projects like the Dhanush, M777 ULH and K9 Vajra, Pinaka, Brahmos and upgraded Grad BM21. He is now a Professor in the Aerospace Department of Indian Institute of Technology, Madras, and is actively involved in applied research. He is an avid writer and has a popular blog at www.gunnersshot.com

Air Marshal (Dr) **R. Sachdeva** (49th NDC) was commissioned into the IAF in December 1981 and is a highly-experienced air mobility and transport pilot with over 7,200 hours of flying. He is a Cat A Qualified Flying Instructor, has commanded an An-32 squadron, a premier flying base and was the Senior Air Staff Officer at Southern Air Command. Significant among his other key assignments have been Assistant Chief of Integrated Defence Staff, Commandant of the College of Defence Management, Chairman Capital Acquisition Plan Categorisation Committee and Centre Director (Aviation) NTRO. He was also the Chairman of the Integrated Space Cell of the Armed Forces, is an expert in Spectrum Management and is closely involved with ICT Roadmap for the three services.

Rear Admiral **Sudhir Pillai** (47th NDC) is a Naval Aviator and has held vital operational and staff appointments at sea and ashore, which include commands of the Coast Guard Patrol Vessel *Ganga Devi*, the Marine Commando Flight, the Frigate *Udaygiri*, the Naval Air Station *Garuda*, and the Guided Missile Destroyers *Ranjit* and *Mysore*. While in command of *Mysore*, he participated in Anti-Piracy Patrols in the Gulf of Aden, leading to the capture of 23 Somali/Yemeni involved in piracy. The International Maritime Organisation honoured the ship with a Commendation for Exceptional Services to Shipping and Mankind. He was the Chief of Staff at Andaman Nicobar Command (ANC) and Chief instructor(Navy) at DSSC and is a prolific writer on maritime and security issues.

Air Vice Marshal **R. Isser** is an experienced military aviator with extensive operational and combat experience in Sri Lanka (IPKF),

Siachen Glacier, Kargil War and Congo (UNPK 2003-04). He has been a HADR Task Force Commander in many rescue and relief operations all over India and internationally, including Uttarakhand 2013, Ladakh 2010, Andhra-Karnataka 2009 and Arunachal Pradesh 2000. As a director of net assessment at HQ Integrated Defence Staff, he has coordinated numerous strategic projects and authored strategy reports on many critical issues. An author of three books, he has more than 50 articles to his credit in national and international journals on diverse subjects such as disaster response, peacekeeping, counter-insurgency, irregular conflicts, etc.

Rear Admiral **P Ashokan**, was commissioned into Navy on July 1, 1984. He joined the submarine arm in 1987 and commanded three conventional submarines before he took over as the commissioning Commanding Officer of INS *Chakra*, which was taken on lease from Russia in 2012. After relinquishing command, he was the Commodore Commanding Submarines (East), and oversaw the scaling up of infrastructure to maintain and operate nuclear submarines. On attaining Flag rank, he was posted to Naval Headquarters where he was looking after nuclear submarine acquisition and infrastructure. His last tenure prior to retirement was in Advance Technology Vessel (ATV) Headquarters, New Delhi, where he was the Project Director (Operations and Training), an assignment that gave him a very deep insight into the indigenous submarine construction capabilities.

INDEX

Actual Ground Position Line (AGPL) 105, 111
Afghanistan 79
  Talibanisation of 203
Afghan War 18
aircraft carriers 172
  aviation in naval operations 158–60
  challenges in 160–1
  contribution of 164–5
  emerging maritime environment in India 165–6
  in India 161–4
  inter-service difference 169
  and sharing of air powers 171
  shore-based air support at sea 170
  vulnerability 167–9
  in world 157–8
Al-Qaeda 21, 75, 77
Andaman Nicobar Command (ANC) 6–7, 275, 283, 302
  Chief of Staff 295–6
  Component Commander 297–8
  Deputy Commander 296
  staff organisation 296–7
  tri-service operating and training environment 298–300
Article 370, abrogation in August 2019 25, 58
Artificial Intelligence (AI) 94, 97, 100
asymmetric warfare 116
Atomic Energy Commission (AEC) 305
attacks (terrorists) on India
  Gurdaspur 22–4
  Pathankot 22–4, 59
  Pulwama 24
  Uri 22–4
AUKUS alliance 153, 155
Azhar, Masood 75, 77

Babbar Khalsa International (BKI) 73, 75
Bengal Initiative for Multi-Sectoral Technical and Economic Cooperation (BIMSTEC) 78
beyond visual range (BVR) capability 117
Bhabha Atomic Research Centre (BARC) 306–7
Bhabha, Homi 305–6
Bhindranwale Tiger Force of Khalistan 73
bin Laden, Osama 75
BJP 22, 57
Bodo Liberation Tigers Force (BLTF) 49
border standoff between India and China in 2020 288
Brodie, Bernard 11
Burton, John 59

Chairman Chiefs of Staff Committee (COSC) 270–1
Chief of Defence Staff (CDS) 264, 289–90, 292–3, 302
  roles and responsibilities of 277–8
China/Chinese
  anti-access and area-denial (A2AD) strategy of 160–1, 168
  Belt and Road Initiative 166
  blending past with present 326–7
  China-Myanmar Economic Corridor (CMEC) 252
  China-Pakistan Economic Corridor (CPEC) 252
  Communist Party of China 69
  controlling periphery 337–8
  dependence on IOR 166–7
  farming land in 341*n*1
  increase in defence capabilities and its implications for India's defence commanders 335–6
  and India, relationship between 339–40
  internal issues in 336–7
  international relations 338–9
  Maritime Silk-Road 166
  modernisation of military 340–1
  People's Liberation Army (PLA) 5–6, 99, 108–9, 113, 117, 150, 167, 194, 288–9, 334, 341
  strategic behaviour of 327–32
  three-warfare strategy of 113
  unrestricted warfare concept of 249–50
  Xi Jinping's efforts for power consolidation and implications 332–4
Citizenship Amendment Act 79
Clausewitz trinity model 15–16
Cold Start Doctrine 18, 92
Cold War, proxy wars during 11–12
Coming Collapse of China, The (Gordon Chang) 325–6
Commander-in-Chief Andaman & Nicobar Command (CINCAN) 283–4
Communist Party of India-Marxist/Leninist (CPI/ML) 65–6
Compact Revolutionary Zone 66
contact warfare 93
conventional deterrence, modes of 137
conventional war
  India's experience 17–19
  between nuclear powers 17
Coordination Committee of Maoist Parties 69
Coordination of Democratic Rights Organisation 69
counter-insurgency (CI) doctrine in India 8, 30–1, 91
  Assam 37–8
  British experience and its influence 31–3
  -intensive land strategy 5
  Manipur 36–8
  Mizoram 35–6
  Nagaland 33–5
  Tripura 38–9
counterterrorism (CT) 8
COVID-19 26
CPML-Party Unity 66

Dal Khalsa 73
deep coalition, Chinese strategy of 250
Defense Advanced Research Project Agency (DARPA), US 243
Department of Atomic Energy (DAE) 305–6

Department of Military Affairs (DMA) 264, 289–90, 292–3
Desai, Morarji 307
Dima Halim Daogah (DHD) 50
Disturbed Areas Act 39
Doctrine of Perpetual Defence (also known as Doctrine of Defence in Depth) 87
drones 79, 95, 97, 117, 145 168, 204, 261

Financial Action Task Force (FATF) 78
fire and move in warfare 122–5
firepower (India)
- effective, features of 129–33
- enhancement of 133–6
- evolution and development of 125–9
- Regiment of Artillery, role of 139–40
- role of 136–9

free-flowing intellectual exercise 7
Free Movement Regime (FMR) in India-Myanmar border 51–2

Gandhi, Indira 73, 307, 311–12
Gandhi, Rajiv 308
General Malik 14–15
General Musharraf 13, 18
geospatial intelligence (GEOINT) 118
grey zone conflicts 93, 97–101
Group of Ministers (GoM) 264–5, 283
gunboat diplomacy 147
Gurion, Ben 289

Haqqani Network 75
Harkat-ul-Ansar 76
Health Usage Monitoring Systems (HUMS) 244
helicopters role in future battlefields
- convergence of technologies 242–4
- multi-domain operations 238–40
- Special Forces (SF), importance of 241–2
- urban challenge 240–1

high altitude (HA) warfare 5, 8, 119–20
- and advantage for India's airpower 118–19
- changing conduct of 113–14
- Himalayas region, strategic history of battles 107–10
- history of 104–6
- India to build its capabilities in Himalayas 115–18
- kinetic and non-kinetic warfare 117
- and modern war-fighting, comparison between 112–13
- strategic geography of mountains 106–7

higher defence organisation (HDO) 3, 7, 263–4
- current challenges of 267–72
- Indian scenario 266–7
- need to enhance efficacy of 278–80
- restructuring of commands 274–5
- tasks cut out for CDS and DMA 272–4

Hiroshima 11
Hizbul Mujahideen (HuM) 57, 76
human intelligence (HUMINT) 118

Ibrahim, Dawood 76
Indian Air Force (IAF) 8, 13, 125, 139, 169
- airborne early warning (AEW) 222
- airborne warning and control systems (AWACS) 216, 222–3

air-to-air refuelling operations (AAR) 216, 222
air transport fleet 212, 214–15
border tension in 1962, 1965 and counter-insurgency 230–2
capabilities in Indian Ocean region 225
casualty evacuation (CASEVAC) 216
combat search and rescue (CSAR) 216–17
communication intelligence (COMINT) 222
developed expertise in diverse force multiplier roles 213
effects based operations (EBO) 120
electronic intelligence (ELINT) 222–3
expansion and modernisation plan 229–30
Garud commando 6, 248
Indian Peace Keeping Force (IPKF) operations in Sri Lanka 234
integrated air command and control system (IACCS) 223
intelligence, surveillance and reconnaissance (ISR) 116, 118, 216
missions of mercy 217
offensive airpower operations 192–4
Operation Meghdoot (1984) 236
role in Eastern Ladakh Crisis in 2020 119
role in India-Pak conflict in 1971 233–4
use of helicopters in Kargil conflict, UNPKO and anti-LWE operations 235–6
war fighting capabilities 213
Indian Army (IA) 5, 30, 33, 86
Battle Schools 39
College of Combat/Staff College 39
Doctrine for Sub Conventional Warfare of 2006 31, 43–4
evolution of doctrine 88
granted Armed Forces Special Powers Act (AFSPA) 39, 53–4
IMA 39
Indian Peacekeeping Force (IPKF) in Sri Lanka 40–1, 90–1
Infantry School 39
Jungle Warfare Schools 39
NDA 39
operations in Kashmir 41–3
proactive strategy 92
Training Command 43
Indian Navy (IN) 8, 139, 169, 177
growth of 153–5
Marine Commandos (MARCOS) 6, 247
Indian Ocean Region (IOR) 5, 151, 153, 165–7, 225, 252
Indian Peacekeeping Force (IPKF) 6
Indo-Pacific (IP) 5, 151–3
Indo-Pak crisis of 2001-2002 17, 19
Information and Cyber Warfare (IW) 117
Institute of Defence Studies and Analysis (IDSA) 14–15
insurgencies/conflict
Jammu and Kashmir (J&K) 5, 13, 55–61
in North East 48–54, 60–1
integrated battle groups (IBGs) 94, 116
Integrated Guided Missile Programme (IGMDP) 312
Integrated Theatre Commands (ITCs) 274–5
need for deliberation 275–6

International Sikh Youth Federation (ISYF) 73, 75
Inter-Services Intelligence (ISI), Pakistan 21, 41, 74–5
Islamic State in Iraq and Syria (ISIS) or Khorasan unit 77

Jaish-e-Mohammed (JeM) 75–6, 201
Jamaat-e-Islami Hind (JIH) 76
Jamaat-ud-Dawah (JuD) 75
Jammu Kashmir Liberation Front (JKLF) 76
Jinping, Xi 288–9, 332–4
jointness of military
- aftermath of Kargil war 283–5
- air war for Kosovo 285–6
- in CDS/DMA era 292–93
- doctrinal framework 290–2
- for future battle 300–1
- joint acculturation 293
- joint education and training syllabi 293–5
- military bureaucracy and parochialism 292
- Operation *Weserübung* 287–8
- Persian Gulf War of 1991 (Operation Desert Storm) 286–7

Joint Operations: A Short Military History (Roger Beaumont) 290

Kapoor, V.K. 87
Karbi Longri NC Hills Liberation Front (KLNLF) 50
Kargil conflict/war of 1999 8, 13–14, 22, 42, 91, 109–10, 126, 136, 197–8, 235–6, 288–90
Kargil Review Committee (KRC) 264, 283
Khalistan Liberation Force 73
Khalistan movement 73, 75
Khalistan Zindabad Force (KZF) 73, 75
Khan, Genghis 85
Krantikari Jansangarsh Ekjutta Samiti 69

Lashkar-e-Taiba (LeT) 21, 75–6
Left Wing Extremism (LWE) or Naxalism 5, 80–2
- decline in violence activities and influence of 71–3
- Extremism Division in Ministry of Home Affairs (MHA) 71
- government efforts to control 70–2
- movement, stages of 65–6
- National Policy and Action Plan in 2015 71
- origin of 64–5
- persistence of, factors for 67–9

Lightning Campaign in East Pakistan 88–9
limited nuclear war 17
limited war, India's concept of 14–15, 17–19
- origin of 10
- survival of 28–9

Line of Actual Control (LAC) 5, 26, 93, 105, 111–12, 114, 118, 154
Line of Control (LoC) 13, 19, 24, 55, 92, 105, 110–11, 118
- cross-border firing 21

LTTE 69, 260

Majumdar, Charu 64–5
MALABAR 152–3
manoeuvre warfare, concept of
- British rejection of 87–91
- conventional domain 94–7
- in future conflicts 93–4

in grey zone conflicts 97–101
history of 84–7
touch decades 91–3
Maoist Communist Centre (MCC), Bihar 66, 68
maritime power 142
militancy 31, 33, 51, 54, 57–8, 73, 309
military air transport operations in India
airborne assault to capture Poongli Bridge 218
assistance during pandemic 221–2
during first India-Pakistan conflict 217–18
force multipliers 216–17
future of 224–7
humanitarian assistance and disaster relief (HADR) 220–1, 226
innovative use of bombing capability 219
landscape and challenges 213–14
mobility and sustenance 215–16
out of area contingencies 219–20
responsibility of IAF's air transport fleet 214–15
special missions 216
special operations and force multipliers 222–3
strategic airlift 220
military civic action 44
military confrontation in Ladakh between Sino-India in 2020 25–8
Military-Industrial Complex 288
Military Strategy (RM's Directive) 269
Mishra, Brajesh 318
Mishra, Vinod 66
Mizo Accord (1975) 36
Mizo National Front (MNF) 35
Modi, Narendra 224, 289, 320
Modi–Sharif meeting in 2015 22
multi-domain operational (MDO) 301
Mumbai terrorist strike (November 26, 2008) 19–21

Naga insurgency 33
Nagaland 5
Nagasaki 11
Nagorno-Karabakh 95
Naresh Chandra Task Force (NCTF) 265
National Defence College (NDC), New Delhi 1–2, 4, 9, 158
Kuutneeti journal 3
National Democratic Front of Bodoland (NDFB) 50
National Intelligence Grid (NATGRID) project 77
National Investigation Agency 77–8
National Liberation Front 73
National Security Guard (NSG) 78, 284
National Security Strategy (NSS) 93, 268
National Socialist Council of Nagaland (K) 49
National Socialist Council of Nagaland (NSCN)—NSCN (IM) 49, 51–3, 60
National Socialist Council of Nagalim (NSCN) 35
non-contact warfare 93
North-West Frontier Province (NWFP) 193
No War No Peace (NWNP) 12
nuclear powers 11, 17, 25, 149, 267, 321
big wars and direct military confrontations between 12
nuclear weapons programme of India 11, 14, 24
coherent nuclear policy 308–9
history of 305–7
Indian Nuclear Doctrine 318–20
neighbourhood enemies 317–18

no first use (NFU) policy 17, 310, 313–17, 321–2
nuclear deterrent, development of 307–8
nuclear doctrinal development 309–12
Pokhran tests 308, 321–2
post doctrinal ideas and ambiguities 320–1
role in Kargil conflict 13
Sundarji-Subrahmanyam theory on nuclear weapons use 313–16

offensive airpower operations 192–4, 207–9
conventional deterrent 199–201
escalatory restraint 194–5
and future conflicts 205–7
historical perspective 195–7
limited wars 197–8
and role of air defence (AD) 198–9
in sub-conventional and grey zone realm 201–5
open source intelligence (OSINT) 118
Operation Parakram 92
Operations Other Than War (OOTW) of US Special Forces 249
Organisations of South Asia 69
out of area (OOA) capability 250

Pak Air Force 25
Pakistan 79
no operational nuclear weapons in 1999 13
use of terrorism for national interests 75
Pakistan Army 21
Pakistan Occupied Kashmir (POK) 55–6, 58, 76
Pannun, Gurpatwant Singh 79
Parliament of India attack (December 2001) 92
Parrikar, Manohar 320–1
People's Democratic Party (PDP) 57
People's Guerrilla Army 66
People's Union for Civil Liberties 69
People's War Group (PWG), Andhra Pradesh 66, 68
policy makers in India, restricted views of military matters 7
political leadership 13
Pre-emptive Initiation of Violence in the Opponents Territory (PIVOT) 92
Progressive Writers' Association 69

QUAD 27–8, 152–3

Ramana, Raja 307
Ram Janmabhoomi movement 75
Rao, Narasimha 308
Rao, N. T. Rama 68
Ravi, R.N. 51
Rawat, Bipin 289
Revolutionary Internationalist Movement 69
Rice, Condeleezza 21
rise, defined 141–2
rotary wing employment 236–7
air-land operations 237–8
high-altitude (HA) campaign 237–8
Royal Australian Navy (RAN) 152–3

SAARC Terrorist Offences Monitoring Desk (STOMD) 78
Saeed, Hafiz 75
Sanyal, Kanu 64
Sarabhai, Vikram 306–7

Sea Lanes of Communication (SLOCs) 145
sealift 148–9, 299
seapower
advocacy of 142
attributes of 147–9
defined 142
global system 143–4
Indian outlook 149–53
military aspects of maritime dimension 144–7
Security and Growth for All in the Region (SAGAR) 166, 224, 227
self-preservation 16
shallow thrusts 19
Shanghai Cooperation Organisation 78
Sheikh, Ahmed Omar Saeed 77
Shillong Accord of 1975 35
signals intelligence (SIGINT) 118
Sikh diaspora 79
Sikh militancy/terrorist groups 73–4
Sikhs for Justice 79
Singh, Beant 74
Singh, Jasjit 14–15
Singh, Lakhbir 75
Singh, Manmohan 69
Singh, N. Biren 54
Singh, Rajnath 321
Singh, Ranjeet ('Neeta') 75
Singh, Wadhawa 75
Singh, Zorawar 107
Sino-Indian war in 1962 125
Special Forces (SFs), India 6, 23, 72, 110, 119, 135, 203, 216, 222, 237–42
Armed Forces Special Operations Division (AFSOD) 248
coercion as a powerful instrument of statecraft, importance of 248–50
conduct of operations 247
contemporary warfare, importance during 250–3
Meghdoot Force 247
National Security Guard (NSG) 248
Operation Hot Pursuit 254–5
Operation Snow Leopard 258–9
security difficulties 259–62
Special Action Groups (SAGs) 248
Special Frontier Force (SFF) 247
Special Operations Joint Command 248
Special Rangers Groups (SRGs) 248
surgical strikes on terrorists launch pads 255–8
task of 247
spirit of the age 104
Stability-Instability Paradox 11, 13
Students Islamic Movement of India 76
Students Islamic Organisation 76
submarine(s)
advantages of using 190
air independent propulsion (AIP) systems 185–6
availability of satellite communication 186
changing operational environment 187–90
contracts and equipment 180–3
growth of Indian 177–8
HDW and Scorpene experience 179–80
indigenisation 179
unmanned undersea vessels (UUV) 183–5
use of sensors and weapons 186–7
surgical strikes by India 23–4
Balakot air strike 24–5

tactical nuclear weapons 17
tactical sensors 118–19
Taliban 20–1, 75, 79
Tata Institute for Fundamental Research (TIFR) 305
Telugu Desam Party 68
terrorism 17–20, 22, 29, 31
  Babri Masjid demolition and Jihadi terrorism 76–7
  counter, steps to 77–9
  Islamic extremism in India 75–6
  and Pakistan factor 74–5
  threat of 73–4
  urban 5, 31
transgressions 26, 96, 108–9, 111, 115
Tukhachevsky, Mikhail 87

UAPA 79
United Liberation Front of Assam (ULFA) 50
United Nations General Assembly (UNGA) 23
United Nations Security Council 143
unmanned combat aerial vehicle (UCAV) 168–9
Unrestricted Warfare: China's Master Plan to Destroy America (Qiao Liang and Wang Xiangsui) 249
urban naxals 69

Vaidya, A. S. 74
Vajpayee, A B 13, 22, 26, 308–9, 320–1

Wani, Burhan 57
war (Indo-Pakistan)
  1947–48 194, 217
  1971 194
Westphalian system of sovereign nation-states 143
World People's Resistance Movement 69

Yi, Wang 251–2

Zargar, Mushtak Ahmed 77
Zedong, Mao 335